D0119864

DEVOTION

ALSO BY ADAM MAKOS

A Higher Call

DEVOTION

AN EPIC STORY OF HEROISM, FRIENDSHIP, AND SACRIFICE

Adam Makos

Atlantic Books
London

This edition published by arrangement with Ballantine Books, an imprint of Random House, a division of Penguin Random House LLC, New York.

First published in hardback in Great Britain in 2015 by Atlantic Books, an imprint of Atlantic Books Ltd.

1 2 3 4 5 6 7 8 9

A CIP catalogue record for this book is available from the British Library.

Hardback ISBN: 978 1 78239 574 4
Trade paperback ISBN: 978 1 78239 575 1
E-Book ISBN: 978 1 78239 576 8
Paperback ISBN: 978 1 78239 577 5

All interior maps by Bryan Makos of Valour Studios, Inc.
Book design by Christopher M. Zucker
Photo credits can be found on p. 444

Printed and bound by CPI Group (UK) Ltd, Croydon, CR0 4YY

Atlantic Books
An Imprint of Atlantic Books Ltd
Ormond House
26–27 Boswell Street
London
WC1N 3JZ

www.atlantic-books.co.uk

To the veterans of the forgotten victory in Korea, 1950–1953

CONTENTS

INTRODUCTION

FROM ACROSS THE HOTEL LOBBY, I saw him sitting alone, newspaper in hand.

He was a distinguished-looking older gentleman. His gray hair was swept back, his face sharp and handsome. He wore a navy blazer and tan slacks, and his luggage sat by his side.

The lobby was buzzing, but no one paid him any special attention. It was fall 2007, another busy morning in Washington, D.C. I was twenty-six at the time and trying to make it as a writer for a history magazine. I had a book under way on the side but no publisher yet in sight. The book was about my one and only specialty—World War II.

The day before, I had heard the distinguished gentleman speak at a veterans' history conference. I had caught part of his story. He was a former navy fighter pilot who had done something incredible in a war long ago, something so superhuman that the captain of his aircraft carrier stated: "There has been no finer act of unselfish heroism in military history."

President Harry Truman had agreed and invited this pilot to the White House. *Life* magazine ran a story about him. His deeds appeared in a movie called *The Hunters*, starring Robert Mitchum. And now here he was—sitting across the lobby from me.

I wanted to ask him for an interview but hesitated. A journalist should know his subject matter and I was unprepared.

He had flown a WWII Corsair fighter, I understood that much. Reportedly he had fought alongside WWII veterans and fired the same bullets and dropped the same bombs used in WWII. He was a member of the Greatest Generation, too.

But he hadn't fought in World War II.

He had fought in the Korean War.

To me, the Korean War was a mystery. It is to most Americans; our history books label it "The Forgotten War." When we think of Korea, we picture *M*A*S*H* or Marilyn Monroe singing for the troops or a flashback from *Mad Men*.

Only later would I discover that the Korean War was practically an extension of World War II, fought just five years later between nations that had once called themselves allies. Only later did I discover a surprising reality: *The Greatest Generation actually fought two wars.*

The gentleman was folding his newspaper to leave. It was now or never.

I mustered the nerve to introduce myself and we shook hands. We made small talk about the conference and finally I asked the gentleman if I could interview him sometime for a magazine story. I held my breath. Maybe he was tired of interviews? Maybe I was too young to be taken seriously?

"Why, sure," he said robustly. He fished a business card from his pocket and handed it to me. Only later would I realize what an opportunity he'd given me. His name was Captain Tom Hudner. And that's how *Devotion* began.

True to his word, Tom Hudner granted me that interview. Then another, and another, until what began as a magazine story blossomed into this book. And the book kept growing. I discovered that Tom and his squadron weren't your typical fighter pilots—they were specialists in ground attack, trained to deliver air support to Marines in battle. So what began as the story of fighter pilots became a bigger story, an interwoven account of flyboys in the air, Marines on the ground, and the heroes behind the scenes—the wives and families on the home front.

Over the ensuing seven years, from 2007 to 2014, my staff and I interviewed Tom and the other real-life "characters" of his story more times than we could count. All told, we interviewed more than sixty members of the Greatest Generation—former navy carrier pilots, Marines, their wives, their siblings. This story is set in 1950, so many of the people we interviewed were still young for their generation. They were in their seventies and early eighties, with sharp, vibrant memories.

At times, I stepped away from *Devotion* to work on my World War II book while my staff kept plugging away on *Devotion*. They had help, too. The historians at the navy archives, the Marine Corps archives, and the National Archives were practically on call to aid our research.

Over those seven years we worked as a team—the book's subjects, the historians, my staff, and I—to piece together this story. Our goal was for you not just to read *Devotion* but to experience it. To construct a narrative of rich detail, we needed to zoom in close. Our questions for the subjects were countless. When a man encountered something good or bad, what did he think? What facial gestures corresponded with his feelings—did his eyes lift with hope? Did his face sink with sorrow? What actions did he take next?

More than anything, we asked: "What did you say?" I love dialogue. There's no more powerful means to tell a story, but an author of a nonfiction book can't just make up what he wants a character to say. This is a true story, after all, so I relied on the dialogue recorded in the past and the memories of our subjects, who were there.

Time and again we asked these "witnesses to history" to reach into their pasts and recall what they had said and what they had heard others say. In this manner, we re-created this book's dialogue, scene by scene, moment by moment. In the end, before anything went to press, our principal witnesses to history read the manuscript and gave their approval.

I owe a debt of gratitude to these real-life "characters" of *Devotion*, people you'll soon meet and never forget—Tom, Fletcher, Lura, Daisy, Marty, Koenig, Red, Coderre, Wilkie, and so many others. *Devotion* was crafted by their memories as much as it was written by me.

There was another level of research that this book required. I needed to see the book's settings for myself—all of them, from New England to North Korea. So I hit the road and followed the characters' footsteps to the places where they grew up, flew, and fought.

That journey led me from Massachusetts to Mississippi, to the French Riviera and Monaco, to a port in Italy, a ship off the coast of Sicily, and back to the battlefields of the Korean War. I had been to South Korea before on a U.S.O. tour, but never to that shadowy land to the north—North Korea.

But before the book was done, my staff and I went there too. We traveled to China and then into that misty place known as "the hermit kingdom," the land where some Americans enter and later fail to re-emerge. Our trip to North Korea is a story in itself, but let's just say I owe its success to Tom Hudner.

As *Devotion* neared completion, I struggled for a way to describe this interwoven story to you, the reader. My prior book—*A Higher Call*—had been easy to categorize. It was the true story of a German fighter pilot who spared a defenseless American bomber crew during WWII.

It was a war story.

Devotion is a war story, too.

But it differs in that it's also a *love story*. It's the tale of a mother raising her son to escape a life of poverty and of a newlywed couple being torn apart by war.

It's also an *inspirational story* of an unlikely friendship. It's the tale of a white pilot from the country clubs of New England and a black pilot from a southern sharecropper's shack forming a deep friendship in an era of racial hatred.

As I was editing the last pages of this manuscript, the answer hit me. I knew how to categorize *Devotion*.

The bravery. The love. The inspiration.

This is an American story.

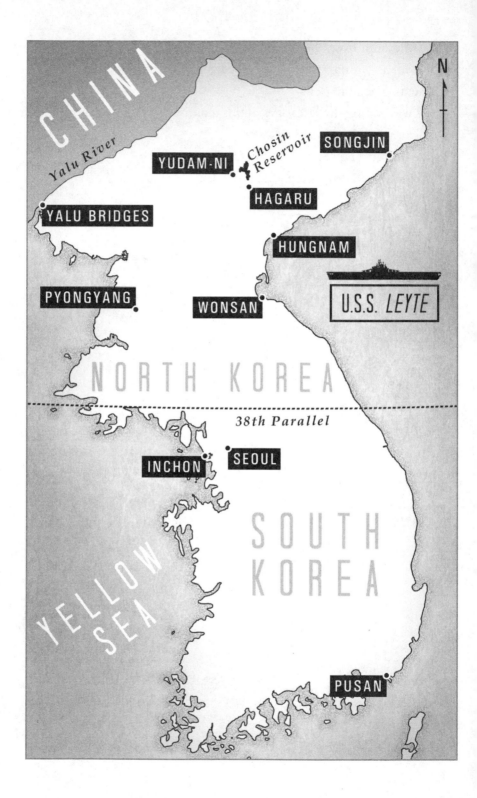

DEVOTION

CHAPTER 1

GHOSTS AND SHADOWS

December 4, 1950
North Korea, during the first year of the Korean War

IN A BLACK-BLUE FLASH, a Corsair fighter burst around the valley's edge, turning hard, just above the snow. The engine snarled. The canopy glimmered. A bomb hung from the plane's belly and rockets from its wings.

Another roar shook the valley and the next Corsair blasted around the edge. Then came a third, a fourth, a fifth, and more until ten planes had fallen in line.

The Corsairs dropped low over a snow-packed road and followed it across the valley, between snow-capped hills and strands of dead trees. The land was enemy territory, the planes were behind the lines.

From the cockpit of the fourth Corsair, Lieutenant Tom Hudner reached forward to a bank of switches above the instrument panel. With a flick, he armed his eight rockets.

Tom was twenty-six and a navy carrier pilot. His white helmet and raised goggles framed the face of a movie star—flat eyebrows over ice-

An F4U Corsair

blue eyes, a chiseled nose, and a cleft chin. He dressed the part too, in a dark brown leather jacket with a reddish fur collar. But Tom could never cut it as a star of the silver screen—his eyes were far too humble.

At 250 miles per hour, Tom chased the plane ahead of him. It was nearly 3 P.M., and dark snow clouds draped the sky with cracks of sun slanting through. Tom glanced from side to side and checked his wingtips as the treetops whipped by. Beyond the hills to the right lay a frozen man-made lake called the Chosin Reservoir. The flight was following the road up the reservoir's western side.

The radio crackled and Tom's eyes perked up. "This is Iroquois Flight 13," the flight leader announced from the front. "All quiet, so far."

"Copy that, Iroquois Flight," replied a tired voice. Seven miles away, at the foot of the reservoir, a Marine air controller was shivering in his tent at a ramshackle American base. His maps revealed a dire situation around him. Red lines encircled the base—red enemy lines. To top it off, it was one of the coldest winters on record. And the war was still new.

✶   ✶   ✶

The engine droned, filling Tom's cockpit with the smell of warm oil. Tom edged forward in his seat and looked past the whirling propeller. His eyes settled on the Corsair in front of him.

In the plane ahead, a pilot with deep brown skin peered through the rings of his gunsight. The man's face was slender beneath his helmet, his eyebrows angled over honest dark eyes. Just twenty-four, Ensign Jesse Brown was the first African American carrier pilot in the U.S. Navy. Jesse had more flight time than Tom, so in the air, he led.

Jesse dipped his right wing for a better view of the neighboring trees. Tom's gut tensed.

"See something, Jesse?" Tom radioed.

Jesse snapped his plane level again. "Not a thing."

Through the canopy's scratched Plexiglas, Tom watched the cold strands blur past at eye level. The enemy was undoubtedly there, tucked behind trees, grasping rifles, holding their fire so the planes would pass.

Tom clenched his jaw and focused his eyes forward. As tempting as it was, the pilots couldn't strafe a grove of trees on a hunch. They needed to spot the enemy first.

The enemy were the White Jackets, Communist troops who hid by day and attacked by night. For the previous week, their human waves had lapped against the American base night after night, nearly overrunning the defenses. Nearly a hundred thousand White Jackets were now laying siege to the base and more were arriving and moving into position.

Against this foe stood the base's ten thousand men—some U.S. Army soldiers, some British Commandos, but mostly U.S. Marines. Reportedly, the base even had its cooks, drivers, and clerks manning the battle lines at night, freezing alongside the riflemen.

Their survival now hinged on air power and the Corsair pilots knew it. Every White Jacket they could neutralize now would be one fewer trying to bayonet a young Marine that night.

"Heads up, disturbances ahead!" the flight leader radioed.

Finally, something, Tom thought.

Tom's eyes narrowed. Small boulders dotted the snow beside the road.

"Watch the rocks!" Jesse said as he zipped over them.

"Roger," Tom replied.

Tom wrapped his index finger over the trigger of the control stick. His eyes locked on the roadside boulders.

When caught in the open, White Jackets would sometimes drop to the ground and curl over their knees. From above, their soiled uniforms looked like stone and the side flaps of their caps hid their faces.

The rock pile slipped behind Tom's wings. He glanced into his rearview mirror. Behind his tail flew a string of six Corsairs with whirling, yellow-tipped propellers. If any rocks stood now to take a shot, Tom's buddies would deal with them. Tom trusted the men behind him, just as Jesse entrusted his life to Tom.

After two months of flying combat together, Tom and Jesse were as close as brothers, although they hailed from different worlds. A sharecropper's son, Jesse had grown up dirt-poor, farming the fields of Mississippi, whereas Tom had spent his summers boating at a country club in Massachusetts as an heir to a chain of grocery stores. In 1950 their friendship was genuine, just ahead of the times.

Tom caught the green blur of a vehicle beneath his left wing. Then another on the right.

He leaned from side to side for a better view.

Abandoned American trucks and jeeps lined the roadsides. Some sat on flat tires and others nosed into ditches. Snow draped the vehicles; their ripped canvas tops flapped in the wind. Cannons jutted here and there, their barrels wrapped in ice.

Tom's eyes narrowed. Splashes of pink colored the surrounding snow. "Oh Lord," he muttered. The day before, the Marines had been attacked here as they fought their way back to the base. In subzero conditions, spilled blood turned pink.

"Bodies, nine o'clock!" the flight leader announced as he flew past a hill on the left. "God, they're everywhere!"

Jesse zipped by in silence. Tom nudged his control stick to the left and his fifteen-thousand-pound fighter dipped a wing.

Sun warmed the hillside, revealing bodies stacked like sandbags across the slope. Mounds of dead men poked from the snow, their frozen blue arms reaching defiantly. Tom's eyes tracked the carnage as he flew past.

Are they ours or theirs? he wondered.

Just the day before, he had flown over and seen the Marines down there, waving up at him, their teenage faces pale and waxy. He had heard rumors of the horrors they faced after nightfall. That's when the temperature dropped to twenty below, when the enemy charged in waves, when the Americans' weapons froze and they fought with bayonets and fists.

Aboard the aircraft carrier, Tom and the other pilots had become accustomed to starting each morning with the same question: "Did our boys survive the night?"

With a deep growl, the flight—now just six Corsairs—burst into a new valley northwest of the reservoir.

Frustration lined Tom's face. The enemy had remained elusive so the flight leader had dispatched the rearmost four Corsairs to search elsewhere.

The remaining six planes followed the road farther into hostile territory. The clouds ahead became stormier, as if the road were luring the pilots into Siberia itself.

Tom scanned for signs of life as the flight raced between frozen fields. Snow-covered haystacks slipped past his wings. Crumbling shacks. Trees swaying in the wind.

"Possible footprints!" Jesse announced. Tom glanced eagerly forward.

"Nope, just shadows," Jesse muttered as he flew overhead.

Tom could tell that Jesse was frustrated too. They both should have been far from this winter wasteland. Tom should have been sipping a scotch in a warm country club back home and Jesse should have been bouncing his baby daughter on his lap under a Mississippi sun. Instead, they'd both come here as volunteers.

It wasn't the risk that bothered them—they were frustrated because they wanted to do something, anything, to defend the boys at the base. The night before, Jesse had written to his wife, Daisy, from the carrier: "Knowing that he's helping those poor guys on the ground, I think every pilot on here would fly until he dropped in his tracks."

Ahead of the flight, a voice barked a command from a roadside field. A dozen or more rifles and submachine guns rose up from the snow. Numb fingers gripped the weapons and shaking arms aimed skyward—arms wrapped in white quilted uniforms.

The White Jackets. They had heard the planes coming and taken cover.

The shadow of the first Corsair passed overhead—yet the enemy troops held their fire. The second shadow zipped safely past, too. The shadow of Jesse's Corsair next raced toward the spot where weapons stood like garden stakes.

As Jesse's shadow stretched over the hidden soldiers, the voice shouted. The rifles and submachine guns fired a volley, sending bullets rocketing upward. Quickly, the weapons lowered back into the snow.

The shadow of Tom's plane flew over the enemy next, then two more Corsair shadows in quick succession. Over the roar of their 2,250-horsepower engines, none of the pilots heard the gunshots. One would later remember seeing the disturbance in the snow, but at 250 miles per hour, no one saw the enemy.

Rather than patrol another desolate valley, the flight leader climbed into an orbit over the surrounding mountains and ordered the flight to re-form.

Tom pulled alongside Jesse's right wing and together they climbed toward the others.

"This is Iroquois Flight 13," the leader radioed the base. "Road recon came up dry. Got anything else?"

"Copy," the Marine controller replied. "Let me check."

Tom and Jesse tucked in behind the leader and his wingman. The trailing two Corsairs slipped in behind them. From the rear of the formation, a pilot named Koenig radioed with alarm. "Jesse, something's wrong—looks like you're bleeding fuel!"

Jesse squirmed in his seat to see behind his tail, but his range of vision ended at his seatback. He looked to Tom across the cold space between their planes.

Tom glanced leftward and saw a white vapor trail slipping from Jesse's belly. "You've got a streamer, all right," Tom said.

Jesse nodded.

"Check your fuel transfer," Koenig suggested. Sometimes fuel overflowed while being transferred from the plane's belly tank to its internal tank.

Jesse glanced at the fuel selector switch above his left thigh. The handle was locked properly, so that wasn't the problem. He studied the instrument panel. The needle in the oil pressure gauge was dropping.

Jesse glanced at Tom with a furrowed brow. "I've got an oil leak," he announced.

Tom's face sank. The hole in Jesse's oil tank was a mortal wound. With every passing second, the oil was draining, the friction was rising, and the plane's eighteen pistons were melting in their cylinders.

"Losing power," Jesse said flatly.

"Can you make it south?" Tom asked.

"Nope, my engine's seizing up," Jesse said. "I'm going down."

How is he so calm? Tom thought. Jesse's propeller sputtered and his plane pitched forward into a rapid descent. Instinctively, Tom held formation and followed him down. Jesse was too low to bail out, so Tom frantically scanned the terrain for a suitable crash site. All he saw were snowy mountains and valleys studded with dead trees. *This can't be happening,* Tom thought. Jesse would never survive a crash in this terrain and if he did, the subzero cold would kill him.

Tom glanced down to his kneeboard map and his face twisted. Jesse was going down seventeen miles behind enemy lines. If he survived the crash, the enemy would surely double-time it to capture him, and if they didn't shoot him on sight, they had an unspeakable torture that they used on captured pilots.

Tom glanced over at Jesse as their Corsairs plummeted toward the mountains. Jesse's eyes were fixed forward as he tried to sort through a hopeless hand of fate.

Tom needed to do something to help his friend, and fast.

Jesse's story couldn't end like this.

CHAPTER 2

THE LESSON OF A LIFETIME

Twelve years earlier, spring 1938
Fall River, Massachusetts

THE CAFETERIA OF MORTON JUNIOR HIGH buzzed with chattering young voices. Boys and girls waited in lunch lines while other students sat at long tables and ate from tin lunch pails. The green linoleum floor reflected more than two hundred conversations and the noise bounced up to a white ceiling made of textured plaster drippings.

Thirteen-year-old Tom Hudner set his tray on a table and sat next to his friends, all boys in the eighth grade, just like him. He wore a white polo shirt and khakis. His chin was strong, and his eyes were blue and honest. Even as young teenagers, Tom and the other boys still sat away from the girls. Morton Junior High was a place of rules and playground codes, and to sit with the opposite gender would invite ridicule. Tom was a rule follower by nature.

He unfolded a paper napkin, popped the cap on his bottle of milk, and began to eat. Tom bought a hot lunch every day for thirty-five cents, a perk of having affluent parents. He chewed silently and listened far

Tom Hudner

more than he spoke. During a lull in the conversation, Tom's gaze shifted. Outside the cafeteria's windows, the school's bullies were gathering in a corner of the courtyard where kids played after lunch.

They were the immigrant kids, dark-skinned sons of the Portuguese fishermen who had settled in Fall River. Tom placed his napkin on the table and stood up to get a better view. The tough Portuguese kids were tossing around a pair of eyeglasses, each boy trying them on and laughing. At the center of the circle, Tom could see a boy haplessly lunging to snatch his glasses back. The boy was overweight and wore his hair slicked to one side. Tom recognized him as Jack. Kids often ridiculed Jack for being quick to cry but Tom was friends with him, and most everyone for that matter.

Tom alerted the boys around him: "Someone should tell the teacher." He looked around, but the teacher was nowhere to be seen. Outside, Jack was turning red and about to cry. The boys around Tom scowled, not because of their affection for Jack.

"Portugee rats!" one said.

"Dirty boat hoppers," whispered another. "They should go back to where they came from."

Tom didn't know the Portuguese kids personally, but they seemed like trouble. The schoolchildren even had a name for the dirty industrial borough near the waterfront that the immigrants called home: "Portugee-ville."

"We should do something," Tom blurted.

Nobody moved.

One of Tom's friends shrugged and looked away. "I'm not getting mixed up in this," he muttered.

"Yeah, I barely know Jack, anyhow," said another.

One by one, Tom's friends sat down. Only Tom remained standing. Outside, he saw that Jack was now blubbering like a baby.

"Come on, guys," Tom pleaded.

"He's your friend, not ours," a boy said.

"If you feel so bad for him, you should do something about it!" another added.

"Okay, fine," Tom said. He sighed and walked toward the door.

Tom stepped out into the pale afternoon sunlight and approached the bullies. "Hey, fellas," Tom said. The Portuguese kids stopped laughing at Jack and turned, some grinning, some glaring. Tom's stride slowed. His mind raced to think.

"You say something?" called one of the bullies.

Tom stopped and tried to smile. "I don't think Jack's enjoying this very much," he said. It was the only thing that came to mind.

One of the bullies emerged from the group and sauntered closer. The teen was short and stocky with an aggressive face and brooding eyes. Tom recognized him as Manny Cabral, the gang's leader. Manny's brown slacks were patched, and his dark T-shirt had a stretched-out neck. He walked over and stood with his nose nearly touching Tom's.

"I think you should stay out of our business," Manny said.

"C'mon, he's crying," Tom said quietly. Out of the corner of his eye, he saw Jack running away, fumbling with his glasses.

"We were only having fun," Manny said, gesturing to his buddies. When he looked back at Tom, his voice lowered. "So what are you going to do about it?"

Tom's heart pounded. He had never been in a fight but felt Manny was suggesting it. He wanted to tell Manny to let bygones be bygones, but Manny spoke first.

"We'll settle the matter later," he said casually. His eyebrow lifted, seemingly with a change of heart. "After school, outside."

Tom gulped.

"You gonna show?" Manny asked.

Tom's eyes darted from Manny to his gang to the circle of students that had gathered to watch the spectacle.

Just say no, Tom thought. But he knew that wasn't an option. If Tom said no, the gang would never leave him alone. An all-American boy in 1938 had no option except to agree.

"Okay, I'll be there," Tom said.

Manny smiled and walked away. His gang followed, all laughing and talking loudly. Tom plodded back toward the cafeteria. His friends' faces were pressed against the window glass.

Tom and his friends returned to their table. The others congratulated Tom for putting Manny Cabral in his place.

Tom looked down at his cold food and shook his head. "I've got to fight Manny after school." Just saying the words made him lightheaded. Tom's friends assured him not to worry; they would back him up.

Tom thought of his father, Thomas Hudner Sr., and how he would react. His father ran a chain of eight grocery stores called Hudner's Markets and always said that the Portuguese immigrants were some of his best workers, people committed to building a new future for themselves. Senior wouldn't be happy about his son getting in a fight—that much was for sure. But Tom remembered something else his father had told him: *Always assume the best of people. But if a guy proves he's no good, then don't hesitate to give him what he deserves.*

*   *   *

When the bell rang at the day's end, Tom's buddies surrounded him in the hallway. They slapped his back as if he were a football player about to take the field. Tom closed his locker and walked out the double doors. Tom's buddies followed him, along with a few supporters.

Fifty yards away stood the white flagpole and a large cluster of students. At the center of the crowd stood the surly-looking Portuguese kids and Manny Cabral. Tom's heart began to race.

He glanced over his shoulder for his friends but they had disappeared. He scanned the crowd and saw that all eyes were on him. Then Tom spotted his friends. They were clear across the street, huddled up, watching and whispering.

Tom was alone.

He stopped, set down his books, and took off his jacket to keep it clean. The crowd murmured. Tom stepped toward Manny Cabral and the crowd hushed. Manny glared blankly as the kids closed the circle behind Tom. Tom raised his fists and turned his palms inward, thinking of pictures he'd seen of boxers. His fists trembled.

"Whip him, Manny!" yelled a Portuguese kid.

"Yeah, beat him good!" urged another.

Tom noticed the strangest thing—despite the presence of his supporters, no one was cheering for him. They were too afraid.

Manny stepped forward and raised his fists like a professional fighter. He dropped his chin and scrunched his face, eyebrows dropping low.

Tom's feet felt light, as if his soul had floated out of his body. Every face in the crowd seemed blurred except Manny's. All of the voices faded. Tom could hear only the blood pumping in his ears. With his fists up and shaking, he began bouncing on his feet—the way he'd seen in the movies. Manny stood stock-still, fists poised to strike.

"Slug him, Manny!" someone yelled. Manny bobbed lightly, as if he was waiting for the perfect moment. Tom was too terrified to throw the first punch. His fists shook. He kept doing all he knew—shuffling his feet.

Manny raised an eyebrow. His expression loosened, he raised his chin and dropped his fists. His fingers uncurled.

Tom stopped bobbing. He kept up his guard.

Manny stepped toward Tom and thrust forward his right hand. His palm was open.

Tom lowered his fists and looked down at Manny's outstretched hand, confused.

"Go ahead, shake," Manny said.

The crowd grew silent. Tom unclenched his fists. He reached out his trembling hand and took Manny's hand in his. They shook up then down just once.

Manny turned to his gang. "He's okay," he said. "It's all right between us." Then he turned and walked away. His gang lingered, speechless, then followed him down the street, toward the docks.

Tom watched the students disperse until he found himself alone by the flagpole. Across the street, his friends had disappeared. Tom gathered his books and jacket and began to walk home. His adrenaline was racing, and he soon began to jog, then run. He ran up Highland Avenue toward his home on the hill. He passed North Park, with its hills and Victorian mansions on the fringes.

At the top of the hill, Tom hung a right and saw his home, a three-story Victorian with gray wooden shingles and tall windows. The Hudner family had prospered even during the Great Depression because the grocery industry was always in demand. Tom's face tightened as he ran up to the porch and entered his home.

Inside, Tom untied his polished Oxford shoes and placed them on a doormat. His mother was away, probably playing bridge, and his father was still at work.

In the back of the house, Tom heard the maid, Mary Getchell, stirring in the kitchen, preparing dinner. She was their housekeeper, thin, gray-haired, and Irish by descent, like the Hudners. The children called her "Nursey."

Tom snuck up the staircase, past his father's pennants from Andover prep school and Harvard University. On the second floor, where his parents and younger brothers and sister had their bedrooms, Tom turned the corner and kept going. He followed another staircase to the third floor, where his room lay opposite Nursey's. Inside, the ceiling of Tom's room was sharply angled and a rectangular window overlooked the street in front of the house. A crucifix hung next to the doorway and a Boy Scout poster hung on the wall. A baseball glove sat perched on his bedpost.

Tom tossed his books on his desk and flopped onto the bed. A model of an old schooner sat on his dresser along with a copy of his favorite book, *Beat to Quarters*, the tale of a British sea captain named Horatio Hornblower. Comic books littered Tom's nightstand, their covers filled with colorful scenes of pirates and sea monsters. Tom loved ships. His favorite movie was *Mutiny on the Bounty*, and at the country club's summer camp his favorite activity was sailing.

As he lay on his sheets, Tom's eyes revealed a racing mind. He could still see Manny's upraised fists and feel the knots of Manny's palm when they shook. The tough Portuguese boy had handed him a challenge, to rise above a human's judgmental nature.

Then the thought hit Tom.

What if Manny had not been such a good guy after all?

Tom stared at the ceiling. Taking a chance — even to do the right thing — had almost cost him his front teeth. *Never again*, he decided.

From now on, Tom Hudner would be playing it safe.

CHAPTER 3

SWIMMING WITH SNAKES

A year later, April 1939
Lux, Mississippi

THE LATE AFTERNOON SUN CAST LONG shadows as a father and his three young sons trudged on the shady side of a dirt road. On one side of the road stood thickets of tall pines and leafy trees with thin white trunks. On the other lay parched brown fields where green plants sprouted.

Twelve-year-old Jesse Brown and his father, John Brown, pulled mules by the reins. Jesse's tattered overalls looped over his slender frame. He was handsome, with sharp eyebrows, steady eyes, and healthy cheeks. A soaked T-shirt hung around his neck and dirt caked his bare feet. The air was hot and muggy.

Behind Jesse came his younger brothers—Lura, who was nine, and Fletcher, who was seven. The younger boys staggered barefoot in the heat, carrying hoes. Each had a fuzz of hair on top of his head and spindly legs that stuck out from overalls that their mother had cut into shorts. The difference was in their faces: Lura's was square and lean whereas Fletcher's was round and chubby.

Jesse Brown

Only Jesse's father wore shoes, but they were falling apart. At five feet ten and 250 pounds, John Brown was built solidly, with a thick chest and muscular arms. Sweat poured down his round face and heavy cheeks. He kept his eyes focused contentedly forward. That night there would be food on his family's table. It was the Great Depression, and Mississippi was the poorest state in the nation. Not everybody was as fortunate.

Jesse's eyes drooped from sleepiness while his brothers struggled to walk in a straight line. Planting season had come in the Deep South and they'd all been at work since 4:30 A.M. Their fields lay in southern Mississippi near the crossroads town of Lux, little more than a gas station and general store in the woods. While the local white children remained in school, Jesse and his brothers were given a spring break from their one-room schoolhouse so that they and the other black children could work the fields.

For eleven hours that day, Jesse and his brothers had chopped plants until their backs ached and their hands were covered in blisters. Now they were headed home to do their chores; there was firewood to chop

and chickens to feed and a garden to maintain. The garden was everything to the Brown family, because it was actually theirs.

As a sharecropper, John Brown didn't own the thirty acres that his
family farmed. He rented the fields from a skinny white landowner
named Joe Bob Ingram, who also owned the town's general store,
where the sharecroppers rented their tools and bought their seed.
Throughout the year, the store ran a tally on each family's purchases.
At year's end when the bill was presented, Joe Bob always adjusted it to
erase the Brown family's yearly profit. For John Brown, it was a no-win
life, one he hoped his boys would escape.

The father and sons approached a roadside footpath that led into
the woods. Insects buzzed about the entrance. Lura and Fletcher
perked up and grinned. With fresh bounce in their steps, the boys approached Jesse and tapped his arm, motioning toward the woods.
Every day they came to Jesse at this same spot, with the same implor-
ing eyes.

"Ask him!" Fletcher whispered.

Jesse knew what his brothers were hinting at and shook his head. He
and his brothers still had to bring in the mules and do their chores.

The faces of the younger boys sank.

"C'mon, ask him—please!" Lura whispered.

Jesse looked down at his disheveled younger brothers. He felt exhausted too. Jesse's face loosened and he steered his mule closer to his
father.

"Pa," Jesse said. "Do we have time for a quick break?"

Fletcher and Lura hurried forward and grinned toward the big man.

John Brown stopped to wipe his brow. He stroked the face of his
panting mule, its eye half-closed. He had served in an all-black army
cavalry unit during World War I, a unit that had been set to deploy
overseas but the war ended before they could ship out.

John Brown looked at his boys and saw their raised eyebrows. His
lips broke into a smile. "I'll handle the mules," he said. "Just do your
chores when y'all get home."

The boys glanced at one another with fresh life in their eyes. Jesse handed his father the reins to his mule and the boys handed him their tools. The family parted.

Lura and Fletcher took off skipping toward the forest path with Jesse following.

"Hold your horses!" Jesse called. At the trailhead he grabbed a sturdy stick from the ground, swung it through the air, and saw that it was good and steady. Jesse warned Fletcher and Lura to stay behind him.

Then he led the boys into the woods.

Jesse walked slowly and swept the path ahead with the stick. The trail wasn't used much and weeds crisscrossed the dirt. The creaking and zipping from insects and croaking from bullfrogs were complicating Jesse's efforts to listen for the hiss of a cottonmouth.

Cottonmouths were the thick brown-black vipers that infested the backwoods, and it was tough to spot one on a trail. They were poisonous, even more than rattlesnakes. The little girl next door to the Browns had been bitten on the foot. She lived, but only after sweating and groaning for weeks while blood bubbled from the wound.

Fletcher tried to race ahead, but Jesse stopped him. "Get back here, Mule!" Jesse shouted. He had nicknamed Fletcher "Mule" because the boy had a mind of his own. Fletcher stopped and grinned.

With his brothers behind him, Jesse resumed the march. He waved the stick at ground level and watched the trail, unblinking. One time, on the same trail, a coiled cottonmouth had threatened Jesse's brothers and blocked their path home. So Jesse beat the snake's head with a stick and killed it. When his brothers investigated the carcass they found a series of big bulges along its belly. Fletcher and Lura took it home and cut it open. Inside, they counted twenty-two frogs.

In the center of the woods, the boys reached a pond of stagnant water dammed off from a nearby stream. The water was brown and a thin layer of green scum floated around the edges. The boys stood a few moments and watched a snake crisscross the pond. Only its triangular head swam above the surface, its blunt snout parting the scum around its black eyes. There were always a few they couldn't see, as well. The boys knew how to get the snakes out of their swimming hole.

Jesse unhooked his overalls and peeled his T-shirt from around his neck, then tossed it aside. He hadn't even stepped out of his pants before Fletcher took off, naked as the day he was born, running down the dirt hill. Legs flailing, Fletcher jumped straight into the center of the pond. Lura followed and Jesse plunged in last.

Muddy water bubbled up from the shallow bottom. The scum shook and waves carried it toward the pond's outer fringes. The cottonmouth didn't like the disturbance. It slithered in retreat up the bank.

The muddy pond felt as warm as bathwater and the brothers splashed and paddled around, hooting and hollering to make as much ruckus as possible. Keeping the noise up was the best way to keep the snakes on the banks.

Dripping wet, the boys walked down the same dirt road as before, talking happily. Even after a bath in the muddy water, they felt clean.

Jesse smiled with amusement as he listened. Fletcher often jabbered about his girlfriends, twin girls who lived next door, whereas Lura knew all the current events from the newspapers left over after his paper route. For this reason, the family had nicknamed Lura "Junior" because he was like a junior Jesse, always reading.

The brothers paused their banter. Behind them, around the bend, a truck downshifted. It sounded imposing. The road was narrow, so Jesse led his brothers to the side and glanced back.

A school bus burst around the corner. It was black on the nose, yellow on the body, and its engine rattled like a laboring air conditioner. The bus shifted gears and picked up speed. Jesse edged his brothers farther into the weeds.

From the windows toward the back of the bus, a half-dozen white faces poked out, sporting mops of brown, blond, and red hair. The kids in the bus shouted a chorus of curses.

"Heya niggers!"

"Dirty niggers!

"Looky here, niggers!"

As the bus roared past, the kids spit at Jesse and his brothers. Sticky gobs of saliva splattered on Jesse and his brothers and stuck to their bare chests and arms as they tried to cover their faces. Dust and hot diesel exhaust enveloped the boys as the bus roared away. The kids in the bus stared back and pointed, laughing and whooping.

Jesse and his brothers frantically tried to wipe away the spit. They found it in their hair. Fletcher began to cry. He and Lura looked to Jesse for an answer. Jesse glared at the cloud of dust where the bus had been. He clenched his jaw and tightened his fists. He seldom lashed out and never cursed; instead he became tense to the point of shaking. He was "PO'd," as he called it.

The brothers resumed their walk home in silence. It wasn't the first time they'd encountered racial hostility, but usually it was just a curse or an angry eye when they walked into a store. Never had anyone spit on them. Never had they felt this dirty.

Lura's flat eyebrows sank over his eyes with disgust. "I know what I want to be when I grow up," he said, breaking the silence. "A Greyhound bus driver—so I can get the hell out of Mississippi."

Jesse nodded. He was thinking the same thing.

CHAPTER 4

THE WORDS

Several days later
Lux, Mississippi

BY EARLY AFTERNOON, the heat struck the sharecroppers full force.

With his back hunched, Jesse Brown hoed between the shin-high cotton plants. Sweat dripped down his back, turning his overalls deep blue. He squinted at the acres of leaves ahead. The rows of green looked endless and the distant pines made the field feel like a prison.

In a nearby row, Fletcher swatted his face constantly. Gnats buzzed his ears and darted for his eyes. Only seven years old, he often lagged behind. Lura, at nine, could keep time with his older brother, but he was away that day with his father, watering the mules or fetching supplies.

Alongside Jesse and Fletcher, six farmhands hoed the furrows. For fifty cents a day, each helped the Browns during planting season. Women wore breezy cotton dresses and worked alongside men dressed in overalls and T-shirts. The adults all wore wide-brimmed straw hats.

Chop. Jesse took a step, then his hoe struck earth again. *Chop.* Jesse thinned the cotton by chopping any weeds between plants. The sun was white-hot overhead. Steamy air settled in the fields and breathing became difficult. Time seemed to stand still.

The sounds of the fields were uninspiring. Hoes jangling the dirt. An occasional sigh or grunt. The *hock* of a worker spitting. No call-and-response songs were ever sung in any field that Jesse Brown worked in. But sometimes there was music. Lost in a daydream, Jesse often hummed to himself. Fletcher and others would glance over to try to discern the tune. Sometimes Jesse hummed a slow folk song and other times a radio jingle.

At one point, it was Jesse who noticed that Fletcher's hoe had gone silent. Jesse looked over and saw the younger boy rubbing his eyes with both fists. This happened often. Jesse walked to the end of the furrow, grabbed a jug of Kool-Aid, and carried it over to his little brother.

"Gnats getting to you, Mule?" Jesse asked.

The younger boy sniffed, wiped his nose against the back of his arm, and nodded. A gnat or two had found its way into his eyes and made them sting.

"They're peeing in my eyes," Fletcher insisted.

Jesse handed Fletcher the jug. Fletcher took a swig. The lemon-lime Kool-Aid was hot but sweet. Kool-Aid was a new invention and it cost just five cents a packet. Fletcher wiped his chin. A timid smile returned to his chubby cheeks.

He and his brother returned to work.

At first, no one heard it coming.

Not Jesse as he hummed.

Not Fletcher as he swatted away the buzzing gnats.

The airplane dived down from the sky. From across the field, Jesse heard a shout. A farmhand was pointing frantically toward the edge of the field. The man dropped to the dirt. Other sharecroppers were falling down too.

A BT-9/NJ-1

Jesse turned just in time to see a sleek blue airplane traveling toward him at treetop height. Its wings were low and yellow, its engine was round, and two large landing gear hung down from the wings—but the plane's propeller wasn't whirling. It was fixed straight across.

It was *aiming* for him.

Jesse ducked and dropped to the earth. Fletcher was already down. The pilot steered down a row of cotton. Jesse lifted his head and his eyes went wide. The plane was stretching larger and larger as it glided toward him.

Jesse buried his nose in the dirt and when he thought he would hear the plane smack the field and slide with a grinding groan, its engine whined, coughed, and bucked to life. Jesse felt the gust of hot exhaust as the plane roared over him.

The plane climbed, whistling toward the clouds. Jesse stood and studied the machine. The plane had a long glass canopy big enough for two men to sit one behind the other. The pilot—whoever he was—jerked the wings and wagged the red-and-white-striped rudder. It was a stunt. The plane had never been in danger of crashing.

"It's that fool Miley boy again!" one of the sharecroppers yelled.

Miley was a neighboring landowner whose son was training to be a pilot in Alabama.

Jesse envisioned the pilot and a redneck buddy having a good laugh at the black folks they had scared senseless. At the far end of the field, the plane turned above the pines. It was circling back for another pass.

"Head for the trees!" shouted a sharecropper.

In the center of the field lay a tall clump of oaks. The farmhands sprinted for safety. Some clutched straw hats as they jumped over the rows of cotton.

Jesse didn't move.

He shaded his eyes with his hand and watched the distant airplane coming around. Fletcher stayed too. If Jesse wasn't going to run, then neither was he, even though he was shaking.

A male farmhand darted out and hollered, "Fletcher! Jesse! Git your asses over here! That boy's gonna kill you!"

Fletcher's knees began to bend in terror, but Jesse didn't flinch. The plane zoomed over the far end of the field and aimed at them. It wasn't gliding now. Its engine was alive. The silver propeller blades whirled at shoulder height and the low-hanging wheels threatened to skim the dirt.

Jesse stood tall and stared right at the oncoming plane. The pilot hugged the earth, his prop wash blowing away the loose plants. The machine grew large in the boys' vision. Its wings stretched. Fletcher hit the dirt and covered his head with his hands.

Just before the plane could cut Jesse in two, its nose pitched up. The pilot gunned the engine and the machine's wheels soared over Jesse.

Fletcher looked up from the soil in time to see Jesse's hands reach toward the wheels as the plane passed above his fingertips. The engine's blast blew soil around the boys. Jesse shielded his eyes and then waved vigorously at the plane as it shrank in the distance. The farmhands ran to his side.

"Did you see that?" Jesse said. "A BT-9! I've only ever read about them."

"You're crazy!" one of the farmhands shouted. "That boy was trying to kill you!"

Jesse laughed and explained that the pilot would never have hit him—at that altitude the pilot would have crashed if he'd tried.

The other farmhands insisted that the pilot was out to get them. "He was up there laughing, yelling, 'Run, niggers, run!'" one man said.

Jesse brushed the comment off with a grin. "He was just having fun. When I get my plane I'll probably do the same thing to you!"

The farmhands broke into laughter. In front of them stood a barefoot thirteen-year-old boy dressed in stained overalls.

"Child, throw that idea straight out of your mind!" said a female field hand. "If Negroes can't ride in aeroplanes, they sure ain't gonna be flying one."

Jesse's smile faded. He returned to chopping but this time he didn't hum. His shoulders tightened and his chin tucked. He was PO'd and not because the farmhands were ignorant but because they just might be right.

Several days later, after the farming was done, Jesse, Fletcher, and Lura walked on the dirt road, heading home to their chores. Dark storm clouds filled the horizon, a brewing summer storm.

Behind them came the distinctive sounds of a gear shifting and an engine rattling like a laboring air conditioner.

Jesse pulled Fletcher off the road into a nearby field and Lura followed. Jesse looked his brothers in the eyes. "If I say to run, then you run—get it?"

The younger boys nodded rapidly.

Jesse scoured the ground until he picked up a dried cornstalk about four feet long. He shook off the dirt and ran back to the roadside, the stalk in hand.

As the school bus neared, the windows slid back and the same angry faces emerged. Jesse stood to the side of the bus's path and choked up on the cornstalk like a bat. As the bus passed, he swung the cornstalk and smacked the first face that jutted from the windows.

The angry face squealed and reeled back inside. The boy's friends yelled at the bus driver to stop. The bus made a grinding sound and stopped. Jesse lowered the cornstalk but kept it in his hands. The boys in the back of the bus swore until a male voice barked, "Shut up!" The bus door banged open.

A white man in suspenders stepped out, spit tobacco juice, and strode toward Jesse. The bus driver was older, yet he had broad shoulders and big fists. Lura shielded Fletcher and glanced nervously up at Jesse, waiting for the order to run. Jesse remained still, his eyes fixed on the approaching driver.

"What in the hell just happened here?" the driver asked, his eyebrows narrowing.

"Sir," Jesse said. "Every day when you pass us, those boys stick their heads out and spit on us."

The driver's eyebrows lifted. He turned and stared at his bus. The boys were leaning halfway out the window, like dogs with dangling tongues.

"C'mon, let him have it!" yelled the crying boy.

The driver turned and studied Jesse from head to toe, taking in the sight of the boy's bare feet and patched overalls. The driver then glanced to Fletcher and Lura, who were cowering in the nearby field and looking up with frightened eyes.

"Well, that won't happen anymore," the driver said.

The man turned and strode back to his bus. The door slammed harder than before. The boys' heads disappeared from the windows. Through the open windows of the bus Jesse and his brothers heard the driver chewing the kids out. Soon enough, the bus started and drove off with a grind and a roar.

When the bus was out of sight, Jesse and his brothers resumed walking home. The storm clouds still brewed in the distance, but things felt different.

After a few silent paces, Fletcher looked over at Jesse. His eyebrows were arched in astonishment. Jesse smiled, shrugged, and raised his hands, palms out.

His younger brothers broke out in laughter.

The rain was falling thick and heavy by the time Jesse and his brothers reached home, a cabin nestled in a thin grove of trees. The cabin was made of unpainted pine boards and was covered by a rusted tin roof. Kerosene lamplight flickered in the windows. The whole structure sat on blocks, a pile under each corner. Behind the home was a garden fence and then some railroad tracks. When trains raced by at night, the cabin shook.

Jesse and his brothers stepped onto the porch, where the mosquitoes had collected, seeking protection from the rain. The boys swatted the pests and entered through the cabin's rickety front door.

John Brown was lumbering around the main room, placing glass jars under leaks from the roof. The cabin's main room was for living, cooking, and sleeping. At night, Jesse's parents slept there on a pull-out bed, while the children slept in a smaller room in back. The shack lacked plumbing; an outhouse served that role.

Jesse and his brothers wiped their bare feet with a rag that was kept near the door. Their brown shoes sat nearby and were being saved for Sundays, when the family attended church services. Jesse's shoes had holes and so did his brothers' shoes, but the holes had been filled with patches of cardboard and painted over with shoe polish.

"Look after your things, boys," John Brown shouted over the rain that pinged against the metal roof. Julia Brown, the boys' mother, was cooking on a wood-burning stove on the other side of the room. She was petite and trim and wore her short black hair curled behind her ears. Her face was strong and certain, with high cheekbones and intelligent eyes.

The boys greeted their mother.

"Hi, loves," she said back. She was unfazed by the clatter on the roof and her toothy smile stretched widely.

John and Julia Brown

Jesse and his brothers ran to the smaller room in the back of the cabin. Between two beds sat a lantern on top of an apple box. The boys' books and magazines lay in piles next to their beds. At night, Lura and Fletcher shared a bed with their older sister, Johnny, who was away helping her boyfriend's family.* On the other side of the room, Jesse shared the other bed with his older brother William, who was shoveling coal for the railroad and wouldn't come home until much later.

Jesse gathered up his dog-eared copies of *Popular Aviation* and stacks of how-to books—how to do magic, jujitsu, woodworking, and athletics—while Fletcher scooped up his mystery novels and Lura rescued his newspapers. The boys moved their effects to the driest corner of the room and then dragged their beds over their books. They had slept in wet sheets before and it was miserable.

---

* Johnny Brown would marry that year. Tragically, both she and her first child would die a year later during childbirth.

Jesse and his brothers ran to join their father in aligning the jars under the leaks. On a clear night, they could see stars through the cracks, but now all they saw were flashes of lightning. With the leaking roof under control, the boys congregated near their mother. The warmth from the cast-iron stove dried their skin. Julia was almost finished with supper. Jesse's favorite dish was his mother's chicken pot pie.

"How was your day, boys?" Julia Brown asked.

Jesse shot his brothers a quick glance and answered for them. He told his mother that they had made good progress on the field. On their walk home, Jesse and his brothers had agreed not to mention the cornstalk incident.

Jesse knew that his actions had been dangerous. In the Depression-era Deep South, a black kid couldn't just hit a white kid without inviting trouble. The white kid might go home and come back with his father and his father's friends, or worse. There'd been a lynching six months earlier, just thirty miles down the road.

After dinner, Jesse, Fletcher, and Lura sat around the table with their mother and enjoyed dessert. The family grew their own sugarcane and made syrup, so sweets were never in short supply. Sweet potato pie was a family favorite.

John Brown rocked his oversized frame in a chair while reading a newspaper. As he read, he sipped sweet tea from a mason jar. A church-going Baptist, he served as deacon for the family's forty-member church and never drank alcohol. Beside him, a wind-up Victrola record player played softly. When the record player slowed, John reached down and cranked it back to life. His favorite record was a musical containing the song "Ol' Man River."

After dessert, the boys and their mother always played what she called "the word game," Julia's attempt to make up for the schooling her boys missed during planting season. Before she married John Brown she had taught public school, and when Jesse and her boys were old enough, she resumed teaching Sunday school at the church.

Jesse, Lura, and Fletcher passed around a dictionary. Each chose a word and read its definition. Julia then attempted to spell it. The harder the word, the greater the challenge, and the boys groaned time and again as she spelled every word correctly. The boys' older brother Marvin was away on scholarship at the all-black Alcorn College, intent on becoming a science teacher. But when he came home, even he couldn't stump his mother. Embedded in the game was Julia's hope that through education her boys could escape the fields forever.

Fletcher took the dictionary. He usually chose a word pertaining to medicine, as his dream was to be a doctor. His mother had always told him he could do anything he set his mind to—provided he got an education. When Lura took his turn, he often chose a word relating to geography. Jesse was usually the most excitable player. He'd look up aviation terms like *dihedral* and *dirigible*. But that night, he was mellow. His mind was in another place as the day's events chewed at him.

"People judge you by the words you use," Julia reminded Jesse and his brothers. "So choose the right words and say them correctly, the way they're spelled. No *ain't*. No *whatcha doin'*." She looked at Fletcher, who laughed because he was the guiltiest.

Frustrated, Jesse pushed aside the dictionary. "Mama, sometimes people don't judge you by the words you use. They just judge you." He folded his arms.

"Of course they do," Julia said. She could see that Jesse was holding something back.

She looked him in the eyes.

"Well, I've been called a 'dumb nigger' by a dozen different people," Jesse said, "and that's just this week."

John Brown looked up from his paper. Fletcher and Lura glanced at the floor.

Jesse's mother leaned across the table. "When someone calls you a 'nigger,' then you feel sorry for him," she said. "You have to pity him because his mind has such a sorry way of expressing itself."

Jesse frowned and looked away. He knew his mother had endured far worse than he had. Before her days teaching school, she had been a missionary who had traveled to every corner of Mississippi and encountered every sort of verbal abuse.

Julia smiled and put a hand on Jesse's shoulder. "Even when folks call you the most hateful things, they're still only words," she said. "Words can have all the power in the world or — none at all. That's up to you."

One night soon after, the Brown family gathered on the porch to brush their teeth before bed — everyone but Jesse, who lingered inside. Julia sprinkled baking soda onto John's toothbrush and Lura's and Fletcher's too. A water basin sat on a nearby chair for them to dip their brushes into. John and the boys began scrubbing their teeth and spitting over the porch railing.

Inside, Jesse faced the family's only mirror, on the wall near the kitchen. That night he began a habit he would practice for years. From time to time, his mother spied his secret routine through the window.

"Hey, nigger!" Jesse said to his reflection in the mirror, lowering his eyebrows. "Run, nigger!" he said.

Jesse's jaw tightened. His shoulders lifted. His eyes narrowed and he glared at himself.

"Stupid nigger boy!" Jesse snapped at the mirror, his mouth contorted into a sneer.

Then Jesse took a deep breath.

Then another. And another. His shoulders dropped, his jaw relaxed, and his lips receded to their normal calm. He gazed into his own brown eyes.

Every night he could sneak away, Jesse practiced cursing himself until his eyes remained steady, until he could shrug away the vilest insult without flinching. He knew those words were sure to come.

For what he dreamed of doing, the insults would be coming in planeloads.

CHAPTER 5

THE RENAISSANCE MAN

Five years later, spring 1944
Near Lux, Mississippi

UNDER HIS BREATH JESSE SANG as he weeded the young watermelon plants. He was now eighteen, and five feet eight. His face flowed to a pointy chin. Lura, Fletcher, and John Brown worked nearby as the sun was setting. It was a weekend evening and only the Brown family was still toiling in the fields.

Sporadically, Lura, Fletcher, and John Brown stopped and looked at Jesse. Each was trying to discern the tune he was singing. It was a strange song, almost operatic, probably something he'd learned in school.

A year earlier, Jesse had moved into the nearby city of Hattiesburg to attend a better high school for blacks and his parents had arranged for him to stay with his aunt and uncle. It was his senior year, yet every Saturday morning he walked home to help his family and every Sunday night he walked back to the city to begin the school week.

The words from Jesse's mouth sounded foreign.

"What in the heck are you singing?" Fletcher blurted from his row. "Ain't nobody happy in these damn fields!"

In the fields, his mother's grammar lessons went right out the window.

Jesse looked up and beamed a guilty smile. "I'm practicing a song for choir," he said. "Leander and I are going to sing in an assembly." Leander was his close friend.

"In front of the whole school?" Lura said and raised an eyebrow.

Jesse nodded sheepishly.

Fletcher was intrigued. "If you're gonna sing in front of all them, at least let us hear it first!"

"Come on, son," Jesse's father called over from his row. "Practice on us."

Jesse suddenly became interested in the leafy plants near his foot. "Nah, I'm too tired," he said.

They were all tired, but Jesse especially. His weeks were grueling. In school, he maintained a top-three ranking in his class, ran track in the spring, played football in the fall, and still every evening reported to the Holmes Club, a bar and honky-tonk south of Hattiesburg. There, he worked until midnight, carrying beers to tables of rowdy soldiers from nearby Camp Shelby. With World War II raging, more than a million men and women had flowed into Mississippi for training. Every so often Jesse needed to dodge a fistfight or deal with a drunken soldier's racial slurs, but he shrugged it all off.

Jesse planned on fighting in World War II himself, if the war continued. He wanted to enlist as an officer, which required a higher education; otherwise, he could end up slinging corned beef hash in a mess tent or driving shells to the front lines, the jobs black soldiers usually received. So Jesse had applied to The Ohio State University in hopes of attending the same university as his idol—Olympic track star Jesse Owens—if the university would grant him admission.

Lura and Fletcher stopped picking weeds. They folded their arms and insisted that Jesse sing before they would return to work.

Jesse knew he couldn't talk his way out of giving them a performance. Besides, they heard him sing every Sunday in the church choir.

Jesse cleared his throat and stood straight, revealing a lean physique beneath his tattered overalls. The rows of watermelon plants separated him from his father and brothers like seats in a theater.

He began to sing.

Ave Maria . . . gratia plena . . .

His baritone voice was deep and smooth, and each Latin word rolled perfectly off his tongue and danced across the field.

Maria . . . gratia plena . . .

The song was "Ave Maria," by Schubert, a musical prayer to the Virgin Mary.

Jesse's last lyric trailed softly to silence. He wiped his brow and an embarrassed grin spanned his face. After a stunned pause, Fletcher, Lura, and John Brown clapped and cheered. Jesse jokingly bowed across the rows of watermelons.

CHAPTER 6

THIS IS FLYING

Nearly three years later, January 1947
U.S. Territory of Hawaii

THE SILVER SNJ TRAINER PLANE flew low and fast over the waters of
Pearl Harbor. The plane was stubby with square wings, an open round
nose, and NAVY painted on each flank. Both canopies were open over
the front and back seats.

In the back seat, Tom Hudner eagerly leaned over the cockpit railing to see the sights of the harbor. He was now twenty-two, and his
chin and jaw had thickened, his face had grown more rugged. Beneath his tan cloth helmet his blue eyes devoured the sights. Afternoon clouds dotted the bright sky and their shadows stretched like oil
slicks across the water. Lush fields with gaps of reddish soil surrounded
the harbor, broken only by the short white buildings of Honolulu to
the north.

Tom's black tie flapped wildly over his tan shirt and gold collar bar,
the insignia of an ensign, the entry-level officer grade in the U.S. Navy.

Navy SNJ trainers

Tom was a sailor now, and this was his first real plane ride. He had flown in the belly of a C-47 airliner when he first came west for shipboard duty, but to him that didn't count.

The growl of the engine filled his ears. He glanced beyond the pilot's head and through the flickering propeller. Ahead, gray navy warships were anchored in the harbor's center. The pilot banked a wing as he approached a cruiser with three square gun turrets. She was the USS *Helena*—Tom's ship—and she looked peaceful with shadows draping her sharp lines and sailors milling about her deck.

The sailors waved upward as the SNJ soared overhead. Tom focused on the ship's signal bridge. This had been his home for the past six months. He was a junior officer on the ship whose job was to decode incoming messages and signal other ships with a lamp.

At the rear of the ship sat a kingfisher floatplane on a small ramp. Tom's pilot friend normally flew the kingfisher when the ship was at sea, and he logged extra flight time when the ship was ashore. Today, he had invited Tom along.

The plane dipped its left wing and pulled into a gentle turn. "There's the *Arizona*," the pilot said into his microphone as he pointed leftward.

Tom looked down the wing and saw the yellow outline of the USS *Arizona*'s deck below the water. The sunken battleship rested beside her moorings. Just five years earlier, more than twelve hundred men had died on the *Arizona* after the Japanese sneak attack, and most were still entombed there.

Tom snapped a salute.

The pilot steered the plane into the island's heart for some sightseeing. Rich green mountains slipped past the wingtips and a dark storm brewed in the background. Tom marveled at the tropical ambiance and knew he had made the right choice when he chose the navy.

Four years earlier, in 1943, he had preregistered to attend Harvard University. His father was a Harvard man and everyone expected Tom to follow in his footsteps. But to his family's surprise, Tom contacted his congressman and secured a nomination to the Naval Academy. He was accepted and had graduated in May 1946, just nine months after World War II ended. In accordance with the academy's rule, all graduates were required to do their first posting aboard a ship, and Tom wound up aboard the *Helena*.

The plane began bucking in the rough mountain air. Tom floated from his seat and felt his gut hanging. His smile retreated and his head felt heavy. The pilot dipped a wing and pointed out a waterfall. Tom looked where he was told and thanked the pilot.

The pilot dipped the other wing and pointed out something else. Tom looked but couldn't tell what he was seeing—his vision was becoming blurry. He glanced forward at the instrument panel and could have sworn that the yellow numbers were spinning. Tom lowered his chin and braced his arms against the cockpit walls. Sweat slipped from his helmet. "Sir, I'm not feeling so good," he said over the intercom.

The pilot leveled the plane. "Sorry, Tom, these mountains have some chop because of the coming storm—I'll turn us around."

Tom tried to focus his gaze ahead, but his vision seemed to float. Through a wave of dizziness, he looked down and saw his knees bouncing. The plane swerved back and forth as the pilot steered through the roughs. Tom felt hot around his neck. He opened his shirt and sucked in deep breaths, thirsty for fresh air.

Tom Hudner, now a naval officer

The plane leapt and dipped again. Tom closed his eyes but his head was spinning. He gagged and then shot a hand to his mouth. He scanned the cockpit frantically for an airsickness bag but found none. He knew enough about flying to know that ground crewmen hated nothing more than to have to clean up a pilot's puke. *I can't do this to them*, Tom thought.

With a hand across his mouth, Tom leaned over the right ledge of the canopy and vomited down the side of the plane.

He threw up again and again. His seat harness barely held him from falling out. He heaved so loudly the pilot turned to check out the action.

Finally, Tom wiped his mouth and flopped back inside the cockpit. He leaned his head against his seatback as the world spun around him. "I tossed my cookies," he groaned.

The pilot laughed. "Next time, eat bananas! They taste the same going down as when they're coming back up!"

Too exhausted to reply, Tom vowed there wouldn't be a "next

time." As far as flying went, he had made up his mind—he just wasn't built for it.

Three months later

Drink in one hand, officer's hat in the other, Tom passed through the officers' club wearing a crisp blue blazer over a white shirt and black tie. The club was furnished like an upscale steakhouse but with the Hawaiian touch of palm leaves and tiki statues.

Tom approached a round table and took a seat with his buddies—Carl, Bill, and Doug. Tom's friends were well mannered and neatly groomed, with their hair slicked back. They were ensigns too, and dressed like Tom. Each night, Tom and his buddies enjoyed scotch and sodas in the club after a day's work for their boss, Admiral Kitts, the commander of the Pacific Fleet. For Tom, the posting was new, his first since the *Helena*.

As it did most nights, the talk centered on flying. Tom's buddies had each served on carriers previously and discussed aviation more than real aviators did. The young men turned to Tom. Their unofficial leader, Carl, had an announcement to make. "Tom, we're done with paper pushing. We're doing it, we're putting in our chits for aviation."

A "chit" was another word for an official letter, in this case requesting admission to flight training. It was common knowledge that the navy needed pilots, because so many veterans had left the service after World War II.

"That's wonderful, guys," Tom said. "I hope you get in."

Carl leaned across the table. "You don't get it—we want you to apply with us!"

The others studied Tom's face, eager for his answer.

Tom's smile dropped and he told his buddies about his airsickness.

They reassured Tom that the airsickness was a onetime thing.

Tom nodded politely, despite his doubts.

"Think about it, Tom," Carl said. "What's the first thing you see when a fella approaches you?"

Tom shrugged.

"Gold wings!" Carl said, slapping the left breast of his blazer, where embroidered wings would go.

"Girls see them too," one of the fellows chimed in.

Tom nodded, but he still wasn't budging.

Carl advised Tom to forget his dreams of captaining a battleship—the fleet was retiring them all. Tom shook it off. He didn't really want to command a battleship as his friends assumed. He enjoyed his current work, decoding and sorting classified messages for the Pacific Fleet. Most of the messages concerned the Chinese Civil War, where the Communists were trying to take over China, a nation of 563 million people.

"Aviation is the new battleship," Carl asserted. "It's the future."

He's got a point, Tom thought. Deep down, Tom knew it might be foolish to spend a military career shuffling papers from a decoding machine. He did appreciate aviation's appeal—the leather jacket, the goggles, the ability to buzz your friends or pick up girls.

"Any red-blooded ensign needs to at least try," Carl said. "If not, there's something wrong with you!"

The others raised their drinks over the center of the table. They looked to Tom, hoping he would raise his own.

Tom still remembered the airsickness vividly—heat climbing up his neck, vision spinning, throat gagging. Tom wanted to say no to his friends but could see the enthusiasm in their eyes. He couldn't let them down.

Tom raised his glass.

"Okay, I'll put in my chit, too."

CHAPTER 7

SO FAR, SO FAST

Two years later, May 1949
Hattiesburg, Mississippi

APPLAUSE SHOOK THE AUDITORIUM of Eureka High School as Jesse finished his speech. Behind the podium, Jesse stood in the dress uniform of the U.S. Navy—golden buttons down the front of a white jacket with black shoulder boards. He was now twenty-two and a newly commissioned ensign. On his right hand he wore a Eureka High class ring.

Jesse nodded to the crowd and struggled to keep his grin from stretching too wide. In front of him sat rows of young black faces, teenage boys and girls dressed in their finest for the baccalaureate ceremony, and behind them stood proud parents and teachers.

Jesse tucked his white hat under his arm and walked off the stage. He wasn't accustomed to applause, much less from his alma mater. The local newspaper had never announced that he'd earned his navy wings the previous October. There had been black pilots before: The Tuskegee Airmen had done the army proud during World War II. But

Jesse Brown becomes an officer in April 1949

the navy was a tougher nut to crack. Until Jesse, only whites had flown from carriers.

After the ceremony concluded, Jesse walked down the school's front steps with the principal, Nathanial Burger, a distinguished man with gray hair and a thin mustache over light brown skin. Jesse settled his officer's hat onto his head. It was a Sunday, around noon, and the sun radiated over the quiet neighborhood. As Jesse and the principal talked on the sidewalk, families streamed around them, eager to shake Jesse's hand.

Everyone had wanted to know: How had he earned his wings when countless black cadets before him had failed? In his speech, Jesse had revealed his secret: his flight instructor, Lieutenant Roland Christensen.

During navy flight school Jesse had met Christensen, a former farmboy from Nebraska who'd volunteered to take Jesse—a former farmboy from Mississippi—as his student after other instructors had refused. Before their first flight, Christensen had told Jesse, "Convince me you have what it takes." He saw Jesse as a man, not as a black man.

A slender young black woman in a yellow sundress emerged from the auditorium. She approached Jesse and hugged him tightly. "That uniform just gives me shivers," she said. Quiet and graceful, she was twenty-two-year-old Daisy Pearl Brown, Jesse's bride of a year and a half. They already had a baby girl together, Pamela Elise, who was five

Daisy Brown, then a high school sophomore

months old. Daisy wore her hair in a bun, pulled up and away from her wide, dark eyes.

Jesse introduced Daisy to Principal Burger, who took her hand and joked, "At this rate you'll be the wife of the first Negro admiral some-day!"

Daisy laughed and thanked him.

"You met at Eureka, didn't you?" Principal Burger asked Daisy.

"Yes, sir," Daisy said. She explained that she had been a sophomore when Jesse was a senior. Every day, Daisy and her girlfriends ate lunch near Jesse's woodshop class.

"I had never dated before," Jesse added, "but I was an excellent girlwatcher. And she was the one I had my eye on." Daisy smiled and the principal chuckled.

"I still can't get past it," the principal said to himself. "A son of Eureka flying from a carrier!"

Everyone was astonished at how far Jesse had come. For two years he had studied up north at Ohio State. He had chosen to study architectural engineering and paid his way through school by working as a department store janitor some nights and unloading boxcars others. He also got help from some unlikely friends. When Jesse had worked at the Holmes Club, he made six dollars a night. But on his last night of work, the owner passed the hat to raise a scholarship for him. The white soldiers of Camp Shelby tossed in wadded-up bills, the bar owner emptied his wallet, and together they filled the hat with seven hundred dollars—enough for a year's tuition.

During his second year at Ohio State, Jesse encountered a recruiting poster on a campus bulletin board. The poster showed a naval officer on a carrier deck as a pilot climbed into a fighter plane behind him. It read: CADETS FOR NAVAL AVIATION TAKE THAT SOMETHING EXTRA . . . HAVE YOU GOT IT? With two years of schooling under his belt, Jesse met the requirements to follow the poster's instruction: APPLY—NEAREST U.S. NAVY RECRUITING STATION. Jesse was never more thankful to have attended Ohio State. That poster would never have appeared at an all-black school.

Leaning forward, Burger had a question just for Daisy. "Has he taken you flying yet?"

"No, sir," Daisy said. "And to be quite honest, I'm not too crazy about Jesse's work—it's awfully dangerous."

"We're working on that," Jesse said, giving Daisy a gentle nudge.

Jesse and Daisy strolled arm in arm through Hattiesburg's "colored" neighborhood. Bound for the bus stop in the center of the city, they walked past weeping willows, a brick corner store, and an antiques emporium the size of a barn. A gray water tower broke the skyline. Jesse's folks had been unable to attend the ceremony; Hattiesburg was too far for them to walk.

Jesse and Daisy arrived downtown, where the sunlight streaked across the tops of buildings, casting sharp shadows. Hattiesburg had a fresh face of luxury—Art Deco hotels, classical columns on government buildings, marble banks—thanks to a lumber boom at the turn of the century.

The couple reached the bus stop on the corner of Pine and Main. There were few cars out and the city was calm.

"Perfect day," Daisy said.

Jesse agreed and kissed her on the cheek.

Some of their best memories had been made around the corner at the Saenger Theatre. They had sat in the balcony, the colored section, and watched Clark Gable and Humphrey Bogart movies. Before Daisy was in his life, Jesse first fell in love at the Saenger—with Lena Horne, the famous black singer who starred in the film *Stormy Weather*.

The stoplight on the corner turned red.

A car full of teenage boys pulled up, windows rolled down. Out of the corner of his eye, Jesse glimpsed the red glow of a cigarette being held by a white hand. The passenger draped his arm out the window and tossed the cigarette butt. Jesse eyed the passengers.

The light turned green, but the car didn't budge. No other vehicle was around.

"Hey, nigger," came a voice from inside the car. "Where ya headed?"

Jesse avoided eye contact. He knew the odds were bad if they wanted to fight—four against one.

"How come you wearing a white man's uniform?"

Time slowed. The light turned red again.

An arm slapped the side of the car. "You hear me, boy? Where'd you steal that uniform?"

Jesse held Daisy's hand tighter.

"Stupid nigger, look at me! I asked you a question."

Jesse looked straight ahead.

"Fine, stay there," said the voice. "Don't move a muscle."

The car peeled away and Jesse followed it with his eyes, remaining tense.

Daisy tried to get her husband to let it go. It was over; they had both endured worse. She reminded Jesse that most people had never seen a black officer before. It was true. Just ten months earlier, President Harry Truman had ordered the integration of the military, yet progress was slow in coming. As of that January, just five of the navy's forty-five thousand officers were black—and Jesse was one of them.

Jesse checked his watch and looked up, annoyed—the bus was late. All they needed was a lift across town, to the apartment of Daisy's mother, Addie, who was babysitting baby Pam.

An engine revved hard and loud behind the couple. Jesse and Daisy turned and saw the same car racing back up the road in their direction. Jesse pulled Daisy close. At the corner the car screeched to a stop even though the light was green. Two boys leaned out from the passenger-side windows with fists full of eggs. They threw one egg, then another at Jesse and Daisy, who were too shocked to react. The eggs passed left and right of the couple and exploded against a brick wall in a shower of shells and yolk. Whoops and hollers poured from the car.

More eggs flew through the air. Jesse shielded Daisy with his body, turning his back to the car. An egg flew past Jesse's officer's hat, another splattered the concrete. Daisy trembled against Jesse's shoulder.

Another egg flew past Jesse's white blouse and cracked on the bus stop bench. Another zipped past his leg.

A car's horn blared. The boys' whooping trailed away. The horn honked again and again. The boys began cursing someone new. Jesse lifted his head from shielding Daisy and saw that another car had pulled up behind the teenagers. Its driver, an older man, was gesturing angrily. One of the teenagers lowered himself into the car while the other hung out, eager for one last toss. The teenage driver peeled out in front of Jesse and Daisy and his passenger threw one last badly aimed egg, which missed by a mile.

Jesse watched them leave.

Daisy was sobbing, and Jesse comforted her. "Aww, Tootie, it's over." "Tootie Fruity" was Daisy's nickname, first given to her by her father.

"But they tried to hit us!" Daisy choked out the words.

"Yeah, but they missed." Jesse stroked her back.

A bus's brakes squealed and Jesse and Daisy felt a hot blast of air as the bus screeched to a stop. The door slammed open.

Jesse removed his hat, walked up the steps, and paid the fares while Daisy waited on the ground. Jesse stepped down and led Daisy to the bus's rear door, where black passengers boarded. Sometimes a sympathetic driver would tell a black person that he or she could board from the front—if there were few whites aboard—but not today.

Daisy sat against the window and dried her eyes. She glanced at Jesse and saw that his shoulders were tense, his eyebrows narrowed. A stern look filled his eyes as he scratched his blouse's sleeve with a fingernail. Daisy leaned over and looked closely at his sleeve. A speck of yellow egg yolk had landed on his uniform. She moistened a finger and tried to wipe it off, but the tiny mark stayed.

"I can't believe it," Jesse stammered. "Who would want to desecrate the uniform of the United States Navy?"

CHAPTER 8

THE RING

Seven months later, December 2, 1949
Naval Air Station Quonset Point, Rhode Island

A LIGHT BLUE COUPE PURRED along the roadway of the military base. Its engine revved as the driver pulled into the nearly full parking lot beside hangars and a seaside runway. The car looked and sounded like a hot rod, but it was a stock 1939 Pontiac short cab, with thick flares over each wheel and a fast-sloping back.

Tom Hudner steered to his favorite spot in the rear corner of the lot. Now twenty-five years old and a lieutenant junior grade, Tom had been stationed at Quonset Point for two months, flying heavy attack planes called "Skyraiders." He had overcome his airsickness by simply taking the controls. Flying, instead of riding, made all the difference.

Tom stepped from the coupe and his breath made small clouds in the December air. For weeks now the season's big radio hit, "Baby, It's Cold Outside," could be heard on every radio station. Suddenly it fit.

Tom slapped a green tent cap over his wavy brown hair and zipped his brown leather jacket over his black tie and tan shirt. Below his leather jacket, Tom wore green slacks and brown shoes. The winter "green" uniform was a pilot's pride and joy, an ensemble that only aviators could wear. All other naval officers wore navy or tan uniforms and black shoes.

The biting wind blew shoreward, carrying the scent of the sea, and Tom flipped up his jacket's black fur collar. The clouds above were heavy with snow. Tom liked the Christmas season. He was from Fall River across the bay, and the cold felt familiar and invigorating—yet strangely different this year.

For Tom and his fellow servicemen, a new, uneasy weight blanketed the season of peace. America was at war in a conflict the papers were calling the "Cold War," because the bullets weren't yet flying, as in a hot war.

Just seven months earlier, in May 1949, the first clash had been decided. The struggle was over Berlin, the vanquished city that the Allies had divided after World War II, each taking a zone. In June 1948, America, Britain, and France awoke to find Soviet tanks blockading the roads, railways, and canals into their zones. The dictator of the Soviet Union, Joseph Stalin, was besieging the democratic zones to force the 2.2 million German civilians there to submit to communism or starve. But America and the democracies devised a way around the Soviet tanks—by flying over them. For eleven months, American and British aircrews flew three hundred thousand runs of food and supplies into Berlin during an operation coined the "Berlin Airlift." Ultimately, the Soviets abandoned their roadblocks, but the lasting outcome was clear: The sides of the Cold War had been drawn.*

Tom thrust his hands into his pockets and walked toward the han-

---

* During the airlift, the Soviet military shined spotlights in Allied pilots' eyes and Soviet fighters buzzed dangerously close to transport planes during 773 documented acts of interference. Seventy-eight Allied pilots and crewmen died in crashes. Historians estimate that the airlift cost more than $2.2 billion in present-day currency.

gar. Beyond, navy fighter planes sat in rows on a concrete parking area with their wings folded upright. Beyond the planes lay a long runway and beyond that the cold waves of Narragansett Bay. The airfield lay on a "neck," as New Englanders call it, a slab of land jutting into a bay.

As Tom opened the hangar door, a rush of exhilaration hit him. He was reporting to "Fighting 32"—pilot slang for Fighter Squadron 32 (VF-32).

He had made it to fighters.

Tom and his new flight leader, Lieutenant Commander Dick Cevoli, leaned over the railing on the hangar's second floor and gazed at the planes below.

Cevoli was thirty, and 100 percent Italian American. His black hair receded at the temples, but his dark eyes beamed youthful enthusiasm. A grin stretched beneath his long Roman nose.

Although the hangar's doors were shut, the metal rafters trapped the cold. Both men kept on their leather G-1 jackets, the standard gift from the navy after earning their wings. The fur collar on Cevoli's jacket had turned reddish with time, the sign of a veteran. Before Tom met Cevoli, he had heard rumors in the officers' club. Apparently, his new flight leader was a former civil engineer turned fighter pilot who had pulled some jaw-dropping heroics in WWII, although Cevoli himself remained tight-lipped about it.

Beneath the bright lights, the planes' dark blue paint glimmered. Black propellers and radial engines poked out from between folded wings. Maintenance men stood on ladders inspecting engines and others used a crane to lower a propeller.

"Anything I can do to help your transition?" Cevoli asked in his snappy New England accent. He had grown up just five miles from the base.

Tom assured Cevoli that everything was fine. "I didn't even need to change my parking spot," he joked.

Dick Cevoli and his wife, Grace,
on their wedding day in 1946

"Everyone brags about his squadron being the best," Cevoli said, "but Fighting 32 really is."

He gestured to the stubby, barrel-shaped planes below. They were F8F Bearcats, the postwar hot rod of propeller planes. A white letter *E* had been painted on the engine cowling of each Bearcat. Every aviator knew that the *E* stood for "excellence." Cevoli explained that '32 had been rated the top squadron in the fleet that year and would wear the *E* during their yearlong reign.

Cevoli glanced at Tom's right hand, where he spotted a thick gold ring. Anyone in the navy could instantly recognize a Naval Academy class ring. A deep blue stone glimmered on top and "1947" was embossed on the side, the year of Tom's class.

"You know we've got a Negro pilot in '32," Cevoli said as he eyed Tom's ring. "First in the navy."

Tom said that he'd read about this pilot in *Naval Aviation News*.

"You'll be flying with me and him," Cevoli added. "He's a good guy." Cevoli explained that the black pilot was an ensign and, even though Tom outranked him, he had more flight hours than Tom. "If it's just the two of you in the air, he'll lead. That's how we do things here, experience over rank, okay?" Cevoli's personality reminded Tom of a high school baseball coach.

Tom said he was fine with the setup. He knew he had just two months of squadron experience.

Cevoli glanced at Tom's ring again and squirmed, like something was still bothering him. "Will you be okay taking orders from a Negro pilot?"

Tom knew what he was hinting at. The ring. The Academy.

The Academy lay in Annapolis, Maryland, relatively far north, but some still called it "Rebel Country." Maryland was technically a border state during the Civil War but slavery had been legal there, and when the men of Maryland signed on to fight, most fought for the South. For one hundred years the navy elite had studied at the Academy, white males who were essentially joining the navy for life. Until that June, there had never been a black Academy graduate. Five black students who had gained admission earlier were hazed out; rumor had it that one was lashed to a buoy overnight in frigid Chesapeake Bay.

A bead of sweat formed on Tom's forehead. He wanted to hide the ring so that Cevoli would drop the questions. Instead, he said the first thing that came to mind.

"At my high school we only had one colored kid and I was friends with him."

Cevoli nodded.

"His name was Tom Brown," Tom added.

Cevoli smiled.

"He was a good guy," Tom concluded. He glanced away and wanted to pound his own forehead. It was the truth, but it sounded contrived.

Cevoli saw Tom's distress and broke the tension. "Well, that's good. I think you'll get along with this fellow, too—our guy's name is Jesse Brown. And if you don't get along with him, no shame in asking for a transfer," Cevoli added. "We can't have guys flying together if they don't trust one another."

Tom nodded.

He and Cevoli glanced back to the planes below, to avoid the awkwardness of further conversation.

Several nights later

It was dark when Tom walked through the front door and past the reception desk of the bachelor officers' quarters. The three-story brick dormitory resembled a roadside hotel, neither fancy nor shabby, and all single pilots at Quonset Point would fondly call it home between tours at sea.

Tom's shoes clicked on the linoleum as he walked down the dim hallway. Between Tom and his room, a door was wide open and light poured forth, as did sounds. Tom could have sworn he heard a girl giggling and a guy whispering. Women were not allowed in the dormitory.

At the Academy, Tom had been a "Red Mike," the name the cadets gave classmates who were too busy to date. Tom considered turning around and waiting in the lobby but he needed to change for dinner.

He took a deep breath, lowered his chin, and walked quickly ahead. As he passed the room, he glimpsed a tall young man with black hair wildly kissing a brunette girl. Both were clothed—barely.

Oh Lord, Tom thought. He walked faster.

Marty Goode

"Hiya!" came a voice from behind him. The black-haired young man was leaning out the door, shirtless and grinning. With that much confidence, he had to be a pilot.

"Oh, hello," Tom said.

"You're a new guy in '32?" the pilot asked.

Tom said he was.

The pilot stepped from the doorway and approached, barefoot and wearing only boxer shorts. He was about six feet tall and lean cut with sharp black eyebrows and blue eyes paler than Tom's.

"I'm Marty Goode," the pilot said, shaking Tom's hand. "Not to be confused with my evil cousin, Marty the Bad!" Marty laughed at his own joke. He was from Brooklyn and had a strong accent.

"Why, thanks for the warning," Tom said, playing along. "I'll keep an eye out for him."

Marty introduced himself as '32's bull ensign—the ensign in the unit with the most seniority. He was proud of his rank, having joined the navy at age sixteen and worked his way up the enlisted ranks into flying school and an officer's commission.

"Well, I'll see you around," Marty said, "I've got duties to attend to!" He winked and hurried back the way he had come, his bare feet slapping the floor.

Tom walked the other way, shaking his head. He may have kept his parking space, but in Fighting 32, he was starting from scratch.

CHAPTER 9

THE POND

A few days later, December 6, 1949
Warwick, Rhode Island

JESSE STEPPED ONTO THE PORCH of his white clapboard cottage and glanced around the neighborhood. Frost covered the ground, and the early morning light streamed over the houses and onto a large frozen pond across the street. The pond was shaped like an hourglass and the sunlight made the ice glow golden.

Beneath his leather flight jacket, Jesse wore green slacks and brown shoes. His hair was shaved high and tight up over his ears. When he placed his tent cap over his head, his hair completely disappeared. It was a Tuesday and cold enough that Jesse had already started his car to warm the engine. The car was a sparkling new 1949 Dodge Wayfarer coupe, forest green with a long curving roofline, whitewall tires, and flares over the rear wheels. Jesse loved the Wayfarer and had saved for years to afford this, his first car. He never worried about leaving it running in the morning; Warwick was a summer resort for New Yorkers and the neighborhood was deserted in the winter.

Jesse walked down the cottage's steps. This was the first home that he and Daisy rented together, 140 Glen Drive, a cottage built in 1945. The home was raised on concrete blocks because it lay on a peninsula. Gray trees leaned over the streets that paralleled the house, their branches empty and brittle.

As Jesse reached his car, the cottage door was flung open. Daisy threw a wool coat on her shoulders and ran down the steps. Jesse looked surprised to see her again. They'd already kissed goodbye inside, as they did every morning. Daisy reached Jesse, wrapped her arms around her husband, and held him tightly.

Jesse chuckled and hugged her back.

Their neighbors, had they been there, might have been peeking out their windows. They had been fascinated with the young black couple and often asked Daisy to speak in her southern drawl. And when Jesse spoke without an accent, they would marvel that both of them came from the same region. The neighbors had been kind. The ones across the street would invite Jesse and his family over to swim with them in the pond. Daisy was afraid of water but Jesse loved to take dips. He would hold Pam's hand as they waded together.

Daisy kissed Jesse a final time and released her grip. Jesse told her he would see her soon and raised a finger to the sky. Today was a flying day. He continually tried to tell Daisy that flying was fun but Daisy wasn't convinced. She knew a pilot could meet a swift end in peacetime, let alone the war that seemed sure to come.

Just four months earlier, the Soviets had successfully detonated an atomic bomb on a test site and shattered America's "atomic bomb monopoly," the reason her citizens slept soundly. Now the U.S. military was planning for the Soviets to launch an atomic sneak attack. The papers called the scenario the "Disaster Attack" and predicted that Soviet bombers would fly over the polar ice cap—down over Greenland and over Alaska and Canada—to atomize cities on both American coasts. The military was hurriedly building radar outposts up north to provide early warning of enemy bombers that flyers like Jesse would be called to intercept.

Jesse slid into the Wayfarer and shut the door. Daisy remained in the driveway, her arms crossed. Their eyes met through the windshield glass and Jesse lifted his hand from the steering wheel in a small wave. Daisy broke into a guilty grin and waved meekly. Jesse backed out of the driveway and drove away past the pond.

Inside Hangar 4, Quonset Point

Alone in the locker room, Tom slipped on his flight suit and zipped it up. The room smelled like soap and reminded Tom of his days at Andover Academy prep school, changing for track, football, and lacrosse. He kneeled and laced his black leather boots.

The day's mission called for training, but even training carried new seriousness. The navy needed her pilots ready to go operational if the Soviets made a move. Tom found it hard to envision himself lining up a Soviet bomber in his gunsight; just five years earlier, the Soviets had been among the Allies of World War II.*

The locker room door swung open. Tom looked up as he laced his boots. Jesse walked in and set his flight bag on the wooden bench that separated them.

"Good morning," Jesse said stiffly. He opened a locker opposite Tom's.

Tom returned the greeting. He knew he was looking at a figure from aviation history but didn't know much more about his new squadron mate. Tom was, however, eager to correct that. He had long forgotten the tough Portuguese boy Manny Cabral but not Manny's lesson—that a man would reveal his character through his actions, not his skin color.

---

* In reality, the Soviets had been Hitler's ally first. Before WWII began, Hitler and Stalin signed a secret non-aggression pact that allowed German pilots to train on Soviet airfields and German warships to anchor at a Soviet base. Stalin sent oil, rubber, and minerals to Hitler, who supplied the Soviets with tank prototypes, fighter planes, and even the blueprints for the battleship *Bismarck*. The alliance lasted for nearly two years until Hitler turned on Stalin and attacked the Soviet Union. Only then did Stalin join the Allied cause.

"I understand we'll be flying together," Jesse said, looking into his bag. His tone was formal. He removed his boots, then his flight suit.

"I'm Jesse Brown, by the way." Jesse gave an awkward half-wave and remained on his side of the bench.

Tom finished tying his boots and stood up.

"Good to meet you, Jesse. I'm Tom Hudner." Tom thrust his open hand across the space between them.

Jesse looked down at Tom's hand, paused, then extended his hand and shook.

Tom pretended not to notice Jesse's reservations and made small talk about the upcoming flight. He paused when he caught Jesse glancing at his Naval Academy ring. Jesse's eyes fixed on the deep blue stone.

Damn it! He's heard stories about the academy, Tom thought as he slipped his leather jacket over his shoulders. His helmet and survival gear were upstairs in the ready room. Tom told Jesse that he would see him at the preflight briefing, then shut his locker and left the room.

Jesse pilots an F8F Bearcat in November 1949.

*   *   *

In tight formation the two Bearcats raced fifty feet above the waves of Greenwich Bay. The morning sky was dotted with clouds, "seasonably cold" as the weatherman called it. With their square wings extended, the Bearcats took on a barrel shape that tapered to slender tails.

Tom flew behind Jesse in the wingman position, a short distance behind Jesse's right wing. Each pilot wore a tan cloth helmet with earphones and goggles on his forehead. Tom's eyes studied Jesse's wingtip as it rose and fell.

The Bearcat fit tightly around Tom. When climbing into the aircraft, he needed to turn his shoulders to sit down. But once he secured the safety straps over his life preserver and leather jacket, he felt like the Bearcat was strapped to his back.

Watch your prop, Tom thought. Four massive, twelve-foot propeller blades whirled like a translucent buzz saw from the nose of Tom's plane. Unlike a jet, if a propeller plane flew too snugly, a pilot could chop off his buddy's wing or tail.

Tom snuck a glimpse at the leaping waves ahead, then back to Jesse's wing. Flying in tight formation required faith. The wingman always watched his leader's wingtip and only the leader looked ahead. If both pilots looked ahead, they could collide.

A blurry pole whipped past Tom on the right. Then another flashed by on the left. The poles were the masts of fishing boats motoring across the bay; Jesse had taken them that low. Tom's eyes narrowed with worry. They were flying due north, the wrong direction. All Jesse had said before takeoff was that he needed to make "a quick detour."

The Bearcat's speed was blistering, yet Tom fought the urge to look ahead. The plane had been built to intercept kamikazes but missed fighting in WWII by just three months. From out of the corner of his eye, Tom saw seagulls whipping past the windscreen like white bowling balls, above and beneath the plane. One bird strike could shatter the canopy, or worse.

Where is he taking me? Tom wondered. They were supposed to fly to Long Island then from landmark to landmark to hone their navigation abilities, skills they might someday use in combat. The brass predicted that the Soviets needed just two more years to mobilize for war. Already, the enemy had America outnumbered.

A spy report published in one of America's top magazines—*Life*— had revealed the enemy's numerical superiority. Reportedly, the Soviet air force boasted 9,000 planes to America's 3,000. The 2.6-million-man Soviet army dwarfed America's force of 600,000. Only the U.S. Navy's surface fleet of 164 vessels topped the Soviet's 127 ships, but an American advantage lay within that fleet—15 aircraft carriers and 5,000 navy and Marine Corps combat planes. The Soviets had no carriers, whereas America had built so many that the navy had mothballed a number of still-operable World War II carriers. Overnight, the navy and Marine flyers had become America's competitive advantage.

Tom glimpsed a gray, rocky coastline racing toward him. A small peninsula reached across the bay from the west. Tom knew it was Warwick Neck because his hometown lay across the bay. The planes roared past a lighthouse and crossed the shore.

"Harrison Tower, this is Lawcase Flight," Jesse radioed. He was calling the civilian airfield that lay ahead, just inland. "Are your skies clear? We're two F8Fs from Quonset Point, passing through."

What the heck? Tom wondered. They were supposed to make every minute of training time count, not play games.

Jesse nosed forward and took his plane even lower, nearly scraping the gray branches of barren trees. Tom followed him down, then spotted an ice-covered pond in the center of the peninsula. The pond was shaped like an hourglass and was bordered by cottages and trees. Jesse aimed for it. Tom glanced between Jesse's wingtip and the pond. A mile beyond the pond, a flat X appeared on the horizon. It marked Harrison Field, a civilian airfield where hobby flyers and panicky student pilots took to the sky.

Tom scowled. He was certain that Jesse was lining up on the pond in order to buzz the airfield, low and fast to rattle the civilians. "Flat hatting," as buzzing was called, was neither approved nor forbidden.

The word was just "Don't get caught." Tom had not gone through the Academy to get booted in a stunt like this, but Jesse was flying lead.

"Harrison Tower to Lawcase Flight."

The tower was calling Jesse.

"Our airspace is clear, come on over."

Jesse thanked the controller, and Tom gritted his teeth.

"Get ready to climb!" Jesse told Tom, his voice crackling with enthusiasm.

The silver pond stretched in Tom's windscreen. It looked like Jesse was going to fly them straight into it.

Daisy's heels clunked down the wooden steps of the cottage as she carried baby Pam outside and set her feet on the cold driveway. A year old now, Pam could walk, just unsteadily. She was bundled in a small coat and a beanie hat. Between the beanie's earflaps was a face with round eyes and chubby cheeks. Daisy kneeled and turned Pam back toward the cottage, in the direction of Quonset Point. Far over the tree line she spotted them — two black crosses zooming toward them.

"There's Daddy!" she shouted, pointing.

Pam smiled at the mention of Daddy and blinked at the horizon.

"Here he comes!" Daisy said. "Look!"

Behind the trees, the Bearcats' wings stretched wider and their whirling propellers purred louder and louder. In a screaming roar the planes blasted over the cottage roof.

Daisy crouched and covered Pam's ears. Tree branches rattled. Daisy turned Pam to follow the Bearcats as the planes raced over the pond. Already far away, the planes pitched up and into a vertical climb. Their canopies glimmered.

"There goes your daddy!" Daisy exclaimed, pointing for Pam.

Pam bounced and cooed.

Daisy took Pam's little hand, and together they waved as the Bearcats shrank toward the clouds.

*   *   *

Stick like glue, Tom told himself as the two planes climbed in formation. He kept his eyes locked on Jesse's wingtip and held even pressure on the stick.

Jesse looked over to check Tom's position. He was grinning.

"Just saying hi to my girls!" he shouted over the radio.

Tom's scowl lifted.

The Bearcat held its speed. It had so much power that it wanted to go up and up and up. Tom's instrument panel vibrated and the engine hummed. Gray clouds slipped downward past his wings.

A smile slowly cracked Tom's face. When the clouds disappeared behind them, Jesse leveled out into a sky of pure blue. Jesse turned the two-ship south toward the sun, the direction they were supposed to fly.

"Air show's over," Jesse said. "Let's go find the Big Apple."

Tom sat back and relaxed. Jesse looked over and explained over the radio that every time he could, he did a low pass for his wife and little girl.

Tom smiled and nodded. *Why didn't he just say so?*

"Anyone you want to buzz?" Jesse asked as an afterthought. "Now's the chance."

"Nope," Tom replied without hesitation.

Then he gave the opportunity some thought. If he could buzz anyone, he'd buzz his dad's country club when the golfers were there. He and Jesse were probably flying over the club at that moment. Tom imagined his dad's friends would look like a bunch of storks from above as they walked in circles looking for a ball. The grin slipped from Tom's face. He couldn't bring himself to do it, no matter how much fun it would be.

Someone might report him.

On the ground, with their Bearcats' massive blades at rest, Tom and Jesse slid from their planes' wings. The Bearcat sat high on its gear and both men dropped four feet, their boots hitting the tarmac. Together they walked toward the hangar, carrying their plotting boards. Jesse was still glowing after buzzing his family and he asked Tom if he had a wife or girlfriend.

"Nope," Tom said. "I'm all business, just focusing on my career."

Jesse told Tom that sounded like a good plan. Tom would later realize that Jesse was just being polite. A man could have both, and Jesse was proof.

As they walked, Jesse looked over at his new wingman. "We may have gotten off on the wrong foot this morning," Jesse said. "I apologize." He added, "In flight school I stuck my hand out a lot of times but the other guy kept his at his side."

Tom nodded sympathetically. "Well, you don't have to worry about that with me," he said.

Jesse nodded with approval.

Inside the hangar at the duty desk, Tom and Jesse filled out their reports. Time up, time down, hours in the air—the usual. Tom caught Jesse looking at his ring again and made a mental note to leave it at home tomorrow or else he'd never make any progress in '32.

"Beautiful ring," Jesse said.

Tom stopped writing and looked up, surprised. Jesse was still gazing over at the ring's deep blue stone.

"I lost mine swimming in the pond by my house," Jesse said, referring to his high school ring.

Tom told Jesse that he had lost his ring, too, during flight training at Pensacola. The one he was wearing was a replacement, not the original.

"You get used to it being there," Jesse said. "It reminds you of something you can be proud of, huh?"

Tom agreed, then returned to filling out his forms, fighting a grin. Even if he was dangerous to his career, Tom felt the potential to really like this Jesse Brown.

CHAPTER 10

ONE FOR THE VULTURES

Nearly four months later, April 4, 1950
Warwick, Rhode Island

IT WAS MORNING and Daisy was crying on the bed in the cottage's dark bedroom. She was dressed with makeup on and was curled up in the fetal position. She knew where Jesse had gone and what he was trying to do, and the thought nearly drove her mad.

After a while, Daisy stood, wiped her eyes, and blew her nose. She snuck down the hallway and cracked the door to the baby's room. Pam was still asleep. At the sight of her child resting, Daisy's lip began to quiver and her eyes again welled up with tears. She shut the door to Pam's room, held a hand to her mouth, and hurried to the living room. A thought repeated in her mind: *What will we do if something happens to him?*

Daisy clutched herself and paced in front of the bookshelf. Jesse had given her a book club subscription for her birthday and she had filled the shelves with Emily Post's etiquette books and romance stories such as *Pride and Prejudice*. She and Jesse were living their own romance story and all Daisy wanted was a happy ending.

Jesse had tried to prepare her for the worst. He often sat her down and reminded her: "On any day that I walk out of this house, there's a possibility that I may not walk back in." It was hard for Daisy to hear and harder still for her to accept.

She stepped to the front window and peered through the curtains. The green Wayfarer sat empty in the driveway. Jesse had taught her to drive on the back roads and she could manage to drive to the grocery store and back. Yet she felt stranded, even if she wasn't.

Daisy curled up in a chair near the window and kept glancing outside, as if her longing would bring Jesse home sooner. Dangling from Daisy's neck was a cross. She held it tightly and prayed for her husband's safety.

That afternoon

The aircraft carrier USS *Wright* plowed through the dark, choppy sea. On the carrier's tower, Tom Hudner weaved through the pilots and sailors who crowded the observation deck, a place darkly nicknamed "Vulture's Row" because it proved the best spot to watch carrier landings, some of which ended in crashes.*

The tower sat mid-ship, so Tom had a good view across the deck. He draped his arms over the edge of the bulkhead and shielded his brow. A gust of wind nearly swept away his tent cap. The *Wright* was a "light carrier," a smaller vessel and less than stable in rough seas.

Gray clouds draped the Atlantic and cracks of blue peeked through in spots. Tom's eyes locked on a sleek dark Corsair several miles away that flew past the ship in the opposite direction. Jesse was at the controls and coming around to land.

Tom's squadron mates shared the railing. Nearby was Ensign Carol Mohring, a lanky twenty-six-year-old with dark hair who'd recently

---

* Throughout this book, the author has translated some navy terminology into civilian-friendly equivalents. Accordingly, the carrier's "island" has become the "tower," the "wardroom" is the "dining room," "knots" have been converted into "miles per hour," and so forth.

Carol Mohring

joined the squadron. Carol clutched a mug of hot chocolate in his hand. It was no easy matter to climb the flights of stairs that led to Vulture's Row using one hand, but somehow he always found a way. Carol's folks were Germans who had immigrated to Pennsylvania and their son looked classically Teutonic with a cleft chin, sharp eyebrows, and wide lips that often appeared to frown.

"How's he doing?" Tom asked Carol.

"He's missed twice," Carol said with the hint of an accent. "Both wave-offs, not even close." Carol spoke matter-of-factly but not without concern—he and Jesse were close friends who carpooled to work together. "He's coming in too hot and high."

Tom knew why Jesse was having difficulties—the Corsair.

That winter, the navy had redesigned Fighting 32 as a ground attack squadron and replaced their lightweight Bearcats with heavyweight Corsairs. Unlike the Bearcat, the Corsair was combat-tested and capable of hauling tons of ordnance.

Despite a reputation as the navy's iconic fighter of WWII, the Corsair had a glaring weakness—its "hog nose." The plane's nose was too long and its designers had placed the cockpit too far back along the fuselage. This compromised the pilot's forward visibility exactly when

he needed it most—during that heart-pounding maneuver that separated naval aviators from every other pilot on earth, the act that Jesse
Brown was about to attempt: landing on an aircraft carrier.

Fighting 32 had come aboard the *Wright* to complete the pilots'
carrier landing certifications in the new Corsairs. To qualify, a pilot
needed to land six times on the carrier. Tom had already certified on
an earlier cruise, but Jesse was still trying. He had made five landings
so far, but the sixth was everything. If he failed on the sixth, he'd be
vectored back to dry land, an hour's flight away, and his days of flying
fighters would be in question.

Carol studied Jesse's plane in between sips from his mug. He was
always on Vulture's Row, trying to learn by watching the others. Carol's file back at Quonset Point held a secret—he had once crashed a
Corsair in training.

The American flag flapped wildly overhead. From the back of Vulture's Row came murmurs of excitement. Dozens of black sailors
leaned across the railing like men at a ballpark hoping to snag a homer.
They wore navy pea coats and white hats and had come from the mess
hall or engine room or the staterooms where they made the officers'
bunks. They had come to watch the navy's first black carrier pilot land,
to see history being made, no different than a man yearning to see
Jackie Robinson steal home plate. But the stakes were higher here. No
one ever got killed trying to steal a base.

Tom could see Jesse sitting tall in his seat, his canopy back. The
plane's landing gear was down and its tail hook dangled behind the tail
wheel. Soon, Jesse would begin his U-turn to approach the carrier
from behind. To the average sailor, everything appeared fine. But Tom
knew something the average sailor didn't—Jesse was in trouble. Each
time a pilot missed a landing, the panic began to build and subsequent
attempts would be more hazardous. The Corsair's reputation didn't
help Jesse any. It wasn't called the "Ensign Eliminator" and the
"Widow Maker" for nothing.

Sailors in brightly colored shirts and skullcaps huddled on the flight
deck and shouted into one another's ears. The wind stormed across

A carrier landing approach

the deck, rippling their blue dungarees. Their uniforms were color-coded according to their roles: Men in yellow steered the planes around the deck; men in red formed the crash crew. Tom saw them glancing at Jesse and knew what they were saying: *Be alert—this guy's shaky!*

Far away and slightly behind the carrier, the left wing of Jesse's plane slowly tilted toward the sea. He was beginning his U-turn to approach from behind. The ship's loudspeaker blared, "Clear the deck!" Tom's heartbeat spiked. The deckhands broke their huddle and ran for cover in the tower and the metal trenches that ran alongside the deck.

The wooden deck was empty but for the nine black cables that spanned the rear, each spaced ten yards apart. The cables were everything to carrier aviation. Although the *Wright's* deck stretched nearly seven hundred feet, a pilot used only the back half for landing, a space about the size of a football field. There, the cables were strung five inches above the deck—low enough that a plane's tires could roll over them, yet high enough that its tail hook could snag one and yank the plane to a stop. Jesse would need to set his twelve-thousand-pound machine down at a precise angle and speed to stand a chance.

If he overshot the cables, three tall crash barriers—cables strung from stanchions—stretched across the middle of the ship to stop him by wrapping around his propeller and wheels. If Jesse overshot the cables and crash barriers, an ominous final barricade remained. At the front of the deck, Corsairs sat parked and empty, almost asking for a collision.

As Jesse's plane continued its turn, a solitary figure took his place on a small platform that jutted from the rear corner of the ship. He wore a silver flight suit and skullcap. He was a landing signal officer—the LSO—a veteran pilot who doubled as a sort of shipboard traffic cop. From the trench below, a sailor handed two paddles to the figure. The paddles were lined with neon pink strips of fabric. The LSO would use the paddles to steer Jesse toward the deck and signal the precise time for him to cut the engine and touch down.

Jesse's Corsair curved fast over the frothy waves, one wing aimed like a dark slash toward the sea. The ship's deck heaved and sighed. *This is going to be tricky,* Tom thought.

Jesse held steady at 110 miles per hour. Any faster and he'd overshoot the cables. Too slow and he'd stall and wing over, into the waves.

Two hundred yards behind the deck, Jesse broke his turn and snapped his wings level. With his nose high and his tail low, Jesse descended faster and faster toward the field of cables. He was flying nearly blind, barely able to see a sliver of the deck. That's exactly how an LSO liked it. *Don't watch the ship!* they were known to tell pilots. *Keep your eyes on me!*

The LSO spread his arms wide like a scarecrow. *You're good!* he was telling Jesse. *Hold steady!* The black sailors leaned farther over the railing, their eyes locked in awe.

The Corsair was a hundred yards from the rear of the ship. Seventy-five yards. Fifty. The LSO flipped his right paddle across his chest— *Cut the engine and land!*

But something didn't look right to Jesse. He hesitated for a split second and violated the cardinal rule of carrier aviation: *"Cut"* means *"cut"!*

Instead, he kept flying. The cables slipped toward him.

Only then did Jesse cut the throttle.

In a blur of speed, he dipped the Corsair's nose forward and dived for the deck. At the last second he lifted the nose and dropped the tail to catch a cable. His hook passed over one cable, then another, until they all had slipped away.

The plane's tires slammed the deck in puffs of white smoke. The tail hook slapped the wood, snagging nothing. The plane's struts compressed and the Corsair sank low onto its landing gear like a coiled spring.

Then it sprung. Upward the Corsair leapt as its momentum carried it forward, straight toward the crash barriers.

Jesse's engine snarled to life with a roar that shook the deck. White smoke shot from his engine's exhaust ports. Tom's eyes went wide. Rather than roll into the crash barrier as he should have, Jesse was compounding his mistake. He was pouring on full power.

Tom couldn't believe his eyes.

He's trying to take off!

Pilots gasped. Sailors covered their faces. Carol spilled his hot chocolate.

Jesse's Corsair leapt over the first crash barrier, then the second. He was on course for a bone-crunching collision with the parked Corsairs ahead. Tom, Carol, and the others sank behind the bulkhead and braced for the sound of crumpling metal.

As the Corsair soared over the final crash barrier, its right tire clipped the wire. The wire spun the Corsair out of control, to the right. Instead of careening into the parked planes, Jesse's plane whistled off the side of the carrier's deck and dropped out of sight.

Across from the tower, deckhands peeked up from their trench. Only the sea could be seen, churning on the horizon. They waited for the sound of a plane punching into the waves but heard only the wailing wind.

Tom and the others rose from Vulture's Row and leaned across the railing to see forward. The red-shirted crash crew poured from the tower with axes and fire extinguishers. On the ship's bridge, the captain and his sailors stood and pressed their faces to the windows.

A deckhand climbed cautiously to the deck, then another and another. Together, they sprinted across the deck to the spot where the Corsair had last been seen. At the edge of the deck they stopped and looked down, scanning the waves for the wreckage.

All they saw were foaming whitecaps floating on the dark sea.

The men looked up to the horizon. Their eyes narrowed. A mile away flew a dark blue plane just skimming the waves.

The men burst into a massive cheer.

The cheers diminished into laughter and clapping as the Corsair shrank in the distance. After several tense seconds, the plane climbed skyward and slowly began turning.

Jesse Brown was coming back around.

Twenty minutes later, in a ready room below the flight deck, Jesse removed his flight gear in silence. The rows of leather armchairs were empty in the room behind him.

Before missions, pilots came to this theater like room for briefings, and they suited up here, too. Soon everyone who had flown that day would gather in the room for a debriefing, to hear the LSO read his critique of each landing.

Jesse had completed the six requisite landings and was now fully qualified in the Corsair. But he dreaded what would transpire in the debriefing. A naval aviator was supposed to land correctly the first time—not the fourth—and Jesse knew how the LSO would describe his barrier bounce: "DNKUA."

It was an acronym, pilot-speak for "Damn Near Killed Us All."

"There he is!" an excited voice shouted.

A rush of pilots burst through the doorway. Jesse turned and saw the tall frame and curly black hair of Marty Goode. Marty's gang of junior ensigns followed close behind. Marty threw an arm over Jesse's shoulder to make a pronouncement. Jesse squirmed to get away, but Marty kept him close.

"They say there are two kinds of aviators in the navy," Marty told his gang. "Those who have hit the barrier—and those who will someday hit it. But I think there's a third—Jesse Brown. When he sees a barrier, he jumps it!"

The pilots laughed. Even Jesse had to smirk. Marty was Jewish and felt kinship with Jesse because they both had endured prejudice. During flight training, a fellow cadet admitted to Marty that before he met him, he thought Jews might actually have horns.

Jesse dropped his shoulders as Marty and the others pummeled him with their questions. As they replayed his barrier bounce with their hands, Jesse's smile faded. Despite the levity, despite the adulation, he understood the reality.

He had damn near killed himself.

CHAPTER 11

A TIME FOR FAITH

The next evening, April 5, 1950
Warwick, Rhode Island

FROM HER SEAT ON THE COUCH, Daisy heard the car pull into the driveway and saw the headlights cut the darkness. She set her book down. A car door shut, then another. Daisy peered through a window and a smile spanned her face. In the driveway, Jesse was removing his sea bag from the trunk of Carol Mohring's car. Both men were wearing long blue coats and white officer's hats.

Daisy scooped up Pam as Jesse's keys jingled in the lock. Jesse stepped inside and his eyes turned moist. He hugged his wife and daughter tightly and seemed reluctant to let go. Finally, Jesse remembered that Carol was waiting on the porch, so he took Pam into his arms and stepped aside, inviting Carol in. Carol took off his hat, greeted Daisy, and tousled Pam's head. He had visited the family many times, but was always shy at first.

After putting Pam to bed, Jesse sat in the living room with Carol and switched on the radio. A big band melody drifted into the kitchen, where Daisy was fixing sandwiches. Daisy enjoyed Jesse's taste in music—Glenn Miller, Nat King Cole, and Etta James—but whenever Jesse tried to pull her to her feet, Daisy drew the line. She was convinced that she was a terrible dancer.

Daisy overheard fragments of somber conversation as the men discussed Jesse's barrier bounce. She leaned closer and snuck a peek. At one point Jesse sat back, wrapped his hands behind his head in frustration, and said, "If I had done anything right, I would have killed myself."*

Daisy's eyes widened.

Carol spoke about the time he had crashed on the carrier USS *Cabot*. He had been coming in to land when he saw the forward deck crowded with planes and lost his nerve, causing his Corsair to skid across the deck and into a trench.

"I nearly crushed several men," Carol admitted. What Carol didn't reveal was that he had only remained an aviator to honor his father, a factory laborer new to America from Germany.

Jesse stayed silent. His greatest fear, one he'd confided to his squadron mates, was of dying and leaving Daisy a widow.

"Makes you think of hanging it up, huh?" Jesse said.

Carol nodded.

In the kitchen, Daisy quickly turned back to the sandwiches, her face frozen with shock. She had always comforted herself by thinking, *My husband is different—nothing will happen to him.*

Daisy added cups of coffee to her platter, entered the living room, and set it on the table. Jesse sat up and tried to force a smile. He nibbled at the corner of a sandwich, like he was eating only to please her.

Daisy returned to the kitchen, her eyes heavy with worry.

---

* Later, in the same living room, Jesse would confess his fear of the Corsair to his friend Vic Breddell, a black enlisted man in charge of cockpit training. "You know, Vic, I think that Corsair will kill me," Jesse said. "I just have that feeling."

Four weeks later, May 2, 1950
Quonset Point Naval Air Station

The USS *Leyte* loomed over the clusters of pilots and their loved ones gathered on the concrete pier. The carrier's tower stood ten stories above a flight deck loaded with planes and the ship's long angular shadow darkened the shallow water.

It was a pleasant spring morning. Sun snuck through the clouds and reflected off the chrome of the cars on land. About one hundred pilots from Fighting 32 and her sister squadrons said their goodbyes. The pilots wore summer uniforms—tan slacks, tan jackets with black shoulder boards, and tan hats with black brims. Their girlfriends and wives wore their Sunday best hats and knee-length skirts.

In the midst of the crowd, Daisy dabbed her moist eyes with a handkerchief and watched Jesse hold Pam's hand as the little girl twirled circles around him. Carol Mohring hovered nearby, reluctant to leave

The *Leyte* (right) alongside the *Wright* at Quonset Point

Jesse's side. In the middle of a throng of giggling college girls stood Marty Goode and a few pilots. The girls wore cream-colored sweaters with the brown letter *B* of nearby Brown University.

Jesse tried to cheer up Daisy. He asked what souvenirs she wanted him to bring home for her.

"Maybe something from Anathens?" she asked, sniffling.

Jesse raised an eyebrow in confusion.

"You know—from Anathens, Greece," Daisy clarified.

Jesse grinned. "Darling, I think it's *Athens*, Greece."

Daisy shook her head. She was pretty sure it was "Anathens," just like "Annapolis." Jesse chuckled but decided to leave it alone. In contrast to Daisy's fretting, he was bursting at the seams to see the world.

Soon, Fighting 32 would board the *Leyte* and their new mother ship would whisk them to the Mediterranean to join the navy's 6th Fleet, the only armed forces in those waters, a unit nicknamed the "Dancing Fleet."

A period of work and play would follow. The pilots would train over the open seas and even launch a mock assault on the sun-drenched island of Crete. But it was the shore leave in Greece, Italy, France, and Lebanon that made the Dancing Fleet a navy man's dream duty. Stories had slipped back to Quonset Point from earlier cruises—visions of white uniforms, champagne, dances, and girls, slinky French ones and tan Italian ones who loved to chase pilots and sailors.

Daisy glanced around as sailors gathered to untie the ship. At the entrance to the pier, other sailors from the base band were unloading from a bus and unpacking their trumpets and drums. Daisy knew her time with Jesse was running short.

The recent headlines had set her emotions on edge. Five days earlier, the papers had revealed the fate of a lost navy plane. A month before, the four-engine Privateer reconnaissance plane—nicknamed the "Turbulent Turtle"—had vanished over the Baltic Sea, north of the Soviet Union.

The newspapers had been following the saga of the lost "Baltic

Plane" and were now reporting that residents of a Danish island had found American flight uniforms washed ashore, and a Swedish fishing boat had pulled up its nets and discovered the landing gear from the plane—riddled with bullet holes. The unarmed navy plane had been shot down, its ten-man crew murdered over international waters. And the perpetrators?

The Soviets.

The senseless brutality troubled Daisy and all navy wives. On New Year's Day that year, a columnist for *The New York Times* had made his prediction for 1950: "Perhaps we will have to get used to the thought that we are in for a long period of worry and uncertainty."

Daisy asked Jesse if he'd be near the Soviets in the Mediterranean. Jesse stroked Daisy's back and assured her that the Soviets were far away and that the *Leyte* would be safe. "The worst that can happen is a sunburn from sunbathing with French girls!" he joked. Daisy playfully punched his shoulder.

On the fringe of the crowd, Tom Hudner puffed away at a pipe as he watched Jesse and the others. His shoulders hung relaxed and a smile lined his face. He enjoyed naval ceremonies, even one as simple as a ship's departure, and he'd quickly forgotten his disappointment that his family hadn't come to see him off. His dad couldn't get away from work, and his younger three brothers and sister had school.

The pipe was a new affectation for Tom; it made him feel like a sailor of old, like Horatio Hornblower from the *Beat to Quarters* novel he had read as a boy. In his own way, Tom was about to sail into the unknown, maybe even into battle. The Soviets' belligerence seemed senseless to Tom, but not surprising. They had been angling for a fight since WWII.

In August 1945—just two weeks after the war's end—Soviet fighters had attacked an American B-29 that was parachuting food and medicine to a POW camp in Korea. Then in September and October they attacked navy planes off the coast of northern China. The following spring they used American P-39 fighters—given to them as lend-lease—to attack an American C-47 transport over Austria. And those were just the aerial clashes in one year's time.

Trumpets and trombones blared lazy notes as the band tested their instruments. A murmur traveled the crowd, then an officer shouted, "Okay, let's hop to it." Couples embraced. Children hugged their father's waists.

Jesse picked up Pam, kissed her, and set her down. He embraced Daisy as her tears dripped onto his shoulder. She wanted to whisper in his ear: *Jesse Leroy Brown, stop risking your life and stay with us!* In her mind, she and Jesse could live out their days in their cottage near the pond. But she knew saying anything would only spoil Jesse's adventure.

When Jesse let go, Daisy pulled herself together. Her eyes flickered with a thought. She knelt by Jesse's leather handbag and pretended to be checking that it was zippered. Swiftly, she slipped a slender book from her coat pocket into his bag without him noticing.

Carol stepped up to Daisy and awkwardly held out his hand. She shook it, and he smiled and turned for the ship. His sea bag, like most of their belongings, had already been loaded.

Jesse kissed Daisy once more before forcing himself to break away. He followed Carol a few paces, then turned back to his wife and shouted, "Don't worry, darling, I'll send you a postcard from Anathens!" Daisy laughed in the midst of her tears. Jesse blew her one last kiss, then walked away.

Tom followed Jesse and the others onto the gangway that arced into the ship. Marty went on excitedly about how sexually liberated French girls supposedly were. Signal bells rang out from the tugboats that were idling at all four corners of the ship.

Glancing up at the carrier, Tom felt small. An American flag flapped against the clouds, radar cones were revolving, and anti-aircraft guns aimed skyward from their turrets. A loudspeaker blared, "All hands to quarters," and sailors began lining up, their numbers wrapping around the deck. They were but a fraction of the 2,700-man crew who provided the flyboys with a mobile airfield from which they could strike any foe in the world as Uncle Sam's fist.

Sailors leaned from the tower above and looked down as the pilots boarded. At the end of the gangway, an officer stood in a blue uniform jacket. Behind him, a square passageway led into the heart of the *Leyte*. The officer held his hand in a frozen salute against the black brim of his white hat. As the pilots passed him, each snapped a salute in response. Jesse did the same and stepped into the dark tunnel and Tom followed him in.

For a better view of the carrier's departure, Daisy led Pam closer to the water where the other young wives and pilots' girlfriends milled about. Daisy edged close to Dick Cevoli's wife, Grace. The two exchanged greetings as Grace cradled her infant son, Steve. Grace was tall with long brown hair and a slender, gentle face. Several times, Daisy and Jesse had visited the Cevolis' cottage in Shore Acres, an idyllic community south of the base. From the cottage's front window, the carriers could be seen at the pier.

Daisy had met Grace and the other young women the summer before, when Jesse brought her to the air group's summer social in the officers' club. Amid clouds of cigarette smoke and the sounds of clinking glasses, the pilots and their wives and girlfriends had lined up to shake hands with the new black couple. On the drive home, Daisy had told Jesse how special the others had made her feel, like she was royalty. After that, Daisy visited the officers' club once a week for happy hour with Grace and the other young women.

Chimes sounded and the band began playing the lively tune "Anchors Aweigh." The women around Daisy began waving up toward the men on the deck, hoping their pilots would appear. The girls tucked away their handkerchiefs to present a fond farewell sight.

Grace Cevoli held her son's tiny hand and helped him wave. Daisy

glanced in Grace's direction and realized that the woman wasn't crying, yet Grace had as much to lose as she did. Daisy dried her nose
with her handkerchief. She was beginning to understand the duty of a
military wife.

Daisy smiled and waved like the others; she would wait for Jesse's
letters and hope that he was right—*the worst that can happen is a sunburn.*

CHAPTER 12

A DEADLY BUSINESS

Twenty days later, May 22, 1950
Off the southwest coast of Sicily

TOM JUMPED FROM THE WING of his Corsair and hurried past the parked planes to where Cevoli was standing. Jesse and a pilot named Koenig exited their planes and rushed in the same direction. The men stopped breathlessly at Cevoli's side. They were all wearing cloth flight helmets and silver aviator sunglasses, having just landed on the deck of the *Leyte* in rapid-fire sequence, twenty seconds apart.

At first, no one said anything as the carrier steamed into the noisy wind. The men glanced at their watches—it was nearly 4 P.M. They searched the hot and hazy blue sky. Far in the distance, thin white clouds hovered over the coast of Sicily like snowy alpine peaks. A destroyer and eighteen other ships surrounded the proud carrier, each bow cutting the waves and trailing white lines on the sapphire blue sea. Together, the ships formed the Dancing Fleet, the navy's largest active force.

Already the fleet had visited Portugal and Greece, and now it was here in Sicily. Just moments before, the four pilots had been aloft, practicing their aerial gunnery by blasting a white banner towed by another plane. The catch was, they couldn't actually see if they had hit the banner until the tow plane came down and dropped the banner into the sea, where it would be reclaimed.

As the pilots waited for the tow plane to return, adrenaline surged in their veins. The four men often flew together, and on paper were assigned to "Cevoli's flight." Traditionally, Cevoli was the flight's best shot, having fired at live planes and ships in World War II, and Jesse was second best, with a year's worth of trigger time over Tom. But it was Lieutenant Bill Koenig, the squadron's newest member, who was the most competitive.

A short, baby-faced pilot from Iowa, Koenig scanned the sky, his pale blue eyes beaming intensity. Today, he was certain, his aim had been on the money. Everyone joked that if there ever was a perfect naval officer, Koenig was the man. His tie was always cinched the tightest, his shoes always the best polished.

Tom had known Koenig for years. They had met during their shipboard duty days and crossed paths again in flight training, only to reunite when Koenig was assigned to Fighting 32, to the same flight as Tom.

"Here he comes!" Tom shouted, pointing to a speck in the sky behind the carrier. Jesse and Koenig and Cevoli leaned forward to see. Before takeoff, mechanics had painted the tips of each pilot's bullets a different color to track their scores.

The shape of a Corsair swelled as it came into view. A three-hundred-yard rope stretched from the plane's belly and behind the rope a thirty-yard banner fluttered like an advertisement over a beach. The Corsair dropped level with the *Leyte*'s deck and buzzed dramatically between the carrier and the neighboring destroyer. The white banner was riddled with colored holes.

Tom's eyes lit up at the sight. Cevoli grinned with the reigning champion's confidence. The men were especially happy not to be towing the banner. Being a tow pilot required nerves of steel. The risk

Bill Koenig

started right from the deck when the tow pilot needed to take off faster and steeper than usual to avoid dragging the banner in the water. Once he reached fifteen thousand feet, the danger factor rose exponentially. The tow pilot needed to fly straight and level while other pilots swooped in from the side to shoot the banner behind him. If a shooter misjudged the trajectory of his bullets, the tow pilot could come under friendly fire. ·

Only Carol Mohring ever volunteered for this job. As the shakiest pilot in the squadron he seemed continually eager to make friends, from carpooling with Jesse to towing the banner, anything to get the other pilots to know him as more than the kid with the German accent.

Carol flew his Corsair ahead of the destroyer and released the hook on his plane's belly. The tow line plummeted and the banner fluttered down like a streamer. Carol's plane accelerated and peeled left to enter the pattern to land.

The banner splashed down into the sea and rolled on the waves. "Come on, come on, stay right there!" Koenig said. His voice had a midwestern "gee whiz" twang. Tom chuckled at his friend's intensity.

Koenig had a point—sometimes the banner became tangled in the tow line and sank, the scores forever lost.

The destroyer veered toward the banner and several crew members appeared on the edge of the deck with a long pole and hook. With one scoop they lifted the banner from the sea. Tom breathed a sigh of relief. Koenig happily shook a fist. Next, the destroyer's crew would count the holes by color, then radio the results to the *Leyte*.

The flyboys practiced often, and with live rounds, for a reason. Their commanders suspected that the opening battle of World War III might be waged in the Mediterranean. The Soviets desperately wanted to gain a "warm water" port there so they could send warships to the Middle East in the event of World War III, to block America's access to oil. That was why the *Leyte* was in the Mediterranean, and why the 6th Fleet was permanently stationed there—to flex American muscle and demonstrate to the Mediterranean nations that America could defend them from the communists.

So far, the strategy was working. A year earlier, America and her allies of World War II—notably, Britain, Canada, and France—had formed NATO, a new alliance against the Soviets. They welcomed Italy and Portugal into the fold and agreed that "an armed attack against one or more of them in Europe or North America shall be considered an attack against them all." Now NATO was working to recruit Greece and Turkey before communism could topple a government and give the Soviets a warm-water port.

"Clear the deck! Clear the deck!" the *Leyte*'s loudspeaker blared. The deckhands scattered to their trenches and the LSO stepped to his platform. A spindly blue rescue helicopter edged alongside the carrier, ready to pluck a pilot from the sea in the event of an accident. Tom and the others took cover in a trench at the front of the deck to watch Carol land.

Carol was in the middle of his U-turn and perpendicular to the ship, about twenty-five yards above the sea. His left wing was angled downward, his wheels and hook were dangling.

Tom lifted his sunglasses for a better look. The distant Corsair's nose seemed to be angled a bit high. Its tail was drooping a bit low.

"His approach is off," Cevoli said. "He needs to speed up."

Tom murmured in agreement. Flying too low and slow was dangerous in a Corsair—and so was the act of acceleration. A pilot needed to level his wings before adding heavy power or else the Corsair's powerful engine would surge and the propeller's massive torque would twist the plane clockwise onto its back.

The LSO stood with his arms at his sides. Carol was still too far away to be directed. The distant Corsair's left wing dipped farther toward the sea. Then it flicked shakily upward.

"He's stalling!" Jesse shouted with alarm.

Carol's wing dipped again, then rose again. The plane was fighting with lift. From a distance, Tom heard the Corsair's engine surge— Carol was pouring on the power—but his wings were far from level.

With a mechanical groan, the Corsair pitched up and began rolling clockwise as if Carol were attempting a barrel roll above the waves. The Corsair kept groaning and turning, wing over wing, until it was upside down with its landing gear aimed toward the sky.

Tom held his breath.

Jesse stood still.

The plane nosed downward. Its glossy belly flashed in the sunlight, its engine screamed, and the Corsair plunged into the sea. A geyser of water burst upward.

Tom raised his hands to his helmet in shock.

The waves settled and the Corsair came into view. It was floating upside down, with two propeller blades jutting from the sea. The crash had stripped away the landing gear.

Silence settled on the carrier deck and then the ship's loudspeaker broke in: "Emergency! Emergency! Plane in the water!" The crash crew poured from the tower as the carrier came to a stop. Tom, Jesse, Koenig, and Cevoli joined the footrace to the rear of the deck. With the deckhands, they watched Carol's plane floating as the waves lapped its wings. Everyone yearned to see a waving hand emerge from the blue. A crash crew medic, Corpsman First Class Halley Bishop, stood by wearing a yellow skullcap and white shirt with a red cross affixed. He clutched his medical bag to his chest, powerless to help. The wreckage was too far away to reach by swimming.

The *Leyte*'s helicopter banked and hovered over the wreckage, its blades blowing the water into a circle. The helicopter pilot waited for a sign of life so that he could lower the rescue harness.

Minutes passed that felt like days. The destroyer USS *Buckley* pulled up beside the wrecked Corsair. Sailors leaned from the railing, holding flotation rings.

"It's all too late," Tom muttered and shook his head. Cevoli agreed.

Nearly five minutes had passed and still the plane was rocking in the waves, as if to remind Tom and the others that theirs was a deadly business.

Tom saw the lesson in front of him. There were specific rules to flying a Corsair and rules to making a carrier landing.

When you don't follow the rules, Tom thought, *this is how you end up*.

Bubbles rose from the Corsair's nose and popped along the surface. The plane twitched as if it was coming back to life. In one motion, the nose sank into the translucent sea and the tail rose slowly until it was standing upright. In a smooth rush, the plane slid into the deep.

Tom and the others avoided Jesse's eyes. They knew of his close friendship with Carol. There was no more talk of the banner and scores.

The helicopter banked away. A white frothy circle floated on the waves where the Corsair had been. Slowly the circle shrank, smaller and smaller until the sea was smooth.

CHAPTER 13

A KNOCK IN THE NIGHT

A month later, June 25, 1950
Off the west coast of Italy

IT WAS JUST AFTER MIDNIGHT, and the *Leyte*'s lights flickered silently against the darkened waves. The ship drifted at anchor under a half-moon.

On the nearby coast, the city of Livorno, Italy, was wide awake. A curving seawall sheltered the city and at the left end of the wall sat an ancient stone lighthouse. A beam of light shot forth from the lighthouse and spun in a circle. Behind the seawall, the city glowed with nightlife.

Had someone been standing on the shore and looking out at the *Leyte*, he or she would have seen the carrier's lights begin to click off in banks. The lights on the tower snuffed out first. Then the lights that ringed the deck. Bank by bank the ship went dark.

Against the shore lights, the *Leyte*'s silhouette stood like a rock in the sea.

*   *   *

Below the ship's deck, hurried footsteps could be heard descending metal stairs. A squadron orderly darted from door to door among the officers' cabins, rapping each wooden door with his fist until a pilot emerged.

Tom thrust his head out from the doorway. His hair was matted and he was wearing a T-shirt and shorts. He seldom slept well on the ship with all the noise.

"Sir, something big's up," the orderly said. "Skipper wants everyone in the ready room in ten."

"How big?" Tom wiped the sleep from his eyes.

"World War III just started." The orderly moved on to the next cabin.

Tom wavered in the doorstep, dumbstruck. Conventional wisdom said that it would take two years before the Soviets could attack. Had the military got it wrong?

Tom threw on his pants, a tan shirt, and a black tie, then bundled his flight jacket around his shoulders. By the time he reached Fighting 32's ready room, it was abuzz with pilots' nervous chatter. He dropped into a seat near Koenig and gave his friend an uneasy glance. Neither said much. Everyone was waiting for the skipper, the squadron leader.

The ready room looked like a small theater with an aisle dividing two rows of red leather seats. A movie screen in the front could be pulled down, under which was a chalkboard. The pilots' flight suits hung from pegs on the left wall.

Cevoli and the squadron's other World War II veterans sat in the front row, sipping coffee while fending off a barrage of nervous questions from the younger pilots. In other ready rooms, pilots from three other squadrons were gathering.

Jesse sat silently near the front row. Since Carol's death, he had become quieter than usual, withdrawn even, and now he was deep in thought. It was nearly 8 P.M. back in Mississippi, where Daisy and Pam were staying with Daisy's mom.

The skipper, Dug Neill

He didn't have to think long. A pilot with a thick jaw and a mustache entered the room. He looked stern, a bit like Clark Gable. He was the skipper. Instantly the coffee-fueled banter went silent and the twenty-one pilots jumped to their feet. The intel officer, a non-flyer, followed, and the skipper motioned for the men to sit. The skipper stepped front and center. He was Lieutenant Commander Dugald Neill, from Long Island, but the man hated his first name and insisted that his pilots call him "Skipper."

"Here's the skinny," he growled. "The Soviets are mobilizing, so we're mobilizing too. Is this the big one? Who the hell knows? All they're telling us is, 'Code 3, be ready on a moment's notice.'"

The pilots glanced at one another, wondering what exactly that meant.

The skipper had been in a war before. During WWII he had been a night fighter pilot and had landed on carriers in the dark. At thirty-one years old, he was already an old man in the eyes of his pilots.

The skipper gestured to the intel officer, who placed a world map against the blackboard. The intel officer spoke up. "The Reds might be preparing to hop the Bering Strait and charge into Alaska," he said. He swept his finger across the map. "Or their armored divisions might be gearing up to race through Germany bound for Paris and up to Denmark and Norway."

Tom had followed World War II as a teenager and could see the parallels. If a new world war was about to happen, it would likely mirror Hitler's blitzkrieg. If the Soviets took France and Scandinavia as quickly as Hitler had, they would move on to England next for a second Battle of Britain.

The skipper stepped toward the map and added, "*Leyte's* concern is the eastern Mediterranean. The Reds will move for Turkey after the other attacks are under way. They'll want to cut our oil pipelines in Lebanon and Israel and take the Suez Canal. If they do that, then they'll immobilize the whole of America."

The skipper turned to his second-in-command, Cevoli, and asked if he had anything to contribute. The fun-loving Cevoli said that everything he was hearing was news to him. He was known for limited contributions to briefings.

Tom and the other young pilots looked uncomfortable. The skipper had worried them without providing any real answers. The skipper nodded to his third-in-command, the operations officer, who sat in the front row.

Lieutenant Dick Fowler rose. A six-foot-four Texan, he was as tall as John Wayne and had a similar face with a sharp nose, thick chin, and blue eyes. During World War II, Fowler had shot down six Japanese planes by the age of twenty, so whenever he gave a tip or critique, people listened. Fowler was just twenty-six but both the younger and veteran pilots called him "Dad." Everyone in Fighting 32 recognized him as the outfit's best flyer.

In a deep and steady voice, Dad announced that the ship had gone on alert and that the planes were being loaded with ammunition. A third of the squadron was to suit up immediately and man their planes. He read out a list of names. Tom and Jesse were called, along with five others. They were to remain in their planes on deck until 8 A.M.

"Dad" Fowler receiving the Navy Cross from Admiral McCain in WWII

If a mission came down, then Dad would brief everyone planeside. Tom and the others became nervous. The squadron didn't fly much at night and most of the pilots weren't qualified for carrier landings in the dark.

"Don't get too alarmed," Dad said, sensing the tension. "You won't likely be launching tonight or anytime soon, until the ship steams east."

Tom and the others nodded and sat back in their seats. Dad's voice had a calming effect. No one had any questions.

"Okay, boys, have at it," the skipper said.

The pilots jumped to their feet.

Dressed to fly, Tom and Jesse stepped from the tower onto the flight deck and hurried to their planes. In trenches along the flight deck, sailors loaded and aimed 20mm anti-aircraft cannons toward the sky.

Waves lapped the *Leyte*. Slowly, the lighthouse's beam swept the ship and revealed the long gray hull.

As Tom sat in his Corsair, a scuffling sound could be heard on the wing. Someone was climbing up. Tom turned, expecting to see Dad Fowler.

Instead, Jesse hoisted himself even with Tom's cockpit. "Hey, Tom," he whispered through darkness. "Did you hear the rumor?"

"Nope," Tom said.

"Some fellows are saying there are saboteurs aboard—Soviet agents who enlisted as sailors." Jesse's voice was high-pitched with concern.

"Oh, brother," Tom said. "Let's hope it's just a rumor."

Jesse nodded, climbed down from Tom's Corsair, and headed back to his own plane.

In the dark silence, Tom considered the war that he might be about to wage. As a Catholic and former altar boy, Tom read everything he could about the communists, who were declared atheists and oppressors of the Church. His concern went beyond religion. An hour's flight away, the people of Eastern Europe lay enslaved.

When the Soviet army liberated war-ravaged Eastern Europe, they had promised the people free elections with Hitler gone. At first, Stalin kept his promise. But when communist parties in Poland, Hungary, Germany, and Austria lost in the free elections of '45 and '46, Stalin set his secret police, the NKVD, in motion. The secret police reopened former Nazi concentration camps, Auschwitz to imprison Poles and Buchenwald and Sachsenhausen to imprison East Germans. The communists built sixteen new camps to hold Hungarians.

Only then did elections start to go Stalin's way. Across occupied Europe, local communists were brought to power, men indoctrinated in Moscow and known as "Little Stalins." From England, former prime minister Winston Churchill watched these troubling developments and famously lamented, "An iron curtain has descended across the continent." That same year, 1950, including the gulags in Russia, the communist camp system reached its highest occupancy—2.5 million prisoners.

*   *   *

The sun cast an orange glow on the sea at 8 A.M. when the relief pilots stepped out from the tower. Tom, Jesse, and the others climbed down from their planes and met their replacements on the deck.

The relief pilots had news.

War had broken out, all right, but it was contained to the Korean peninsula. The communist North Koreans had attacked the democratic South Koreans.*

Jesse breathed a sigh of relief. At least it wasn't World War III. Behind Tom, a pilot asked, "Where's Korea anyhow?" Tom looked to see if the guy was joking. He wasn't. "It's just west of Japan," Tom said carefully, to avoid sounding judgmental.

Tom himself wasn't initially alarmed by this new Korean war. It sounded like a civil war—north versus south—or a regional dispute. Even if America intervened, the Pacific Fleet could handle the job with one hand tied behind their backs.

Tom glanced at his watch. He still had time to sleep.

---

* Stalin was a driving force behind the Korean War. After NATO stonewalled communism in Europe, Stalin turned to Asia. He appointed a "Little Stalin" in North Korea named Kim Il Sung and told him in 1949: "You must strike the Southerners in the teeth. . . . Strike them, strike them." Soviet tacticians then drew up the battle plans for the North Korean invasion of the south and Kim Il Sung assured Stalin: "The attack will be swift and the war will be won in three days."

CHAPTER 14

THE DANCING FLEET

A week later, July 3, 1950
Aboard the USS *Leyte* off the French coast

DOORS SLAMMED and fast talk filled the air. Tom and Koenig navigated the jam of pilots in the narrow hallway and yelled for their buddies to hurry.

Tom and Koenig wore civilian blazers over polo shirts; the others were only half-clothed as they darted to and from their staterooms. The air crackled with youthful energy. It was early on a Monday morning, but the pilots weren't preparing for the work week. They were headed ashore to Cannes, a city in southeastern France on a legendary strip of beaches called the Riviera.

Tom and Koenig entered a pale green room at the front of the ship and found themselves in a world of chaos. Record players and radios blared, lockers and trunk doors slammed. Jesse and his fellow ensigns bustled between sinks and their bunks with shaving kits in hand. Marty stood in the center of the room with his hands over his head. He wore a T-shirt and tan slacks and grinned as another ensign taped packs of cigarettes around his waist.

This was "Boys' Town," the rowdy bunkroom where the ensigns lived.

Marty caught Tom and Koenig staring, mouths agape. "Nab a carton at the ship's store," Marty shouted. "Sell 'em ashore and you can leave your wallet aboard!"

Tom slapped his forehead. It was a customs violation to bring more than two packs of cigarettes ashore, yet Marty already had a dozen packs taped to his body. The young ensign seemed unafraid of risking a mark on his military record, probably because he had done this before, in Italy, where he made a fortune. A carton of cigarettes that cost eighty cents aboard ship could fetch eight dollars ashore.

"Hurry! We're going to miss the bikinis!" an ensign shouted. The pilots had heard that French girls were all wearing a scandalous new bathing suit, one its designer bragged was so small it "could be pulled through a wedding ring."

A flash of tan uniform brushed between Tom and Koenig and into Boys' Town. The skipper stopped, stood with his hands on his hips, and stared around the room. His mustache accentuated his glare, particularly when his eyes landed on Marty. Marty's eyes opened wide. His buddy stopped taping.

"If you get caught," the skipper growled, "I ain't gonna do a thing for you."

"Aye, aye, Skipper," Marty said, straight-faced. None of the pilots doubted that the skipper meant what he had said—if caught, Marty would be left to rot in a local jail. But the gleam in Marty's eyes revealed that he wasn't planning on getting caught.

"Don't forget," the skipper said loudly for all to hear, "you're in a foreign city, and you look like foreigners, so stick together." He glanced at Tom and Koenig as he departed, as if to say, *Look after them.*

Several of the ensigns joined Tom and Koenig at the door and glanced at their watches. One yelled back to his buddies, "Hey, hurry up so we can lie in the sun and get as black as—" The ensign covered his mouth. An awkward silence descended on the room.

Koenig scowled at the offender. Tom shook his head in disbelief. All eyes snapped toward Jesse to see his reaction.

Jesse turned from his bunk and looked around. "Don't wait for me, I'll catch the next boat," he said. "Besides, I've got a head start on my color!"

The cabin erupted with laughter and even Jesse joined in. With relief, the offender grinned an apology to his squadron mate.

The wind rushed through Tom's hair as the *Leyte*'s officers' launch carried him and his buddies toward the tropical coastline. The boat skipped the waves. Tom clutched a dark gray hat beneath his knees. His aviator sunglasses blocked the mid-morning glare.

Behind the launch, the *Leyte* lay at anchor, her nose pointing to open waters to speed an emergency departure if necessary. The Dancing Fleet had dispersed and sent ships to nearby ports with a plan to gather in open waters after thirteen days—the longest layover of the cruise.

Wooden speedboats raced past Tom and the others, their cockpits filled with happy couples, the boats' chrome-ringed windshields sparkling.

The frolicking seemed to sour Koenig's mood. Behind his sunglasses, his youthful face scrunched. "We shouldn't be here," he yelled in Tom's ear over the engine's roar. "There's a war raging and we're pleasure cruising."

Tom nodded. The news from Korea was ominous. After a week of fighting, the North Korean communists had already captured the South Korean capital of Seoul and driven South Korean and American army troops into retreat. The American commander, General Douglas MacArthur, was calling for reinforcements and air support, but monsoons had turned the South Korean airfields into swamps.

Reportedly, Australian P-51s and U.S. Air Force F-80 jets were flying missions all the way from Japan to offer whatever help they could.

Tom shared Koenig's frustration. Rumor had it the carrier *Valley Forge* had just deployed for Korea, yet the *Leyte*'s orders were inexplicable — to "keep dancing."

Tom leapt from the boat to the dock and slapped his fedora onto his head. The hat was a felt Borsalino and hand-made, just like the one Humphrey Bogart wore in *Casablanca*. Jesse, Koenig, and the others donned fedoras, too. Tom looked around him and grinned. *We look like a bunch of gangsters*, he thought.

In Italy, they had all bought hats on the admiral's orders. The admiral wanted his officers to look good, since the Dancing Fleet had its headquarters in Cannes.

The pilots hurried along the dock.

French dockhands held ropes while boatloads of young sailors came ashore. At the end of the dock, souvenir vendors displayed their wares and tour guides waved pamphlets. They were all hungry for some of the $2 million the fleet's sailors spent annually in Mediterranean ports. The American government was, in fact, the biggest spender in Europe. Since 1947, America had sent $15 billion in economic aid to Europe under the Marshall Plan, 85 percent of which were gifts to stimulate the reconstruction of war-ravaged Europe in the hopes that democracy — not communism — would rise from the ashes of World War II.

Tom squirmed past the vendors and onto the sidewalk. He and Jesse and the others gawked at the Riviera, a place they had seen only on travel posters. White clouds billowed over the tropical city and church bells clanged. Alabaster buildings with red roofs were shaded by gently blowing palm trees. Steam drifted down through the green and rocky mountains in the background.

The beach curved along a half-moon bay and white umbrellas dotted the sand. Men and women sunbathed and others waded into the clear turquoise waters where the ocean floor was visible.

Tom smiled at the sight of paradise. The travel posters had boasted, "If you love life, you'll love France," and already he was a believer.

As the pack of pilots crossed the palm-lined boulevard, the discord began. Some of the pilots removed their fedoras against the admiral's orders. Earlier they had joked that they looked like an Olympic sports team in hats and blazers. Tom pinched his Borsalino to straighten it and Jesse and Koenig kept theirs on, too.

Beside the boulevard, the pilots stopped to confer. A long line of outdoor restaurants and boutiques built in the 1800s awaited them. Sailors with cameras around their necks drifted around window-shopping tourists, some Americans who were finally returning to France after the war. Locals darted between the foreigners, their heads down.

Marty excused himself to complete his black market transaction. Other pilots departed the group to rent a short-term apartment— a place to nap and change and entertain girls.

Tom fished a pamphlet from his pocket, a guide to local culture that he had received from the ship's tour director, the chaplain. Tom read aloud how the Man in the Iron Mask had been imprisoned in an is-land fortress just a half-mile from shore. Tom suggested they go there.

But someone said they should visit a casino instead. Tom wasn't eager to gamble in the morning, nor was Koenig or Jesse. But the re-maining pilots loved the idea. "We've got to be careful where we go with Jesse," Tom quietly reminded the ensign who'd championed the idea. Tom didn't want to see Jesse embarrassed if a casino doorman refused him entry. The ensign reluctantly agreed.

Jesse must have sensed the tension, because he announced that he was going to shop for perfume for Daisy. Koenig had plans of his own. The others remained fixated on the casino, so Tom, Koenig, and Jesse made plans to later take a boat together back to the *Leyte*.

The group broke up and the pilots went their separate ways. Koenig strolled away in one direction while Jesse set off in the other.

Alone, Tom slapped his guide pamphlet against his hand, unsure of what to do and filled with disappointment.

The skipper said to stick together.

CHAPTER 15

THE REUNION

That same morning
Cannes, France

A HANDFUL OF YOUNG MARINES in tan uniforms and tent caps stood
on the sidewalk behind the beach. They were not there to swim. They
were girlwatching.

The beach was crowded with willowy female bodies lying on striped
beach chairs. Behind the sunbathers, waiters emerged from cabanas
carrying trays of beverages.

"Hey, fellas, have a look-see!" one Marine said, directing his buddies' attention to a girl in a sundress who had found a spot to camp for
the day. She wrapped her towel around herself and pinned it underneath her arms. Her sundress fell surreptitiously to the sand and she
wiggled into her bathing suit.

Another young Marine, with red hair and a small, downturned
nose, leaned around his buddies. A shy grin spanned his fleshy face.
He was twenty-one-year-old Private First Class John Parkinson. His
buddies called him "Red."

John "Red" Parkinson

"Is she putting on a bikini?" he asked.

The other Marines shielded their eyes but couldn't tell—the girl's towel was hiding everything. Spotting a bikini in 1950 was a rare but exciting event. The tiny swimsuits were rumored to slip off sometimes, because girls weren't used to wearing them yet.

The girl's towel floated to the sand, revealing a disappointing sight for Red. The girl stood in a one-piece bathing suit. The Marines groaned and Red struck his forehead with his palm. But the Marines didn't give up. They started walking down the sidewalk, still scouting.

Red and the others were Fleet Marines, the boys shown in recruiting posters wearing dress blues. The public assumed that Fleet Marines were lifelong military men, the saltiest of the salty, but in reality, this new crop of Marines was made up of military rookies—eager products of the postwar middle class who'd just graduated high school and seldom skipped chapel. But when it came to ogling a girl in a bikini, boys would be boys.

Before joining the Marines, Red had never even seen a beach. When he was seven, his mother left the family's Brooklyn tenement one day and never came home. Red's father worked on the New York waterfront and couldn't care for the boy, so he sent Red to live with family friends at a farm in New York's Catskill Mountains.

Red's adopted family, Uncle Anton and Aunt Anne, were Czech immigrants who raised him to be a farmer, too. When Red turned nineteen, he told them that he wanted to see the world before settling down. With their consent, he hitchhiked to the nearest recruiting center and became a Marine—because theirs was the only office open. The other recruiters had all gone home.

"Hey, fellas, I see something promising," one of the Marines announced. His eyes locked on a petite brunette with dark sunglasses and black hair that curled beneath her ears. She was draping a towel over a beach chair. She looked young and unusually chesty for having such a small waist.

"Wow, she looks just like Elizabeth Taylor!" Red said. Taylor was the reigning starlet of Hollywood's new generation. She was only eighteen years old, but already she was acting alongside seasoned actors such as Robert Taylor and Van Johnson.

The other Marines laughed at Red. They said there was no way that Elizabeth Taylor would be *alone* on any beach, let alone in Cannes.

Red studied the girl more closely. Headlines called Taylor the most beautiful actress in the world and the girl on the beach was certainly good-looking.

"Maybe it's her twin sister," one of the guys ventured. Another urged Red to go investigate. Another joined the chorus until Red finally relented.

He took a deep breath and started walking toward her.

*   *   *

Sand poured into Red's black shoes. He approached the girl from the side and pretended to be looking for a beach chair. As he walked past, he saw that she was wearing a white one-piece with a pink flower pattern. The suit's top tied around her neck and the bottom curled discreetly around her hips. Beneath her sunglasses, she had a pale, China-doll face with arcing black eyebrows and a nose that turned up at the tip. Red's eyes locked on an unmistakable beauty mark on her right cheek and his heart took off racing.

Holy cow! he thought. *It might really be her!*

Red walked a safe distance then looked back to his buddies. They raised their hands and shrugged: *Well?*

The last thing Red wanted to do was annoy the girl, and he didn't know what to ask her, anyway. His thoughts flashed back home to his uncle Anton.

How would Uncle Anton handle this? Red wondered. The hard-working Czech was his hero, a man with strong Slavic features and muscles like a bull. Day after day they'd milked cows and harvested cauliflower, potatoes, and hay, and Uncle Anton had always impressed on him one golden life lesson—*If you're going to do something, then do it right, or don't bother doing it at all.*

Red turned around and doubled back toward the girl. He stopped near her feet.

"Miss Taylor?" he said.

The girl lifted her sunglasses. Underneath were crystal blue eyes framed by thick black eyelashes. There was no mistaking the eyes of Elizabeth Taylor. The papers said that in the right light they actually sparkled violet.

"Why, hello," she said. Her playful voice trailed away with an aristocratic up-note, a hint of her English heritage.

Red introduced himself, stammering.

"Why, it's nice to meet you, Red." The starlet sat up in her chair. "Are you a Marine?"

"Yes, ma'am," he said, sticking out his chest.

"Please, call me Elizabeth," the starlet said.

Elizabeth Taylor in Cannes with sailors of the *Leyte*

She asked Red if he was enjoying Europe. Red told her how at each port he hurried to the train station to go sightseeing. Before joining the Marines, he'd never seen a building bigger than a silo, but now he'd been to Berlin, Switzerland, and even to the top of the Eiffel Tower. Elizabeth asked what he thought of each experience and seemed genuinely interested.

The other Marines came stumbling through the sand. They joined Red and introduced themselves to Elizabeth. She seemed to love the attention. Red told her he had seen *National Velvet,* and the other Marines said they had seen her other blockbuster, *Courage of Lassie,* about a girl's dog who runs away and serves in World War II. Elizabeth asked the men about themselves and grew even more animated—just like she was a girl at home hanging out with friends in an ice cream parlor.

"Miss Taylor, not to impose," a Marine said. "But would you happen to have change for a hundred-dollar bill?" He assumed movie stars carried stacks of money.

"Oh," she said, "maybe Nicky can help you." Her voice turned meek. "He's up at the Carlton Hotel."

She was talking about her new husband, twenty-three-year-old

Nicky Hilton, son of the famous hotel founder Conrad Hilton. Elizabeth and Nicky had been married for only two months.

"Thanks, Miss Taylor," a Marine said. "We'll go ask him." The latecomers peeled away to seek their change, and Red found himself alone again with the starlet. They talked for a few more minutes, then Red excused himself. As much as he was enjoying talking to Elizabeth, he knew that if he didn't catch up to his buddies, he might not find them again.

"It was nice to meet you," Elizabeth said, giving a little wave that made Red smile. He waved in return but couldn't help noticing that Elizabeth seemed sad to lose the company.

Several hours later, wealthy guests filled the terrace café of the luxurious Carlton Hotel, but Jesse sat alone.

Between sips from a glass of ginger ale, he scribbled another letter. He'd already written a small pile that he'd sealed in envelopes. Around him posh travelers chatted in white wicker chairs and sipped flutes of the local pink-colored wine. The air smelled of flowers and music drifted through the terrace.

The terrace lay at the front of the palatial hotel. At seven stories tall, the Carlton was the tallest building in Cannes, with black turrets on the front corners of its roof. Jesse had discovered the hotel in a *Guide to the Mediterranean* book that Daisy had slipped into his bag before the carrier departed Quonset Point.

The hotel's terrace proved the best place to write letters. A waist-high wall of carved white stone enclosed the space and made it feel almost private, while a sun canopy provided just enough shade. Down several marble steps and across the boulevard lay the beach.

Jesse had written to Daisy and his family, as usual. The navy's mail delivery service was top-notch: Planes whisked mail to the States so quickly that a letter often reached its destination in five days. Jesse's squadron mates joked that he deserved his own zip code because he sent and received so much mail.

Halley Bishop

"Hey, Ensign Brown!" a voice called from the sidewalk.

Jesse turned to see the V-shaped face and shy eyes of the crash crew medic, twenty-six-year-old Corpsman Halley Bishop.

"Hey, Doc," Jesse said.

Halley wore a sailor's white uniform with a Red Cross armband around his left sleeve and he carried a canvas medic's bag over his shoulder. Today his duty was to patrol the boulevard in search of drunken or injured sailors, but it was too early for trouble, so he'd come to see the legendary hotel.

Jesse invited the young medic to have a seat, but Halley hesitated and glanced over both shoulders. Navy tradition forbade enlisted sailors from associating with officers.

"It's okay," Jesse reassured him while clearing his pile of letters aside. Halley pulled up a chair, removed his hat, and swept back his brown hair, which was so lengthy that it barely met regulations.

A waiter in a white jacket and bowtie delivered a bowl of olives. Jesse told Halley that he wanted to buy him a drink. Halley again checked for officers. He had grown up in an orphanage in North Carolina, where he had learned a healthy respect for authority.

Speaking only in French, Jesse asked the waiter for another ginger ale. Jesse looked to Halley, who threw his hands up and asked Jesse to order him the same. In high school, Jesse had become fluent in French.

The men chatted without pretense. When the waiter delivered their drinks, Jesse admitted that he liked ginger ale because it gave the appearance of alcohol and thwarted his friends from pressuring him to drink. Halley was struck by Jesse's ease and humility.

Jesse caught Halley by surprise with a question. He asked the young medic if he had ever learned a good way to break bad news, such as news of a death. During WWII, Halley had seen plenty of death as a "doc" with the Marines on Peleliu.

Halley shook his head. He explained that the officers, not medics, wrote letters to families of the dead. Halley asked Jesse if Carol Mohring's death was eating at him. They both had watched the plane sink.

Jesse motioned to the envelopes and said that he'd finally brought himself to break the news to his wife, Daisy.

Halley leaned forward sympathetically. "Ensign Brown, if I've learned anything, it's that death's gonna get us all, but we've got some say in how we go. You die flying a Corsair, well, that says enough. Ensign Mohring was a brave man."

Jesse thought for a moment and nodded. His face loosened and he posed a new question for the young medic.

"How about another round of ginger ale?"

Morning turned to afternoon, and the sun grew hot on the terrace canopy.

Alone, Jesse finished the remnants of his lunch while Halley was away at the restroom. When the young medic returned to the table, he took his seat in a hurry. "Ensign Brown," he said, "you're never gonna believe this. Guess who just sat behind us?"

Jesse shrugged but noticed that his surroundings had gone silent.

Everyone on the terrace was looking in the same direction and whispering. Jesse glanced over his shoulder. Several tables away sat Elizabeth Taylor and her friends.

Elizabeth had wrapped her hair with a colorful bandanna and was wearing a lace sundress with a low neckline. She looked as if she had just come from the beach.

Jesse turned back to Halley with a grin. Halley smoothed his hair with his hands and said that he was going to talk to her. His eyes turned steely, the look of someone who'd stitched up men in combat. Before Jesse could stop him, Halley was walking toward the table of ladies.

"Hi, Liz, I'm Halley," he said. "You may remember me? We went to school together."

Elizabeth looked up. "Oh really?" she said with girlish innocence. "Were you at University High?"

"That's the place!" Halley said with relief.

Elizabeth stood to shake his hand. "So good to see you again!" she squealed and pumped his hand vigorously.

For the next ten minutes, Halley and Elizabeth stood and chatted about where life had taken them since their school days. They came to the conclusion that they had attended not one but two schools together. Halley told Elizabeth about his pilot friend and Jesse caught the pair looking at him. The sudden appearance of a slender young man with black hair and a widow's peak brought the discussion to a halt. He was Elizabeth's husband, Nicky Hilton. Hilton wore a polo shirt tucked into khakis and a gold watch and he seemed impatient to talk to his wife. Halley politely excused himself but Elizabeth asked him to wait. Hilton told Elizabeth that he was going to the races with his friends, then turned and left abruptly.

Elizabeth shook her head, dumbstruck. When she regained her senses she called the waiter over and asked for a bottle of wine. The waiter returned with a cold bottle wrapped in a towel. Elizabeth told the waiter that the wine was for her friend Halley, who reeled in surprise.

"That's awfully nice, Liz, but I don't take to wine," he said. "I'm just a simple beer guy."

"Then give it to your pilot friend," Elizabeth said, leaning to look at Jesse. "Tell him it's a present."

Halley smiled. He took the wine and told Elizabeth he hoped that they would reunite again. She gave him a hug.

Halley returned to the table and handed Jesse the bottle of wine. "A gift from Elizabeth Taylor," he said.

Jesse took the bottle in his hands.

"Did you really go to school with her?" he asked.

A guilty grin stretched across Halley's face. "Nah," he said. "Unless she was in the same orphanage!" Jesse chuckled and told Halley that he was something else.

Jesse examined the label and noticed that Elizabeth was glancing in his direction. He gave her a small salute. She smiled and lifted her glass in return.

Tom and Koenig saw Jesse approaching the dock with a bottle of wine in one hand and shopping bags in the other.

Tom smiled. "Since when do you drink?" he asked.

"Oh, I don't," Jesse said.

Koenig raised an eyebrow. "You know you can't bring that aboard ship, right?"

Jesse nodded. He saw a group of Marines stepping from a boat and stood. When they walked past, Jesse handed them the bottle and jokingly welcomed them to Cannes.

"Gee, thanks, sir," a Marine said, looking confused as he and his buddies examined the bottle.

Jesse told Koenig and Tom the story about meeting Elizabeth Taylor.

"You mean she got married?" Tom asked, faking dismay. "And here I was saving myself just for her."

The men laughed, unaware that Tom's dreams were actually far from dashed.

CHAPTER 16

ONLY IN FRANCE

Four days later, July 7, 1950
Off the coast of Cannes

THE MORNING SUN STREAKED across the flight deck and over the Corsairs that were parked mid-ship.

Beside the nose of a plane, Tom jotted notes on a clipboard while Marty crouched with a flashlight near the landing gear. Flight operations were on hold while the *Leyte* was at Cannes, but maintenance work continued.

"So sloppy," Tom muttered. He frowned at the clipboard, where blocks of numbers were missing from a chart.

Marty called out a string of serial numbers and Tom recorded them. Every pilot in the squadron had a side job; Tom and Marty were "assistant maintenance officers." Their role was to review the squadron mechanics' work and keep tabs on aircraft readiness.

"Man, you should have seen her, Tom," Marty exclaimed as he searched for a serial number. "Blonde with green eyes, long legs, a real doll!" Marty's mind was ashore on Cannes where he had met a French girl.

"Sounds nice," Tom murmured.

Marty was going ashore to see her that night and he had invited Tom along. "If you aren't having a fling in this place, there's something wrong with you," Marty added.

Tom grunted. The stay in Cannes was already a third of the way over, yet Tom had more pressing concerns—namely, the planes' logs. Some weeks earlier he had spotted a problem: Each Corsair was issued with a maintenance log, similar to a person's file in a doctor's office. The planes' manufacturer, Chance Vought, often sent maintenance orders to squadrons, and when mechanics changed parts they were supposed to notate their work in the logs. But Fighting 32 got its Corsairs from a Marine reserve squadron where the mechanics had been lazy.

Tom had alerted the skipper and volunteered to bring the logs up to date by gathering serial numbers from the planes and cross-checking them with the manufacturer's catalogues. The job fell to Marty to help him. It was tedious work, but Tom wanted the mechanics to know what parts were due to wear out so that no one would crash—himself included.

The sound of airy conversation and slapping flip-flops came from across the deck. Tom looked up from his clipboard.

Past the Corsair's wing walked a girl in a short white sundress with an officer in dress whites by her side. Tom's and Marty's eyes both went wide. It was Elizabeth Taylor.

Some distance behind the starlet an entourage followed—men and women, young and old, some officers and some of her friends. Her husband, Nicky Hilton, was among them. He looked like a typical youth in a red polo shirt as he chatted with his escorts.

Elizabeth spotted Marty and Tom and strolled over.

"Well, what are you doing down there?" she asked Marty. Her sundress was decorated with colorful beads and her handbag was made of white leather.

"Just making sure I don't get a flat tire," Marty joked.

Elizabeth flashed a smile. Marty stood, wiped his hands on his slacks, and introduced himself.

Tom kept his distance, happy to let Marty do the talking. He had seen one of Elizabeth's movies and thought that her acting was good but not great. Still, she was stunning.

"Are you mechanics?" Elizabeth asked.

"Us? No," Marty said with a laugh. He explained that they were pilots, but checking the planes was part of their job. Tom nodded in agreement as he held the clipboard to his chest.

Elizabeth apologized and added that she couldn't imagine flying one of those planes. Marty offered to show her the cockpit and her eyes lit up—but the officer interceded and said they needed to move along in order to see the entire ship.

Before the officer could steer Elizabeth away, she invited Marty and Tom to visit a casino with her and Nicky that night, and she told them to bring their friends. Marty said he would be there and Tom agreed too. The sound of the flip-flops faded as Elizabeth's escorts led her toward the rear of the ship to pose for a photo with the rescue helicopter.

Marty looked at Tom with glee. "I guess you'll be meeting my girl now!"

That night, in nearby Monaco

Big band music floated through the Monte Carlo Casino as Tom slid his chips onto the green velvet of the roulette table.

"Put one here, one here, and one there!" Elizabeth said. Sitting by Tom's left side, the starlet pointed to the table's numbered grid. An orchid was nestled in her black hair and her strapless white dress fit elegantly. Tom happily obeyed. Across the table, Marty grinned at the sight.

Before this night, Tom had never been inside a casino, let alone the world's most famous one in Monaco, a short train ride from Cannes. The parlor was stately, with high ceilings, ornate chandeliers, and walls flourished with gold. The music reminded Tom of smooth jazz, his favorite.

Tom leaned back, pleased with his gambling partner's advice. Elizabeth knew all the rules, even though she was too young to gamble legally in France or the United States. Her husband, Nicky, had taught her, but tonight he was absent, supposedly away with friends.

Around the table, navy pilots and their girls placed their bets. Some of the girls were pilots' wives—young, childless "ship chasers" who came to Europe on vacation. Elizabeth had invited them all. The starlet glanced eagerly up the table and waited for the dealer to spin the wheel. *She's far too beautiful and too young to be married,* Tom thought.

Elizabeth's blue eyes narrowed when an elegant blonde took her place across the table and cozied up to Marty's side. Tom's eyes, the pilots' eyes, all eyes immediately locked on the blonde. She curled her arm around Marty's waist. Her nose was small and sharp, her eyes green and sultry. She was Marty's French girlfriend and she'd just stolen the spotlight from Elizabeth Taylor.

Tom looked at Marty, cocked his head in amazement, and thought, *Maybe he's some sort of Casanova after all?*

The dealer spun the wheel and called out, "Mesdames and messieurs, no more bets!" Shaken from their daze, Tom, Elizabeth, and the others began cheering and clapping. The ball landed and the dealer placed the marker on the winning number. A combination of laughter and groans erupted.

From the other tables, sophisticated women in pearls and men in tuxedos turned toward the pilots' table, perturbed. They looked down their noses at the young military men in blazers and the women in simple dresses.

The pilots couldn't have cared less. As the game continued, several of the wives congregated around Elizabeth, who chatted away, seemingly "one of the girls." Earlier that week, the wives had found Elizabeth alone and depressed and had welcomed her into their group. They then spent the ensuing days together at the wives' hotel, gossiping and sharing clothes. Elizabeth even told her new friends that she was secretly jealous of them because of the men they'd married. She admitted that her new husband was having an affair and she was already planning to get divorced but couldn't leave Cannes without Nicky because they had come to Europe on a shared passport.

During a change of dealers, Tom stood to stretch his legs. Marty approached and whispered into his ear, "I feel like I've stepped into the middle of an unspoken competition!" He was talking about the rivalry between his girl and Elizabeth. Tom complimented his friend's eye for beauty. Grinning broadly, Marty rushed away to refill his drink.

Tom nursed his scotch and flipped a chip in his hand as he waited for the game to resume. He was already running low on money and the night was still young.

Someone bumped Tom in passing and knocked the chip from his hand. It tumbled end over end and down the wooden seatback of Elizabeth's chair.

Oh, brother! Tom thought.

Elizabeth didn't notice. Her back was to him as she conversed with the wives.

Tom slowly leaned over Elizabeth's seat and glanced down. The chip had come to rest between the seatback and the starlet's shapely behind. Tom reeled backward and looked away. Fortunately no one had caught him looking.

Of all the places! he thought.

The others were returning with full drinks and Tom knew that the group wasn't going anywhere anytime soon. He needed that chip to keep playing. Tom flexed the fingers of his left hand. He slid his hand across the top of Elizabeth's chair as if he was resting his arm. Swiftly he plunged his hand downward, snatched the chip, and pulled it out. He dropped his arm to his side and stood still like a soldier, his eyes fixed straight ahead.

Elizabeth must have felt the rustle of Tom's sleeve. She turned and looked up at him, her eyebrows raised, her blue eyes sparkling. She cocked her head playfully.

She thinks I tried to grope her! Tom thought. He glanced down at her, blushed, and sheepishly held up the chip so that she could see it.

Elizabeth laughed, slapped Tom on the arm, and turned back to her conversation.

Several pilots claimed they saw him there in the casino, the pilot who resembled Clark Gable.

The skipper.

They said that he drifted in through the smoke and wandered the room with his hands in the pockets of the plainest civilian clothes, as if he had come from a lowbrow bar. How he got past the casino's doormen was a mystery.

He must have seen Marty playing roulette with his French girlfriend.

He must have seen Marty kissing the girl.

He must have seen the young pilot look like he was head over heels in love, a dangerous cocktail that could cloud an aviator's mind on the ground—and in the air.

There could be no other explanation for his reaction to come.

The next morning

Tom looked up from a paper-strewn desk inside one of the *Leyte*'s cavernous hangars at the tail of the ship. Across from him, Marty hummed as he cross-checked serial numbers with the catalogues.

Behind Marty, planes filled the hangar deck. Situated one level below the flight deck, the hangar deck stretched the length of the ship. Lights dangled from beams and sliding walls in the ship's sides allowed the breeze from Cannes to drift through the massive chambers.

Tom had never seen Marty this cheerful and knew exactly who his friend was thinking about. The sound of approaching footsteps drew

Tom's attention upward. The skipper was coming. Tom began to stand but the skipper stopped him: "As you were."

"Hiya, skipper," Marty said. The skipper nodded in return.

"Boys, we've got a heck of a problem." He told them that the mechanics were having trouble starting a plane and suspected that there could be water in its gas tank. "Could be sabotage," he added. Tom and Marty glanced at each other with concern.

The skipper's eyes settled on Marty. "Ensign Goode, I've got a job for you and it's important."

Marty nodded, eager to please.

"I want you to inspect every airplane and fuel tank to figure out if there's water in the gas and how it got there," the skipper said.

Marty's smile disappeared.

"No going ashore until it's done," the skipper added.

Tom could see Marty's mind churning, calculating his predicament. The squadron had fifteen planes, each with a main fuel tank and an underbelly drop tank. *Thirty tanks*, Tom thought. It would take Marty forever and the *Leyte* was due to leave Cannes in seven days.*

Tom raised his hand a bit. "Sir, I can assist Ensign Goode?"

Marty's face lifted with hope. He grinned from Tom to the skipper.

"Nope," the skipper said. "I've got other tasks for you."

Tom nodded and Marty's face fell in despair.

"Carry on," the skipper said and walked away.

"This is a bad dream," Marty muttered. He could not call his girlfriend—there were no ship-to-shore phones. He needed to get ashore to see her, to give her his address, at least. His only hope was to work fast.

Over the ensuing days, Marty rushed around the ship carrying glass test tubes to the ship's lab. When the report came back, the news wasn't good. Water had found its way into the tanks of *all* the aircraft.

---

* Elizabeth Taylor visited the *Leyte* several more times in Cannes. She dined in the wardroom with the pilots, attended a dance in the hangar deck, and dropped by the sick bay when Halley was on duty to give him autographed photos for his friends. To this day, Halley regrets that he gave them all away and forgot to keep one for himself.

With just a few days remaining in Cannes, Marty reported to the skipper's office to explain the situation. He had even built a wooden box to display the test tubes. Marty concluded that the ship had taken on contaminated gas at Livorno.

"Fine work, Ensign Goode," said the skipper from his desk. "Now you can supervise the removal of the contaminated fuel from *all* our planes."

When Marty stepped from the skipper's office, he buried his face in his hands.

Several days later, Marty and an assortment of wistful sailors and pilots leaned over the railing of the *Leyte*'s fantail and watched Cannes shrink in the distance. In the morning light, the carrier's wake bubbled a golden V on the sea, like two arms reaching out.

Marty's eyes hung low with despair. He hadn't made it ashore to see his girlfriend again and now the *Leyte* was steaming east for war games on the island of Crete. Other men had French girlfriends, so why the skipper had singled him out for punishment, Marty didn't know.

It was all too late. Up and down the coast, destroyers and tenders of the Dancing Fleet were pulling out from their ports to rendezvous in open waters.

Beneath the horizon, the *Leyte*'s wake surrendered its reach and became blue with the sea.

CHAPTER 17

THE FRIENDLY INVASION

Four days later, July 19, 1950
The Island of Crete

THE MARINES BRACED in the landing craft's belly as the boat scraped the sandy bottom of the shallow water. The engine surged, the propeller gurgled. In the middle of the men, Red Parkinson grinned while cradling a bazooka almost as tall as he was. It was 7 A.M. and shadows filled the craft.

Red looked between the camouflaged helmets of the Marines in front as the ramp dropped. Golden light rushed inside and Red squinted. Before the men lay a glimpse of heaven—a Mediterranean beach and beyond it, green fields against a backdrop of scrubby hills.

"Hit the beach!" the boat driver shouted.

"Weapons Company, move out!" an officer yelled and the Marines surged forward. "Let's get 'em!" joked a Marine. His buddies laughed. Red followed the others off the boat and into the shin-deep water. The Marines stepped toward the beach, every splash darkening their tan leggings and baggy green pants.

Besides the M20 Super Bazooka that Red carried, he wore a full backpack and a carbine rifle slung across his shoulder. He carried two bazooka rockets in a bag around his neck and a pistol, canteen, and knife on his hips. His chinstrap was loose and the brim of his helmet kept sliding over his eyes. *Keep going!* he told himself. *Uncle Anton would be proud!*

In the center of the beach stood an officer with arms outstretched. Red slowed to a trot as he passed. "Don't crap in the bushes!" the officer shouted. "Use the slit trenches! Stick to footpaths—this is borrowed property!" Red grinned and kept charging. To his left, he could see the village of Kalives.

Red's legs grew rubbery as he scaled a bluff. On the other side he found his five buddies, who had stopped to catch their breath. Red happily took a knee. Now assembled, the boys comprised an antitank platoon. They were separated into two squads. In his squad, Red carried the rocket launcher, another Marine served as his loader, and another carried extra ammo.

Ahead, beyond the fields, lay their objective—a wide hill where Red and his buddies were ordered to set up a roadblock to intercept imaginary Soviet tanks. To the far right of the hill stood a fort built in the time of Napoleon.

Two Greek soldiers paced past Red and the others. They wore dark green uniforms and tipped their small brimmed caps in greeting. The Greeks were allies who had come to observe. Just nine months earlier, they had fought a bloody civil war against Greek communists that produced more casualties among their people than WWII had. Among the losses were twenty-eight thousand children abducted by Greek communists and dispersed across communist lands to be raised under political indoctrination, in lives of manual labor.

"We gotta get moving, or we'll miss the air show!" said one of Red's buddies. The men moved out, eager to scale the hill to get the best view of the *Leyte*'s planes flying over.

The Marines followed footpaths over a creek and through a field of knee-high leaves. Red carried his bazooka in both hands, evenly distributing its fourteen pounds. The weight made his arms tired, and the muggy heat made him sweat. The Marines ahead suddenly veered off the path. Red found them crouched at the edge of a field of melons.

"Hey Red!" an ammo bearer shouted. "You're a farmer. Can we eat 'em?"

Red studied the leaves from where he stood. "Yup, they're watermelons! Get one for me, too!"

The others plucked watermelons from their stems. One of Red's buddies approached him with a melon but stopped when he noticed that Red's hands were full.

"Just shove it in my pack!" Red said with a grin. The Marine laughed and jammed the extra weight inside.

Atop the hill, Red and his buddies stopped at the road and ditched their backpacks on the sandy ground. Red opened his shirt and rolled up his sleeves.

He and his assistants crouched behind scrub bushes and Red aimed his bazooka up the road that led to the hilltop fort. His assistants each held shells. The other bazooka squad set up a few yards away and platoons of riflemen took up positions along the hill. A few men scampered across the road to spread triangular marker panels on the ground—vibrant orange "road signs" that would show the pilots above how far the friendly lines stretched.

One of Red's buddies checked his watch. Thinking aloud, he wondered where the flyboys were.

"Probably overslept in their floating hotel," another man joked.

Red removed the rockets from around his neck and tipped his helmet back. His buddies yawned. The action in Korea was far from their minds, even as friendly forces were reeling in retreat and the papers were predicting a longer war, maybe six months, maybe nine.

Someone suggested that it was time for a snack. Red set his bazooka on a rock, the others left their ammo, and the men returned to their

Bob Devans (left) and Red Parkinson

packs. On the edge of the hill, overlooking the sea, they drew their long Ka-Bar knives and carved into the watermelons.

Red sank his teeth into a slice, gushing seeds. *This is the life!* he thought. The Marines enjoyed their feast and the view of the fleet at anchor, a few miles out.

One of Red's buddies lowered the slice of watermelon from his face. "Uh-oh," he mumbled, looking downhill.

Their platoon leader, Corporal Bob Devans, was approaching. Devans was just twenty years old and short, with an upturned nose and sleepy eyes on a square face. He had joined the Marines straight out of high school.

Devans's eyes settled on his men. Red and the five others didn't even try to scamper away or hide the melons. Devans shook his head in frustration.

"Fellas, you know better. Where'd you get 'em?" Devans asked.

"Down by the beach, Bob," a Marine admitted.

"I'd tell you to put 'em back, but it's too late for that," Devans said.

Red and the others nodded with watermelon seeds stuck to their chins.

Devans scanned the hilltop and saw that everyone was in position for the mock air strikes. Everyone who knew him agreed—he had "presence." In high school, Devans had been an actor in school plays such as *Janie* and *The Waltz Dream*.

"Keep the melons," Devans said. "Just get back to your positions and at least *act* like there's an enemy coming."

Red and the others scrambled to their positions.

The clanking of wheels echoed across the quiet hilltop. Red perked up and glanced toward the fort. He saw that his buddies were starting to doze.

"Soviet tank, T-34!" Red shouted, slapping his assistants on their helmets. Red raised his bazooka and aimed. The assistants perked up and glanced in the direction of Red's aim.

Up the road, two small Greek boys were pulling a rickety cart loaded with watermelons. The Marines chuckled. They watched the boys carry melons from their cart to the other Marine squads. Sometimes the boys returned without melons, counting coins in their palms.

The youngsters worked their way down the road to Red and his buddies. They approached, presented their melons, and recited the only English they knew: "Two for dol-la!" They were deeply tanned, with mops of black hair. The youngsters' eyes suddenly went wide, locking on the watermelon rinds scattered around the Marines. Red glanced guiltily at his buddies and asked if anyone had brought any money.

None had.

"We. Don't. Have. Any. Dollars," Red told the youngsters. The boys raised their palms in confusion.

One of Red's assistants hollered for Corporal Devans.

"Oh, you've done it now," Devans said as he approached from behind. He knelt in front of the youngsters, who backpedaled in fear. "Hey, hey, don't be scared," Devans said. He pulled a phrase book from his pocket and jabbered something in Greek. The youngsters laughed. Devans chuckled and looked at his phrase book again. In each port, Red and the others had seen Devans using the local language, like an actor practicing his lines.

Devans tried a different phrase and the boys nodded and pointed toward the beach. They babbled an excited reply. Devans turned and addressed his platoon.

"It's official—you ate their livelihood," Devans said. "They're brothers and that's their farm by the beach." Devans fished a dollar from his pocket and handed it to the youngsters. The boys grinned and returned to their cart.

Devans turned to Red and the others with a parting thought: "You owe me a slice!"

Behind the Marines, a droning sound came from the heavens above the sea. Red and his buddies turned and looked up. At eight thousand feet, four blue cross-like shapes flew in formation, followed by another formation, and another. More than forty planes were crossing the sky.

"It's the Ks!" a Marine shouted.

"About time," said another.

The Marines could spot the *Leyte*'s planes by the tall, white letter K on their tails. Tom, Jesse, and Koenig were up there flying Corsairs in Cevoli's flight. Dad Fowler had a flight of his own; so did the skipper and the other squadron leaders from the *Leyte*.

The Corsairs nosed over, one after another, and flew downward at a gentle angle, their bent wings taking shape in the sunlight. Red and his buddies stood up. The planes were aiming for an imaginary target in the arid fields across the road—maybe a hill, maybe a hay pile.

"Bring it in close!" a Marine urged the planes.

The lead Corsair descended and stretched in size, the entire plane glimmering from nose to tail.

A Marine made imaginary strafing sounds with his lips—"*Bup! Bup! Bup!*"

The plane leveled off at three thousand feet and passed high over Red and his buddies with barely a grumble. The Corsair kept flying inland, as if striking a target miles away.

One after another, the other three Corsairs emulated their leader's mock attack. As each gently swooped overhead, the Marines cheered with a little less enthusiasm. "Come on, bring it in lower!" a Marine shouted at the planes. It was no use. One by one, the Corsairs pulled up at the same invisible spot then flew away. The young men groaned.

"I want my money back," one joked.

"They probably don't want to spook the goats," Red commented.

More Corsairs came in and made attacks so tepid that the Marines turned back to their watermelons. High over the island, the formations turned and motored back toward the sea. They had been ordered to avoid flying low over areas populated by civilians or livestock but the Marines didn't know this.

One young Marine was particularly peeved. He shielded his eyes and spoke for the others.

"That was the worst air show I've ever seen!"

CHAPTER 18

AT FIRST SIGHT

Three weeks later, August 11, 1950
Beirut, Lebanon

THE NIGHT WAS YOUNG and the party was in full swing around the pool of the ritzy St. Georges Yacht Club, a six story hotel decked in Arabic patterns.

Mixed groups of government dignitaries, local girls from well-connected families, and naval officers stretched around the pool. The party, hosted by the American ambassador to Lebanon, was to welcome the navy to the capital city of Beirut.

A waiter refilled Tom's and Cevoli's champagne glasses—not for the first time. "I think the ambassador's trying to get us drunk!" Tom said with surprise. Cevoli chuckled and agreed. Neither had ever seen so much champagne being slung around.

An orchestra played beneath a poolside cabana, softly enough that the buzz of refined conversation could be heard. Palm fronds swayed in the lamplight, and beyond the pool lay a staggering background: the *Leyte* at anchor.

As Tom and Cevoli strolled around the pool, Tom stuck to the sidewalk. From the top of his hat to the cuffs of his pants he was dressed all in white. Tom loved the crisp perfection of the formal uniform. His jacket was punctuated by gold buttons and framed by black shoulder boards; on his chest, his golden aviator wings shone in the light. But the uniform was difficult to keep clean. On the boat ride from the *Leyte* to the party, Tom had been very careful where he chose to sit.

Cevoli glanced across the pool and burst out in laughter. "Look!" he said. "He's dragging Jesse off again!" Tom looked in time to see the ambassador, Lowell Pinkerton, lead Jesse by the arm toward a throng of local dignitaries and their wives. Wearing a sandy-colored suit, Pinkerton looked like a bald Teddy Roosevelt with a thick mustache and a similar aura of enthusiasm.

The partygoers swarmed Jesse to shake his hand. The curious expressions on their faces suggested that they had never seen a black officer, let alone one in dress whites. The men and women leaned forward to hear Jesse's every soft-spoken word.*

Between yawns, Tom glanced at his watch. The party still had an hour to run before it concluded at midnight. For Tom, Jesse, and their squadron mates, the parties and glad-handing were becoming tiresome. After Crete, the Dancing Fleet had sailed to Athens, then Istanbul, before dropping anchor at Beirut the day before. Prior to now, Tom hadn't left the ship because the crowds in Lebanon—on the eastern extreme of the Mediterranean—were unfriendly to Americans. After two more days in Beirut, the fleet was scheduled for a last stop in France and Tom was counting down the days.

Then, out of the corner of his eye, he saw her.

At first he caught a flash of brown hair and a pastel pink dress and he heard her high heels clattering as she walked past. Tom's eyes followed her lithe legs upward until he came to her wavy hair. The girl glanced over her shoulder and caught him looking.

---

* Jesse handled his role with dignity, yet he harbored a quiet desire. In a letter to his cousin, Jesse had written: "But I'll give you a small clue. The happiest moment of the whole cruise will be when they say, 'Let's go home.'"

Dark eyebrows arched over blue eyes. Her lips were red and her smile beamed all-American friendliness.

Tom felt a rush of light-headedness.

Is she looking at me? he thought.

Tom glanced behind him. Only Cevoli was anywhere near him. Tom watched the girl turn away and blend in with a group of civilians at the far end of the pool.

Cevoli shook Tom to bring him back to earth. Tom saw his flight leader grinning broadly.

"She's probably with one of them," Tom said, motioning to the group the girl had joined. Cevoli disagreed. A married man, he assured his young wingman that only a single girl would emit such a look.

Tom glanced back. The girl laughed and tossed her hair, then shot another glance in his direction.

Cevoli looked down at Tom's flute of champagne. "Drink up!" he said. "That's an order."

Tom chuckled nervously and downed the glass. "Drink mine too," Cevoli said, handing his glass to Tom, who threw it back in one gulp. "Good, you're fueled."

Tom began to waver. He reminded Cevoli that they would be sailing from Lebanon in two days.

Cevoli leaned close and put a hand on Tom's shoulder. "I shouldn't have to tell you this," he said. "But in our line of work sometimes you only get one chance."

Tom nodded. Here one day, gone the next—every aviator knew the hazards.

Cevoli took both empty glasses from Tom's hands. "Why are you still here?" he asked.

The girl turned and stepped from her group before Tom had reached her. "About time!" she said, laughing. She was certainly American.

Taken aback, Tom grinned. "I saw you from over there," he said and pointed to where Cevoli stood. He told the girl he couldn't help but wonder who she was. A bemused look spanned the girl's face. Tom's was probably the most honest pickup line she had ever heard.

The two exchanged pleasantries. As they talked, Tom discovered that the girl worked for the embassy. She was well educated and knew all about the Korean War on the diplomatic front, where Britain and India were now calling on the Soviets to stop the North Korean attacks. *Gosh, she's fascinating,* Tom thought.

"Have you seen the lounge yet?" the girl asked at one point. Tom hadn't, so she grabbed him by the hand and pulled him toward the hotel.

One level beneath the hotel sat the lounge and a view unique to the Middle East. Behind the bartender, a massive pane of glass provided an aquarium-like side view into the hotel's swimming pool.

In a booth, Tom and the girl sat close together at a table covered with empty champagne flutes. The party was thinning out and the lounge was dark and moody but for the waves of blue light along the walls.

The girl studied Tom's face as he smoked a cigarette. Tom pulled the cigarette from his lips and flicked away the ash. He had smoked it down to half its original size.

"Okay, ready for some magic?" he asked.

The girl nodded.

Tom placed the cigarette between his lips and cupped his hands over his mouth. Wisps of smoke rose from the cracks between his fingers. He began making pained expressions with his eyes, as if he were being burned, but he kept his hands clasped over his mouth. Finally, the smoke stopped rising and Tom relaxed. He cupped his palms inward and lowered them from his face, as if he were hiding something. The cigarette was missing from his lips. The girl's eyes followed Tom's hands as he slowly slid them toward her, then fanned them open.

His palms were empty. The cigarette was gone.

The girl's eyes leapt with amazement to Tom's face.

Tom smiled and shrugged. When he refused to tell her how he did it, she punched him playfully on the arm.

"I want to give you something," Tom said.

The girl cocked her head and leaned closer. Tom unfastened his collar and began unbuttoning his jacket, one gold button after another.

The girl sat back in confusion.

Tom slid a hand into his jacket and fiddled inside. From the outside, he grabbed his golden flight wings and pried them from his uniform. The wings were a naval aviator's most valuable possession.

Tom handed his wings to the girl. "For you," he said.

The girl studied the wings in her palm and glanced up, her eyes glimmering. She embraced Tom tightly. When she released him, a dumbstruck grin lined Tom's face.

The girl gazed into Tom's eyes. He gazed into hers.

"This was a lovely night," Tom said. The girl nodded, maintaining eye contact. Tom glanced down to his watch and added, "But I've got a boat to catch." The girl's face dropped. She had expected a kiss.

As Tom gave the girl a hand and led her from the booth, he was sure he had played everything right. They'd made plans for a date the following night and Tom had already decided: He'd take bigger chances tomorrow.

All navy men were supposed to reach the docks by midnight and time was running short. Tom stumbled sloppily down the road from the hotel, his hat in his hand and his coat unbuttoned. The road led down to a small marina on the left where the *Leyte*'s shuttle boats idled. Whistles shrieked from the darkness.

Tom knew that the Shore Patrol, the navy's police, were out rounding up sailors, pilots, and Marines who appeared drunk or in danger of breaking curfew—men like him.

Now you've done it, Tom thought. His polished dress shoes slapped the road faster.

Entering the marina, Tom saw the docks where the *Leyte*'s boats were bobbing, but the Shore Patrol stood in the way. They were sailors wearing black armbands with the white letters *SP* on them. Batons dangled from their belts.

The SPs had formed a human chain to steer clusters of drunken sailors and Marines toward the boats where other SPs took positions to ensure that no one fell in the water. Some of the drunken men were topless, having swapped their shirts for a final drink. Others were wearing ridiculous souvenirs—kepis, fezzes, fur shawls—and a few were carrying their incoherent buddies. During an earlier shore leave in Athens, a pilot had even brought a goat on a leash back to the docks.

Tom stood as soberly as possible and approached the SPs' human chain.

"Excuse me," he said to an SP.

The SP turned, saw Tom, and said, "Evening, sir, you're just in time." The SP stepped aside.

Tom thanked him and fell in line with the drunken sailors.

In the officers' launch, Tom took a seat in the middle. The vessel was nearly empty. Behind Tom stood a sailor at the helm, waiting for stragglers.

Tom sprawled across the damp bench and felt the wood, cool against his cheek. He no longer cared if he soiled his dress whites. Another officer entered the boat, saw Tom, and laughed as he claimed a seat.

"It's not the booze," Tom said, clutching his sore stomach. "I ate a cigarette."

The following afternoon

A puttering noise shook the steel ceiling. Tom clutched his pounding head and sat up in his bunk, baffled at the sound. Without windows, his cabin aboard the *Leyte* was dark and timeless. The sound came in strokes: *whomp, whomp, whomp. What in the heck?* Tom thought. It was the sound of a helicopter, but flight operations were supposed to be suspended while the carrier was in port.

Tom glanced at his watch and cursed. Noon had come and gone. It was a Saturday and he had nowhere to go until his date that night, but apprehension still nagged at him. He looked to his roommate's bunk below but saw that his friend, a pilot named Whalen, had already left the cabin. His buddies were undoubtedly ashore already, and something was happening on deck.

Tom slid heavily to the floor and winced. His brain throbbed with a headache. He found his white uniform draped over a chair and went to unpin his golden wings, to transfer them to his tan uniform—but they were missing. Tom slapped himself on his forehead.

What was I thinking?

He knew he could buy replacements back in the States, but that first pair carried irreplaceable meaning.

Tom dressed to go above deck to find out what else he was missing.

Slowly, Tom climbed the steps and emerged onto Vulture's Row. The helicopter's racket rose from the *Leyte*'s flight deck.

A few pilots stood along the railing, but none were from '32. Jesse was probably below deck, helping the chaplain prepare for religious services the next day. Tom took a spot beside the other pilots and shielded his eyes—the midday sun sprayed sharp and white across the sea.

"Holy cow," Tom muttered. Beside the *Leyte*, a few football fields away, a massive aircraft carrier lay at anchor. Tom looked to a pilot next to him.

"It's the *Midway*!" the pilot shouted over the helicopter's puttering. "You missed it, she just came in."

Tom glanced at the helicopter. The rotors were whirring, an indication that it was going to take off again. In the water between the two carriers, landing craft were carrying helmeted Marines from the *Midway* to the *Leyte*.

"What's going on?" Tom yelled to the pilot.

"Our orders just came in," the pilot replied. "We're leaving for the States today, then on to the Far East—you know what that means!" His face lit up with excitement at the prospect of getting into the thick of the Korean War. He explained that the Marines were probably going to Korea, too—the *Midway* had scooped them up from across the fleet and was transferring them to the *Leyte*. The cruise had been cut short.

Tom draped his arms over the railing as the thought hit him: *I'm never going to see her again.* On the deck below, officers were making their way to the helicopter carrying thick map cases and the fleet's code books. Soon, the admiral would follow them to the *Midway* and he'd transfer his flag, making the *Midway* the new flagship of the Dancing Fleet.

Tom looked leftward, past the carrier's tail and toward Beirut, where the SPs were probably rounding up every sailor on shore leave. Tom thought about her, the vivacious brunette he'd never see again. In 1950, before the age of commercial jet travel, Lebanon seemed as far from home as the moon.

Tom's face drooped with self-disgust. He was furious with himself for breaking his own rule. He was a bachelor committed to his career and he knew better than to have chased after that girl. Now his infatuation wilted in the heat of a new reality: He was going to war.

Tom's eyes lifted. He glanced toward the shore and up to the St. Georges hotel, where he'd spent the best night of his life with the girl in the pink dress.

The embassy! he thought. *I can write to her there!*

I can still get my wings back!

CHAPTER 19

ON WAVES TO WAR

The next day, August 13, 1950
The Mediterranean

SEVEN HUNDRED YOUNG MARINES from the *Midway* filled the cavernous bays of the *Leyte*'s hangar deck. They had changed from their green fatigues into tan uniforms with ties and ditched their helmets. Some milled between parked planes, some marveled at the carrier's vastness, and some cleaned weapons on the side.

In a stretch of the hangar deck that was free of planes, two Marines tossed a baseball. One was PFC Ed Coderre, a short eighteen-year-old with an oval face and black hair. Coderre wound up, crow-hopped, and threw the ball like a bullet across the deck.

Crack! His buddy snagged the ball with a five-fingered glove.

"Good catch!" Coderre shouted, his voice carrying a Rhode Islander's clip. Of French Canadian descent, Coderre had black eyebrows that arched so sharply that they looked threatening, yet his dark eyes beamed friendliness. His buddy nodded and returned the toss.

Crack! Coderre caught the ball, then rotated it to grip the seams.

Ed Coderre

Every throw and catch had to be perfect or the ball could wind up overboard. The ship's crew had slid open the deck's side doors for some fresh air, and the waves of the Mediterranean could be seen slipping behind Coderre's buddy. At top speed, the *Leyte* was steaming for Crete.

Coderre savored each toss and crack of the leather mitt. He knew that he wouldn't get many more chances like this. Throughout the cruise, he had served on the USS *Worcester* and played on the cruiser's ball club during games at various naval bases. Coderre was a center fielder and the team's star. Everyone who watched him play agreed—he had the talent to go pro. But only his friends knew that the pros had already been after him. During Coderre's high school days, the Red Sox had scouted and tried to recruit him—but Coderre had already promised his four buddies that he'd join the Marines with them. After his hitch, however, Coderre knew he'd be free to take the Red Sox up on their offer.

Coderre wound up to throw, then abruptly lowered his arm to the side. He shook his glove from his hand, let it fall, and snapped to attention. His platoon leader, Second Lieutenant Robert Reem, was approaching.

The burly lieutenant was twenty-four, with a thick jaw and eyebrows that hung low over kind eyes. He had enlisted during World War II and at some point someone, recognizing his leadership potential, gave him a special appointment to the Naval Academy.

Reem waved for Coderre to relax and told the other Marine that he needed a word with Coderre, alone.

"I've got good news and bad news," Reem said.

Coderre nodded intently.

Reem said that the battalion had been given a chance to send one enlisted man to prep school for the Naval Academy; he had nominated Coderre and the other officers had concurred.

Lt. Robert Reem

Coderre's eyebrows rose. He'd always dreamed of becoming an officer, but never imagined he could attend the Academy too.

"Here's the bad news," Reem said, shaking his head.

He said that the *Leyte* would be delivering the Marines to a transport ship at Crete, and then they would sail to Japan for staging—not home as some of the men were hoping.

"So, battalion's pulling the Academy thing off the table," Reem added, "but I'll fight like hell to bring it back up once we get home."

Coderre's face dropped but he thanked the lieutenant for looking out for him.

"It's rotten, but what can you do?" Reem said. "I won't even get to see my wife to say goodbye." The lieutenant's eyes sank. His wife, Donna, was the daughter of an admiral. The slender, older gentleman had invited Reem to his house in upstate New York, and together the two had listened to the 1947 Army-Navy game on the radio. When Donna had walked into the room, her black curls bouncing, Reem fell instantly in love. These days, the young couple called Lancaster, Pennsylvania, home.

"I'm just glad to be staying with the unit, sir," Coderre said.

"Me too," Reem said. He smiled and walked away.

Coderre's buddy hustled to his side. "What was that all about?" he asked.

"For two seconds there I was heading to the Naval Academy," Coderre said. "But plans have changed."

"Who cares?" his buddy said. "You've got the Red Sox—that's what I'd do."

Coderre's stomach knotted as he remembered where they were heading.

"Yeah," he said reluctantly. "There's always the Red Sox."

Ten days. Tom passed between Corsairs, a stainless steel pot of coffee in hand, and all he could think was, *Ten days.*

The skipper had told the squadron to prepare for ten days in America before the *Leyte* could be replenished to sprint to the Far East. No longer was it a theory—the Corsairs around Tom would soon be operating in hostile skies. Tom dived into his maintenance officer duties with greater urgency and had the mechanics working around the clock. To show his appreciation, Tom kept them fueled with coffee.

From the corner of his eye, Tom noticed a handful of the new Marines clustered behind a Corsair's folded wing. The Marines were looking toward the cockpit as if something was wrong. Tom approached them. "Can I help you fellas?" he said.

"Yes, sir," a Marine said from the front of the group. "We're trying to figure how a pilot gets up there?"

Tom realized they were talking about how the cockpit sat so high above the ground and practically behind the wing. He told the Marines it just took a little agility.

"I'm sorry, I didn't know you're a pilot, sir," the Marine said. Tom followed the Marine's eyes down to the coffeepot in his hand and in doing so, he noticed the blank spot on his chest where his gold wings should be. He had vowed to buy a replacement pair as soon as he reached American soil.*

"Here, I'll show you," Tom said.

He set the coffeepot down and, in a quick bound, sprang from the foothold in the flap and onto the wing. He steadied himself against the folded wing and invited a Marine up with him. Tom guided the youngster up and then pointed out the cockpit and explained how a pilot would crank up the seat to see above the gunsight.

Tom told the Marines that the Corsair could withstand two thousand pounds of weight per wing. He jumped up and down to show how it didn't budge. The tour concluded, Tom slid down the wing and landed with a spring, then coached the Marine down.

The Marine was all smiles. "I built a Corsair model when I was a kid," he said. "But I never thought I'd get that close to one!"

---

* Tom would later write to the girl to whom he gave his original wings, but would never receive a reply.

"I used to put firecrackers in my models!" another Marine joked.

Tom's eyes flickered with mischief. "I used to build balsa planes as a kid," he said. "I'd light them on fire and toss them out of my bedroom window."

The Marines laughed. It was ironic, coming from a pilot.

The rear of the ship resembled a yard sale.

Along a side wall, a dozen Marines were inventorying their rifles, bazookas, and other equipment. Red Parkinson followed Corporal Devans from one boy to the next, while scribbling notes on a piece of stationery. Each Marine had two sea bags to sort, one that would be sent home from Crete and one they would carry to Japan.*

"Bob, my jungle kit is missing," a Marine said, glancing up from a mound of cartridge pouches. Devans nodded to Red, who scribbled down: *one jungle kit.*

Another fellow's helmet cover was missing. Another had lost his canteen cover. Devans sighed. Most of the gear had been lost during the landing on Crete.

"I can't find my Ka-Bar," a Marine reported. Devans dropped his hands to his hips and shook his head. The knife could be replaced but that wasn't the point.

"I suggest you look harder," Devans said. "I've got to report everything to the gunny."

The Marine nodded vigorously.

At the end of the line, Devans called both antitank platoons together and asked them to take a knee. He squatted in the midst of them. Devans had turned twenty-one just weeks before but carried himself with the presence of a man twice his age.

---

* Red and others would soon be assigned to the legendary 1st Marine Division—the WWII conquerors of Guadalcanal and Peleliu. However, budget cutbacks had thinned the division from 22,000 Marines to 8,000. To rebuild the unit to its WWII strength, President Truman mobilized the Marine reserves, recalled embassy guards, and pulled the Fleet Marines from their ships.

"Fellas, why are we missing more Ka-Bars than anything?" Devans asked.

The others remained silent.

"It's because you traded 'em for hooch or sent 'em home to your kid brother," Devans said. Several boys glanced at their feet. "Where we're going," Devans added, tapping the steel deck, "you're gonna want your knife."

Red nodded. He had seen the newspapers call the Korean War a "police action" but knew better. In Korea, the communists had squeezed the forces of democracy into the southeastern corner of the peninsula, an area called the Pusan Perimeter. No matter how the bureaucrats in Washington labeled the conflict, war was war and the free world was losing.*

Devans had a last message for the others, this one softer in tone.

"If you get killed over there, your sea bags get sent home. Make sure yours is cleaned out of anything you don't want your folks to see."

The boys remained silent.

Devans stood and the others hurried back to their bags with awkward urgency. Devans and Red remained behind.

"Red, I forgot—did you lose anything?" Devans said.

"Nope," Red replied, sticking out his chest proudly. Devans slapped Red on the shoulder and walked away to tend to his own effects. Rumor had it Devans wrote to a girl back home and sent a chunk of every paycheck to his parents, who were struggling financially.

Red returned to his buddies and found them digging through their personal effects. Word had traveled throughout the deck and other Marines were now scouring their sea bags. On the floor lay piles of pulp fiction comics and pin-up magazines. A few boys unearthed stacks of love letters, wrapped in rubber bands.

---

* Earlier, on June 29, a reporter had asked President Truman: "Mr. President, would it be correct . . . to call this a police action under the United Nations?" Truman replied: "Yes. That is exactly what it amounts to." However, by mid-August, despite the arrival of reinforcements, the American and U.N. forces were in danger of being driven into the sea. The Joint Chiefs decided to send in the 1st Marine Division to change the war's momentum.

"Don't want Mom to see this!" a Marine said, holding up a brassiere. Red and the others laughed.

At the bottom of his sea bag, Red found a flyer for a French cabaret show. A sheepish grin crossed his face and he quickly crumpled the flyer in his palm to spare Uncle Anton and Aunt Anne any shame.

The Marines scoured the deck for trash cans until a resourceful boy spotted a solution. He carried his stack of contraband to the open platform at the rear of the ship and tossed the pile overboard.

Other Marines noticed and flocked to the opening where ropes had been strung. A line formed at the ropes as the Marines somberly showered dirty magazines, souvenir women's undergarments, and photographs down to the sea. When Red got his turn at the ropes, he tossed his wadded-up flyer into the breeze and watched it mix with the contraband that speckled the sea.

A few Marines lingered at the ropes and looked pensively at the sea, as if they could already feel the chill of Korea, the place that would end their lives or make them men. The things that made them boys drifted farther and farther behind the ship until they slipped beneath the rolling waves.

CHAPTER 20

THE LONGEST STEP

Sixteen days later, August 29, 1950
Fall River, Massachusetts

TOM SET HIS SEA BAG on the Persian rug in the entryway of his parents' home. The smell of a simmering dinner drifted in from the kitchen and familiar photos lined the staircase wall. It was a Tuesday evening, yet it felt like a holiday to Tom. He had one week of leave remaining before the *Leyte* sailed for the Korean War.

"My darling!" his mother shouted as she approached from the hall. Mary Hudner's hair was gray and curled above her dark eyebrows. A fashionable dress draped her trim figure and her pearl necklace shined.

"Hello, Mother!" Tom said as they hugged.

His mother led him to the living room and sat him in an overstuffed chair opposite a fireplace. Tom told his mother about the Mediterranean and she shared stories from the Fall River social scene. Tom's father was away at one of the family's grocery stores.

In the midst of chatting, Mary's eyes sparkled as she remembered something. She hurried to a side room, reemerged with an envelope,

Mary and Thomas J. Hudner Sr. with their children. Tom is standing behind his father.

and handed it to Tom. In the upper left corner stood a red crest in the shape of a shield and the words "Harvard College."

Tom flipped over the letter and raised an eyebrow when he saw that it had been opened.

"I'm sorry," his mother apologized. "I just had to see if it was important."

Tom read the letter: "We're awaiting your application as we form our new classes for fall. . . ." His brow furrowed. He had shown early interest in attending Harvard but assumed that the college would have forgotten about him when he never submitted an application. Tom lowered the letter and looked at his mother. "Don't they know I've already got an education?" he said. "Why are they still writing to me?"

Mary smiled. "Well, you were a fine student."

Tom fought back a smile. His grades hadn't been that good. If anything, it was his prep school pedigree that had opened the door to Harvard.

Mary asked Tom if he would consider pursuing a graduate degree at Harvard. She knew her son had fulfilled his two years of service to the navy and could foreseeably seek a discharge.

"Nah," Tom said. "I'm going to make a career of the navy."

Mary looked away with dismay. Her son was due to sail for war and she hoped that Tom might yet follow the path his father and grandfather had laid out for him.

Tom handed back the letter. "Don't worry, Mother, they'll stop sending them sooner or later."

Two days later, a lanky gray-haired woman removed the crumb-speckled plates from the dining table as Tom and his father sat in silence. The woman was Nursey, still the family's maid. Seated on his father's right, Tom had dressed up for dinner, as was the family's custom. He wore a dark suit and fidgeted with his unlit pipe. A chandelier dangled from the high ceiling.

At the end of the table, Thomas Hudner Sr. smoked a cigarette. Behind him, a tall window revealed the dark street. Thomas Senior resembled a thinner version of President Truman. His gray hair was slicked back and he wore wire-rimmed spectacles and a three-piece suit. His wealth had come through hard work, hand in hand with his father, to build their grocery chain.

The family had just celebrated Tom's twenty-sixth birthday and now Senior wanted to talk with his son in private. The war was on his mind. That day the first British unit had arrived in Korea, and troops and medical units were following from eighteen other U.N. nations. The international response was unprecedented: American forces were about to lead the first U.N. army into battle.

When Nursey left the room, Senior encouraged Tom to light his pipe. Tom hesitated, having never smoked inside the house.

"Oh, just light it," his father chuckled. "Can't be worse than these." He nodded at his own cigarette.

Tom lit his pipe. His after-dinner routine had changed vastly over the years. As a boy, Tom usually snuck away after meals with his pockets full of cooked vegetables. From the porch he'd toss his vegetables into the bushes.

"So, how are you feeling about where you're going?" Senior asked, lighting another cigarette.

Tom lowered his pipe. "Well, we have to show the communists that enough is enough, or their aggression will never stop," he said. "So Korea's as good a place as any."

Senior asked if Tom's buddies felt the same. Tom chuckled and said that one of the pilots actually transferred out of the squadron rather than accompany them to Korea. Tom explained that he and his friends barely knew the pilot—the young man kept to himself, and the news had come as a total surprise. Senior's face twisted with distaste.

"He requested transfer to a noncombatant unit," Tom added. "So they sent him back to Quonset until they can figure out what to do with him."*

---

* The pilot who transferred out of '32 told the author that he had always wanted to fly multi-engine aircraft in an air-sea rescue role but was talked into requesting fighters during flight training. When news broke that the *Leyte* was headed to Korea, the pilot asked the skipper for a transfer. The skipper understood and pushed the young pilot's request up the chain. The navy, however, reacted less kindly. Several months later, the pilot was forcibly discharged.

"He chose to be in fighters, didn't he?" Senior asked.

"Yes, sir," Tom said.

"And he raised his hand to protect and defend the American people, didn't he?" Senior added.

Tom nodded. They all had taken the oath. "In his defense," Tom said, "there's lots of ways to serve, and they don't all call for trigger pulling."

Senior nodded. He had been an officer himself during World War I and he regretted being stuck in a staff job while everyone else was deployed. "So you don't exactly need to go to Korea, do you?" Senior asked. "You can call Quonset and transfer out like that other fellow?"

Tom shrugged. "Yeah, I suppose I could."

Senior flicked the ash from his cigarette. Tom took a puff from his pipe.

"But none of the other fellows are backing out," Tom added. "We all figure it's dangerous if we just let the North Koreans take the South. What message would that send the Soviets? If we don't take a stand, in a few years we'll be fighting for America's survival."

Senior looked at Tom and swallowed hard, fighting back emotion. His next words would mean the world to Tom.

"I'm proud of you, son."

A day later, in Mississippi

The evening sunlight settled over the Hattiesburg projects as Jesse and Daisy sat on the front steps of her mother's apartment.

Up and down Robertson Place, people sat on their porches. The affordable housing units were each two stories tall and built of red brick. Lamplight leaked from some windows; radio music trickled from others.

Dressed in a white shirt with short sleeves and slacks, Jesse held Daisy's hand, his eyes distant in thought.

Daisy smiled and pretended not to notice. She wore a brightly colored dress and a floral fragrance drifted from her neck, the rose and jasmine scent of the Coeur Joie perfume that Jesse had sent home from Cannes.*

The couple had done most of their dating on the porch, under the eye of Daisy's mother, Addie. Addie was a generous, loving woman, yet strong too. Her husband had died young, leaving her a thirty-year-old widow with five children. To put food on the table, she had taken to cleaning homes, while Daisy, the eldest of the children, helped raise her younger siblings.

During Daisy's school days, her mother would shoo Jesse off the porch by 10 P.M. But this time, Addie stayed inside. The young couple's time was fleeting. It was Friday night and on Sunday Jesse had to fly east to rejoin his squadron for the cruise to war.

Jesse turned to Daisy and took her hands. His grip was firm, his eyes serious with passion. Jesse had joined the navy—not the airlines—so that he could fly and fight for his country. He had prepared himself for where he was headed.

Jesse told Daisy that they needed to talk. At first, Daisy wondered if he might try to spring a ring on her. Jesse had been unable to afford a ring when they became engaged, nor could they afford a honeymoon. Recently he had begged Daisy to allow him to buy her a diamond ring, but she had refused, because money was still tight.

"Tootie, this isn't easy," Jesse said. "But if something should happen to me over there, I've been thinking, you should go to college and get a degree."

Daisy reeled back, shaking her head. She begged Jesse not to spoil the night. But ever since his barrier bounce on the carrier, he'd been trying to broach this subject with her. Before he'd left for the Mediterranean cruise, he'd even sent her back to Mississippi and allowed the lease of their Rhode Island cottage to expire. He wanted Daisy to be close to her family if something happened to him.

---

* Jesse sent home so much expensive French perfume for Daisy and his mother that a local store offered to re-sell any bottles the women didn't need or want. Daisy refused and kept them all. As this chapter was written, she still had one of the original bottles that Jesse had sent her and a few drops remained.

Jesse dropped Daisy's hands and pulled a small notepad from his pocket. He handed it to her. Daisy skimmed the pages with bewilderment.

"Survivors' benefits, Social Security, everything we've talked about," Jesse said. "I've mapped it all out. You'll also find there's a private life insurance policy I took out."

Daisy stopped thumbing through the pages and looked blankly at him. A *private insurance policy?* she thought. *Since when?*

Jesse explained that he had invested in a policy that, if he was killed, would issue a monthly payment for five years. "If something happens, darling, use the money for tuition—even if you go just part-time," Jesse said. "Before five years is over, you'll have your degree and won't need to work in somebody's kitchen."

Daisy stared, her mouth open with shock. Jesse took his wife's hands again, and Daisy shook from her stupor.

"Will you become a teacher, like my mama?" Jesse said. "She'll tell you—it's one of the best professions there is. Will you promise me, darling?"

Daisy remembered what she had learned at Quonset Point, from Grace Cevoli and the other seasoned military wives: *An aviator has enough worries at work, he doesn't need any more at home.*

Daisy also knew that this would be Jesse's last deployment—her husband had joined the navy through the reserves in 1947 and had just seven months remaining in his commitment. In March 1951 he'd revert back to the reserves and civilian life, and then he'd resume his studies at Ohio State to finish his degree. Daisy knew that Jesse would still put in his weekend a month for the navy to get his flying fix, but she looked forward to having him as a husband, almost full-time. All she had to do was endure seven more months.

A calmness settled across her face. Daisy squeezed her husband's hands. "I promise," she said. "If anything happens I'll become a teacher."

Jesse's face lifted. "Good." He leaned back with relief. "That way you'd be able to take care of yourself if you can't find another man in five years!"

Daisy laughed and hit Jesse's arm. She loved it when he teased her.

The next morning, the rural airfield was quiet as the Brown family and their sharecropper neighbors picnicked on the grass. Forests surrounded the field. Over the trees to the south, a dark storm brewed in the Gulf, but over Hattiesburg the clouds remained billowy and white.

It was Saturday, a workday, yet the Browns and their neighbors sat on blankets and sipped sodas. Jesse's mother, Julia, bounced baby Pam. In suspenders that stretched over his shirt, John Brown talked with other fathers. Daisy mingled with old friends while barefoot children chased one another.

The Palmer's Crossing municipal airport was largely deserted with the storm brewing. A mechanic or two in greasy clothes strolled between the large, flimsy hangars. A tin Standard Oil sign hung near a fuel pump, and an assortment of biplanes and Piper Cubs were parked in rows on a worn patch of concrete.

A buzzing sound arose in the sky to the south. The sharecroppers stood as a red Cessna appeared above the trees. The plane was new, a sleek model for private pilots. A square wing sat atop a tapered body and short landing gear jutted out from the fuselage.

The Cessna descended toward the runway but the approach seemed too high, as if the pilot would need to circle around again. The plane's engine suddenly cut to idle. The nose snapped rightward, the left wing dipped downward, and the plane dropped like a rock. Onlookers gasped and Julia Brown covered her mouth, but Daisy just shook her head: She knew this trick.

Low above the runway, the plane's nose suddenly snapped back to normal and its wings leveled. The Cessna rode a cushion of air down until its front tires and tail wheel kissed the concrete. *Tweek, tweek, tweek*. The plane barely bounced.

The pilot taxied the Cessna onto the empty concrete near the small crowd. He gunned the engine and swerved the plane around so that the tail was facing the people. The propeller kept whirling. Doors popped open on either side of the fuselage and Fletcher, Lura, and a young friend hopped down to the ground. The boys covered their eyes as they darted behind the tail, their T-shirts flapping. Lura was now twenty, and a smile filled his face. But Fletcher, now eighteen, wasn't faring as well. His face was frozen in fear. He flopped onto the grass near his family and his mother, father, and Daisy huddled around him.

"Jesse let me try to land," he panted. "But I was too high and couldn't get the plane down, so he took over and dropped us from the sky! Called it a 'slip' or something—it scared the hell out of me!" Everyone laughed, especially Daisy.

The pilot's door opened on the left side of the plane and Jesse leaned halfway out. He wore sunglasses and a headset. A smile spanned his face and his polo shirt flapped. A friend had loaned him the Cessna and already Jesse had given half the community of Lux their first plane ride, including some of the hired hands who once predicted that he'd never fly an airplane.*

Jesse signaled with three fingers. Finally, with nervous grins, three sharecroppers shielded their eyes and approached the plane. They disappeared inside and the Cessna taxied away.

When Jesse landed next and disembarked the last flock of passengers, he leaned out from the door. "Daisy!" he shouted. Daisy shook her head and pointed to someone else. One of her friends gently elbowed her and another nudged her forward. Finally, Daisy threw up her hands in defeat. She ran to the plane and hopped in, and Jesse took off.

Fifteen minutes later, the plane taxied back to the concrete patch and its engine cut to silence. The Brown family and their neighbors

---

*Lura Brown remembers that Jesse had come home on leave soon after earning his wings and had taken some local boys flying, kids from Hattiesburg's poverty-stricken black neighborhood. Two of the boys became military pilots in the 1950s and one of them rose to the rank of colonel.

flocked to the plane. Jesse jumped down and circled to the passenger's side to unbuckle his wife. Together the couple emerged from beneath the wing and the crowd broke into an applause that went on and on, as if no one wanted it to end.

A day later, Sunday, September 3

Jesse leaned across the steering wheel and peered through the thick rain as he drove along the drenched Mississippi roadway. The rain slapped against the green Dodge Wayfarer's hood. The roads were slick but the car's whitewall tires managed.

From the passenger's seat, Daisy held Jesse's uniform jacket across her lap as her eyes focused on the car ahead, the one her husband was following. Two red taillights beamed in the gloom. Thick forests bordered the road. It was mid-morning and the rain had turned the world gray.

Now and then, Jesse glanced in the rearview mirror as he held his speed. In the back seat, a young black couple named Ike and Gwen Heard gripped the doors. In a coat and tie, Ike resembled a nervous dignitary being chauffeured to a state function. He was young, Jesse's age, but his thin mustache and high hairline made him look older.

Ike was Jesse's cousin and his boyhood best friend. Already he'd become a college professor at a school near Houston, Texas, where his wife was from. Gwen's face was round and youthful. The young couple was visiting from Texas and accompanying Jesse and Daisy to the airport so that Ike could drive Daisy back to Hattiesburg—provided they all arrived in one piece.

In the rear window of the car ahead, a small hand emerged over the seatback. Then another hand. Baby Pam's pudgy face and short black hair popped into view. Pam waved from the car ahead.

"Ooooh! She's up again, she sees us!" Daisy said over the pattering rain.

"Hiya, baby!" Jesse said and waved.

From the back seat, Ike and Gwen leaned forward to catch a glimpse.

Pam bounced a few times, then dropped from sight. A second passed, then again the chubby hands clamped the seatback and Pam hauled herself back into view. The baby waved and the adults waved back.

In the car ahead, Jesse's mother, Julia, turned in the passenger's seat to check on Pam while Jesse's aunt drove. Julia was taking Pam to the aunt's house in Meridian, north of Hattiesburg, so Daisy could focus on seeing her husband off to war.

Jesse was not bound for Meridian but for Birmingham, Alabama. A hurricane had settled over Mississippi and washed out the flights. Luckily, Jesse had found a flight out of Birmingham, so he could reach Norfolk, Virginia, in time to ferry his plane aboard the *Leyte* the next morning.

A road sign for Meridian flashed past Jesse's window and his smile faded. He knew the turn was nearing. Jesse waved faster at Pam and blew his daughter kisses. Daisy saw tears sneaking down his cheeks.

Outside the window, signs indicated that the split in the road was upon them. Jesse cranked the turn signal upward and a right arrow blinked. Jesse eased the steering wheel to the right and the car followed the road east toward the Alabama border. Through the rain, Jesse and Daisy watched the other car stay straight on the road to Meridian. From his side window, Jesse waved at Pam. The baby's face turned to follow him, her eyes welling with confusion.

From the passenger's seat, Jesse's mother blew him a kiss before a misty patch of woods came between the two cars.

Jesse focused his eyes forward and wiped them dry.

As rain fell on the terminal, Jesse parked the Wayfarer at the Birmingham airport. The rounded tails of airliners stood out in the gloom. Daisy checked her watch. It was just after noon; they had made it with time to spare. Everyone in the car was quiet for a moment, then Gwen broke the silence. "Well, Ike and I are going into the terminal. We'll listen for the boarding call to give y'all some time."

Ike stepped out, popped an umbrella, and offered Gwen a hand. The couple scurried through the rain to the terminal.

In the front seat, Daisy and Jesse took hold of each other. Jesse stroked his wife's hair. "I could sit here forever and never find the words to describe how much I love you," he said.

Daisy's eyes turned wet as she met her husband's gentle stare.

Jesse spoke again. "No man ever loved a woman more than I love you."

Daisy broke into tears on Jesse's shoulder and soon felt his tears on the back of her neck.

Twenty minutes later, maybe more, Daisy lifted her head from Jesse's shoulder and wiped her eyes. *An aviator has enough worries at work, he doesn't need any more at home!* she thought. She apologized for the waterworks. "I'm crying because I'll miss you," she said, "not because I can't handle myself."

Jesse nodded lovingly.

"What I'm saying is," Daisy added, "you do what you need to do over there, love, and don't worry about me—I'll be here when you get home."

Jesse smiled, wrapped an arm over Daisy, and pulled her close. "When I get home, we're going on our honeymoon," Jesse said. "I'm taking you to the Bahamas and we're going to have the time of our lives."

They held each other until Gwen appeared and waved from the terminal's doorway. Jesse's boarding time had arrived.

Jesse and Daisy shared a last kiss.

Jesse slipped his uniform jacket over his shoulders and climbed from the car. He slapped his officer's hat on his head and tossed his sea bag over a shoulder. As he hustled toward the terminal he glanced back at his wife through the rain. At the terminal doorway, he gazed one last time, then walked inside.

The door to the Wayfarer opened, startling Daisy. Gwen slipped into the back seat, then Ike dropped into the driver's seat. Daisy noticed tears on Ike's face and she put a hand on his shoulder. The young man bowed his head and began sobbing.

"I'm so sorry," Ike mumbled between sobs. "I just feel like I'm losing my best friend." In the back seat, Gwen broke down in her handkerchief.

Daisy sniffled and felt herself losing the composure she had regained. She wrapped an arm around Ike and said, "Ike, Jesse flies with some fine fellows, the best our country has. He's not alone in this— don't you fret."

Ike's sobbing slowed but his chest still heaved. Daisy noticed his hands shaking. She suggested that he sit in the back seat with Gwen for a bit while she got them back on the road. Daisy had never driven on a highway before but knew they had to begin the four-hour drive if they were to reach Hattiesburg by nightfall.

Ike nodded somberly and moved to the back seat. Daisy slid into the driver's seat and started the car. She clicked the wipers to life and cleared the glass. She knew that Jesse was probably aboard his plane, strapped into his seat, and no good could come from waiting any longer. Daisy cranked the car into gear. She drove out of the parking lot, away from the misty terminal and the aircraft tails. Exhausted with emotion, Ike and Gwen soon fell asleep in the back seat.

Behind the wheel, Daisy kept driving. Her chin was firmly set, her breathing steady, her eyes dry and alert. Without any help, she drove them all the way home.

CHAPTER 21

THE LAST NIGHT IN AMERICA

Two weeks later, September 18, 1950
San Diego, California

IN THICK LEATHER SEATS, Tom and Koenig relaxed in the hotel's cocktail lounge. Cups of coffee sat on the table between them. A massive painting of a peacock spanned the wall behind them. This was their last night on American soil, for a while at least.

Tom lowered his pipe from his mouth. "Look what the cat dragged in," he whispered. Koenig scrunched up his newspaper and glanced between the lobby's yellow pillars. Eight young pilots in tan uniforms were sauntering in, jabbering loudly.

They were the squadron's ensigns. Without a word, Tom and Koenig shrank in their seats. Both knew what would happen if the ensigns spotted two "old" lieutenants trying to enjoy an uneventful night—the young pilots would try to pressure them into drinking. In Tom's mind, there was a time for that, but it wasn't now. The *Leyte* had just steamed 4,700 miles from Norfolk through the Panama Canal to San Diego, and the next afternoon the squadron was casting off for Korea. On their last night in America, all Tom and Koenig wanted was some peace and quiet.

"Hey, Hud! Bill!" an ensign shouted and waved from the entrance to the lounge.

They'd been spotted.

Tom rose in his seat as the ensigns approached. Koenig folded his paper.

Tom and Koenig greeted the group and noticed some new faces among the regulars. Six new pilots had recently joined the squadron, bringing the unit to a war-ready strength of twenty-four flyers. The skipper already regretted the new pilots because they were fresh from training, when he had been hoping for WWII veterans.

"Dad's hosting a martini muster over at the bar," an ensign said. "You need to join us!" Another young pilot announced their objective—to try to out-drink Dad.

Tom cringed. His stomach was still shaky. The night before, the squadron had gathered in a suite in the same hotel and had drunk until the sun rose. At roll call that morning on the Leyte's deck, Tom and Koenig had stood wobbly but others were absent, including the man who never missed an assembly—the skipper.*

Koenig told the ensigns that he and Tom would have to pass on the invite. The ensigns mockingly groaned.

Dad Fowler and Jesse entered the lobby and headed for the barroom at the other end. Jesse's bar hopping? Tom thought. Now I've seen it all!

The young pilots broke from Tom and Koenig and flocked to Dad's side.

Tom returned to his pipe and Koenig to his newspaper. The headlines indicated that the 1st Marine Division had just made a surprise landing behind enemy lines at the port of Inchon, halfway up Korea's

---

* One of '32's new pilots, Bill Wilkinson, wrote home with observations of the skipper: "He gets pretty noisy at parties and the proprietors always end up asking him to leave. He sure is the life of the party, and it's a darn good thing he always wears civilian clothes ashore. He may be a party boy, but by golly it ends there. The next morning you'd never know him from the same man the night before. He's strict, stern, and very official aboard ship and with the pilots, which is the way it should be, I guess."

western coast. Already, the Marines were moving to liberate Seoul and cutting off North Korean supply lines to choke the enemy's assault in the south. Reporters speculated that the Marines' bold landing could turn the tide of the war.

Inside the barroom, sailors, ladies, and businessmen sat along the bar and filled curved booths, drinking beer and cocktails. Rhumba music piped in from the ceiling and beams of light snuck up the walls from scalloped light covers. The room was dim, yet friendly.

At the head of a long wooden table, Dad sat and told jokes with Jesse at his side. One of Dad's favorites went like this: "What's an aviator's favorite breakfast after a night of drinking? A puke and a smoke!" The young pilots roared in laughter and rocked back in their chairs. The ensigns looked up to Dad, the squadron's third-in-command and John Wayne–like figurehead.

In the Mediterranean, Dad had appointed Jesse as his assistant operations officer, and the job fell to Jesse to review and tally the pilots' flight logs. The two became fast friends. Both were southern gentlemen; Dad hailed from rural roots outside of Houston. During high school he'd been captain of the debate club and worked as a carpenter's assistant for his father, who taught him a guiding principle: "The color of a man's skin makes no more difference than the color of his eyes."

A young waiter went from pilot to pilot, scribbling drink orders onto a pad. Dad told the waiter to make his drink a double and encouraged the others to do the same. He was trying to build a bond with the young ensigns, one they would need in combat.

The waiter approached Jesse last. Sometimes Jesse would order a gin and tonic, then jokingly add, "Just hold the gin!" But before Jesse could place his order or crack his joke, the waiter walked away. Jesse glanced to see if the man had realized his mistake and would come doubling back. He didn't.

"Excuse me!" Dad said loudly. The waiter turned on his heels. Dad pointed to Jesse. "You missed this gentleman's order."

The ensigns' chattering wound down.

The waiter approached and leaned in toward Dad's ear. In a low voice he said, "Sir, I apologize, but we don't serve Negroes."

Jesse glanced away with disappointment. Dad held up his hand to stop the waiter from leaving. "How about an exception?" he said, keeping his cool, a skill he had practiced as a law student before WWII.

The waiter whispered something about "hotel policy." The ensigns mumbled in disgust. They hadn't realized that racism remained prevalent in California. Bus lines and movie theaters were safe—throughout the state, blacks could sit anywhere. But the YMCA allowed blacks to swim only on Thursdays and most bowling alleys refused them outright. The National Guard was still segregated and restaurants and bars could legally refuse black patrons. They never posted "whites only" signs—they simply stopped blacks at the door.

Dad's jaw tightened and he scowled at the waiter. "You're either going to serve him, or you aren't going to serve any of us."

Jesse stood. "No need for trouble," he said. "I'll see you fellas back at the ship." He quickly walked toward the door.

Dad curled his fists.

The waiter's voice turned shaky. "Sir, I apologize, but we'll happily serve the rest of your party."

Dad abruptly stood, nearly flipping over his chair, and announced to the table: "We're outta here! Let's go, boys. Up, up, up!" He was six foot four and the black shoulder boards of his uniform made his frame seem even bigger. The waiter stumbled back.

The pilots snapped to their feet and grabbed their jackets. Throughout the bar, other patrons turned toward the commotion. Dad lowered his chin and stormed up to the bar where the waiter was whispering to a tall bartender.

Dad addressed the wide-eyed bar patrons.

"Tomorrow, that young man is leaving to fight the Reds," he said, gesturing to the lobby to which Jesse had fled. "And these people won't even pour him a drink!"

The bar patrons—sailors among them—turned to the bartender

with angry eyes. The bartender shrugged. "Mister, we already explained our policy. Explaining it again ain't gonna change it."

"Oh, stuff it!" Dad growled. The bartender had no clue that he was facing a man who'd shot down six Japanese planes by the age of twenty. Dad unclenched his fists, turned, and walked away. He didn't want to risk winding up in jail and having the *Leyte* sail without him.

In the lobby, the ensigns fell in behind Dad.

"This is the only time I've ever regretted wearing the uniform of the U.S. Navy," he muttered, "because it keeps me from going back there, jumping the bar, and kicking that guy's ass."

From his seat in the lounge, Tom had seen Jesse stride through the lobby. His friend's eyes were locked forward. His hands were buried in his pockets. And he was heading for the revolving front door alone. *That can't be good,* Tom had thought.

Not a minute later, Dad and his pilots followed, the ensigns glancing disgustedly back toward the bar.

"What the heck?" Tom muttered. Koenig lowered his newspaper.

One of the ensigns broke from the group to alert Tom and Koenig. "They wouldn't serve Jesse!" he said.

Tom shook his head in disbelief. *He can fight for his country but can't order a drink?*

Koenig's face turned red and he glanced around wildly in search of a manager, eager to leap to Jesse's defense.

Tom hadn't planned to leave the lounge and didn't have to. He could still enjoy the uneventful night he wanted—hot coffee, a fully packed pipe, and peace and quiet. Neither he nor Koenig could change the hotel's racist policy or fix the state's hypocrisy.

But there was something they could do.

Tom stood. "Let's get the hell out of here."

"With pleasure," Koenig said tossing his paper aside.

CHAPTER 22

THE BEAST IN THE GORGE

Nearly two weeks later, October 1, 1950
The front lines, South Korea

RED PARKINSON KNEELED on the rural Korean road and slid the bayonet's blade into the rocky soil. His hand trembled, his blue eyes blinked. He sank the blade in deeper and fished around. *Nothing.* Red slid the blade out and sat back on his heels. *Whew!* Dust clung to his fleshy cheeks. The walls of a wide mountain gorge towered above him on both sides. In the rugged terrain north of Seoul, the Marine column had been stopped.

In front of Red and behind him, sixty Marines cursed and grunted as they probed the road with their bayonets. Dressed in pale green fatigues and helmets with brown and tan camouflaged covers, they were searching for box mines, essentially wooden boxes containing eighteen pounds of explosives. A mine had already claimed one Marine tank. Red and the others were assigned to the battalion's Weapons Company (3rd Battalion, 7th Marine Regiment); they were bazooka

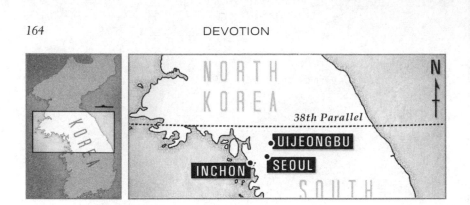

operators and machine gunners, not bomb disposal experts. Still, any disturbed soil had to be searched.

Red glanced up periodically from his work and scanned ahead. He felt vulnerable, having stashed his bazooka and pack beside the road. The midday sun warmed his back while the cool breeze chilled his sweat. Trees with yellow leaves dotted the roadsides and beyond lay pastures and steep terrain scattered with white boulders. War had spared nature, but not the small South Korean settlements beside the road. Here and there lay white pagodas with shattered blue roofs and footbridges smashed into rustling creeks.

Corporal Devans paced behind his platoon, his eyes locked forward. Scouts had spotted North Korean troops five miles ahead at the town of Uijeongbu, where they had paused in their retreat. The North Koreans had planted the mines to delay the Marine column—and it was working. As Red and the Weapons boys inched forward, Ed Coderre, Lieutenant Reem, and other riflemen patrolled ahead through the neighboring pastures. Corsairs occasionally raced above the gorge and the air crackled with tension.

Red shuffled on his knees and stabbed the earth again. His bayonet hit something hard. His eyes went wide. He wiggled the blade and dug down with his fingers. Out popped a rock. Red wiped his brow with relief.

The duty felt like punishment after he'd come so far. After steaming from Crete to Korea, Red and the other Fleet Marines had joined the 1st Marine Division during the fighting for Seoul.

That was nine days ago.

Bob Devans (lower left) and Charlie Kline (lower right)

Since then, the twenty-two thousand Marines had liberated Seoul and thrown the North Koreans into retreat. Friendly forces were now breaking out of the Pusan Perimeter and driving the enemy from the south. As soon as the communists were pushed back above the 38th parallel—the prewar border—everyone expected the war to end. With the border just twenty miles to the north, Red didn't mind the idea of coming home soon, as long as he came home with some good stories to tell Uncle Anton.

Behind Red, a voice began quoting a Bible verse. Red turned and spotted PFC Charlie Kline talking to himself as he probed the soil. Sandy blond hair peeked out from under Charlie's helmet. His eyes were blue and his thick chin jutted out as he smiled. Tall, hefty, and twenty years old, Charlie was a fired-up Baptist from Philadelphia who loved to sing "Go Tell It on the Mountain."

"Being right with the Lord is necessary for protection in this life and the next!" Charlie proclaimed. "Ain't that right, brother John?"

Red averted his eyes. "Uh, yup," he muttered.

Charlie was one of the most all-American guys Red had ever met and, at that moment, one of the most annoying. Since landing in Korea, Charlie had been harping about "being right with the Lord." At first, Red had told Charlie to give it up, but Charlie only became more persistent. So Red had decided it was easier just to agree.

Red knew his friend meant well; they just regarded God with different fervor. Red had never prayed before, in fact. His mother had been an atheist and on the farm he took after Uncle Anton—a Methodist who milked cows on Sunday morning instead of going to church— whereas Aunt Anne never missed a sermon.

Tat tat tat! Burrrip!

Flashes of gunfire zipped between the trees on the flanks. Red and Charlie hit the deck. The riflemen on the flanks had hit resistance. Whooshing sounds fell from the heavens, followed by explosions cracking beside the road. Shock waves flattened the foliage and soil burst into the air. Red and Charlie wrapped their arms over their heads.

"Mortars!" Devans shouted as he sprinted for cover. "Get off the road!"

Another mortar dropped in, then another. Red scrambled back, seized his Super Bazooka, and dived into a ditch with Charlie and Devans. Over the gunfire and explosions came a growling noise from the road up ahead. The mortars stopped falling and the sound of squeaking wheels took the place of explosions.

"Tank!" a faraway Marine shouted. "Tank, incoming!"

Red's heart pounded. His mind flashed back to Crete, where he'd joked about an approaching tank when really the sound had been two boys with a melon cart. Now the pebbles on the roadside seemed to vibrate at eye level. Red cradled his bazooka and parted the weeds for a better view.

A hundred yards away the machine turned the corner, and Red's eyes went wide. "Jesus help us," Charlie whispered. The tank was green like a dragon and the hole at the end of its cannon looked like a lone eye sweeping side to side. It was a Soviet-built T-34, the first live example that Red had ever seen. Its sloping turret looked deformed, too tall and thick for the machine's angular body.

The tank stuck to the road and clanked past the Marines out in front without firing a shot. A machine gun protruded from the front of its hull and swiveled as its gunner scanned for targets.

The tank kept rolling along, its suspension clanking. It was now only ninety yards away from Red, Charlie, and Devans. The tank's tracks spit white rock forward, and dust billowed from the rear as it ground up the road.

Eighty yards.

Seventy.

Frozen in place, Red watched the T-34 churn closer. Charlie's chin trembled. The tank was well within the Marine lines.

Sixty.

Fifty.

A T-34 destroyed near Seoul

More than a hundred Marines surrounded the machine but only one was in a position to stop it. Only a bazooka man could slay the T-34, the best Soviet battle tank of WWII, one that Stalin had given the North Koreans. Red's face twisted as a realization struck him. The only bazooka man in position was him.

Tat tat tat!

"Get down!" Devans shouted. Red and the others flattened against the base of the ditch as bullets snapped overhead.

Tat tat tat!

With a groan, the beast lurched to a stop forty yards away in the middle of the road and let out another burst.

Tat tat tat!

Red glanced up and saw that the tank was focusing on a target. Its machine gun spit fire toward a pasture to the left, where a lanky Marine was running uphill, tearing through the undergrowth. Bullets bit the earth around him, nipping at his heels. The Marine carried a spool of phone wire in one hand and his rifle in the other.

That's Bill Morin! Red realized. Morin was from upstate New York, like Red. He was a party Marine who loved scotch and looked like Dean Martin. Everybody loved him.

Higher on the hill, a mortar squad crouched behind boulders. "Take cover!" they shouted at Morin. "Get down, you idiot!" Morin dived behind a clump of small trees. Bullets snapped the branches overhead and kicked up the soil around him.

With a roar, the tank belched black smoke and wheeled in place to face the pasture where Morin was cowering. The enemy machine gunner now had a straight shot. Gunfire burst from the machine gun's muzzle toward the trapped Marine.

You can save him! Red thought.

Red hoisted the Super Bazooka onto his shoulder. "Load me up!" he shouted to Charlie over the tank's gunfire. Charlie grabbed a rocket from his pack and shimmied up to Red.

Red fixed his eyes on the tank. It was broadside, an ideal target profile. Large scratches marred its green hide where bullets had skidded across it in the past. White Soviet-style numbers lined the turret. Dust and grease matted the wheels between the tracks.

Stay put! Red thought.

Charlie slid the eight-pound rocket into the rear of the bazooka tube and connected an electrical wire to the rocket. He smacked Red on the shoulder to tell him he was armed and dived out of the way, expecting Red to fire from the ditch.

But with Morin's life on the line, Red had no intention of shooting from cover and maybe missing. He leapt to his feet and scrambled up onto the road. In one motion he slid to a knee, lifted the bazooka, and braced the tube on his right shoulder. Red leaned his face rightward and peered through the circular gunsight.

Red clenched his breath and swung the crosshairs onto the machine's rear quarter, over an auxiliary fuel drum that had been strapped to the tank's side. Behind the drum stood nearly two inches of armor that shielded the machine's fuel tank and engine. Red's bazooka could punch through eleven inches if need be.

Now!

Red squeezed the trigger. A coil behind the trigger produced a spark that raced up the grip and into the rocket. The rocket's propellant ignited with a *whoosh*, and the projectile shot from the bazooka's mouth in a flaming bolt of orange.

Crack!

The shell punched into the T-34 and the twenty-six-ton beast shuddered on its tracks. A split second passed.

KABOOM!

The tank's hatches burst open and a shock wave blasted Red onto his back. The fuel vapor had exploded in the vehicle's fuel tank with the power of an artillery shell. Black smoke streamed from the hatches and flames boiled over the engine compartment.

From his backside, Red saw the North Korean tank commander writhe out of the turret, his quilted blue uniform and padded helmet engulfed in flame. The tanker fell to the ground and burned. None of the other crewmen emerged.

The gunfire in the pastures trailed away as flames engulfed the tank. A blowtorch-like sound rose from the hulk and the turret's white numbers became charred.*

Still in the road, Red set his bazooka down and took in the sight. Behind him, his buddies began cheering and whistling.

Did Morin make it? Red wondered. He glanced to the clump of trees on the hillside. Morin stood and dusted himself off. He stared at the tank then over to Red. "What the hell took you so long?" he shouted. A grin stretched across Red's dusty face. Morin waved and gathered up his gear.

Charlie approached and shook Red by the shoulder. "Hallelujah!" Charlie yelled as he watched the tank burn. "Hallelujah!" He turned to Red and pointed a finger at his friend's heart. "Be right with the Lord and *he* will protect you!"

Red smirked and placed a hand on Charlie's shoulder. "Shucks, Charlie. I thought an eight-pound rocket was protectin' me."

Charlie shook his finger. "Steered by the Lord!"

Red laughed.

Devans approached the duo, pleased as could be. Between glances at the tank, the men debated why the lone tank crew had made a suicide attack. They concluded that the tank commander was saving his cannon shells for any American tanks while trusting his machine gunner to handle the infantry.

A fresh column of Marines marched past Red and his friends. The advance had resumed, thanks to the enemy tank: The road was obviously clear of mines if the tank had safely traveled it. "Atta boy!" a Marine said, slapping Red on the back. "Nice shot!" said another. An officer paused to say that he would recommend Red for a medal. The men steered around the burning tank and marched with fresh vigor.

Devans returned to his duties and Charlie went to retrieve his

---

*The North Koreans acquired 150 T-34s in 1948 as gifts when the Soviets withdrew their forces after occupying North Korea since WWII. A year later, Stalin provided the North Koreans with 40 million dollars' worth of credit to purchase Soviet artillery, tanks, and firearms to use to attack South Korea.

friend's gear. Red remained in the road, his gaze settled on the dead North Korean tank commander, whose body had shrunk into the dirt.

Red had aimed at a machine, but he had killed maybe five men in the process. After a long pause, Red shook off any lament for what he had done.

Better them than Morin.

"You okay?" Charlie asked. He held out his friend's pack and carbine, waiting up so they could advance together.

Red nodded as he shouldered his gear. He was more than okay. He had stood against a tank and lived to tell the story.

Red's eyebrows lifted as a thought crossed his mind.

Maybe Charlie's on to something with that "being right with the Lord" stuff? Red picked up his Super Bazooka and slung it over his shoulder.

Nah, he decided. *That surely ain't it.*

CHAPTER 23

INTO THE FOG

Two days later, October 3, 1950
Near Tokyo Bay, Japan

FOG FLOATED FROM THE FORESTED HILLS of Yokosuka Harbor and blanketed the *Leyte* at anchor. For mid-afternoon, the harbor seemed asleep. Lights glowed dimly from the docks and empty mooring posts jutted from the waves.

The misty ceiling hung level with the *Leyte's* tower and obscured any glimpse of distant Mount Fuji. Despite the conditions, at the front of the carrier's deck, crewmen uncovered the blades of six blue helicopters in preparation for flight.

Below deck, Tom passed through the officers' dining room with his dress coat draped over an arm. Located near the front of the ship, the dining room maintained a gentlemanly aura, with its carved wood ceiling and white tablecloths. Between meals, a few officers sipped coffee. They were likely debating the topic of the times: Should the

U.S. commander, General MacArthur, allow U.S. and U.N. forces to follow the North Korean army across the 38th parallel and crush them once and for all? Most Americans were unaware, however, that Soviet and Chinese diplomats had just issued a warning—if U.S. forces did cross the 38th parallel, China planned to attack. In fact, two days earlier, the Chinese had publicly declared: "The United States Government, because of its frenzied and ruthless imperialistic aggression, has been proved the most dangerous enemy of the People's Republic of China."

At the end of the room, Tom encountered a green canvas curtain that hung from the ceiling and segmented off a quarter of the dining room. He searched for the opening in its folds. Behind the fabric, the telltale sounds of revelry could be heard.

Tom parted the curtain and stepped inside. Cigarette smoke stung his nostrils. More than twenty pilots crowded the small space. At a table, Jesse and Cevoli were playing backgammon, as usual. Another pilot kept the record player spinning, while others passed a coffeepot around to refill their mugs. Maps spanned a wall and a teletype machine's green TV screen flickered with the weather and shipboard announcements. Everyone kept an ear tuned for the announcement that they could go ashore.

This was "ready room forward," '32's new hangout. Before leaving the States, the *Leyte* had taken on extra pilots, so the squadrons' ready rooms had to be reassigned. In an unlucky twist, '32 had drawn this space and been made to swap their leather seats for hardback chairs and their theater-style lounge for a space similar to a catering station at a banquet.

Tom slid into a seat next to Cevoli and Jesse. In a nearby corner, six pilots were tossing on jackets and life preservers in preparation to fly. They were older, saltier-looking men who wore green infantry fatigues beneath their leather jackets. Revolvers dangled from their hips and brown paratrooper boots wrapped their ankles. They were some of the Marine Corps' first helicopter pilots, men trained to fly the Sikorsky HO3S, used for rescuing downed airmen.

An HO3S departs the *Leyte*

The chopper pilots remained tight-lipped as they suited up. They and the fighter pilots had shared the ready room since Norfolk, yet they seldom intermingled. The younger fighter pilots were the problem. They assumed that any man stuck flying a flimsy "eggbeater," as they called helicopters, had to be a flight school dropout. Sensing the disdain, the chopper pilots generally ignored the fighter pilots.

Now, in their last time together, the two groups maintained their sullen distance—all except for two pilots. Between tosses of dice, Jesse exchanged quips with First Lieutenant Charlie Ward, a stocky chopper pilot whose thick red cheeks squeezed his grin tight. Ward was a former wholesale chemical salesman from Troy, Alabama, and his hair was already graying at age thirty-two.

"Heya, Mississippi, do you remember . . ." Charlie would say, then ramble something in a drawl so thick the others would wrinkle their noses.

Charlie Ward (far right) and some of the first Marine helicopter pilots. Aircraft designer Igor Sikorsky is seated (lower left) beside Marine General O. P. Smith.

But Jesse would understand every word. "You said it, Alabama," he would reply.

The two had met during the journey over, when Ward was briefing the fighter pilots about helicopter rescue capabilities, even admitting that his craft had difficulty operating in the thin air over five thousand feet. "If you gotta crash, do it at sea level," Ward had said. "If you crash in the mountains, I ain't coming for you!" The room had erupted in laughter.

Afterward, Jesse and Ward had struck up a friendship whereby Jesse discovered that Ward and another chopper pilot had actually flown Corsairs during WWII. Now Ward was about to enter his second war. After a hop across the bay to Kisarazu Air Base, he and the other chopper pilots would join Observation Squadron 6 (VMO-6), their unit in Korea.

"Have you fellas popped a head outside?" Tom asked the chopper pilots. "You can stir the soup out there, the fog's so thick."

Several of the men stopped dressing and turned toward Tom. Their thoughts were written on their faces. *Another fighter jock trying to teach us how to fly?* Only when they saw the genuine concern on Tom's face did they relax.

"Nah, that won't stop us," a chopper pilot said. "We'll just go under it." His buddies nodded.

Cevoli shook his head in amazement. More than one fighter pilot raised an eyebrow.

"I'll admit, I don't know the meaning of the word *fear*," Charlie Ward said, thumping his chest. "Not because I'm brave," Ward continued, "but because I jus' don't understand big words!"

Everyone broke out in laughter.

Ward was his unit's go-to man for comic relief. At parties he'd strum a ukulele and sing profane Irish ditties. But beneath the bravado, he had misgivings about the primitive machine he was tasked to fly. Ward was married with children and had already crashed one helicopter. He knew that his new mount was underpowered and almost too flimsy to fly on a windy day—let alone if someone was shooting at him.

One by one, chopper pilots filtered from the ready room.

"Hey—take it easy, Mississippi!" Ward said, slapping Jesse on the shoulder.

"Be safe, Alabama," Jesse replied.

Tom shook his head in disbelief. The chopper pilots were really going to try to take off.

"See ya later, fellas!" Ward said over his shoulder as he brushed through the curtain.

I sure hope not, Tom thought.

He had nothing against Charlie Ward—he just hoped that he would never need the man's services. If Tom had gone on deck to watch the helicopters fly away between the fog and waves, he'd have seen that Ward was wrong about himself: He *was* brave, even borderline crazy.

And one day those traits would matter. They would meet again, Tom Hudner and Charlie Ward, in a place where only a crazy man would go.

CHAPTER 24

THIS IS IT

Several nights later, early October 1950
The Sea of Japan

WITH EVERY LIGHT EXTINGUISHED, the *Leyte* steamed through the darkness. A sliver of moon hung in the sky, casting barely enough light to trace the ship's deck. Ever since Japan, the *Leyte's* crew had run her all blacked out in order to hide from enemy submarines. The North Koreans didn't have subs, but the Soviets did, and sometimes they trailed American fleets.

On either side of the *Leyte*, the outlines of countless ships could be seen, each vessel holding its course to avoid collision. The *Leyte* now belonged to the 7th Fleet, one of the largest flotillas assembled since WWII.

Together, the ships steamed toward the hostile waters of North Korea.

✳　✳　✳

Below deck, in a cabin near the front of the *Leyte*, Jesse and Koenig examined their new flight helmets. Koenig sat on the lower bunk, his face full of wonder as he turned the white helmet in his hands. A map of the Pacific lined the wall behind him. Jesse sat at a desk and gazed at his helmet with a forlorn expression.

He knocked the helmet's shell with his knuckles and frowned at the hollow clunking sound. The helmets were made of plastic and black padding lined the edges. Gone were the old cloth helmets—this was a helmet that Buck Rogers might have worn in space.

Jesse glanced over at Koenig. "Remember Carol's crash report?" he said. Koenig nodded somberly. Jesse glanced back at the helmet and added, "Crying shame."

Investigators had determined that Carol might have survived his crash if he had been wearing one of the new helmets. At the time, however, hard helmets had only been issued to jet pilots, so the investigators' report urged the navy to issue the new helmets to all pilots as quickly as possible.

Jesse stepped to the stainless steel sink beside the door and peered into the mirror. He snugged his helmet down over his head, adjusted the black goggles over his forehead, and fastened the chinstrap under his jaw. Koenig eyed his friend with curiosity. Jesse had moved into his cabin for the Korean cruise to make room in Boys' Town for the new pilots.

Jesse's eyes narrowed to slits like a western gunslinger's. He grimaced sternly and bit his lower lip. The ceiling light shone from behind, casting his face in menacing shadows. Slowly Jesse's eyes lifted and his cheeks loosened. He broke into a wide smile and shook his head at his reflection. "All I see is a white helmet, white teeth, and eyeballs showing through!"

Koenig broke out in laughter, and Jesse did too.

Several days later, October 10, 1950

Tom and Cevoli peered from Vulture's Row as dawn stretched over the *Leyte*'s deck. Below, propellers whirled from sixteen Corsairs as the

Teenage Tom Hudner (seated) with his siblings.

Nineteen-year-old Tom during a visit home from the Naval Academy in 1944.

Daisy holds Pam during a 1949 visit to Hattiesburg.

Jesse as an ensign, September 1949.

Jesse and Daisy with Pam at their Rhode Island cottage, summer 1949.

Marty Goode
aboard the *Leyte*.

In February 1950, Jesse rehearses his
reading in the Quonset Point chapel.
His reading was Romans 12, "A Living
Sacrifice."

A *Leyte* LSO signals
"Hold steady!"

While training
spring 1950, M
catches the las
cable before t
crash barrier.

hting 32 during the Mediterranean cruise. Front row, left to right: Key, Hudner, Ferris, ...nin, Cevoli, Neill, Fowler, Jester, Whalen, Koenig, Lane. Back row, left to right: Brown, ...gent, Byron, Stevens, Cotchen, Mohring, Goode, Sheffield, Nelson, Miller, Gelonek.

Leyte deckhands prepare a Corsair for takeoff.

The beach at Cannes during the *Leyte*'s visit.

Elizabeth Taylor, Nicky Hilton, and friends tour the *Leyte* in Cannes.

Elizabeth Taylor dines with the *Leyte*'s officers.

6th Fleet Marines practice an amphibious landing in the Mediterranean.

Red Parkinson (far right) and his antitank platoon on Crete.

During maneuvers, a Marine aims an M20 Super Bazooka.

Ed Coderre during a visit home to Rhode Island in 1949.

Enjoying watermelons on Crete. Foreground, left to right: Charlie Kline, Red Parkinson, Bob Devans.

...rines assemble ...ard the ...*te* during the ...diterranean ...ise.

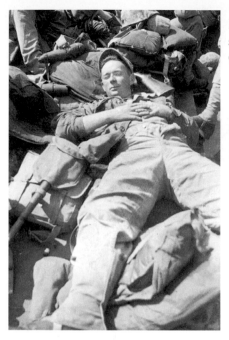

Red Parkinson naps as his LST ship passes through the Suez Canal, bound for Korea.

Before Jesse's deployment, he and Daisy drove home through Tennessee, where Daisy snapped this photo.

Days before deploying, Jesse plays with Pam outside Daisy's mother's apartment.

Bill "Wilkie" Wilkinson during flight training.

Wilkie snapped this photo during a practice flight before Korea.

heir cabin aboard the *Leyte*, Jesse
is a letter home while Bill Koenig
ds.

On the *Leyte*'s first day at war, her crew
watches one of '32's planes launch.

Squadron 32 at the front of the pack, waiting for the takeoff signal.

In the hangar deck, sailors muscle a Corsair onto an elevator.

"Dad" Fowler as a twenty-year-old Hellcat pilot in 1944.

Tom in the cockpit during the Korean cruise.

Dad Fowler launches down the center line. "I always tried to fly like he did," Wilkie would write.

pilots warmed their engines. The sun danced golden on a sea so blue that Tom could have sworn that the *Leyte* was off the coast of California. It was around 6:30 A.M. as the carrier steamed northward.

On the horizon, the carrier *Philippine Sea* cruised alongside the *Leyte*. A cruiser and destroyers flanked the flattops. Somewhere beyond the horizon lay North Korea's eastern coastline. The fleet was one hundred miles above the 38th parallel, deep in enemy waters.

The planes crowded the rear of the *Leyte*'s deck to keep the front clear as a runway. With wings folded, the Corsairs of '32 and her sister squadron, '33, sat side by side in a gaggle that pilots called "the pack." Gray rockets hung from each plane's wings and deckhands crouched by the tires, waiting for the signal to pull the chocks and free the planes for takeoff.

Earlier that week, the forces of democracy had crossed the 38th parallel to pursue the North Koreans and the Chinese had remained on the sidelines, despite their saber rattling. Now, within striking range of North Korea, the *Leyte* was about to enter the war.*

It was a brisk sixty degrees atop Vulture's Row so Tom wore his jacket's black fur collar flipped up and his tan tent cap snugged tight. He could see the skipper at the front of the pack and Dad nearby. Jesse and Koenig waited in the second row of Corsairs. Tom couldn't see Jesse behind his plane's folded wings, but he knew his friend was probably praying. The first time the deckhands had seen Jesse's head bowed in the cockpit, one had climbed onto the wing, believing something to be wrong. Now they knew better.

Only eight of the squadron's pilots were flying, men whose turn had come in the rotation.

"You'll never forget this moment, Tom," Cevoli said, gazing at the planes as if envisioning himself as a young Hellcat pilot in 1944.

---

* The CIA assured the secretary of state that the Soviets would hold the Chinese back from intervention. An October 1950 CIA report read: "While full-scale Chinese Communist intervention in Korea must be regarded as a continuing possibility . . . barring a Soviet decision for global war, such action is not probable in 1950." When reporters asked the secretary of state if the Chinese would enter the war, he declared that it would be "sheer madness."

"The engines throbbing, your heart pounding," Cevoli continued. "You'll never forget seeing your buddies fly away while you're stuck here, left behind, waving goodbye." Cevoli broke into a sly grin. Tom chuckled. He wasn't bitter about missing the first combat mission because he had plenty of other work to do. The squadron had been issued some new Corsairs in Norfolk and Tom needed to start over with their maintenance logs.

From the second row of the pack, a pilot waved at Vulture's Row and pointed straight at Tom. Tom and Cevoli squinted. "It's Wilkie," Tom said. Wilkie was one of the new ensigns the squadron had picked up in Norfolk. Curious, Tom aimed a finger at himself. *Me?* Wilkie nodded and beckoned for Tom to come to him. Tom's face filled with confusion. If Wilkie had a mechanical problem, there were mechanics already on the side of the deck. But the young pilot kept beckoning.

Tom hurried down the steps from Vulture's Row. Cevoli should have stopped him—the flight deck was a dangerous place during engine warmup, but Cevoli wasn't one to wield authority. Some of the squadron's pilots whispered that he was second-in-command only in name, because he spent more time joking and playing backgammon than doing his paperwork.

At the base of the tower, Tom opened the steel door and stepped onto the flight deck, wearing borrowed goggles. A blast of wind buffeted him. The carrier was steaming into the wind at nearly 40 miles per hour so the pilots would have lift when they launched.

Ahead lay a daunting obstacle: Propellers whirled from the noses of four Corsairs in the front row, like thirteen-foot buzz saws. Tom knew he needed to hurry—any minute, the deckhands would receive the signal to pull the chocks.

Tom took a step forward and felt his feet slide. Oil from countless engine drippings had slickened the wood. Choosing each step carefully, as if he were wearing bowling shoes, Tom crept toward two Corsairs in the center. He turned sideways and began shimmying through the narrow gap between them. Their 2,250-horsepower engines popped and sizzled and their yellow-tipped blades reached for him. Tom felt

Bill "Wilkie" Wilkinson and his wife, Mary, a month before the war

hot engine exhaust on the back of his neck and thought, *This is nuts!* As he snuck between the planes' folded wings, young deckhands looked up at Tom from the wheels as if he were indeed crazy.

Tom broke into the open space behind the first row of planes. Their prop blast buffeted his back, pushing him toward the second row of spinning propellers. Tom braced on the slippery deck. He knew the rule: *If you fall, stay down—spread your arms and legs to stay flat!* If a man rolled into a propeller, it wouldn't be pretty. Ahead, Wilkie glanced around the nose of his Corsair and beckoned. Tom lowered his chin and continued.

Scampering up on Wilkie's wing, Tom grabbed the canopy railing and held on for dear life. Farther up the nose, the propeller spun and its prop wash made breathing difficult. The smell of spent gasoline filled Tom's nose and hot plumes of exhaust licked his ankles. Angry machines and whirling propellers surrounded him.

Wilkie grabbed Tom's arm to steady him. "Thank heavens!" he shouted, his voice clipped with a New England accent. Beneath Wilkie's helmet and goggles was a slender face with blue eyes and a thick chin. "Wilkie" was twenty-two-year-old Bill Wilkinson, a rookie who had gone straight from Yale University to navy flight school and who had gotten married mere weeks before the *Leyte* sailed.

"What's the matter?" Tom shouted.

Wilkie explained that he had run a check of the magnetos and seen that insufficient electricity was flowing through the engine cylinders. "I might have a bad spark plug!" Wilkie added. The engine had thirty-six spark plugs, two per cylinder.

Tom leaned into the cockpit to see for himself. He didn't doubt Wilkie's judgment; everyone in the squadron knew that the youngster had as much flight time as a veteran. As a boy, Wilkie had soloed at sixteen after working nights in a grocery store to pay for flying lessons. Following his solo, he refused to play contact sports, only allowing himself to ski, in order to avoid injuries that could compromise his pilot's physical exam.

As he scanned the instruments, Tom kept his goggles lowered because the planes' prop blasts sometimes flung wooden deck slivers through the air. With Tom watching, Wilkie turned a knob to test the current.

Tom turned to Wilkie. "Yup, RPMs are low!" he shouted. Wilkie's face sank with dismay. He'd called for Tom, the assistant maintenance officer, for a reason. If he told a mechanic about the problem, he'd be forced to shut down the engine and sit out the mission. That wouldn't help his case with the skipper, who already disliked the new guys.

Several deckhands huddled behind the wing of Wilkie's plane, trying to surmise what Tom was doing up there.

"A spark plug's probably fouled with carbon buildup!" Tom shouted to Wilkie. He told the young pilot to rev up the engine and then thin back the fuel mixture, to allow less fuel and more oxygen into the cylinders. This would make the cylinders burn hotter, which could burn away any carbon on the spark plugs.

"Don't touch the throttle, just let it cook!" Tom added. He slapped Wilkie on the shoulder and climbed down to the deck. Tom wound his way to the tower, turned, and watched.

The yellow tips of Wilkie's propeller spun faster as he revved the engine to a higher power setting. Only the top of the young pilot's helmet showed as he studied his instruments. Tom glanced at his watch as the minutes slipped past.

"Clear the deck for launch!" the loudspeaker sounded.

Wilkie's head suddenly lifted in the cockpit. He looked over to Tom and flashed a thumbs-up, followed by a wave. All thirty-six plugs were firing correctly. Tom returned the wave, entered the tower, and shut the steel door with relief.

"Plane recovery in progress!"

Three hours after takeoff, the loudspeaker blared throughout the hangar deck as Tom performed his maintenance duties. Amid a row of parked planes, he lowered his clipboard and glanced at his watch. It was nearly 9:30 A.M. *They're back*, he thought.

The loudspeaker blared again: "Repair 8 to the flight deck!" Tom set down his clipboard. Something was wrong if the crash crew was being called in. Mechanics began moving in small groups toward the rear of the deck. Tom asked one of the sailors what had happened.

"A damaged Corsair is coming down, sir," the sailor said, "Number three elevator." The sailor hurried away, eager to see the first battle-damaged plane.

Tom followed the exodus through the string of hangars, his eyes wide with alarm. His friends were on that flight—Jesse and Koenig, and the new guy, Wilkie. At the rear of the deck Tom joined the sailors in glancing anxiously at a square platform in the ceiling. The contraption was the plane elevator, a means of delivering aircraft to and from the flight deck. Chains clinked and the elevator began descending. Sunlight poured in and water showered from the elevator. A Corsair sat at the platform's center, dripping wet. Tom studied the sky through the opening in the flight deck. There wasn't a rain cloud in sight. Tom glanced back to the dripping plane. *What the heck?*

The elevator settled into the floor and the men crowded closer.

"Good grief," Tom murmured. Black holes spanned the Corsair's left wing and deep dents marked the engine cover, as if fists had punched the plane. The large white number 203 on the nose was pitted and scraped. Corsair 203 didn't belong to one pilot or another; everyone alternated planes.

Tom ducked under the nose to check the other wing. It was also full of holes. He began a mental checklist. *We're gonna need two new wings.* Tom shook his head. It was awful soon to be dipping into the spare parts. As he ran his hand along the punctures in the wing, his eyes narrowed.

A gooey brown substance bled from the holes. Tom swiped a finger and examined it. "It's mud, all right," he announced. The deckhands murmured, unsure how mud could wind up in an airplane.

The bullhorn interrupted their thoughts. "Now hear this!" a sailor's voice bellowed. "Now hear this! A message from the skipper of Fighting 32." This was the new routine—after each combat mission, the flight leader would report the results to the ship's crew.

A pause followed as the microphone changed hands. "This is Lieutenant Commander D. T. Neill, skipper of Fighting 32," the gruff voice announced.

The skipper explained that he had led '32's patrol over Wonsan Harbor that morning. "We had good hunting, although pickings were slim," he said. "We knocked out some shore batteries and trucks on some islands."

Tom nodded to himself. The mission was important. The 1st Marine Division was due to land at Wonsan Harbor to open a new front

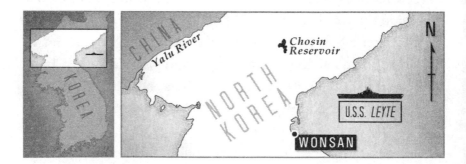

on Korea's east coast, as they had in the west. But until the navy softened up the harbor's defenses, the Marines weren't going anywhere.

"Overall, we encountered little resistance," the skipper added. "Just
one plane banged up and no one hurt—a mighty good start."

Now Tom was really curious. He had seen the damaged plane and
wondered: *Who took the first lumps?*

The film projector's beam cut through the darkness and onto the blank
screen in front of Tom and his squadron mates. Shadows crossed the
screen as other officers took their seats, hands laden with coffee or
soda. Zippos flickered and cigarettes glowed.

In the rear of the dining room, sailors loaded film onto a projector's
reels. The dining room had been transformed into a theater and Fighting 32's ready room had been dismantled, the curtains parted, the tables wheeled aside to make room for the ship's officers, both pilots and
sailors. Thirty-two's ready room held one advantage come time for the
nightly movie: The squadron always got the best seats. Now the pilots
filled up the first two rows and Tom sat with Jesse and Koenig. In the
hangar deck, enlisted sailors would be watching a film of their own.

The projector's wheels began turning, the beam of light flickered,
and voices hushed. Every few days, a helicopter landed aboard the
Leyte to circulate the latest movies.* An intelligence officer snapped to
his feet. "Gentlemen, we have a treat for you tonight," he announced.
"You're about to see a smattering of gun camera film from today's missions, courtesy of Fightin' 31, Fightin' 32, and Fightin' 33!" Exagger-
ated whistles and clapping arose from the audience; Tom leaned
forward in his seat.

The screen filled with life. In blotchy color, the gun camera flew
low over a stretch of rugged seaside hills. The camera filmed ahead,
unobstructed, from behind a panel of glass in the plane's right wing.

---

* When *Father of the Bride* played, starring the ship's darling, Elizabeth Taylor, all view-
ings were standing room only.

The men were seeing an island in Wonsan Harbor, from treetop height.

The footage showed one strafing attack after another against coastal pillboxes, a warehouse, a sampan—anything of military value. The screen flickered with each new splice of film, each shot from a different plane. The audience clapped and hooted, and some jokesters imitated explosion sounds.

A fresh clip appeared from a new camera angle. Rough waves flowed toward the viewer as the pilot raced for a concrete watchtower on a beach. Marty's wingman elbowed him. The film belonged to one of them—they had struck the same target.

The camera shook as the plane's guns fired. Orange bolts arced toward the tower and sparks flickered up and down the concrete structure. The audience cheered. Just before the plane could collide with the tower, the camera lifted and filmed the blue sky as the pilot climbed over the target.

A grin stretched across Marty's face. Despite the strikes on the watchtower, somehow, the enemy there had fired back. Marty whispered to his wingman, "Remember when you asked Dad, 'What are all those flashes?'" The wingman nodded. "'Why, someone's shooting at you,'" Marty said, imitating Dad's deadpan reply.

The screen flickered again, and the island appeared from a bird's-eye view, looking down. The camera dived toward a cave on a rocky promontory. The barrel of an enemy cannon took shape where it jutted from the cave. Koenig's youthful face lifted with life. "Jesse, it's your cave!" he said. Jesse's eyes perked at the sight of his film.

Of the targets that day, the enemy's artillery was at the top of the aviators' list. The enemy would roll the cannons from the caves, snap off some shots at American vessels, then roll the cannons back inside and disappear. Until the artillery was knocked out, the Marines couldn't land.

As Jesse's plane dived closer, the island stretched in the film's frame. The cave's mouth grew wider and enemy soldiers appeared, scurrying like ants. In a yellow flash, a long narrow rocket streaked from Jesse's wing. The weapon trailed black smoke and flew unguided toward the cave like a bottle rocket.

As the rocket neared the cave's mouth, the audience leaned forward to see the impact. The camera suddenly flicked upward and filmed the sky as the pilot climbed away. The audience groaned. They wanted to see the explosion.

"Did you hit it?" a pilot called out. "Any secondaries?"

Before Jesse could reply, his defender spoke up. "He sure did!" Koenig said. "Right in the kisser!" Koenig told the men around him how flames had leapt from the cave and smoke had poured out the holes in the roof. Jesse just shrugged and smiled. Several seats over, Dad nodded with approval—Jesse's technique had been sound; a pilot was supposed to pass at least eight hundred feet over his target to avoid being hit by shrapnel or debris. The skipper didn't even smile or turn to congratulate Jesse. A naval aviator was supposed to hit the target.*

The screen flickered again and a small black truck appeared on a gravel road. The truck was likely a Ford or Chevy given to the Soviets during WWII and later resold by them to the North Koreans. Scrubby trees obscured the truck as it motored between the stands. The pilot was attacking so low he nearly skimmed the earth.

"It's Koenig!" a pilot whispered.

Koenig swept his hand nervously over his brush cut.

This one's gonna be a doozy! Tom thought.

The truck rolled into a clearing and the audience braced for the machine guns' golden sparks—the pilot was clearly too low for rockets. The camera raced closer and the truck grew larger. "Fire, Bill!" a pilot joked. "Fire!"

Tom grinned and saw Koenig's eyes locked on the screen. The cam-

---

*The following day, October 11, the skipper would experience engine trouble and make an emergency landing at the newly secured Wonsan airfield. A South Korean general presented him with captured North Korean and Soviet battle flags, which he brought back to the *Leyte* as souvenirs.

era raced so close that fabric could be seen rustling over the truck's bed.

In a yellow flash, a rocket shot through the camera frame, toward the truck. The audience gasped. An orange fireball burst and filled the screen. Tom shot back in his seat. Mud and pieces of truck were flung skyward and seemed to hang there as the camera punched through the debris cloud. Darkness momentarily filled the lens. When the plane emerged and light returned to the picture, a dark crack ran through the camera lens, and mud slid down over the picture.

The audience roared with laughter. Koenig sheepishly covered his head with his hands as his buddies shook him.

"And that, my friends, is how you waste a $75,000 Corsair to kill a $500 truck!" someone announced. "I'll take that math any day!" joked another man.

Koenig turned to the hecklers and played along: "Yeah, but you don't know what that truck was carrying!"

In the front row, Dad folded his arms. On their return to the ship, he had made Koenig land last so that he wouldn't block the deck if his plane crashed from the damage. When Koenig did land, so much mud had covered his plane that the crash crew needed to wash down the Corsair before sending it below for repairs. He was the first to damage his plane but he wouldn't be the last; by the deployment's end, six more of the squadron's Corsairs would be damaged by pilots who flew through their own shrapnel.

After the gun camera viewing, the nightly movie rolled. In the midst of the film, Jesse leaned over to Koenig and whispered, "Bill, are you going to start carrying your camera?" Koenig had bought a compact camera in Japan but no one had seen him take any photos yet.

"No," Koenig said. "If I have to bail out or ditch I could lose it."

"Too bad," Jesse said, fighting a smile. "I thought it could come in handy the next time you smash the one in your wing!"

Koenig rolled his eyes.

Through the light that spilled from the projector's beam, Tom saw his buddies: some hazing one another, some fixated on the big screen. He had spent countless hours imagining this, their first day at war, and he had expected something scarier and bloodier. Deep down, Tom wanted to become a veteran of a "real" war, one that mattered, like World War II.

A thought crossed his mind, followed by a pang of guilt.

This is it?

CHAPTER 25

TRUST

Nine days later, October 19, 1950
Near Songjin, North Korea

AT FIRST THE VALLEY was gentle and calm.

The dawn's warm light spread across the trees that covered the mountains, revealing leaves ablaze in autumn yellows, reds, and browns. Shadows clung to the mountains' furrows and mist floated through the peaks. The sea was close, just a few ridges beyond.

From the south came a sound, soft like the buzz of a mosquito but lower in pitch. Then the sound grew louder.

A dirt road ran along the valley floor and connected small farms and fields. On the road, a young Korean boy and his sister pulled their goats by the reins. The children stopped when they heard the sound and turned in its direction.

Farther up the road, an elderly farmer repaired a fence in his field. He heard the sound, lowered his tool, and looked to the south. The sound was still growing, though the morning sky remained empty.

Still farther up the road, several middle-aged women carried baskets

across a stone bridge. They also paused and turned south. The sound
was clear now, a roaring, throaty buzz.

At the opening to the valley, they appeared—eight Corsairs silhouetted against the morning sky. The planes flew low, hugging the road,
lower than the telephone poles. Their propellers whirled and a bomb
hung from each plane's belly.

The children scurried to the roadside as the lead plane burst past at
a blurry 250 miles per hour. The children covered their ears. Within
the plane's cockpit, a white face peered out from a helmet. One after
another, seven more Corsairs roared past and bathed the valley in
noise.

The planes ripped past the farmer, who shrank but held his ground.
In his lifetime he had likely seen Japanese occupiers, then Soviet "lib-
erators," then homegrown communists, and now the men in blue
planes, whoever they were.

The women on the bridge lowered their baskets and crouched low,
fearing a strafing. In a flash, all eight Corsairs raced over them.

Without firing a shot, the blue planes thundered up the road.

At the controls of Corsair number 200, the seventh plane in line, Tom
Hudner cringed. He had seen the North Korean people below, their
faces frozen in confusion or fear. *These people must hate us,* Tom
thought. He wished he could tell the peasants that flying low was the
best way to hunt for targets while avoiding anti-aircraft fire.

Black residue from gunfire clung to the six gun barrels in Tom's
wings. His rocket rails were empty, their missiles spent on an enemy
convoy that morning. Now he and the others were saving their bombs
for a sizeable target.

A week earlier, the port city of Wonsan had been liberated, then the
city of Hamhung, where the South Korean army had discovered the
bodies of seven hundred political prisoners executed by the North Koreans. Now the forces of democracy were pushing the North Koreans
up the eastern coast, killing and capturing them with light opposition.

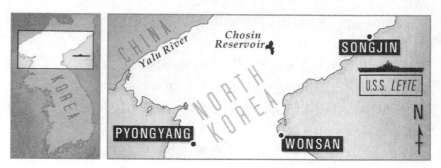

To support the advance, the *Leyte* and *Philippine Sea* had leapfrogged ninety-three miles north to operate off the coast of Songjin, a city behind enemy lines.

The radio crackled with sporadic chatter. "I see smoke coming out of that tunnel!" a pilot announced. "I've got a train up here," said another. "Let's knock out those sampans," suggested another voice. Tom glanced outside his canopy for the source of the voices but the other pilots were probably a mountain or two away. An informal race had begun between the carriers and their squadrons to hit whatever targets they could find before Songjin was picked clean, as Wonsan had been.

Tom's eyes rose with concern to a rearview mirror along the canopy rail. His face relaxed. *Good, he's still there*, he thought. One hundred yards behind him, Marty Goode flew low over the terrain. Marty was last in line, the flight's "Tail-End Charlie." Behind a flickering propeller, the young ensign was sitting tall in his seat, his white helmet nearly brushing the canopy. Tom was Marty's leader for the hop because Cevoli and Jesse had the day off and Koenig was flying in the plane ahead as wingman to a senior pilot.

Tom wished that Marty were flying in front of him so that he could keep an eye on him. Tom knew Marty as the young, unpredictable ensign who had boasted that he had once come in late to work and was ordered to wash fifteen Bearcats as punishment. When his flight leader stepped from the hangar to review his work, he saw sparkling planes. But really, Marty had only washed the sides of the planes that were facing the hangar.

To the right, an orange light blinked at the foot of a fast-approaching mountain. Tom's eyes narrowed—the light resembled a bonfire. The light pulsed, growing larger and larger. "What the heck?" Tom muttered.

In a blur, a glowing sphere arced over Tom's canopy and past his tail. *Zip!* Tom flinched in his seat. *Zip!* Another sphere curved wildly over the left wing, then one under the right. Tom's head whipped from side to side to track the golf ball–sized projectiles. *Tracers!*

Someone was shooting at him, probably a Soviet-made 37mm gun. Tom had flown five combat missions so far, but this was the first time he'd taken anti-aircraft fire.

The enemy gun fired steadily as the flight neared. The tracers appeared to be aimed at Dad Fowler's plane in the lead, but the inexperienced North Korean gunner wasn't leading his target, so the shells drifted toward the formation's rear.

Zip!

Another orange sphere whipped over Tom's wing. *Is anyone else seeing this?* he wondered. Tom glanced in a mirror and saw Marty shifting in his seat as shells whipped around him.

Tom pulled the lip microphone close to his mouth but stopped short of speaking. He knew the skipper's rules: *Don't clog the airwaves! Speak only when urgent.*

Tom's eyes shifted forward. The planes ahead were still holding course, low over the road. Dad wasn't panicking, nor was his wingman, Wilkie, nor was Koenig or any of the others. Everyone was flying in eerie silence.

Tom shrank in his seat. The enemy gun was nearing, about to pass by on the right. It was still blinking, brighter than ever, and was becoming unnerving. Tom remembered the words of a veteran pilot who had briefed the squadron before the first mission: "Enemy flak isn't very accurate—however, you've got to call it accurate when you're hit."

Tom could hold his tongue no longer.

"Lead, this is 200!" he said. "We're taking fire back here!"

"Copy that 200," Dad said calmly. "You may take evasive action if you so desire." Boredom colored his voice. The valley was too tight for all eight planes to take evasive maneuvers, but one or two could manage.

Tom gritted his teeth.

If he began weaving now, he'd reveal his fear. Aviators were taught not to panic because it was unsafe—and worse, "unprofessional."

Tom steadied his eyes forward on Koenig's tail as shells continued to whiz around his wings. Through the windscreen, Tom watched Dad fly past the gun without taking a hit. The other Corsairs followed without question.

After Tom had safely cleared the gun, he glanced in the mirror. Marty was still there.

At the end of the valley, Dad broke radio silence.

"Lead to flight," he said, "Target spotted, twelve o'clock."

Tom strained his eyes, trying to see what the veteran had spotted. Ahead, the land twisted leftward into a rocky gorge between two mountains. In the gorge stood a flat concrete bridge.

Dad's plane peeled up into a climbing rightward bank and the others followed, one by one. At five thousand feet, Tom leveled off behind the others. Undulating mountains filled the bottom of his windshield and low-hanging clouds filled the top. The Corsair's nose glowed as the sunlight filtered softly through the clouds.

Dad rocked his right wing twice, the signal for the flight to break into right echelon formations. Dad held his position as three pilots nestled beside and behind his right wing, forming a diagonal line in the sky. The second formation assembled next, behind the first. Koenig cozied up to his leader, then Tom banked left and settled beside Koenig. Tom glanced past his right wing and saw that Marty had parked himself tight. The assembly was complete.

Dad led the formations away from the bridge. An enemy soldier below would have sworn that the Americans were heading home, but

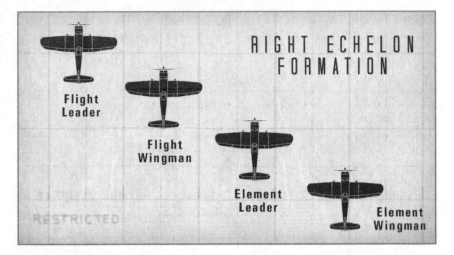

Tom knew otherwise. The bridge below enabled supplies to reach the retreating North Korean troops and its destruction could possibly hasten the war's end by minutes, hours, or days. Dad was simply positioning the flight to attack.

Tom glanced over his left shoulder, past his fist on the throttle, past the huge white star on the wing. Beyond the wingtip, the bridge slipped perpendicular to the flight. It was narrow, probably twenty feet wide, and strung over a small stream. Black railroad tracks crossed its length and vanished into a mountainside tunnel on the right.

Dad peeled left and dived to kick off the attack. He disappeared from sight. Five seconds later, his wingman followed. Then came the next pilot in line, then the next. In fifteen seconds the first formation was gone.

Tom's formation leader raised his fist and made two pumps. *Prepare to attack!* Tom reached with his left hand for the bank of switches to the left of the gunsight. He flicked up a switch to activate his guns and bomb, then another that made his gunsight's rings glow.

The formation leader patted the top of his helmet and pointed to Koenig to signal: "I'm beginning my attack and passing the lead to you." The leader peeled left and dived.

Already, Dad and his formation were dropping their bombs. Tom heard the pilots spotting one another's results. "Did mine hit?" Dad asked. "No sir, just missed," Wilkie replied. Deflated voices reported more failures: "No dice!" "Close one!" "No go!" The first formation had struck out.

After five seconds, Koenig turned to Tom, tapped his helmet, and peeled away. Tom was next. His breathing quickened as he silently counted off. Tom turned to Marty and saw the young ensign's blue eyes blinking nervously. When the count reached five, Tom patted his helmet, and Marty rapidly nodded.

Tom racked the control stick left and pulled back. In a violent, eager rush, the Corsair peeled leftward. The world rotated clockwise in the windscreen—sky and clouds turned to autumn foliage as Tom completed the turn with his Corsair aimed in a sharp dive toward the mountains.

Five thousand feet below, gray smoke bubbled across the bridge, obscuring portions. Koenig's Corsair was pulling from its dive. "Near miss, Bill," Dad called out, now in position to spot for the others. Under heavy Gs, Koenig was too busy to reply.

Open air now lay between the bridge and Tom's plane. Tom peered through the gunsight and maneuvered the control stick to align the crosshairs with the bridge. He floated from his seat momentarily. When the smoky bridge was an inch above his crosshairs, the estimated aiming point for the steepness of the dive, Tom stopped steering.

Hold her steady! he thought. The needle in the airspeed indicator wound upward as the speed mounted.

320 miles per hour, 330, 340.

Tom nursed back the throttle. His ears popped. *Keep the wings even! Fight the crosswind!* The needle in the altimeter spun backward.

4,500 feet, 4,000, 3,500.

The bridge swelled in the shaking crosshairs.

3,000 feet, 2,500.

Now!

Tom mashed the red bomb release button with his thumb.

Clunk! The bomb released.

Climb! Tom thought. He had to put distance between himself and the explosion. Tom hauled back on the stick and slammed the throttle forward. *Climb! Climb! Climb!* The altimeter reversed its spin and spiraled upward. Gravity sucked Tom's cheeks back and pulled him into his seat. He squinted against the sun and grimaced while squeezing his neck muscles to keep from blacking out. The Corsair soared up from the valley.

Behind Tom, the bomb exploded. *Thump.*

"Tom, you missed," came Dad's voice over the radio.

"Damn it!" Tom muttered.

Tom turned against his straps and glimpsed Marty pulling from his dive. Tom watched for the explosion from Marty's bomb. Nothing happened.

"Marty, you didn't drop at all," Dad reported.

Leveling off, Tom studied the bridge from the side. The concrete appeared untouched.

"Join up, and let's head for home," Dad said. He sounded annoyed at himself. The results were an embarrassment to the squadron.

Behind the others, Marty climbed to catch up. His black eyebrows were furrowed in frustration. The pylon beneath his plane's belly had malfunctioned and still gripped his bomb. Mechanical malfunction or not, he couldn't land aboard the carrier with a hung bomb.

Marty's face twisted as he reached to the panel beside the gunsight to disarm the bomb. With the flick of a switch he could turn the bomb inert, then jettison it. He hesitated, his finger over the switch. If he dumped the bomb, the others might assume he'd messed up or worse—he'd panicked. More than anything, Marty wanted to look good for his buddies and Dad in particular.

Dad was the best pilot in the squadron and maybe on the entire ship. Others would line Vulture's Row just to watch him land because he came in so smoothly, without a twitch of his landing gear, all the way to the deck.

More than anyone, Marty wanted to win Dad's approval. Once, during carrier landing practice, Marty's engine quit in midair. From the carrier, an officer radioed and asked Marty if he wanted to ditch alongside the ship. But Marty knew that Dad had just landed and was watching, so he tried for the deck without power. Marty caught a hook but landed askew and nearly rolled into a trench opposite the tower. When Marty dismounted, Dad approached him. Marty expected the veteran to say, "That was a damn fine landing, considering everything." Instead, Dad shook his head and said, "That's about the worst landing I've ever seen," and walked away.

Now, as Marty flew with a live bomb beneath his feet, he had yet to realize that Dad's hard-nosed manner was a veteran's way of leading, to let a young pilot know he had room to improve and further to go.

Marty removed his hand from the bomb arming switch and sat back in his seat.

"This is 217 to Lead," he said into his microphone. "I'd like to make another run on the target."

Silence ensued over the airwaves.

Wide-eyed, Tom orbited in formation with the others. *Talk about sticking your neck out,* he thought. He had heard Marty's request.

Dad's voice was silent for a moment; then he said, "Okay, go ahead."

Tom and the others saw Marty's Corsair rocket up past them and toward the clouds. At five thousand feet, the young ensign winged over and dived back toward the bridge.

Tom kept his eyes fixed on his wingman—Marty had really set himself up. If his bomb released and missed, he'd look worse than if he hadn't tried at all.

Marty's Corsair shrank tiny in sight as it plummeted toward the bridge. A green speck fell from its belly and punched into the smoke. The Corsair pitched upward as a flash crackled through the smoke behind it. A new plume of gray rose from the cloud, this one containing a swirl of white dust—the dust of shattered concrete.

As the smoke and dust settled, the bridge reappeared. Stone pillars still stood—but without a concrete ceiling to connect them. Slabs of bridge lay folded into the stream. Marty had scored a direct hit.

A grin stretched across Tom's face. He wanted to congratulate Marty but held his tongue to respect radio silence.

After several more orbits, Tom watched Marty slide into formation on his wing. When he caught Marty's eye, Tom smiled and flashed a thumbs-up. Marty cracked a grin. He nodded to Tom, then returned his focus to flying formation.

Dad wheeled the flight eastward and the sea appeared on the horizon. For several minutes, the pilots flew in silence until Dad's voice crackled over the radio.

"Nice job, Marty."

Three simple words.

"Thanks, sir," Marty replied. He tried not to sound too high-pitched with excitement. Coming from Dad, those words were possibly the highest compliment he had ever received.

Tom glanced over his right shoulder and saw Marty concentrating on maintaining close formation. Tom turned forward again and didn't glance back until the end of the flight.

He knew Marty would be there.

CHAPTER 26

HE MIGHT BE A FLYER

That evening, after the bridge attack

THE OFFICERS DUG INTO THEIR SUPPERS in the *Leyte*'s dining room. Silverware clinked and savory smells filled the air. As usual, Tom sat across from Jesse and Koenig. The men wore tan slacks and shirts open at the collars, and printed menus lay between them. Conversations buzzed, as officers planned their return to civilization. In a week, the *Leyte* was leaving for six days of R&R in Japan.

Behind Tom, the skipper dined at a separate table with the ship's senior officers. At the head of the table sat the *Leyte*'s executive officer—the second-in-command. He was the honorary host of each meal. In adherence with naval tradition, the captain dined in the tower.

Black stewards slipped behind the seatbacks and lowered silver trays of food in front of the officers. The stewards wore clean, high-collared jackets and their hair was neat and closely cropped. A war correspondent recorded a typical *Leyte* meal: "Bean soup with crackers, grilled beef steak, mashed potatoes, mushroom gravy, creamed peas and carrots, buttered cabbage, lettuce and tomato salad, peach pie, bread, butter, and orangeade." Only the squawk boxes on the walls and the watertight doors reminded the officers that they were aboard a warship, not at a banquet.

Marty's blue eyes beamed as he ate with vigor. He had received plenty of backslapping after the mission, although he hadn't sought it. His destruction of the bridge had been recorded as a squadron victory and that was enough for him. That day, *Leyte* planes had claimed five bridges and five trains.*

The day's most triumphant moment actually came just before supper. The pilots had been relaxing in their ready rooms when the teletype machines blinked: "Enemy capital, Pyongyang, fallen to U.S. Army 1st Cavalry Division. U.N. Forces now occupying." The pilots had cheered at the news. A glance at the map revealed that the boys on the ground had the enemy cornered in North Korea's mountainous northwest. All that remained was to push the communists out of the country—just seventy-five more miles. Four days earlier, during a meeting with President Truman on Wake Island, General MacArthur had even predicted a timeline to the war's end: "I believe that formal resistance will end throughout North and South Korea by Thanksgiving."

Tom picked at his plate and listened courteously when the conversation turned his way. In his mind, he could still envision the glowing spheres whipping past his canopy. *What if the gunner had fired a split second earlier?* he thought. A harsh reality jabbed at him—even if he did everything right, one lucky shot could change everything.

At first, only Jesse and Koenig noticed.

Something was amiss in the dining room.

---

* The skipper would notice Marty's proficiency. Two days later, Marty passed through the dining room after a mission. The skipper lowered his sandwich and called him over. "Ensign Goode, how many landings are you up to?" the skipper asked. "About forty without a wave-off, sir," Marty replied. The skipper looked surprised and said, "You know, someday you may make a naval aviator."

As the stewards leaned plates of food in front of Jesse, they remained tense and tightlipped. Jesse quietly scooped his portions. Normally, the stewards were chatty. "Good hunting today, Ensign Brown?" they'd ask. Or, "I watched you take off this morning!" Jesse was their hero and not just because he was the only black carrier pilot. Whenever Jesse passed through the dining room in his flight gear, he always greeted them as they folded napkins and polished silverware. The steward who cleaned Jesse's cabin had told the others how Jesse always made his own bed, did his own dusting, and left him with little work to do. The stewards knew Jesse's full name, Jesse Leroy Brown, and behind the scenes they affectionately called him "Jesse L."

But now, something had changed. The stewards hurriedly moved from Jesse to the next man. Jesse's eyes followed them and his face pleaded—*What did I do wrong?*

This had happened before. During flight training, Pensacola's black stewards had viewed Jesse as an upstart, a black man trying to break into a white flying club. Come mealtime, the stewards often pulled their serving plates before Jesse could finish ladling out his food. They had glared at him while serving the white cadets at his side, and allowed the other men all the time they needed to fill their plates. After Jesse earned his wings, the ill treatment had ended. Or so he had thought.

With the main course concluded, the stewards removed dirty plates and filled the officers' coffee cups. Tom and others lit pipes and cigarettes. As the stewards served dessert, they continued to avoid Jesse's eyes. Some even fought to keep from grinning.

Confusion filled Jesse's face. Koenig lowered his cup to the table. "What the heck is going on?" he asked. Jesse shook his head. Across the table, Tom shrugged. He hadn't noticed.

A group of stewards drifted from the kitchen and congregated by the back wall, followed by cooks in T-shirts and stained aprons. Their eyes settled on Jesse. The kitchen door swung wide and a steward emerged carrying a small cake on a tray. Some of the officers' heads turned. When the steward reached Jesse's table, Tom saw an unlit candle on the yellow sponge cake.

Jesse's eyes grew wide and Koenig relaxed in his seat. Tom grinned. *Last week was Jesse's birthday!* he remembered. The ship's paper had run a blurb announcing that Jesse had turned twenty-four on October 13.

"Excuse me, sirs," the steward said to Tom and the man beside him. The steward leaned in and lowered the cake in front of Jesse, who shook his head in disbelief.

"Hey, Jesse," Cevoli shouted from down the table. "How did you swing a cake and party with 150 guests? There's a war on, you know!" Jesse and the others laughed, but Cevoli had a point: The kitchen never celebrated just one man's birthday.

The chief steward approached Jesse with a small box in his hands. He was an older black man with a small mustache. His jacket's left sleeve had three red V-shaped chevrons and the white eagle of a petty officer first class. The stewards and cooks stepped from the back wall, eager to see.

"Ensign Brown," the petty officer said, "me and the boys chipped in and got you a little something." He handed Jesse the box. Jesse grinned and surveyed the faces of the kitchen staff. They were smiling, now free to show their excitement. Jesse removed the packaging and flipped open the box top. Nestled inside was a steel watch with a white face and a tiny silver crown for a logo.

A Rolex.

Jesse's jaw hung open.

"Holy cow!" Koenig murmured.

Along the table, officers leaned in. The watch had a black leather band and a silver winding crown. *That's a chunk of change!* Tom thought. Rolexes were the priciest items in the ship's store at sixty dollars — equivalent to nearly six hundred dollars in present-day money.

Jesse slid the Rolex over his left wrist and fastened the snap. He held the watch up to catch the light and marveled at its glimmer.

"Thank you for lifting us up," the petty officer said to Jesse. "Now, on this ship, when a black man passes you in the hallway, you never know, he might be just a cook — or he might be a flyer."

Jesse looked at them all, from the petty officer to the messiest line cook. "Thank you all so very much," Jesse said. "I hope I never let you down."

"No, thank you, Ensign Brown," a steward replied. The others murmured in agreement. "Enjoy it, sir," said another. "God bless." One by one the cooks and stewards broke from the gaggle with a nod or wave and returned to their duties.

A steward remained behind. He leaned forward with a lighter and lit the candle on the cake. The flame's tiny light flickered on Jesse's cheeks.

In a bashful voice, Koenig broke into song: "Happy birthday to you . . ." Tom and the officers joined in, and the steward sang, too. Jesse grinned as the chorus of warm voices reached a crescendo.

As the song ended, applause arose. "Thanks so much, guys," Jesse said. He thanked the steward and waved to the officers up and down the table. "Thank you all."

With everyone watching, Jesse leaned forward and blew out the candle.

CHAPTER 27

HOME

Sixteen days later, November 1, 1950
Sasebo, in southwestern Japan

THE SUN WAS SETTING as four "bikeshaws" raced between the wooden storefronts on a Japanese street.

In the lead vehicle, Tom and Cevoli held on to their hats. Two wheels spun beneath their seats while ahead of them a Japanese driver furiously pedaled a third. The bikeshaw was similar to a rickshaw, but instead of towing the cart a man pedaled from a bike seat and steered with handlebars.

Hoots and hollering followed Tom and Cevoli. Three bikeshaws trailed them, each filled with pilots. Dressed in blue blazers and white hats, the pilots seemed out of place for racing. *I wish I had a camera!* Tom thought.

American sailors leapt from the street to the sidewalk as the bikeshaws raced past. The sailors, too, were bound for downtown. Colorful signs with black Japanese symbols decorated the neighboring storefronts and a background of craggy mountains stood dark against the setting sun.

Tom and Cevoli's bikeshaw inched from the pack. "Maintain formation, Cevoli!" a pilot shouted from behind. "Stop clogging the airwaves!" retorted another pilot. Tom and Cevoli laughed.

Sporadically, their Japanese driver glanced back and flashed a toothy smile. He was young, too, and wore pants wrapped with cloth at the ankles. A threadbare cap with a short brim and pointy top sat on top of his head—the military cap of a Japanese veteran of World War II.

Cevoli shouted encouragements and the young driver laughed and pedaled harder. After six days ashore in Japan, Cevoli had already put the war behind him. Sasebo had once been an Imperial Japanese Navy base, but now, to the U.S. Navy's 7th Fleet, it was a welcome playground.

The bikeshaw driver turned onto a crowded pedestrian street and stopped at the curb. He announced in broken English that they had arrived. "Black Market Alley!"

Tom hopped down onto the city's most energetic street.

Shops filled both sides of Black Market Alley and lighted signs blinked. Sailors milled about, jovial, loud, tipsy. Japanese vendors hawked lacquer boxes and silk pajamas. Smoke rose from grills, and the air smelled of sizzling meat and plum wine.

Tom and Cevoli paid their driver and the young man bowed. The other bikeshaws emptied Jesse, Marty, Wilkie, and other high-spirited pilots who flocked to Cevoli and Tom.

This was their last night in Japan before the *Leyte* sailed in the morning. Although the ship's destination remained unannounced, Tom and the others had their suspicions. They had last heard that the army and Marines were mopping up in Korea, and the air force was rotating home its B-29 bomber squadrons that had run out of targets. And when the *Leyte* had anchored in Sasebo, spare parts and new Corsairs were supposed to be waiting—yet the docks were empty. When Tom inquired, he discovered that his requests for spares had

been denied, the delivery of new planes canceled. The facts steered
Tom and the others to the same conclusion: *We're heading home.*

Together, the pilots waded into Black Market Alley, eager to knock
out their Christmas shopping early. The Korean War was short—and
they'd survived.

Tom absorbed the sights around him as old women hobbled past in
wooden clogs. Sailors sat on stools while Japanese artists painted their
portraits. Other sailors tried to sweet-talk Japanese girls, only to hear
the commonplace rejection: "Never hoppon, Joe!"

Along the street, Japanese shoe shiners crowded the curbs and polished the shoes of sailors. Most of the shoe shiners wore the same
pointed military caps. The postwar Japanese society viewed its veterans
as bad memories, so many veterans had to settle for menial jobs.

In clusters, Tom and the others ducked into shops to explore.

Beneath a store's high ceiling and dangling lights, Jesse examined a
string of pearls as sailors jostled past. At his side, an ensign named Lee
Nelson leaned across the counter and studied several cases of pearls.
Nelson was of Scandinavian descent, blond-haired and blue-eyed with
boyish features. A pilot in '32, he also doubled as the squadron's ama-
teur cartoonist.

The Japanese merchant pointed out the differences among the
pearls. Nelson was interested in buying a necklace for his wife, a
Northeast Airlines stewardess also named Lee. Like everything in
Sasebo, the pearls cost a third of what they would elsewhere.

Jesse trickled the pearls back into their case. He had decided to save
his money for the diamond ring he intended to buy for Daisy. Since
hearing the rumors that the *Leyte* would be making a beeline for
home, Jesse had been all smiles. The first thing he planned to do was
to buy the ring and then present it when he and Daisy were vacation-
ing in the Bahamas.

Nelson told Jesse that he wanted to check for a better price at another shop. The pilots excused themselves from the negotiation and

stepped into the street. Jesse and Nelson pulled their white officer's caps down over their heads and headed toward the next pearl broker.

A jeep honked in the distance, and a whistle pierced the night. Another whistle sounded, this one from the opposite direction, then another. Flocks of Shore Patrol sailors emerged from the crowds at both ends of the street. SPs ran from building to building, while others stopped American servicemen in the street and shouted messages into their ears. The servicemen nodded; even the drunk ones straightened up.

The SPs worked their way closer to Jesse and Nelson. Jesse had always tried to avoid the SPs. During flight training, they often trailed him and Daisy from street to street in Pensacola, unaware that Jesse was an off-duty pilot cadet.

An SP spotted Jesse and Nelson. He pointed and alerted his partner. The two uniformed men hustled toward the pilots, their whistles and night sticks bouncing. At the last second, they stopped and saluted.

"Sirs, liberty is suspended," the SP said. "Everyone needs to head back to their ships ASAP—something big is happening."

Jesse asked if something was wrong.

"Shit's hitting the fan in Korea," the SP said. "That's all they're telling us, sir." The SPs hurried off to the next navy men.

Jesse's face fell. He'd just written to Daisy to tell her that he might be coming home.

A full-scale roundup was under way. Along the street, SPs pried sailors from movie theaters, steak dinners, geisha houses.

Tom and Cevoli emerged from a shop, each man wearing newly purchased binoculars around his neck. Tom's eyes swept the street with alarm.

Even before the SPs reached him, the whistles told Tom what every fighting man dreaded.

Home was going to have to wait.

CHAPTER 28

THE FIRST BATTLE OF WORLD WAR III

Two days later, November 6, 1950
Northeastern North Korea

MARINE HOWITZERS ON THE VALLEY FLOOR barked and sent shells rocketing skyward. Flashes exploded against the charred hilltop. *Crack! Crack! Crack!* Each blast echoed through the valley. Plumes of smoke rose into the gray afternoon sky.

A seemingly endless string of five thousand Marines watched from the valley floor near the village of Sudong. They were the lead element of the 1st Marine Division. Some Marines stood beside jeeps and trucks parked along a winding dirt road; others stepped from nearby tents. Hands on hips, cigarettes dangling, they stared at the fireworks show on the large, round hill to the north. Korean refugees plodded past the Marines, bound in the opposite direction. The refugees, too, stopped to watch. The top of the hill was charred black, but brown trees still bristled from the bottom.

Before this, the Marines had been making good progress marching north. Their orders were to push the North Koreans over the Chinese border—just eighty miles away—and go no farther.

Then, the massive hill appeared in their path, at the opening to a pass through the mountains. The hill stood 891 meters above sea level, so men called it "891."

From atop 891, a formidable force had fired down on the Marines and stopped the column in its tracks.

Now the Marines fired back.

Anyone watching could see and feel the Marines' fury, but not all eyes were fixed on the hill. . . .

Red Parkinson took a few steps from his buddies and unslung his carbine. His eyes settled across the road, where a mass of North Korean refugees was resting.

One of the refugees, a man in a peasant's long coat, had strayed from the group. With his back to the others, he strolled over to a handful of Marine trucks parked by the roadside. Marines were unloading boxes to set up a supply depot. The refugee lightly waved a finger, as if counting the trucks.

Red's eyes narrowed. "Charlie, take a look at this," he muttered. Charlie Kline stepped to Red's side. The refugee held a palm to his chest and bowed his head, scribbling something.

"Can you believe this joker?" Red said. "He's taking notes."

"He's awful curious," Charlie said.

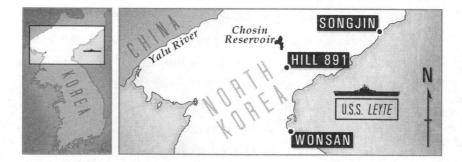

Several Marines gathered around Red and Charlie. Red lowered his carbine and shouted, "Hey, you!" The refugee glanced over his shoulder and slipped something into his pocket.

Red took a step toward the man, and the refugee took off running.

"Halt!" Red shouted.

But the refugee kept sprinting through a field.

Red raised his rifle and took aim.

The refugee was twenty yards away. Then thirty. Then forty.

Bam! Red fired, and smoke rose from the carbine's barrel. A puff of filling burst from the back of the refugee's coat. The man lost his footing, steadied himself, and kept running. *Bam, bam, bam!* Red fired again. More filling jumped from the man's back but he kept going. The carbine's pistol-like bullet had little effect. In disbelief, Red lifted his face from the stock.

"Out of the way, Red!" said another Marine. He calmly leveled his M1 Garand rifle on the running man. *Bang!* A chunk of filling flew and the refugee flopped to the ground.

Charlie and the other Marines hustled toward the fallen refugee while Red stomped over to the nearest tree. He was finished with the lightweight carbine and knew of a field hospital where he could find spare M1 Garands. With a crimson face, he flipped the carbine upside down in his hands, grabbed it by the barrel, and swung it like a bat against the tree. "Piece of junk!" he shouted. The rifle shattered and Red tossed the bits by the roadside.

Within the circle of curious Marines, Devans crouched and rolled the body over. He had recently been promoted to sergeant and Red had been made a corporal. Red caught up and saw that the dead man was Asian, probably in his twenties. His face appeared full, and he was well-fed, almost too well-fed to be a refugee. Devans scratched his chin.

Charlie glanced at Red with a raised eyebrow. "A refugee wouldn't run like that," Red said. Devans flapped the young man's long coat open. Beneath was a second layer, a quilted white jacket that was reversible, brown on the inside. Red had heard of this attire. He felt a knot form in his gut.

Devans fished through the man's pockets and retrieved a notepad. Red peered over Devans's shoulder as he thumbed through pages filled with drawings.

"Well, I'll be," Devans said. "He's got our positions marked up and down the road!"

The Marines muttered in disgust. "Sarge, is that one of them?" a Marine asked. The others looked to Devans.

"He's no refugee," Devans said, shaking his head. "He's not North Korean, either. Take a look at that jacket."

All eyes settled on the white jacket. One man spit and another nervously fished for a cigarette. Something about the dead man's attire told them that the fighting wouldn't be over by Thanksgiving, as General MacArthur had boasted.

The men remained silent and somber. No one congratulated Red for spotting the suspicious character. Instead, their eyes followed the sounds of gunfire back to 891, where something ominous was brewing.

Soon after, around 4:30 P.M., on the hill

"Come on, Coderre, *reach!*" Lieutenant Reem shouted over the gunfire.

Ed Coderre glanced up from the base of a small embankment and saw Reem reaching down to him. Beneath his helmet, the lieutenant's eyebrows hung low over his steady eyes.

Deep in a hillside gully, Coderre had never felt so far from his baseball diamond back home in Pawtucket, Rhode Island. Gunfire barked from uphill and green tracers zipped down over the gully.

Coderre lunged and seized Reem's hand. Reem was burly like a fullback and he yanked Coderre up and over the bank. "Get your squad moving," Reem shouted. "We gotta reach the crest together!"

Coderre nodded and scrambled to a crouch. Centuries of water runoff had scooped the gully into the hillside, creating U-shaped walls that curved twenty feet above the men. *Snap! Snap!* Lines of tracers wove over the gully and cracked through the dead trees above. The enemy was raking the hill's lower slopes. Coderre flinched, his black eyebrows arching high with alarm. Reem noticed and yelled with a shrug, "They're just firing blind!"

Blind fire can still kill you! Coderre thought.

"Head down," Reem said. "Keep moving."

"Yes, sir!" Coderre said with a New Englander's clip.

Reem slapped the young Marine's shoulder and dashed uphill. The two had shared a bond of friendship ever since Reem had nominated Coderre for the Naval Academy.

Higher in the gully, the platoon's riflemen waited for Coderre and the machine gun squads to catch up. Together, they comprised the 2nd platoon of How Company (3rd Battalion, 7th Marine Regiment). The sun was setting behind the crest, and the platoon still had three-fourths of the hill to climb.

Coderre shuffled to the lip of the embankment and glanced down. In the shadows below, a dozen men from the machine gun squads were stumbling beneath the weight of their guns, tripods, and ammo cans. Five of them belonged to Coderre's squad. That morning, Reem had promoted Coderre to corporal and squad leader.

"Come on, fellas, pick it up!" Coderre shouted over the gunfire. A wiry Marine hustled to the embankment with the squad's Browning M1919 .30-caliber machine gun over his shoulder. He was Wick, the squad's mechanical specialist, who maintained the weapon when he wasn't carrying its ammo. Beneath his helmet, Wick's face was narrow and his eyebrows were light brown. The hole-filled barrel sleeve rose and fell as he huffed and puffed.

"Toss me the gun!" Coderre said. With both hands Wick tossed up the weapon. Coderre caught it, his arms sinking beneath the thirty-one-pound weight. He set the gun aside and gave Wick a hand, then helped the other squad members over the ledge.

"The LT says pick up the pace!" Coderre told them. Wick reached for the gun but Coderre stopped him—"I'll take it for a bit." Still breathless, Wick thanked him. For Coderre, helping others came naturally. Back home, his father was a fire academy instructor and his godfather, a policeman. Coderre himself had bagged groceries as a grocery-store clerk and was a Boy Scout before joining the Marines with his buddies.

Above, Reem signaled for the forty Marines to move out. The men began grunting and clawing up the steep slope.

Coderre shouldered the gun and climbed. His father had taught him how to carry a fire hose, but that was nothing compared to the block of steel on his shoulder. Coderre planted a hand in the soil and bent forward against the slope as his legs pushed his short frame upward. He wore two pistols in holsters on his hips and was glad to have traded away his carbine for a second pistol.

Every now and then, Coderre glanced uphill. Green tracers still swept the darkening sky. He knew who was shooting at him and the thought sent a chill down his spine.

Five days earlier, while the air force was rotating home its B-29 bombers and the navy boys were on R&R in Sasebo, the Chinese had launched a surprise attack in the western valleys of North Korea. Under darkness, on November 1, they struck the army's 1st Cavalry Division. Like the hordes of Genghis Khan they descended and wiped out a six-hundred-man battalion in a night.*

No one knew exactly how many Chinese had slipped into the war or what their intentions were. The North Korean prime minister, Kim Il Sung, had bragged publicly that the Chinese had joined the fight, although the Chinese denied that the troops belonged to their military. Any Chinese soldiers in Korea, they said, were "volunteers." Only

---

* MacArthur's staff initially discounted the reports of Chinese troops. Throughout the war, MacArthur never actually spent a full day in Korea—he always flew back at night to his HQ in Japan. On October 30, he sent General Charles Willoughby, his military intelligence chief of staff, to Korea. Through a translator, Willoughby interrogated sixteen Chinese prisoners and reported back that they were simply "stragglers."

one thing was certain: The North Koreans weren't fighting alone any-more.

The gully ended and became level with the hill. Shell craters and blackened trees filled the last seventy-five yards to the top. Coderre snuck a glimpse of the crest, a rough gray line against the twilight. Nothing moved. The Chinese guns had gone silent. *Are we being lured up?* he wondered. The Marines crept into the volcanic-looking land-scape.

In the midst of the broken terrain, word filtered back: "Take a knee." Coderre handed the gun to Wick and collapsed. He took a swig from his canteen. The sky was turning darker and the air colder, so Coderre zipped up his jacket. He questioned the wisdom of starting the attack so late.

From the fringe, a Marine whispered a challenge. Another Ameri-can voice replied with a password. From the left, How Company's 1st platoon silently emerged from a parallel gully. Led by the company commander, the additional forty men slipped in beside Reem's pla-toon. Coderre eyed the newcomers. Counting both platoons, the Ma-rines had eighty men on the hill.

Reem and How Company's commander glanced upslope and planned their assault. From behind, Coderre watched and marveled at Reem's endurance. After twenty-seven days on the line, the young lieutenant seemed tireless. In reality, he just hid any sign of fatigue from his men. In a recent letter to his wife, Reem had confided: "I am getting mighty tired chasing Reds up and down the hills of Korea. I'd like to come home and be with you, Donna." In closing, he promised, "I'll be careful."

A sergeant scampered down to Coderre and his squad. "We're going to hit the left flank of the crest," the sergeant said. "First platoon's tak-ing the right. We'll sweep around, they'll sweep around, and we'll hit the Reds from behind. The lieutenant wants the machine guns close to him!" Coderre and the others nodded.

Coderre checked his pistols—both hammers were cocked and ready. Even after the artillery barrage, he couldn't fathom the logic of sending eighty men against an enemy of unknown strength. Everyone knew that the stakes of this battle were high.

Several days earlier, the 7th Marines' commander, Colonel Litzenberg, had called Reem and other officers to his command post to tell them: "Gentlemen, you may soon be fighting in the opening battle of World War III."*

How Company's commander swept his hand rightward. Reem motioned for his men to move leftward. "Home by Christmas!" Coderre whispered to his squad. "Home by Christmas!" they retorted. Their new rallying cry was undoubtedly sarcastic.

Both platoons surged into the volcanic landscape and peeled apart.

Reem and his riflemen led the way toward the left end of the crest. Coderre sprinted, stumbled, and tried to follow the lieutenant's silhouette against the dim sky.

Seventy yards to go!

Coderre dodged burned trees and jumped small craters. He and his squad ran down into the big craters and up the other side.

Sixty yards.

Coderre's thighs felt numb and his boots heavy.

Fifty yards.

A whistle pierced the air, coming from the crest. Then another sounded and another. Coderre slowed, his eyes drawn uphill. Shadowy figures stood along the crest; there had to be a hundred of them, maybe more.

---

* One could argue that the Korean War was really a world war—World War III—in which the nations of the world converged to fight on one peninsula, instead of around the globe. Twenty-three nations committed troops or weaponry to Korea, among them the world's largest industrialized nations—the United States, Britain, Canada, China, France, and the USSR; all took up arms, just without formal declarations of war.

Pop, pop, pop!

Across the crest, enemy muzzle flashes crackled like flashbulbs. Bullets kicked up burnt earth and the Marines hit the dirt. Coderre crawled into a crater with his squad as green tracers sprayed overhead and crossed streams.

"Should we set up the gun?" Wick shouted.

Coderre shook his head. With riflemen between them and the crest, they had no field of fire.

Mysteriously, the Chinese tracers slacked. Coderre peeked over the lip. Fifty yards uphill, figures ran through trenches, earflaps bouncing from their hats. Coderre drew his pistol but didn't have a shot. *Show yourselves!* he wanted to shout. Black shapes began arcing through the twilight, each shaped like a soup can attached to a stick. Coderre turned to his buddies with wild eyes. "Grenades!" he shouted.

Across the cratered terrain, stick grenades exploded, some in mid-air, some against the ground. Dirt showered and splinters sprayed from trees.

"Corpsman!" wounded men screamed.

"Corpsman!"

A Marine medic darted from one shell hole to the next to aid the wounded. Other Marines broke cover to help their buddies.

The rain of grenades ended abruptly and more shadowy figures stood from the crest.

Bup, bup, bup!

They sprayed submachine guns toward the Marines who had stirred from their holes.

As some of the shadowy figures dropped to reload, others stood and fired. This was a Chinese tactic—to use grenades to scatter a foe so that their submachine gunners could pick off anyone in the open.

Bup, bup, bup!

Wick turned to Coderre. "You recognize that gunfire?" he shouted.

Coderre tuned an ear. The gunfire's bark was deep and familiar.

"Those are our guns!" Wick shouted.

How is this possible? Coderre thought. The Chinese were using American-made Tommy guns, the weapon of choice for Chicago gangsters and army paratroopers.

Bup, bup, bup!

As bullets slapped the dirt around Coderre, his eyebrows furrowed in frustration. He holstered his pistol and snapped a grenade from his belt. Hopping to a baseball catcher's crouch, he pulled the pin. *Click!* Coderre threw the grenade at the crest. The grenade exploded amid the Chinese lines. Wick saw the throw and turned to his friend. "Here — use mine!" he said, handing Coderre his grenade. Coderre tossed Wick's grenade. "Load him up!" Wick yelled to the squad. The men shuttled their grenades to Coderre. In machine-like fashion he pulled the pins and heaved. Explosions burst across the crest.

Reem popped up from a crater. "Let 'em have it!" he shouted, momentarily exposed to the flashes of enemy fire. The Marine riflemen answered. Their M1 rifles barked and empty clips plinked. Browning automatic rifles blasted through twenty rounds and sent magazines clattering. In the face of resistance, the Chinese gunners sank from sight.

Reem stood and pointed his carbine toward the crest. "Move up! Move up!" he yelled. "Before they regroup!"

Reem knew that the Marines had to win this battle. No one was sure if the Chinese had entered the war to stay — or just to help their fellow communists escape. The reason didn't matter. Colonel Litzenberg had said it: The results of this first battle "will reverberate around the world" and send a message to the Chinese and Stalin himself.

En masse, the platoon sprinted for the crest. Coderre gave chase. His heart raced, filling his ears with the sound of thumping blood. The Marine riflemen climbed the crest and fired from cover. Chinese voices shouted. Whistles blew. Wounded Marines rolled down and others crawled into their places. Beneath the crest, Reem jumped into a large shell hole and yelled, "Squad leaders, on me!"

Coderre and others slid into the crater. Reem crouched with his back to the crest. "OK, we're going up and over!" he shouted above the

gunfire. "Coderre, take your gun there"—he pointed to the crest—
"and suppress from the center, rightward, but watch out for 1st platoon!"

"Yes, sir!" Coderre said.

As Reem turned to another squad leader, a dark shape flew from the
crest. It arced through the twilight, down over Reem's shoulder, and
landed in the crater. *Ting!*

Grenade! Coderre thought.

"Grenade!" Reem shouted.

Coderre backpedaled, tripped, and fell to the crater's floor, his helmet rolling away. The crater was dark and cluttered with rocks. From
his backside, Coderre saw Reem drop to his hands and knees and desperately search the ground for the grenade. The others flung themselves against the crater's walls; Coderre braced for the spray of steel.

At the last second, Reem spotted the grenade and dived for it. He
swept his powerful arms, pulling the grenade under his chest.

A blinding white flash cut the darkness and a shock wave rippled—
Ka-thump!

A burnt, oily smell cut the air as Coderre raised himself from the dirt.
He coughed and wiped his eyes but saw only shadows. A high-pitched
ringing filled his ears.

A figure dashed up, knelt, and shook him. Wick's face materialized
but remained blurry. "We gotta get you out of here!" Wick said. His
mouth was shouting but his voice sounded miles away. He fumbled for
a bandage.

Blood dripped down between Coderre's eyes. He gingerly touched
his forehead: A deep gash lay beneath his widow's peak. Coderre ran
his shaking hands down and felt the cuts where shrapnel had raked his
neck. A wave of nausea hit him.

Wick slapped a bandage onto Coderre's forehead and plunged a
morphine syrette into his friend's arm.

"The lieutenant?" Coderre mumbled.

"He's gone!" Wick shouted.

Coderre shook himself free of Wick's grasp and peered across the crater. Blue smoke hovered above the floor, and on the fringes Marines slowly stood. In the center, Reem lay sideways, facing Coderre. The lieutenant's eyes were open but he didn't move. His chest was torn open and his hands were missing. Gone was the wedding ring that his wife, Donna, had slid onto his finger.

"No! No!" Coderre muttered. "This can't be!"

Wick pulled Coderre to his feet and dragged him downhill, away from the chaos. Over his ringing ears, Coderre heard gunfire cracking and distant shouts. He glanced behind him and saw Marines charging over the crest.

Wick and Coderre slid downhill for a ways, tried to stand, stumbled, and slid again. Green tracers zipped over them and flamed out in the sky. Coderre's legs felt like putty. Every time they fell, Wick cradled him and helped him stand.

The morphine clouded Coderre's brain. "The lieutenant saved my life," he mumbled. "Yes, he did," Wick said. The duo slid and stumbled. "He jumped on a damn grenade!" Coderre added. "Ed, I know!" Wick said. Coderre felt light-headed. He wanted to fall and roll, but Wick held him back. The gunfire sounded softer with each step.

"I don't get it," Coderre mumbled.

"Get what?" Wick said.

"Why did he do that?"

Wick stepped onto the valley floor with Coderre hanging limply from his shoulder. A Marine medical team rushed over with a stretcher. Coderre asked for a cigarette, but no one listened. Hands lifted him onto the stretcher. He felt himself floating as he stared at the dark clouds with gaps of night sky. Before Coderre could thank Wick, his friend was gone, climbing back uphill.*

---

* How Company Sergeant Jack Coleman remembers how he and a handful of Marines held the top of 891 until their ammunition ran out. During the pitched fighting, Sgt. Charlie Foster said to him, "They'll never believe we made it this far!" So he and Coleman removed their gloves and placed them on rocks to mark their advance. Foster

As the Marines carried Coderre toward an aid tent, his eyes blinked wide with alarm. "My throwing arm!" he said. His mind flashed to Fenway Park and the Red Sox. He struggled to see his right arm.

"Don't worry, it's still there," a Marine said.

Another glanced at Coderre's wounds.

"You're lucky," he said. "That grenade just missed your eyes."

Coderre's face sank with despair. He wanted to tell them how his lieutenant had just saved his life but couldn't find the words. They'd never understand. He couldn't even understand it.

As the Marines carried him into the tent, the question raced through Coderre's mind:

Why did he do that?

---

was killed shortly thereafter. The following day, after the Chinese had vacated the hill, Coleman would recover his friend's body—and his gloves.

CHAPTER 29

THE SKY WILL BE BLACK

Twelve days later, November 18, 1950
Aboard the USS *Leyte*

THE READY ROOM WAS QUIET and the pilots of Fighting 32 were fidgety. All that remained was one last briefing. It was 8:00 A.M. and the pilots—just six of them—were about to make the world's most dangerous commute.

Tom had been chosen to fly. With his leather jacket stretched over his seatback, he leaned forward to study a crinkly green map on the wall. His eyes locked on a blue line that snaked up the side of Korea and divided North Korea from China.

The Yalu River. Tom took a drag from his pipe to cool his nerves.

Tom and the others snapped to their feet when the skipper entered. The man wore the winter seasonal getup: a leather jacket and green pants. He motioned for his pilots to sit and stepped front and center. He had just come from a briefing with the ship's intelligence officers.

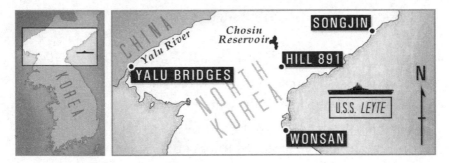

"Well, the Chinese are still MIA," the skipper said, approaching the map. "And it's quiet across the front. The army's sitting tight in the west," he said, tapping the map. "And in the east the Marines are marching north again without resistance."

Tom shook his head in disbelief. The brass had identified twelve Chinese divisions in Korea—at least a hundred thousand enemy soldiers. Yet after one week of combat they had mysteriously disappeared into the mountains.

"Just because the Chinese aren't engaging doesn't mean they're gone," the skipper continued. "Our night fighters are reporting headlights coming *into* Korea—not out." He explained the belief of the Intel boys—that the Chinese were bringing in fresh troops and supplies.

Tom's eyes glanced back to the map. Slung across the river was the key to the Chinese route into Korea: the Yalu bridges.

The skipper nodded to a sailor in the rear who was manning a slide projector. The lights dimmed. Tom clenched his pipe in his teeth and opened his notepad. Nearby, Jesse and Koenig readied their notepads too. Cevoli rocked in his chair ambivalently; he'd take notes on his palm.

"Today, the strike package is paying a visit to the twins," the skipper said.

Click.

A grainy aerial photo of two bridges appeared on the screen. They spanned the Yalu, side by side. The bridge to the south held a highway that ran across its twelve humps and the other one held railroad tracks.

Both bridges had been damaged enough to halt traffic but neither had fallen.

The skipper explained that the enemy was repairing the bridges under darkness and soon both would be back in operation. Tom wanted to groan. Supposedly the Chinese had five hundred thousand troops on their side of the river just waiting for a lift across and the North Koreans had six thousand trucks on their side, eager to serve. Only the damaged bridges were preventing them from uniting.

No targets held greater importance in all the war. Ten days earlier, General MacArthur had ordered air force B-29 air strikes against the bridges but the heavy bombers had missed the narrow targets, so they handed the job to the navy, which hadn't done much better. The problem lay in the rules of engagement—American pilots were forbidden from crossing the river and violating Chinese airspace, so they had to fly up or down the river and attack the bridges at their thinnest.

"Today, we're going after the highway bridge," the skipper continued. "But this time we're going in ahead to suppress the flak—we'll leave the bridge-busting to the Skyraiders."

The pilots nodded with approval. Skyraiders were heavy attack planes, like flying tanks, that were better suited for the job. Despite having just one engine, a lone Skyraider could carry nearly the same bomb load as a B-17 bomber.

The skipper explained that '32 would lead the strike package, with '33 following and the Skyraiders trailing them. He nodded to the projectionist.

Click.

A photo appeared of Sinuiju, a city on the Korean side of the bridges. Sinuiju now served as the acting North Korean capital for the regime in retreat.

The skipper explained that there were plenty of anti-aircraft guns in Sinuiju—the most in all of Korea—so '32 was going in first, to silence as many guns as possible, before the Skyraiders made their dives.

Tom glanced nervously at his buddies. Koenig ran his hands over his crew cut. Jesse didn't blink from the image on the screen. Veteran

An AD Skyraider

pilots who'd been to Sinuiju swore that the flak was as bad as anything in WWII.

Click.

The next photo showed three red circles over the city grid, near the bridge. Each circle was numbered and represented a battery of three Soviet-built 85mm cannons.

The skipper said that each pair of pilots was assigned a battery to strike. The skipper and his wingman would take battery number one, in the city. Tom and Cevoli were assigned battery two, between the city and the bridge. Jesse and Koenig got battery three, nearest the bridge. "Considering the current level of ruin, Intel believes the area is civilian-free," the skipper added.

He narrated several more slides, then ordered the sailor to turn off the projector. The lights flicked on. The squadron's duty officer stepped forward and ran through a clipboard list of radio codes, call signs, and rescue procedures. He took his seat and Tom closed his notepad. The skipper resumed his place.

"Today's gonna be rough," he said. "They know we're coming, they know from which direction. The sky will be black and we're just gonna have to plow through it."

Tom and the others nodded.

The skipper's eyes filled with determination. "Let's give the Sky-raiders some clear skies, and let's tumble a damned bridge already!"

Koenig stood, his face tight with tension.

Jesse noticed. "You should sit this one out, Bill," he whispered, "You're not 100 percent."

"I'll tough it out," Koenig said. "Just have to hit the head."

Jesse and Tom watched Koenig walk, hunched over, toward the lavatory. Cevoli asked what was wrong and Jesse explained that Koenig had been in and out of the lavatory all night, with flu-like symptoms. "I'm a little worried about him flying," Jesse said. Everyone knew the rules: A pilot was not allowed to fly if he'd had fewer than eight hours of sleep within the previous twenty-four hours.

Cevoli frowned. He summoned the duty officer and told him to find Koenig in the lavatory. "Tell him to get back to his rack," Cevoli said, "and let's get a replacement."

Jesse strode to the bulletin board where the duty officer had slapped up photos of the targets. He opened his notebook and began sketching his own map of the streets and buildings around his target. During his four missions since Sasebo, a new cautiousness had come to define Jesse's flying. He seemed obsessed with doing his job perfectly and get-ting home safely, as if he had never been more eager to live—or afraid to die.

With their helmets on and their hands full with their maps and oxygen masks, Tom and the others traversed the dining room. The breakfast crowd had thinned.

Layers of flight gear covered the pilots. A knife and an emergency light hung from their yellow life vests and revolvers bounced in their shoulder holsters. Beneath his leather jacket, Tom wore a tan flight suit and Jesse wore green. White silk scarves were wrapped around each man's neck to prevent chafing.

Wilkie stepped into the dining room, dressed to fly. "Heya, fellas," he said. "Am I on standby or what?" On important missions, a spare pilot would usually man a plane in case someone encountered mechanical trouble.

Cevoli grinned. "Actually, you're coming with us, Wilkie. Just a quick hop to the Yalu."

Wilkie's chin dropped. Jesse said that Koenig was sick.

"But what are we hitting?" Wilkie said. "I don't know the bomb line or approach sector or—"

Jesse interrupted by resting a hand on Wilkie's shoulder. "You're with me," Jesse said. "Just drop when I drop and you'll get through just fine."

Wilkie relaxed a little. "Okay, but what's the target?"

"Flak suppression, Sinuiju city," Jesse said.

Wilkie's face sank again.

The pilots resumed their march and Wilkie followed silently. Earlier, he'd written to his parents: "It's all been fun so far, as we've just hit buildings, vehicles, etc. Hope I don't have to kill men, as I'm not looking forward to that part at all, but someone has to do it, I guess. Just hope I'm not the one, as I can't see this killing crap at all. Just ain't built that way, I guess."

Now Wilkie's blue eyes were lost in thought. There was no way to bomb a flak gun without killing the men operating it.

Mere minutes after taking off, Tom leaned forward in his seat in the Corsair's cockpit. Something was wrong. His eyes narrowed—in the sky ahead and to the right of the carrier, Cevoli flew with his landing gear still lowered and his flaps dangling. Tom caught up and nestled beside his leader's right wingtip. Cevoli looked over to Tom and shook his helmeted head.

"Lead, this is 214," Cevoli radioed.

The skipper and his wingman were orbiting above at four thousand feet, waiting for the others.

"Go ahead, 214," the skipper replied.

"I've got a hydraulics malfunction," Cevoli said. "My gear won't retract."

"Roger, take departure," the skipper replied tersely. "Hudner, form up on me."

Oh brother, Tom thought. No one wanted to fly under the skipper's scrutiny.

"Tom can handle our target," Cevoli said, glancing at Tom.

Tom forced a smile.

He'd been counting on following Cevoli's lead and simply dropping his bomb when Cevoli dropped. But now the veteran pilot had decided for him. On the most important mission of the war, Tom would lead his own flight: a flight of one. The consequences of hitting the target—or missing—would all be his.

Cevoli waved at Tom and peeled away.

Two hours later, at twenty thousand feet over North Korea

Tall in his seat, the skipper looked from his cockpit to his wingman, then to Tom. He pointed his finger like a gun and motioned forward: *Target sighted!*

Between breaths from his oxygen mask, Tom peered ahead. The midday sunlight magnified every scratch in the windscreen. In the distance, warm brown mountains folded down to the muddy blue Yalu. Cities lined both banks, and between the cities were the bridges.

Cloaked in radio silence, the Corsairs swept over the outskirts of Sinuiju, the city on the Korean side. The tightly blocked Asian neighborhoods looked clean and hospitable in the midday glare. But as the formation neared the bridges, the city turned scorched and shadowy, like a vision of Stalingrad during WWII. Ten days earlier, a B-29 raid had burned 60 percent of the city below.

Tom's eyes lifted. Across the river, an industrial city was wide awake on the Chinese side. Smoke rose from factories and paper mills. Over there lay the warehouses of food and ammo that kept the Chinese armies functioning in North Korea. Over there marched five hundred thousand fresh Chinese troops ready for war.

Tom scanned the fields on the Chinese side and gritted his teeth. Reportedly, anti-aircraft guns dotted the fields. For weeks, the North Koreans had been moving their guns over to sanctuary in China. From there, they could fire on American planes, but the Americans couldn't legally fire back. Tom couldn't fathom how the Chinese could look the nations of the world in the eyes and deny that they were involved in the Korean War.*

A black puff of smoke burst far ahead and below Tom's plane. Another puff leapt from thin air, then another. The puffs began soiling the sky. Each was an exploding flak shell. The hairs on Tom's neck stood up. The enemy gunners weren't aiming for the Corsairs—the puffs were collecting into a black cloud six thousand feet beneath them. The gunners were laying their flak in the Skyraiders' flight path. Tom glanced in his rearview mirror. The formation of Skyraiders looked like dots on the horizon, lower than the Corsairs. They were just minutes behind.

The skipper pumped his fist—*Prepare to attack!* Tom lowered his goggles and reached to the left of the gunsight. He flicked a switch and his gunsight's concentric rings glowed yellow. He armed the guns and bomb next. Beneath the Corsair's belly hung an olive-painted bomb with a message in chalk, scribbled by a deckhand, something like: "With love, from the USS *Leyte*."

The bomb was special, a proximity bomb. A silver cylinder pro-

---

* The U.S. military was cautious not to escalate the conflict with China because the Chinese had signed a mutual defense treaty with Stalin in 1949 that stipulated that an attack on either would spark a war with both. Before the first bridge strike, naval admiral C. Turner Joy reminded his pilots: "Our government has decided that we cannot violate the air space over Manchuria (northeastern China) or attack on Manchurian territory regardless of the provocation. If such attacks were made, the world might be thrown into the holocaust of a third world war."

truded from its nose, and within the cylinder was a radio fuse that would emit a sound wave and trigger the weapon just above the ground. The radio fuse was sensitive and fickle, though. Once the bomb was released it would arm, and a passing cloud could trigger an accidental detonation.

The skipper broke radio silence. "Prepare to deploy dive brakes." Tom reached left and seized the landing gear lever. The lever could be lowered into either a slot on the right marked "landing gear" or one on the left marked "dive brake." A Corsair didn't have traditional air brakes to stabilize the plane as it dived, but the wheels would suffice.

"Deploy dive brakes now!" the skipper said. Tom lowered the lever leftward. Across the formation, the front wheels descended from each Corsair, and the planes bucked and slowed.

The flak cloud slipped beneath the Corsairs and Tom's breathing became heavy. To reach their targets, the pilots would have to dive through that abyss. Tom peered through the cloud and saw the highway bridge's twelve humps rising from the river like a sea serpent. His eyes narrowed on the city blocks just inland from the river. This was his target area. A moonscape of bomb craters pocked the streets there.

The skipper reached his target first. When his Corsair pulled parallel with the first flak battery, he announced: "Commencing flak suppression!" A split second later, his plane peeled leftward into a dive, followed by his wingman's.

Tom held his course toward the bridge with Jesse and Wilkie close behind. Several seconds of flight would place him parallel with his target, the second gun battery. Sweat coursed down the padding of Tom's helmet. His eyes blinked nervously. Before the navy's first bridge strike, Admiral Joy had issued a statement to his fleet. "Our naval pilots have been given a most difficult task," he wrote. "May God be with them as they accomplish it."

Tom banked the control stick leftward and peeled away. The river slid across his gunsight and shadows crossed the instrument panel. Tom kept banking and allowed the Corsair's nose to fall into an eye-watering dive. Wind knifed through gaps in the canopy seal and Tom felt the plane running with him, its weight on his back. The speed mounted—320 miles per hour became 330, then 340.

Below and to the left, Tom saw the skipper and his wingman diving side by side toward the black cloud. With gear down, the planes resembled Stuka dive bombers. The cloud seemed alive, a roiling kill zone. The skipper and his wingman plunged into the abyss. Shells flashed like lightning. A puff of flak erupted behind the skipper's left wing and jarred his plane. Metal pieces of Corsair skin fluttered through the air. The wound was light, so the skipper kept diving.

Darkness wrapped Tom's cockpit as his plane punched into the abyss next. Shells flashed left and right. *Ka-boom! Ka-boom!* Nineteen pounds of jagged steel leapt from each explosion. Tom shrank in his seat and held his breath. Black puffs dissolved against the windscreen and the stink of burnt gun powder filled the cockpit. Shock waves split the air and rocked the Corsair's wings, tossing Tom against his shoulder straps. *Come on, old girl!* Tom urged.

The black cloud suddenly slipped behind and the Corsair popped into the clear. Tom sucked oxygen from his mask. The city now filled his windscreen. His eyes snapped back to his target area. The altimeter needle spun backward as the Corsair dived through 12,000 feet, 11,000, 10,000.

Streams of orange tracers rose from the city and arced toward Tom. His eyes went wide. He reeled back against his headrest and winced. *Zip, zip, zip!* The glowing orange bolts zoomed past his windscreen. Across the rooftops and in the city's shadowy rubble, enemy gunners were sitting at Soviet-made 37mm cannons, cranking wheels, blasting through vertical magazines of foot-long shells.

New tracers cut past Tom's windscreen from the right. *Zip, zip, zip!* Tom tracked the fiery bolts as they whipped over the canopy and under his wingtip. He glanced right and tracked the fire to its source. "Holy hell!" he muttered. The fields on the Chinese side of the river were ablaze with flashes of North Korean gunfire. He had nearly forgotten. Tom's brow furrowed and he held his dive as the tracers crisscrossed around him.

Below, Tom glimpsed the skipper and his wingman at 2,500 feet, now pulling from their dives. Condensation slipped from their wingtips as they peeled right to escape the city. Behind them, their bombs exploded and secondary explosions crackled. Tom depressed the radio button on the throttle and stammered, "You hit something, Lead!" No reply came—the skipper was flying for his life.

Tom turned back to his gunsight. His index finger curled around the stick's crescent-shaped trigger. *Not yet!* Tom thought. *Too high!* The city still blended together.

The Corsair rocketed down through 9,000 feet, 8,000, 7,000. Tom couldn't see the flak cannons, but he saw them flashing. The gunners weren't running.

In the city below, three cannons sat in an intersection, their fifteen-foot-long barrels aiming skyward at the same angle. Behind the guns, North Korean soldiers passed an 85mm artillery shell from hand to hand to reload. They wore Soviet-style helmets and tan uniforms. Sirens blared and rubble lay around them.

When all three cannons had been reloaded, an officer raised a red-and-white flag and his men covered their ears. He lowered the flag.

Ka-boom!

In unison, the cannons fired. Shock waves blasted from their muzzles and dust rippled across the street. Spinning shells as wide as baseballs rocketed up toward Tom Hudner.

Crack! Crack! Crack!

As the shells exploded behind him, Tom didn't flinch. A gleam of certainty filled his eyes—he had seen the enemy muzzle flashes and held his crosshairs on that spot. His finger tightened on the trigger. The altimeter needle spun backward as the Corsair dived through 6,000 feet, 5,000, 4,000. The intersection took shape.

Now! Tom squeezed the trigger. With an ear-shattering roar, all six machine guns bucked like jackhammers in his wings. Fiery streams of orange tracers belched from the wings and empty shell casings tumbled forth.

Tom squinted against the blinding light. Three hundred yards ahead, the molten orange streams converged and the .50-caliber bullets rained into the intersection. With metallic rage, the bullets pierced and thudded and ricocheted into anyone and anything.

Tom lifted his finger from the trigger as the city stretched in his windscreen. The altimeter needle whipped backward through three thousand feet.

Drop! With his thumb, Tom mashed the red button atop the stick. Beneath the Corsair's belly, the proximity bomb clicked loose. Tom hauled back on the stick, and the plane lifted from the dive as the bomb whistled down.

G-forces gripped Tom's lungs and blackness squeezed his vision. He sipped air from his mask and muscled the stick back farther toward him. The wings groaned and creaked, threatening to rip away, and the landing gear whistled through the air. Just above the charred rooftops, the Corsair leveled out.

Behind Tom, a flash burst—*Ka-boom!* Twenty-five yards above the intersection, Tom's bomb had exploded and sprayed a cone of hot metal down onto the gun battery. Shock waves rippled from secondary explosions. High above, Jesse's voice crackled: "Looks like a hit, Tom!"

Tom shook the vision back into his eyes, raised his gear, and steered for the river to follow the Yalu south to safety. Green tracers chased his tail but the Corsair was flying too fast and too low. Tom tore his oxygen mask from his helmet and sucked in fresh air. Relief filled his face.

Behind him, another gun battery was silent.

Meanwhile, seven thousand feet above, fifty feet separated Wilkie's and Jesse's Corsairs as they dived with gear extended through the web of fire. Wilkie squinted through his gunsight. "Crap!" he muttered in his mask. He could see the bridge to the right but couldn't spot their target, where the highway rolled into the city. The cannons had stopped flashing—their crews had likely fled.

Wilkie glanced left and saw Jesse's face fixed forward, his helmet and mask unmoving. Behind his goggles, his eyes were steady and oblivious to the tracers around him.

Jesse's wings erupted with light as gunfire leapt from his muzzles. He must have spied their target. Wilkie's eyes tracked Jesse's tracers into the urban maze. The bullets careened into a shadowy street, but Wilkie still couldn't spot anything military-looking. He lifted his finger from the gun trigger.

The Corsairs plummeted through 6,000 feet, then 5,000, then 4,000. Wilkie hovered his thumb over the bomb release button. Jesse's words were still fresh in his mind: "Just drop when I drop and you'll get through just fine." As the city came into focus, Wilkie's eyes flashed with horror. Just above his aim point he spotted a walled compound. Within the walls, civilians were scattering. Small civilians.

Children.

"Oh, shit!" Wilkie muttered. Down to 3,500 feet, 3,000 feet. The compound resembled a school—and it lay just a few streets above his aim point, in his flight path, not in Jesse's. Wilkie began breathing heavily. His mask squeezed his cheeks. If his aim was off, he'd hit the school.

From the corner of his eye, Wilkie saw a green blur fall from the belly of Jesse's plane as his bomb released. Jesse pulled up, but Wilkie kept diving. The bomb-ravaged city swelled in his windscreen, yet the rubble still obscured the cannons. Wilkie could see the children clearly. Some were scattering—some looked frozen in their tracks.

Wilkie shifted his thumb away from the bomb release button and hauled back on the control stick. With the bomb still slung tight, the Corsair swooped from its dive so low it rattled the roof tiles.

Ka-boom!

Several streets behind Wilkie's tail, Jesse's bomb exploded. A split second later, Wilkie ripped over the school and saw the Korean children looking up, unharmed. Wilkie tore his oxygen mask from his face and breathed deeply. He checked his rearview mirror. Gray smoke rose from Jesse's bomb blast: He had placed his bomb precisely.

Wilkie raised his gear and throttled forward to catch up to Jesse, who was darting toward the river. Spurts of green tracers tracked Jesse's tail and soared over Wilkie's canopy from behind. Enemy gunners were tracking them both. Wilkie ducked his head and took the Corsair lower, almost hugging the rooftops. He could smell the burnt city below.

The tracers slackened abruptly and Wilkie lifted his head. He looked around. The enemy gunners had shifted their fire to new targets—the six Corsairs of Fighting 33 were coming down.

The bomb.

Wilkie had nearly forgotten. He reached forward and flicked a switch to deactivate the radio fuse before the bomb self-detonated. The young pilot glanced ahead of each wing as the charred enemy capital slipped beneath him. His face clenched with frustration. He couldn't dump the bomb, not with civilians living in the rubble.

The radio crackled and drew Wilkie's attention.

"Bogeys! Eleven o'clock high!" a nervous voice announced.

"Roger, I see 'em!" replied another voice.

The voices came from Skyraider pilots, high above the city.

Wilkie glanced over his right shoulder, ahead of the Skyraiders. Above the bridges, white contrails crept eastward through the sky at thirty thousand feet. There were fourteen of them, coming from Chinese airspace. Wilkie squinted. At the tip of each contrail flew a silver machine with a stubby nose, swept wings, and a bubble canopy.

MiG-15s.

Soviet jet fighters.

The MiGs were the Soviet's newest technology, built using German research captured in WWII. The MiGs had first shown up two weeks earlier, when the Chinese entered the war, and they seemed to guard the bridges. Reportedly, Chinese "volunteers" were behind the MiGs' controls, but no one really knew.

Wilkie glanced forward to his leader. Jesse was low above the river, following it south, away from the bridges. In front of him flew the skipper, his wingman, and then Tom Hudner. Wilkie shook his head in dismay. No one was in position to intercept the MiGs—it would take eight long minutes to climb to their altitude.

F9F Panthers

Wilkie glanced above. Open air stood between the MiGs and the lumbering Skyraiders. The Soviet jets were poised to attack.

Then the radio crackled: "Tally-ho! Let's take 'em, boys." Wilkie recognized the voice and broke from his gaze. Over his left shoulder he spotted new contrails coming from Korean airspace. The contrails trickled from eight blue jets with sleek noses, straight wings, and high tails.

F9F Panthers.

Navy jets from Fighting 31, the *Leyte*'s jet squadron.

Above Sinuiju, the Panthers flew head-on into the MiGs and a dogfight erupted. The jets twisted and chased one another's tails, their contrails intertwining.

Wilkie wanted to watch and cheer his shipmates on, but he had to escape the city. When the muddy water slipped beneath his wings, he broke left and followed the river. Thirty feet above the Yalu, he raced past warehouses and fisheries and leapt over fishing boats. In twenty miles, the river would dump into the Yellow Sea between Korea and China.

Wilkie glanced behind him and caught a glimpse of the dogfight—a MiG was twirling from the sky and the remaining enemy pilots were turning toward Chinese airspace, leaving the Panthers behind, unable to give chase. Wilkie's shoulders lowered with relief. The Skyraiders were nearly over the bridge, unmolested.

Jesse's Corsair gradually stretched in Wilkie's windscreen—he had slowed so that his young wingman could catch up. Wilkie nestled into formation on Jesse's right wing. Jesse glanced over at Wilkie, his eyes lowering to the bomb, still attached. Jesse's eyebrows rose with surprise. He grinned and shook his head as if to say, "What can you do?" Mechanical malfunctions were often the cause of hung bombs. Wilkie forced a tight-lipped smile—he'd explain later.

At the Yalu's mouth, the muddy river slid behind the Corsairs and the waves of the Yellow Sea assumed their place. High above, the skipper and the others were assembling.

Wilkie followed Jesse into a climb to re-form.

As he flew, Wilkie kept an eye on his altimeter needle. When the needle wound above 2,500 feet, he took a deep breath and hoped that the skipper wasn't watching. With his thumb, Wilkie mashed the bomb release button. The bomb jettisoned, fell, and splashed harmlessly into the waves. His record was intact—he hadn't killed a soul. But something felt hollow about it, after the bravery his friends had shown. Wilkie shook his head in frustration.*

At twelve thousand feet above the Yellow Sea, Tom followed the plane ahead in a leftward orbit. In another patch of sky, '33's Corsairs circled. Higher yet, the Panthers' contrails patrolled the blue.

Tom breathed steadily, having reaffixed his mask. He kept an eye on

---

* Today, the pilots who flew this mission agree that the North Korean military had intentionally placed the flak guns near populated schools and civilian centers to throw off the American raids, just as they had placed their anti-aircraft weapons across the Yalu, knowing that the Americans wouldn't risk an attack.

the distant bridge. From a distance, it resembled a prop in a toy railroad diorama. Its tiny humps spanned a river that looked spray-painted
and set against brown papier-mâché mountains.

The Corsairs had done their job—the flak cloud over Sinuiju had
thinned from black to a pale shade of gray—and now ten dark specks
could be seen motoring through it. The specks were the Skyraiders,
the navy's flying tanks.

Tom leaned forward in his seat. He had flown a Skyraider prior to
joining '32. The plane was anything but graceful—its nose seemed too
small, its canopy too forward, its body too wide—but it could pack a
punch. Each of the distant specks was carrying a thousand-pound
bomb and a two-thousand-pounder.

"Lead to flight," the Skyraider leader radioed his pilots. "Deploy
dive brakes on three—three, two, one!" Beyond the sight of Tom and
the Corsair drivers, dive brakes extended like small doors from the
Skyraiders' flanks and bellies.

The lead Skyraider peeled from formation and dived, revealing two
square wings and a body shaped like a cross. Between glances at the
plane ahead of him, Tom's anxious eyes tracked the attack. The cross
dived toward the middle of the bridge and then abruptly pulled up.
Behind it, two minuscule splashes leapt from the river.

"Near misses!" a pilot reported.

It's okay, Tom thought. *They're just getting started.*

More crosses dived and new splashes jumped from the river. The
radio crackled with disappointment.

"No-go!"

"No dice!"

"Damn close!"

A flash of light burst from the middle of the bridge and smoke billowed.

"A hit! It's a hit!" a pilot announced.

A smile cracked Tom's face. The following crosses shifted their attacks to a span closer to the Korean bank. Bombs kept falling, the river
kept splashing. A new flash burst and fresh smoke rose.

"On the money!" a pilot shouted.

Tom shook his fist.

The smoke swelled across the bridge so thickly that the last crosses bombed blindly.

One after another, the crosses ran for the Yellow Sea and slowly re-assumed the meaty shapes of Skyraiders. More specks appeared on the eastern horizon. Skyraiders from the carrier *Valley Forge* had come to pummel the other "twin," the railroad bridge. But all eyes were turned toward the highway bridge.

Behind the Skyraiders, the smoke settled. In the middle of the bridge, one hump leaned into the Yalu, shattered. Nearer to shore, another hump sat sunken on the river's bottom. The Skyraider leader radioed all *Leyte* planes: "A-1 job, boys."

Tom couldn't restrain his grin. He patted his jacket's hip pocket and felt his pipe. It was wrapped in a tobacco bag, packed with leaves, and ready to light. This time, Tom didn't need to cool his nerves—this smoke would be ceremonial. When the Corsairs and Skyraiders de-scended to approach the carrier, he and the others would remove their masks and light up pipes, cigarettes, and cigars. But that was still to come.

For now, they left the Yalu smoking.

CHAPTER 30

A CHILL IN THE NIGHT

That afternoon, after the bridge strike
Aboard the USS *Leyte*

THE AIR GROUP'S FLIGHT SURGEON PUSHED a stainless steel cart, wheels squeaking, through the *Leyte*'s dining room. Music drifted from the squawk box on the wall and officers chatted at tables. Over the squeaking wheels, the clinking of a dozen glass bottles could be heard coming from the cart. The officers' ears perked up, and their eyes followed the sounds as the flight surgeon steered toward '32's ready room.

Inside the ready room, the conversation swirled around Tom, Wilkie, Jesse, and the skipper's wingman. Their buddies pumped them with questions about the bridge strike. Word of the bridge's destruction had traveled the ship along with the news that the *Valley Forge* Skyraiders had damaged the railway bridge, too. The strike had been so successful and the ground war was so quiet that the *Valley Forge* would detach from the fleet the next day to steam home.

Tom smoked his pipe between answers and Wilkie smoked cigarettes at Jesse's side. The men were freshly showered and had donned clean uniforms. On the fringes, Cevoli and Marty eagerly followed the conversation.

Word of the mission would soon travel the world. In Japan, General MacArthur would review the strike photos, then President Truman in Washington. The carrier pilots had possibly prevented five hundred thousand Chinese troops from entering Korea and may have helped win the war. They also had just fought the Soviet Union, although only the Soviets knew it.

Soviet pilots, not Chinese pilots, had been behind the controls of the attacking MiGs, and one had been killed in the dogfight, a lieutenant named Tarshinov. On Stalin's orders, Soviet pilots had begun flying combat from China. They flew in disguise, wearing black Chinese uniforms and badges showing the face of the Chinese Communist leader, Mao Zedong. And they were forbidden from flying far beyond the Yalu, so that if a pilot were to be shot down, he would not be captured by U.N. forces. Stalin was not prepared for all-out war with the forces of democracy, but the MiGs still allowed him to fight.*

All conversations ended when the flight surgeon wheeled his cart into the ready room. Tom grinned at the sight, while other pilots gazed sadly.

"Okay, fellas, who flew today?" the flight surgeon asked. Tom, Wilkie, Jesse, and the skipper's wingman raised their hands. The skipper was away, probably typing up his report of the mission.

---

* For the remainder of the war, Soviet-flown MiGs would battle American pilots. American pilots would report seeing defeated enemy pilots in their parachutes, *sans* helmets, with red hair flowing—an unusual appearance for "Chinese" pilots. At any given moment, twenty thousand Soviet advisors, pilots, and gunners were fighting in the Korean War, mostly behind the front lines. The author interviewed a former Soviet flak gunner who was serving at the Yalu in 1953 when Dwight Eisenhower was president. The gunner admitted, "We used to say, 'Get to your guns, quick, the Eisenhowers are coming!'"

The flight surgeon slid a drawer from the cart, revealing tiny glass bottles of brandy.

The *Leyte* was a dry ship with one exception—the flight surgeon. His bottles of brandy were known as "medical rations," and he issued them to help pilots relax after combat, to protect their psychological well-being.

"I'll take a scotch," Tom said.

The flight surgeon shook his head good-naturedly and handed Tom a brandy.

"Gin and tonic?" Wilkie said, and the other pilots laughed. The flight surgeon handed Wilkie a brandy.

The flight surgeon had other squadrons to visit, and every time the pilots would jokingly place orders as if he were carting around a fully stocked bar.

The flight surgeon handed a bottle to Jesse, who quietly accepted it. A few pilots raised their eyebrows. Once the flight surgeon had departed, Jesse passed his bottle to Cevoli, who uncapped it and toasted Jesse. This was their routine.

Tom drank his brandy and felt it warm his throat. A fuzzy calm flooded his brain and he slumped down in his seat. Wilkie's face twisted as he sipped—he didn't like the taste, but drank it anyway.

A pilot turned to Tom, Wilkie, and Jesse. "It's not fair," the pilot joked. "You're going to all get medals, too!"

Tom dismissed the idea—he wasn't one for medals to begin with. Tom was the same pilot who wouldn't sew the squadron patch onto his leather jacket because it would be "showing off."

"Nah, I doubt you'll get anything," said another pilot. "The skipper doesn't believe in medals."

The circle turned quiet. It was true. After almost two months of combat, the skipper hadn't nominated anyone for an award.

"He has his reasons," Marty said.

Tom and the others turned to Marty with surprise. *Marty Goode, defending the skipper?* Tom thought.

At Cannes, everyone knew that the skipper had kept Marty from his French girlfriend and they all assumed that Marty hated the man. But

Marty had come to realize the skipper had, in a roundabout way, been protecting him. Now, in the war zone, Marty was glad that he *didn't* have a French girlfriend to worry about, halfway across the globe.

Marty leaned forward and the others leaned closer.

"I heard the skipper's kid brother was an aviator in the last one," Marty said in a hushed tone. "Story goes, the fleet was under attack off Saipan and the skipper's brother raced straight into a mess of sixteen torpedo bombers and fighters to break up the attack. That was the last they ever saw of him."

The pilots remained silent, some wondering how Marty had heard the story.

"You know what award they gave him?" Cevoli chimed in. "An air medal."*

Someone let out a whistle of disgust. An air medal or even the Distinguished Flying Cross was a paltry tribute to a kid who had given his life that way.

"So that's why the skipper won't hand out medals willy-nilly," Marty said. "The bar's set pretty high."

The pilots quickly shifted the conversation, which suited Tom just fine.

Later that night, the cabin was dark but for a single lamp that hung over the desk where Jesse was sitting. Jesse was keeping the lights low because Koenig was still sick with the flu, tossing and turning in his bunk, trying to fall asleep. Gong-like sounds echoed through the steel ceiling as steam pipes clanged. The floor hummed from the ship's four propellers.

Jesse cleared his desk of any letters and clutter. He wrote to Daisy almost nightly and told her about his missions but never admitted that the enemy had actually shot at him.

---

* The skipper's brother, Ensign Peter Neill, went missing on June 19, 1944, at the age of twenty-three. He remains classified as "missing in action" to this day.

Since Sasebo, Jesse had added to his nightly routine. He'd begun a long-distance college course in international law—but he wasn't studying. He was a subscriber to *Architectural Forum* magazine—but he wasn't reading. He opened a drawer and removed a wide pad and some pencils and rulers. He flipped the pad open.

In the center of the paper, he had begun to draw a house. Only the first floor had taken shape so far. He'd drawn a front door that led onto a porch with an awning over it. He'd penciled in windows and wooden sidings. At the top of the first floor, the house faded away to blank paper.

Jesse leaned over the desk, focused his eyes, and used the rulers to steady his pencil as he drew. He and Daisy had spent days planning the house together. They called it their "dream home."

The dream home was simple. A single story. All-American styling. Painted red, Daisy's favorite color. They had agreed to build it whenever the opportunity arose. Jesse had barely four months remaining in his active duty commitment. In March, he'd revert to the reserves and resume his studies to become an architectural engineer, who selects the building materials for an architect. Afterward, he would build the dream house. He and Daisy planned to stand on their porch and see Pam off to her prom.

That night, like others, Koenig saw Jesse sketching. Jesse smiled to himself when he drew a line perfectly. He erased vigorously if an angle wasn't perfect. He stared deep into the drawing, as if he could see the house filling with color and coming to life, as if he could see the front door swinging open and Daisy standing there.

With every passing night, Jesse sketched faster, as if the drawing were his ticket home.

Several days later

In the darkness a lantern sat on the snow. Twenty yards ahead sat another lantern—then another, and another for as far as the eye could see. The flame from each lantern flickered against the frigid night, spreading just enough light to see by.

A white shape lumbered along the path of light. *Crunch, crunch, crunch.* The shape was a man—short, stocky, and wrapped in a quilted white jacket and pants. His chin was lowered and his face was bundled by the earflaps of a winter cap. Tanned brown skin showed around his eyes.

He was a Chinese soldier. Close behind him marched his fellow soldiers in a silent, seemingly endless parade. Each soldier resembled the man ahead of him and behind him. The only difference was their weaponry—submachine guns around their necks or rifles slung over their backs or bags of grenades across their shoulders.

Beneath their feet, the Yalu River was frozen solid. The bridges that the navy had destroyed had been rendered meaningless. Under darkness, the communist troops marched across the ice and into North Korea.

A man who called himself "Feng Xi" had goaded the Chinese into the Korean War. Feng Xi was Stalin's diplomatic code name. Fully aware that the Chinese still suffered from the wounds of World War II, Stalin preyed upon their worst fears. He told the Chinese leader, Mao Zedong, that the Americans would transform Korea into a "bridgehead" by which a "future militaristic Japan" could once again invade China. To prevent this outcome, Stalin urged the Chinese to commit five or six divisions to battle in Korea. Mao pledged nine.*

The soldiers' breath hung in the subzero air. On each man's back was a backpack and bedroll and across his chest hung a bag of rice. Stubby, slipper-like canvas shoes covered his feet. The ice creaked and groaned.

---

* Stalin told Mao that if Chinese intervention led to a war between the forces of democracy and communism, "Together we will be stronger than the USA and England, while the other European capitalist states . . . do not present serious military forces. If a war is inevitable, then let it be waged now, and not in a few years when Japanese militarism will be restored as an ally of the USA."

For the average Chinese soldier, this was just another march in a lifetime of war. He had once been a rural peasant, drafted to fight the Japanese in World War II and then his countrymen from 1947 to 1949 in the Chinese Civil War. He couldn't read but was street-smart, stoic, and indifferent to pain. He had been trained to fight in close quarters — to "hug the enemy." For him, there was no honorable discharge except for crippling wounds or death.

By then, more than three hundred thousand of these soldiers had snuck into Korea, far more than the one hundred thousand that American commanders had imagined. The brass had consistently underestimated the Chinese. They'd failed to realize that the first Chinese attack had been only a test, something the Chinese called the "First Phase Offensive," a study of the Americans' weaknesses, an exchange of blood for information.

Now armed with knowledge of American tactics, thousands more fresh Chinese soldiers crossed the Yalu, their feet polishing a path on the ice. Soon, they'd join their comrades to set the largest trap in modern history.

In rugged mountain terrain, in bitter winter conditions, they would attempt to destroy all the American forces in North Korea.

Several days later, November 26, 1950

In the warm confines of the ready room, Jesse shook the dice and threw them onto the backgammon board. His eyes drifted to the strangers in the rear of the room. Cevoli sat by Jesse's side and glanced in the same direction. So did Wilkie and other pilots. No one was flying—the Leyte had departed the fleet to resupply from tender ships—and now the pilots were distracted.

At the back of the ready room, the Leyte's PR team was setting up near the curtain. A sailor erected a camera's tripod while another tested flashbulbs. A PR officer flipped through a notepad to review his interview questions. Jesse and the pilots of Fighting 32 were about to become American celebrities.

"So when's this piece gonna run?" Wilkie asked the PR officer.

"Oh, in a few weeks, I'd wager," the officer said. "It'll go coast to coast."

"That's great," Wilkie said. "I'll tell my wife to snag some copies."

Life magazine had decided to run a photo essay about Jesse. *Life* was one of America's biggest magazines, seen or read by half of all American adults in any week. The magazine simply needed some photos of Jesse and quotes by him. The Navy Department in Washington was eager to help and had relayed the request to the *Leyte*.

Everyone in '32 was thrilled for Jesse—except Jesse himself. The PR officer made small talk with Jesse to loosen him up for the photo shoot, but Jesse wasn't biting. "Isn't it too soon to be celebrating?" he asked. "Shouldn't we wait until we're out of this mess?"

The PR officer brushed off Jesse's concerns. "It's perfect, you'll be famous by the time you get home!"

Embarrassed, Jesse turned back to his game.

The "mess" that Jesse referenced had begun two days earlier. In northwestern Korea, the forces of democracy had left their defensive positions and resumed their drive to the Yalu, giving the Chinese the opportunity they had been waiting for. From the mountains, the enemy had attacked, launching the "Second Phase" of their plan. Now the U.S. 8th Army—four full divisions—was stopped in its tracks after covering just fifteen miles and South Korean divisions were disintegrating on the flanks. History was repeating itself.

The lights and camera were ready. The PR officer asked Jesse and Cevoli to pause their game and smile. They did.

Pop, flash!

The officer was unsatisfied. *Life* magazine required something better. The officer asked Jesse to wear his leather jacket, so the folks back home would know that he was an aviator. Jesse sighed and reached for his jacket.

A month earlier, after the first mission, a sailor from the PR department had interviewed Jesse for a press release. "There's nothing special about me," Jesse had said. "I'm just another pilot." In search of a better quote, the sailor had turned to Captain T. U. Sisson, the forty-nine-year-old captain of the *Leyte*. No one knew how Sisson felt about Jesse. Sisson was from an aristocratic southern family, and his father had been a congressman and a champion of segregation. But Captain Sisson had surprised any doubters by straightening the record about Jesse. "He's one of the best pilots of the air group," Sisson said.

Jesse slipped into his jacket. On one breast was a nametag: J. L. BROWN, U.S.N. On the other, Jesse wore the squadron patch: a blue disc with a golden lion and the squadron motto, DIEU ET PATRIA—"God and Country."

Cevoli wore a tent cap but Jesse didn't have a hat, so someone tossed him a ball cap. He slapped it on.

"Okay, look excited," the officer said.

Cevoli grinned and Jesse forced a smile.

Pop, flash!

The officer urged Jesse to show more animation. "Your wife will see these photos," he said, "and someday your grandkids!"

Cevoli shook Jesse by the shoulder to loosen him up. "Hey—this is good PR for the navy," he said.

"Okay, okay." Jesse scooped up the dice, shook them in his fist, and flashed a wide grin.

Pop, flash!

"Great!" the PR officer said. He flipped open his pad and began to interview Jesse. When the officer asked if there had been any prejudice aboard ship, all eyes turned toward Jesse, curious to hear his answer.

"There hasn't been one instance," Jesse said.

The officer nodded, impressed. "So what's your secret?"

Jesse thought for a second. "I never try to force myself on people. If they're going to be friendly, then they will be pretty soon."

The officer chuckled. Cevoli and the others nodded—it was true. A journalist would later read Jesse's answers and publish his conclusion: "The key to Jesse's popularity was his assumption that no race problem existed and, as a result, none did."

The PR officer closed his pad and turned to Jesse with a last request. "Can you suit up like you're going to fly?"

Jesse took a deep breath and went to retrieve his gear.

The flight deck was quiet with flight operations suspended. Here and there, mechanics used the reprieve to check their machines. The sky was calm and cold. Jesse followed the officer and cameramen across the deck. He had dressed as requested, in helmet and goggles, a green flight suit, and a yellow life vest. He wore a pistol on his side.

The officer led Jesse to a Corsair with rockets loaded on a folded wing. The cameraman asked Jesse to pretend to check the rockets. Jesse reached up to verify that the rocket was secure on its rail.

Pop, flash!

The officer directed Jesse into a Corsair cockpit and sent a deck-hand up on the wing. Jesse acted like he was strapping in.

Pop, flash!

The photo shoot wound its way up to the tower and onto a high deck at the front. With the parked Corsairs below, the photographer directed Jesse to stare ahead, into the wind. As Jesse gazed toward the horizon, he couldn't relax. His face was uneasy, his eyes tense, his mouth tight.

He tried. He knew the camera was on him. But at that moment, far beyond sight, the western half of Korea was embroiled in battle, and in the eastern half the Marines were marching deeper into the frozen mountains.

As if he sensed the peril beyond the horizon, Jesse didn't even fake a smile.

Pop, flash!

CHAPTER 31

A TASTE OF THE DIRT

A day later, November 27, 1950
Wonsan Airfield, North Korea

THROUGH THE FRIGID LATE-DAY GLOOM, a line of Corsairs taxied along the airfield by the sea. The planes wove in S-turns, their noses zigzagging as their pilots tried to see ahead. Lights glowed from their wingtips: green on the left, red on the right.

Corsair 202 bounced on its tires against the bomb-scarred taxiway. At the controls, Tom's vision jostled. To his right lay Wonsan Harbor, and to his left a chain of scrubby hills overlooked the field. Gray clouds drooped low, swollen with snow. It was nearing 4 P.M.

Tom leaned in his seat and worked the brakes to swing the Corsair's nose back and forth. Up ahead, Cevoli led the way, his rudder flapping. Fourteen more Corsairs rolled behind Tom. One by one they passed a wooden hangar, its roof and walls shattered like matchsticks. Inside sat abandoned North Korean fighter planes, former Soviet Yak-9s.

A ground crewman parked Cevoli on a patch of concrete beside a bullet-pocked control tower. Tom swung in beside Cevoli, Jesse pulled up next, and the remaining Corsairs followed.

Tom cut the engine. He leaned his helmet back against the headrest and took a deep breath. Sweaty and tired, he had never been happier to reach land. The flight had just returned from a strike in northwest Korea when a blizzard set in over the *Leyte*. Unable to land on the ship, Cevoli steered the sixteen Corsairs—eight from '32 and eight from '33—to the Marine air base at Wonsan. The pilots knew this area, having flown their first mission against islands in the harbor.

As the propeller fluttered to a stop, Tom surveyed his surroundings through the canopy. The airfield resembled a POW camp. Grimy wooden barracks stood side by side and smokestacks rose from a maintenance garage. American tents now dotted the grounds, but few men were in sight. Over the engine's hot ticking, Tom heard a popping noise in the distance. Then a crackle and more popping. He removed his helmet to be certain—it was gunfire.

A young Marine ground crewman hustled to the plane to see if Tom needed assistance. The Marine wore a hooded parka and a helmet with a camouflage cover. A carbine dangled from his shoulder. *What the heck?* Tom thought. The Marine was dressed for battle.

Tom cranked open the canopy. Cold air and the scent of the murky sea swept inside. The gunfire sounded louder now. Tom slipped a knit cap over his head and leaned outside. He traced the sounds of battle behind the plane's tail. From the hills above the field came staccato bursts of noise and tracers that arced and fizzled. Tom's eyes filled with worry. *Did we land in the wrong place?* Wonsan was supposed to be ninety miles behind the front.

"Sir, you may want to come down," the Marine shouted to Tom. "You're presenting an awfully big target!"

Tom dismounted hurriedly, careful to remain shielded by his plane.

"What's happening out there?" he asked.

"The Reds are making a play for the field," the Marine said. He explained that a contingent of North Korean guerrillas and Chinese troops were attacking and the army's 3rd Infantry Division was holding them back, but barely. Tom shot him a questioning look. The Marine was suggesting that this could be the start of a new Red offensive.

Tom dashed to Jesse's Corsair, a plane away. He found Jesse, Cevoli, Koenig, and a handful of Marines crowded around the tail. During the flight's strike on Chinese troop bivouacs, a flak burst had hit Jesse's rudder, partially stripping the fabric skin. The right side of the white letter *K* now dangled in ribbons.

"Think you can still make the deck?" Tom asked Jesse with concern. The damage could hinder a carrier landing.

"Sure," Jesse said as he tugged and tested the remaining fabric. "I made it this far without a rudder."

Marty approached the group with several pilots in tow. "Any of you fellas get shot at coming in?"

Several pilots nodded.

Cevoli told the Marines around him that if the weather didn't soon shift from the *Leyte*, the flight would need to spend the night here. The pilots glanced uneasily at one another. The temperature was falling, and many of them had already flipped up their collars against the cold.

A Marine approached the group. "Sirs, if anyone wants chow, they're serving supper early." He gestured to a green tent about a hundred yards behind the tower where infantrymen waited in line.

Marty and Cevoli said that they were hungry and a few others agreed.

"I'll stay near the tower and wait for word from the ship," Jesse said. Tom said that he was staying too. *It's a bit hairy to be wandering off,* he thought. Koenig was of the same mind. In the harbor, ships were running for open seas for fear that the Reds would sack the port.

Marty, Cevoli, and others departed for the chow line. After several paces, Cevoli turned and shouted over the distant gunfire, "If the Reds rush the field, just go!"

Tom and Jesse glanced at each other with unease.

*   *   *

The chow line was long and slow, and no one seemed worried about snipers. Outside the tent, Marty smoked to keep warm while he and the others waited with exhausted Marines and army soldiers. The infantrymen wore battered helmets. Their uniforms were soiled, their boots muddy.

The line shifted forward and Marty ducked inside the tent. A blast of warmth and a savory smell greeted him. At the end of the line, cooks in winter jackets stood behind tables that held plastic tubs. As each fighting man reached the cooks, he held out a mess tin. One cook ladled mashed potatoes inside, another drizzled gravy, and a third forked up a juicy steak and dropped it into the tin.

Marty turned to a Marine. "You fellas always eat like this? I think I joined the wrong branch!"

The Marine grinned. "No, sir, this is a treat for us, too. The cooks figure if we get overrun tonight, we're not leaving anything good for the Reds."

Marty glanced down at his feet, embarrassed at his question. He collected a plate and utensils and was about to reach the cooks when a tent flap was flung open and a Marine air traffic controller stepped inside. The controller hurried to Marty and the other pilots. "You can launch!" he said. "*Leyte* just called—they found a window in the storm!"

Marty set down his plate and tried to restrain his grin—the ground pounders were watching. "Hey, just take a steak with you!" a young soldier suggested. Marty politely declined and his face turned sheepish— he knew that a bottle of brandy, a hot shower, and a meal on china were awaiting him.

Adrenaline pumping, Marty and the others sprinted for their planes.

In the cockpit, Tom set the throttle forward and flipped switches to bring the engine to life. He pushed the starter switch forward and held it. A whine leaked from the engine and the four propeller blades began clunking counterclockwise. Tom pushed a lever to open the fuel lines.

Come on, old girl, kick over! he thought. He had never felt more eager to reach the sky.

Tom held his breath as the propeller revolved faster and faster. The engine wheezed, coughed, then caught with a roar. White smoke poured from the exhaust ports and the propeller whirled into a blurry circle. A grin cracked Tom's face. He cranked the canopy shut.

Tom glanced left and saw Cevoli's propeller cranking to life. To the right he saw Jesse, his propeller already humming. Jesse peered in Tom's direction as he watched for Cevoli to roll.

Jesse's face looked uneasy and Tom felt it too. Darkness was falling and his heart pounded to escape this place—yet he felt reluctant to be running. His Corsair and the others could help defend the field, yet they had been ordered away to safety.

A symphony of motor noise shook the frigid air—all sixteen Corsairs were ready to roll. Cevoli's plane lurched forward. He steered down the taxiway and along the harbor, his tail bouncing on its small wheel.

Tom checked his wingtips. Beyond the left wing stood the Marine who had urged him to dismount. The Marine saw Tom looking and raised a hand in farewell. Tom nodded in reply. He wanted to open the canopy and shout, "We'll be back!" But he couldn't be certain of that.

Tom released the brakes and let the Corsair roll. He swung onto the taxiway and left his fellow Americans behind, to face whatever was out there, lurking in the dark.

CHAPTER 32

WHEN THE DEER COME RUNNING

That same night, around 9 P.M.
Ninety miles north, at the Chosin Reservoir

BENEATH A FULL MOON, Red and Charlie shivered. A bitter wind howled and a lean-to "shelter half" flapped at their backs. Here in the northern reaches of Korea, it was twenty below zero.

The duo huddled together on the floor of a frozen valley, Charlie on the left, Red on the right. They wore knit hats with small brims, hoods over their hats, and helmets over their hoods. Red wrapped a T-shirt around his face, and Charlie tucked his nose beneath his parka's collar. The cold crept down their necks. The air smelled crisp and metallic.

Thirty other shelters vibrated in the field but not a soul stirred. This was the encampment for sixty Marines, a third of Weapons Company. The 188-man company had been divided into three detachments and the other two had been dispersed to support units on the hills.

Around the encampment, snow-covered hills glowed blue in the moonlight. Red and Charlie could see Marines moving up there, their bodies silhouetted against the clouds. All told, the division had sent 9,500 Marines into the valley. Now they camped on hills in every direction except to the east, where the shacks of Yudam-ni village stood near the silvery ice of the Chosin Reservoir. This land felt lifeless, even prehistoric, and led one Marine to wonder, "Maybe we'll see a saber tooth tiger or dinosaurs?"*

Red unzipped his parka and cringed as the cold raced in. He reached a gloved hand inside and yanked out a can of fruit cocktail, then hurriedly zipped back up. Red eyed the can. "Just warm enough!" he whispered.

Charlie had given Red the fruit cocktail—the prized item from his C-rations—as a birthday present. In return, Red had given Charlie a tin of cocoa, because it was Charlie's birthday too. By some twist of fate, both had been born on the same day and now Red had turned twenty-two and Charlie twenty-one.

Red pawed open the can's lid. For hours he had been warming the can near his armpit.

He lowered his T-shirt from his nose, drew his Ka-Bar knife, and speared a chunk of fruit. Red's shivering shook the blade as he raised it to his chapped lips. The fruit danced on the blade's tip. Red clenched the fruit with his teeth, careful not to touch his tongue to the frozen steel, then chewed with contentment.

He leaned closer to Charlie and offered to share.

"All yours," Charlie murmured beneath his collar.

Red knifed up another chunk and ate between glances forward at a gap between two hills. The hill on the left stood a massive 1,403 meters above sea level and was occupied by Marines, who had named it "1403." To the right, across the two-hundred-yard gap, the other hill was small and vacant.

The gap was the gateway to the northern no man's land, a place of endless mountains. Sixty miles beyond lay the Chinese border. A road

---

* "The country around Chosin was never intended for military operations," Marine general O. P. Smith would later lament. "Even Genghis Khan wouldn't tackle it."

ran through the gap, and if the enemy appeared, Red and the detachment were to serve as a roadblock. A mile behind them, the road
passed the Marines' headquarters tents in Yudam-ni.

Charlie clutched his carbine against his chest, its sling clinking as
he shivered. Red held his M1 Garand across his lap, closer than usual.
That morning, the Marines had arrived from the American staging
base at the foot of the reservoir. As they entered the valley, they ob-
served herds of deer bolting from the woods, and radio men began
picking up Chinese chatter. Then the Marines captured several Chinese deserters who confessed, "Two of our armies now surround you."

Boots crunched against the frozen grass. Red tensed and spotted a
short silhouette approaching behind the lean-tos. The figure was bundled in a long parka that stretched to his knees and was cinched at the
waist by a cartridge belt. *Who the heck would be out for a stroll in this?*
Red wondered. The figure stopped and crouched beside Red.

The cleft chin, upturned nose, and sleepy eyes of Sergeant Devans
came into view.

"You fellas staying warm?"

The twenty-one-year-old sergeant's voice quivered from the cold.
Ice encrusted his shoulders and helmet cover. He was checking on the
dozen men of his two antitank platoons.

"Jesus, Bob," Red said. "Quit playing mother hen and get to cover!"

Devans grinned. "You're drinking regularly?" His breath cast small
clouds.

"Yessir," Charlie mumbled.

Red nodded reluctantly—he hated the order to drink; he didn't feel
the urge and hated having to urinate in such cold. But the Marines
had been warned to avoid dehydration.

"No one's eating cold rations, either?" Devans asked. He didn't
want his men to become constipated.

"I've already got breakfast cooking," Charlie said and patted his
side, where he had tucked a box of rations beneath his parka.

Devans chuckled. His eyes turned serious. "It's no birthday without
a cake, fellas, so let's make up for it when we get home?"

Charlie happily agreed whereas Red simply played along; he had no illusions of seeing American soil anytime soon. Of the homesick Marines in the antitank platoons, Devans had been pining for home more than anyone, recently. Red knew why his sergeant was in a hurry to get back to Wilkes-Barre, Pennsylvania. Her name was Audrey Johns.

Devans was in love with Audrey, his former high school classmate. She was perky, like the actress Doris Day, but had black hair that curled over her ears. They had met on the sidelines of the football field, where Audrey was captain of the band majorettes and Devans carried the flag in the color guard. But Devans was shy and he waited until their senior year to ask Audrey on a date. The two had then dated until Devans shipped off to join the Marines, his lifelong dream. Even from afar, he still loved Audrey. On the ship to Korea, he had confided to a Marine from the same hometown: If he survived, he would return home in his dress blues to win Audrey back, even if that meant leaving the Corps for good.

Devans stood slowly, ice crackling on his parka. "One of you should be sleeping. The other, stay vigilant."

Red and Charlie nodded.

Devans buried his hands in his pockets and hobbled down the line to check on the others.

Red readied his knife to dip it into his fruit cocktail but stopped. His brow furrowed. "Dammit!" he said. The cocktail was frozen solid. Red chipped at the remnants, scowled, and threw the can over his shoulder.

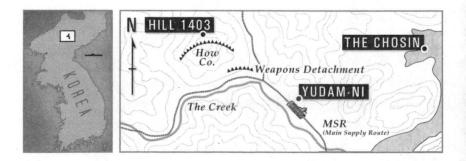

On the *Leyte*'s second day at war, Marty (far left) and others review maps in the ready room before a strike.

Captain Sisson (left) and the skipper display captured enemy flags that the skipper brought back after his emergency landing at Wonsan.

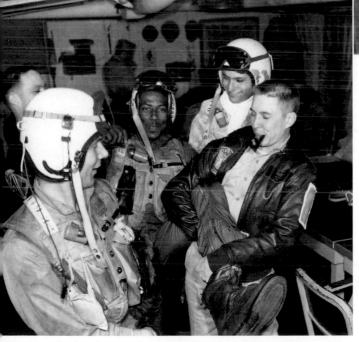

er missing his landing on the first try, Jesse had to pay the tomary fine to the squadron coffee fund. Left to right: Lee son, Jesse, Marty Goode, and Bill Koenig.

The *Leyte* and *Valley Forge* at anchor in Sasebo harbor. In the distance lies the British carrier *Unicorn*, on reprieve from operations off Korea's western coast.

Sailors and locals mix in Sasebo's Black Market Alley, also affectionately known as Robber's Row.

En route to the Chosin, the Marine column waits as its artillery pounds Hill 891.

These Chinese soldiers were captured near Hill 891. Here they wear their reversible uniforms with the brown facing outward.

A *Leyte* Skyraider returns from a mission at the time of the bridge strikes.

The *Leyte*'s "special mission" Skyraiders and Corsairs on a mission in early November.

esse as seen through a Corsair's windscreen in late November 1950.

e bridges of the Yalu. After the *te* Skyraiders' strike, smoke braces the Korean end of the hway bridge. Planes of the *Valley ge* will pummel the railway dge next.

During the November 26 photo shoot for *Life*, Dick Cevoli (left) and Jesse play backgammon.

The photo shoot took Jesse onto the flight deck . . .

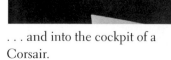

. . . and into the cockpit of a Corsair.

The *Life* photo shoot ended with this last shot of Jesse high on the *Leyte*'s tower.

After the snowstorm that forced Tom and Jesse to land at Wonsan, *Leyte* deckhands work to clear the deck.

The Chosin Reservoir at the time of the battle.

Stalin propaganda posters were prized souvenirs. This Marine liberated one from an enemy bunker near the Chosin.

Marines press onward through the Chosin's relentless cold.

Marines keep the Chinese at bay during a rare daytime firefight at the Chosin.

Marines watch the effect of air strikes against enemy troops near Koto-ri.

Nicolas Trudgian's painting *Off to the Chosin* depicts Tom's takeoff on December 3.

Gareth Hector's painting *Wingmen to the End* depicts Jesse and Tom as they support the Marines' withdrawal from Yudam-ni.

An HO3S from Charlie Ward's unit prepares to lift off from Hagaru. A wounded man's feet can be seen jutting from the open window.

Matt Hall's painting *Devotion* depicts the events of December 4.

ing the withdrawal to the port of Hungnam, iving often walked while the dead rode.

Marines of this mortar squad manage to smile during the evacuation of Koto-ri.

Marines follow the precipitous mountain trails toward the port of Hungnam. "Retreat, hell! We're not retreating," General O. P. Smith famously said. "We're just attacking in another direction."

With sailors assembled to spell the ship's name, the *Leyte* returns to San Diego in February 1951.

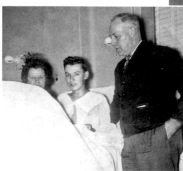

Coderre's parents visit him in a Rhode Island hospital in 1951.

In April 1951, Red Parkinson strums a guitar while on deployment in central Korea. This photo soon appeared on the cover of *Newsweek*.

Charlie lifted his face from his parka like a turtle from its shell. "Could be worse, brother John." He motioned to the left with his head.

High on Hill 1403, dark shapes climbed in the cold. They were Marines from How Company hauling the last of their unit's supplies to the crest. Red, Charlie, and their detachment were assigned to How Company as heavy weapons support. Word had it that the temperature was even lower on the hilltop.

Red shook his head and pulled his T-shirt over his mouth. "Poor mucks," he muttered.

Meanwhile, on the hillside, Ed Coderre climbed in misery. The bitter wind flung ice shards at his face. He pried each boot from the snow and lowered it with a crunch. His shoulders sagged, his gloved hands carried heavy boxes of ammo. Beneath his helmet, his breath puffed from within the sides of his hood. Up here in the open wind, it was minus thirty degrees.

Coderre crested the hill and ducked into a machine gun pit that faced no man's land. A half-circle of rocks was piled chest high and packed with snow. Coderre dropped the ammo boxes and 250 bullets jingled in each box. How Company's defenses stretched about a hundred yards across the hilltop. In the moonlight, one gun pit was visible to the left of Coderre's position, another to the right. From each, covered gun barrels aimed down a rocky slope. A fourth gun lay at the right end of the line, but a rise in the ridge hid it from view.

Coderre took a knee to catch his breath. He had just climbed Hill 1403 for the second time. As squad leader, he didn't need to carry ammo, but this was the front line and he wanted his guys at the gun, ready to fire.

In the middle of the pit, the squad's mechanical specialist, Wick, hunched over the .30-caliber machine gun. Bundled tight, he worked the weapon's bolt repeatedly, to keep it from freezing solid. At Wick's side, a six-foot-four, 250-pound Marine huddled with his arms folded, his thick neck sunk into broad shoulders. He was the squad's gunner, Tex Burnett, from Tyler, Texas.

Behind Coderre, an ammo bearer and assistant gunner stepped from the darkness and into the pit. They delivered their boxes of bullets and sank down against the wall. Along the line, men hid from the wind and the swirling snow. The neighboring gun crews were hunkered in their pits and eighty riflemen were interspersed along the line. In pairs, the riflemen lay behind piles of rocks. One man in each pair stayed awake, while the other dozed in a sleeping bag.

Coderre removed a glove and quickly pulled a pack of Lucky Strikes from his pocket, then a lighter. The cold stung his fingers, but Coderre reminded himself he'd felt this before, back in Rhode Island, when he'd watched his father battle house fires in winter. Coderre turned his back to no man's land and flicked the lighter to life. The flame stood sideways in the wind. He lit a cigarette and it glowed. A moment later, the wind whistled and the ember snuffed out.

Tex feigned admiration. "Quickest smoke I ever saw."

Coderre chuckled and stuffed the cigarette and lighter back into his pocket.

Around 10 P.M., Coderre dismissed Wick and the ammo bearer so that they could get some sleep. Wick looped his pack over his shoulders and grabbed his bag of spare gun barrels. He and the ammo bearer plodded downhill on a trail. Forty yards below the crest lay a ledge where Marines were sleeping, shielded from the wind.

Tex and the assistant gunner nestled behind the gun to take the first watch. Coderre shielded his eyes and scanned the terrain.

An outpost lay ahead and the silhouettes of two Marines were visible. Their job was to provide early warning of the enemy. Farther to the right, a fire blinked in no man's land. Its glow illuminated the silhouettes of two other Marines warming themselves. Coderre shook his head and wondered how some greenhorn officer had granted them permission to build a fire.

How Company hadn't seen a serious fight since Hill 891, and a sense of security had permeated the ranks. The men joked about watching for polar bears more than the enemy.

Coderre turned to Tex. "If the Reds hit us, don't forget about our outposts when you open fire."

Tex nodded, his teeth gritted. He didn't seem worried.

Beside a windbreak of rocks, Coderre slid the snow aside with his boots and stretched out his sleeping bag. He was twenty yards behind the gun pit, close enough to keep an eye on it throughout the night.

Coderre sat against a rock to unlace his boots. Now that he was stationary, the beads of sweat around his feet were turning to ice crystals. He began to remove the boots but stopped. *Wait till daylight*, he told himself. If he removed the boots now, they'd freeze, shrink, and take forever to put back on. Night was when the Reds often struck, when the Americans were denied the advantages of their long-range rifles and airpower.

Coderre unlaced his boots so that his feet could breathe, then slid them into his sleeping bag. The bag smelled musty. It was a mountain-grade bag, and in extreme cold it could keep a Marine from freezing to death. Coderre zipped the bag partway to allow for an easy exit and lowered his helmet over his eyes.

A scar now lined his forehead from the night that Lieutenant Reem had died by jumping on the grenade. After Coderre had rejoined the unit, he had written a statement about the lieutenant's sacrifice and submitted it so that Reem might receive a medal. But nowhere in the write-up could Coderre answer the question that tormented him: *Why? Why would a man jump on a grenade when he could have saved himself?*

The ground beneath Coderre was cold and rocky. As snow slapped his helmet, he shivered and blinked sporadically. He was afraid to close his eyes, having heard the rumor that a man's eyelids could freeze shut.

*   *   *

Thump! The wind carried the sound. Coderre pulled back his hood and listened.

Thump!

It came from the right end of the line, beyond the rise.

Coderre crawled from his bag and stood. *Am I cracking up?* With boots unlaced, he stumbled into the gun pit and found Tex and the assistant gunner beside the gun, their faces buried in their arms. "Ready the gun," Coderre whispered.

Tex and the other Marine lifted their heads. Coderre glanced to the right. In the neighboring gun pit, Marines were stirring.

Tex pulled the cover off the barrel. The assistant brushed away the snow that had accumulated on the ammo belt. Tex cranked back the bolt and released it as quietly as he could. The gun was loaded. Tex and the assistant looked at each other with confusion. Coderre moved to Tex's right and leaned over the lip of the pit. He turned an ear to no man's land and heard only the howling wind.

On the right end of the line, flashes burst behind the rise in the hill. Grenades cracked. *Chinese!* Coderre thought. He couldn't see the end of the line but knew an attack was under way.

Beyond the rise, screams pierced the frozen air. Marines were trapped in their sleeping bags, their zippers frozen by their breaths, and the Chinese were bayoneting them.

A Marine appeared on top of the rise. "They're inside the line!" he shouted, then turned back to fire his rifle.

"Son of a bitch!" Tex said, eyes transfixed. The machine gun on the right end of the line wasn't even firing.

They took the gun! Coderre thought.

Along the line, Marines squirmed from sleeping bags and tugged feet into icy boots. Some fumbled with their weapons; the bolts of their BARs and carbines had frozen. Other Marines rushed to the rise to stem the breakthrough. With their backs to Coderre, they fired down on the enemy, their rifles spitting fire in the dark.

A bugle blared from no man's land like the signal for a cavalry charge. Coderre, Tex, and others turned forward and searched the moonlit fields. Another bugle wailed the same tune. Then another and another as a dozen horns bled a haunting symphony.

A chorus of a thousand high-pitched Chinese voices arose: "*Sha! Sha! Sha!*" Kill, kill, kill! Cymbals began clanging and whistles began shrilling. The noise blended into a terrifying cacophony. Tex glanced to Coderre with wild eyes.

A deeper sound emerged from the dark distance, the pounding of countless feet on the frozen ground. Men were sprinting. Vibrations coursed through the soil and the earth seemed to shake.

Whoosh! From behind the Marines, mortar shells arced overhead, trailing red streaks. The shells popped above no man's land and turned night into an eerie shade of day. They were star shells, flares that dangled from parachutes and showered bluish light onto the earth. Coderre's eyes opened wide. "My God!" he groaned.

Two hundred yards away, Chinese troops stretched the field and stampeded toward him. Hunched over burp guns and rifles in their puffy white uniforms, they looked like thick, muscular animals. Earflaps bounced from their caps and their bodies cast short, inhuman shadows. The White Jackets poured down from the opposite hill. Coderre's voice felt choked, his feet heavy. Tex and the assistant stared with horror at the sight of three thousand enemy soldiers of the Chinese 89th Division.

The neighboring machine guns erupted to Coderre's left and right. Long streaks of flame leapt from their muzzles and red tracer bullets zipped into no man's land. Along the line, riflemen took cracks at the enemy horde. Coderre turned to Tex: "Fire!"

Tex hesitated. "What about our outposts?"

"They're already dead!" Coderre roared.

In no man's land, the outpost warming fire had vanished; the men had been bayoneted.

Tex centered his body behind the gun, braced, and squeezed the trigger. *Thump, thump, thump.* The gun fired slowly, nowhere near the usual six shots per second. Tex released the trigger and the flames vanished. He slapped the gun and cried, "Come on, you son of a bitch!"

Green enemy tracers snapped overhead from the opposite hills. The stampede was closer—a hundred and fifty yards, then a hundred, then seventy-five. Tex squeezed the trigger again, but still the gun fired sluggishly.

"It's frozen!" Coderre shouted. "Give it time!"

Tex resumed firing, rhythmically, inching the gun across his field of fire. As the gun warmed, the firing rate climbed and the ammunition belt slipped across the assistant's hands faster and faster. The gun bucked and hot tracers zipped into the onrushing stampede. Chinese soldiers clutched their wounds as bullets knocked them backward and spun them sideways. Across the Marine line, the firing tempo was building, too.

Spent shell casings amassed beneath the gun. Coderre shifted to Tex's left and opened new boxes of ammunition. He fed the belts up to the assistant, who fumbled to load them with gloved hands. *Wick!* Coderre thought. *Where the hell is he?* Coderre glanced over his shoulder but only saw rocks bathed in flashes.

The fury of the Marine line roared louder and louder. Blinding light poured from the three machine guns and the dozens of rifles. Coderre covered his ears, certain his eardrums were about to burst. Smoke floated through the frozen air carrying the burnt smell of gunpowder.

Tex stood taller as he fired, a six-foot-four target aglow in muzzle flashes. Sixty yards in front of the lines, Chinese bodies began to pile up. White Jackets leapt over their dead comrades and fired from the hip. Their bullets cracked against the gun pit, tossing bits of rock and snow. Coderre ducked but Tex remained tall. Coderre grabbed Tex's arm and pulled him low before a Chinese bullet could find him. Bodies piled up fifty yards away, then forty, then thirty.

Whoosh! From behind, a red streak arced over the Marines, then another and another. Towers of light burst in no man's land, tossing

Chinese soldiers. A cheer rose from the Marine line—the shells came from Weapons Company's 81mm mortars, back in the valley. More hot shells streaked overhead and pinned down the enemy stampede.

Coderre seized the opportunity. "Cut it out!" he shouted to Tex, making a chopping motion. Tex ceased firing. The gun barrel was glowing red—any hotter and the bullets would cook off without the trigger being pulled. "Barrel change!" Coderre shouted.

The assistant searched the floor of the pit for the spare barrels, then turned to Coderre with horror. "Wick has them!" he said.

"Dammit!" Coderre said.

Tex grabbed Coderre's arm. "When this lets up, we're in trouble!" he said, gesturing to the shells streaking overhead. If their gun was silent when the stampede resumed, the Chinese would charge them unimpeded.

Coderre unzipped his parka, reached inside, and drew one of his .45 pistols. He wore both pistols under his parka to keep them from freezing. Coderre racked a round in the chamber. "I'm going after Wick," he announced.

Alone, he set off on the trail down the hill.

With his pistol raised, Coderre rounded a rock outcropping and stepped onto the ledge where Wick and the others had camped. The ledge was shadowy, but Coderre could have sworn he saw bodies among the piles of debris.

With unlaced boots, Coderre waded cautiously through the clutter. Snow filtered from above. He stepped over empty sleeping bags and Marine boots. Coderre shook his head: If Wick and the others had escaped, they had fled in their socks.

Coderre knelt over a body. He felt a padded jacket and flipped the man over. The dead soldier was Chinese, his face misshapen from a blow to the head. Several other dead men in white jackets lay nearby. The Chinese had assaulted the ledge thinking it was How Company's command post.

On hands and knees, Coderre searched for the barrels. He shook packs abandoned by the Marines and his face lifted when he heard the gun barrels jingle. "Thank God!" he said. His eyes locked on a nearby pair of boots and his grin faded. They were likely Wick's. Whatever Wick's reason, Coderre hoped that his friend had escaped.

Coderre departed the ledge. On the trail he stopped and glanced over the moonlit valley.

At the base of the hill, the Weapons boys were firing up the road toward the gap. Behind them, the 81mm mortars were flashing and sending red-hot shells arcing up. From every hilltop in the defensive ring, red American tracers poured out and green Chinese tracers zipped in. As the streaks crisscrossed like a Christmas light show, Coderre realized that the enemy fire was coming from almost every direction. *We're surrounded*, he thought.

Coderre lowered the bag and his pistol in despair.

Commanding voices sounded from below and drew Coderre's attention. Sixty yards downhill, How Company's command post sat behind a rock cluster. Coderre heard the Marines stirring—officers organizing the defenses and sergeants shouting to round up men. If Wick had escaped, he was down there.

It's so close, Coderre thought. He could drop the barrels and run down. The Marines there would welcome him and no one would ask questions—they'd need every man to defend the command post. Sixty yards away lay his chance to survive the night.

Coderre glanced uphill at the alternative. Forty yards above stretched a vision of Armageddon. Backlit against star shells, Marines were fighting for their lives. Explosions thundered and painful screams bellowed. From their foothold on the right flank, Chinese voices screeched, "You die, Marine! You die!"

The bag of barrels grew heavy in Coderre's hand. Up there lay certain death.

But Coderre thought of Tex and the assistant gunner, glancing over their shoulders, having wagered their lives that he would return. He could envision the other Marines firing forward and rightward but never checking the man at their side because they knew he would stand his ground too. Marines had run from the hillside that night— Coderre had seen their empty boots—but none had run from the crest.

Coderre tucked the bag of barrels under his arm, raised his pistol, and began to climb. If he had to die tonight, he would try to save his friends first.

It was as simple as jumping on a grenade.

Back at the gun pit, Coderre found Tex and the assistant firing their carbines over the lip. The machine gun sat abandoned. Marine mortar shells were still falling and bursting—for now. Tex and the assistant turned. "Thank God!" Tex said. "We thought they got you!"

Coderre holstered his pistol and passed a fresh barrel to Tex, shouting, "Hurry, change 'em out!" The assistant turned the gun and slid the overheated barrel from the sleeve. Tex slid the fresh barrel into place and twisted it tight.

Coderre glanced ahead of the line and his jaw fell. Thirty yards away, a grotesque pile of quivering White Jackets stretched as far as he could see.

Tex swung the gun forward, chambered a round, and aimed across the pile.

Once by one, the towers of light stopped bursting in no man's land.

"No, no," Coderre muttered.

The star shells stopped popping and their flares fizzled to darkness. The mortar tubes were probably overheating. Only the Marines' tracers cast a red glow across the slope.

A commotion drew Coderre's attention to the right. On the rise, a Marine rifle stopped flashing. Another flash extinguished, closer to

Coderre, then another. The sounds of desperate hand-to-hand combat arose in their place. Coderre watched the wave of darkness spread toward him, snuffing muzzle flashes.

The neighboring machine gun stopped firing and its squad leader shouted an order. A Marine unlimbered the weapon and tossed its hot barrel over his shoulder. Another took the tripod. The squad retreated toward Coderre's position, some men backpedaling and firing carbines toward the rise. "The right flank is gone!" the squad leader shouted as he passed.

Coderre drew his pistol, his heartbeat thumping in his ears. In the moonlight, he spotted them—more than fifty white shapes pouring down the rise. The wave of Chinese troops spilled over the vacant gun pit and charged, their bayonets catching the moonlight.

The first white shape emerged from the dark, bayonet leveled. Coderre settled his pistol's sights on the soldier and fired. The White Jacket crumpled and slid. Coderre squinted, momentarily blinded from the muzzle flash. He blinked, picked another target, and fired. That soldier went down too. Tex and the assistant stepped to Coderre's side and emptied their carbines into the wave. White Jackets collapsed, others veered around their dead comrades. Coderre swung his pistol left and right, firing again and again. A White Jacket tumbled from the crest. Coderre pulled the trigger again—*click!* The clip was empty, all seven bullets spent. He drew his second pistol. With pistols in both hands, Coderre faced the onrushing enemy and braced himself.

A rifle cracked behind Coderre's shoulder and the nearest White Jacket flopped backward. With weapons blazing, Marine riflemen surged around Coderre. They had come from the left end of the line. From a shoulder, from a knee, they fired into the enemy ranks. Faced with a wall of fire, the wave of White Jackets crumbled and ebbed.

"Fall back to the secondary position!" a sergeant shouted. A fallback position had been chosen on the left flank, a bit downhill. Around Coderre, the riflemen lifted their weapons and retreated. Coderre nodded to Tex. The burly Marine unhooked the machine gun and passed it to the assistant. Tex then folded the tripod and slung it over his shoulder. "Go! Go! Go!" Coderre shouted and waved. His men joined the exodus.

Coderre holstered his pistols and ducked into the pit. He grabbed a box of ammo and was searching for another when new whooshing sounds descended from the moonlit clouds. Coderre glanced up and realized what was coming down—*Chinese mortars!*

Explosions burst along the line, flinging shrapnel and rocks. Tex and the others hit the deck. A shell landed outside the pit and its shock wave tossed Coderre against the pit's wall, spilling his boxes of ammo. Coderre's vision spun. The mortars abruptly stopped—their purpose was just to soften the line. Sounds of pounding feet arose from no man's land: another stampede.

Get up! Coderre told himself. He stood and cried out in pain. The backs of his thighs felt like they were on fire. He hobbled to the opening of the pit. Down the line, Tex and the others stood slowly.

Before Coderre could call for aid, Chinese faces appeared above the rocks between him and the others. White Jackets began pouring over the line. Two heavy crunches sounded behind Coderre and he glanced over his right shoulder. On top of the gun pit, a White Jacket clutched a Tommy gun and searched for a target. His eyes locked on Coderre and his face scrunched with anger. He swung the gun down toward the young Marine.

Coderre dived outside the pit as flashes erupted behind him. Bullets thudded, and one ricocheted off the rocky ground and into Coderre's left calf. Coderre felt a hot stab of pain and screamed. Before the White Jacket could correct his aim, a Marine's bullet struck him in the chest and spun him off the pit.

Coderre lifted himself from the snowy ground with his elbows. Down the line, the White Jackets were swarming the Marines. In the middle of the melee, Tex stood like a giant, swinging the tripod and bashing aside the short Chinese soldiers. In his delirium, Coderre almost smiled.

Another White Jacket leapt down from the pit and a pair of feet landed just beyond Coderre's face. Another pair of feet followed the first. The White Jackets ran toward the melee where Tex and the others were fighting for their lives. With a grunt of pain, Coderre pushed himself up to his knees and reached into his parka for a pistol.

Ting!

A clatter of tin on rock sounded behind him. Coderre knew the sound of a Chinese grenade all too well.

Crack! In a violent flash, his world turned dark.

CHAPTER 33

BACKS TO THE WALL

Meanwhile, on the valley floor

RED THREW HIS BAZOOKA OVER HIS SHOULDER, gripped his rifle, and ran from the encampment with Charlie, Devans, and the other men of the Weapons detachment. Their frozen breaths puffed and their long parkas flapped with every step. A balled-up sleeping bag bounced from each man's back.

The Marines had left everything else behind—backpacks, shelters, rations—to fall back to a secondary position. Beyond the encampment, dead Chinese soldiers lay on the road in the gap. The White Jackets had never expected the detachment's roadblock.

One hundred yards behind the encampment, the Marines reached a frozen creek that snaked across the valley. Red slid down the five-foot bank and stopped short of the iced-over water. Charlie followed, as did Devans. Trees stood above both banks. The moon shone brightly and the trees' shadows darkened the creek bed.

Above the bank, Marines handed two .30-caliber heavy machine guns down to their buddies' waiting arms. Cylindrical water jackets covered the gun barrels to aid in cooling. The Marines had replaced the water with antifreeze. Other Marines slid to the creek bed and unslung their sleeping bags.

Red carried his Super Bazooka to the creek. The weapon was useless, its sights smashed in the previous attack. Red heaved the bazooka to the opposite bank and it landed with a heavy crunch. Several Marines turned with raised eyebrows. Everyone knew that the Chinese would be back in force. "What?" Red said. "It's broken. I'm not sharing my toys if I don't have to!" The Marines broke into nervous laughter.

Red returned to the bank, where a battle line had formed. The sixty Marines were spread across ninety yards, everyone crouching low. On the far right, the road ran past the creek toward the Marine headquarters. Devans called his platoons together. The twelve men moved low and gathered around. "Okay, let's hope they didn't see us regroup," Devans said in a hush. "This is the end of the line. If they get past us and take HQ, the whole valley may fall."

Oh, great, Red thought. Nearly 9,500 Marines were relying on them.

Devans instructed the platoons to each place a man on watch and for everyone else to remain silent and hidden until the enemy returned. His men glanced nervously at one another and Devans noticed.

"Remember, fellas," he said, glancing around the circle. "We're Marines. If we stick together, we can't be beaten." Red and the others nodded and straightened up a bit.

Before Devans could depart, Charlie grabbed his arm. "Sarge, I left my rocket launcher out there." He gestured to the encampment. "Can I go get it quick?" Devans looked down and shook his head in disbelief. "I thought one of the other fellas had it," Charlie added.

Red scoffed.

"You're not going out there, Charlie," Devans said. "Too risky."

Charlie nodded reluctantly.

Red crawled to the lip of the bank to take first watch. One hundred yards away in the field, the wind flapped the abandoned lean-tos. Gunfire still crackled around the valley. On 1403, sporadic explosions revealed ghostly figures darting across the crest. They were likely Chinese, although Red couldn't be certain—at last report How Company was clinging to the left side of the slope. Behind the other hilltops, green and red lights danced like auroras.

Red raised his T-shirt over his nose and tucked his rifle close. For now, all he could do was watch.

Four hours later, the snow was falling and filtering down through the trees to the creek bed. Huddled between Charlie and Devans, Red watched the snow settle onto the ice. The Marines called the particles "diamond dust" because they were so fine. At his side, Charlie dozed, and Devans struggled to keep his eyelids open. Snow collected on their shoulders and helmet covers. Along the lip of the bank, fifteen Marines remained on watch, their chins tucked from the wind. Hill 1403 had turned quiet.

One of the Marines above suddenly raised his head. He whispered to the man next to him. Another Marine perked up, then another. Red's eyebrows lifted. The men sank quietly from the lip and began shaking their buddies. Up and down the line, Marines reached for rifles. Devans rose to a knee. Red nudged Charlie.

"What did I miss?" Charlie muttered.

In a crouch, a tall Marine hustled down the line from the right. He gripped his rifle with one hand at the midpoint as if he were stalking a deer. His face was tight and tough; his black hair was gray on the sides. He was Gunnery Sergeant Alvin Sawyer from the backwoods of Kentucky. The gunny was forty-eight years old and a WWII veteran.

At each cluster of men, he whispered in a thick Kentuckian accent, "They're a-comin'! Stay low!" Weapons Company's officers had deployed to the hills with the other detachments, leaving the gunny in charge. The gunny stopped at Devans. "Bob, keep your boys down," he whispered. "Post weapons and fire on my call."

"Yessir," Devans said as the gunny moved on. Red and Charlie glanced nervously at each other.

Gunny Sawyer

"Post weapons"—the Marines whispered the command from one man to the next and began creeping up the bank. Red lowered his M1 over the lip. To his left, Charlie and Devans steadied their carbines. Two machine gun squads laid their machine guns onto tripods and took aim. All eyes settled on the encampment. Through the falling snow, only the lower half of the lean-tos were visible.

Red's eyes went wide. Black canvas shoes slowly stalked the encampment, crunching the diamond dust. About a hundred White Jackets were circling the lean-tos—Red could see their padded pants lashed at the ankles. Metal clinked from their slings. Red shrank lower against the earth. Charlie's teeth chattered faster.

A whistle pierced the night.

In a frenzy, the White Jackets charged the encampment. Flashes blinked through the falling snow as the Chinese sprayed burp guns into the lean-tos. Others bayoneted the canvas shelters. More legs and feet rushed into the encampment, another hundred White Jackets. The enemy stomped fallen lean-tos, eager to kill sleeping Marines.

The White Jackets lifted the fallen shelters and chattered with surprise. The Marines weren't there. Some of them began ransacking the Marines' backpacks.

"My bazooka!" Charlie whispered. Red shook his head in exasperation. Other Marines gritted their teeth and hoped that the enemy wouldn't steal their war loot. Many had liberated propaganda posters of Stalin from North Korean bunkers and public buildings.

Up the line, the gunny turned to his radio man and the radio man whispered into a field phone. On the other end of the line was Weapons Company's 81mm mortars, located behind the creek.

Thump. Thump. Thump. Shells leapt from Marine mortars with hollow-sounding puffs and rocketed over the creek, trailing sparks in the frigid air.

A Chinese officer looked up and screeched an order. His men turned outward and raised their weapons. Red could feel their eyes searching for him.

"Don't look!" Devans hissed. Red scrunched his eyes tight.

The star shells popped in blinding flashes over the encampment. Red slowly opened his eyes. Bluish-white light beamed down, revealing two hundred White Jackets, all momentarily blinded. Around them, the falling snow sparkled.

"Fire!" the gunny bellowed.

Flames leapt from the Marine line. Red lowered his face to his rifle and took aim but couldn't pull the trigger. His eyes welled with alarm. He lifted his face from the stock and glanced at his trigger finger. His finger wouldn't curl. *It's frozen stiff!* he thought. Beside him, Charlie flexed his hand, stricken with the same problem. Red figured out another way. He took aim and jerked the trigger back with an outstretched finger. The M1 cracked and spit flame. Red jerked the trigger again and again.

The two Marine machine guns raked the encampment. White Jackets fired blindly, then fell, dropping their weapons. Bullets punched enemy troops backward over lean-tos. Tracers thudded dead bodies and sizzled. Red and others slowed their firing to watch. A group of White Jackets dived for cover behind lean-tos, but tracers followed them and zipped through the fabric, leaving smoking holes.

Charlie elbowed Red and glanced to the right. Up the line, a machine gunner was singing between bursts—"If I knew you were coming I'd've baked a cake!" He stopped to fire a burst. "Baked a cake!" He fired again. "Baked a cake!" Red grinned—he knew the tune, singer Eileen Barton's *Billboard* hit.

"Cease fire!" the gunny shouted. After a few long seconds, the Marine line turned black and silent. Red shook the ringing from his ears.

Star shells swayed and revealed mounds of dead Chinese soldiers. Rifle barrels jutted haphazardly from the mounds, like garden stakes after a storm. Moans arose from the withering wounded. Some chanted prayers. One by one, they went silent.

Red and the others listened and stared as the last light fizzled.

A half-hour later, the moon was gone and the snow blew thicker as Red placed clips of bullets on the lip of the bank. Other Marines stacked grenades and checked their weapons.

Beside the creek, several young Marines tugged bullets from rifle clips and reinserted the bullets in machine gun belts. The gunny had pulled the youngest men from the line to help the machine gunners, who were running low on ammo.

Down the line to the left, Devans moved between Marines, collecting spare grenades and placing them in a bag. Hill 1403 had gone quiet. Word had come that How Company had been ordered off. Everyone in the creek bed knew it—the White Jackets could now turn their full fury against them.

Devans handed the bag of grenades to Charlie. "I need you to open up the ice on both ends of the creek," Devans said. "It'll slow them down if they try to flank us."

"Sure, Sarge," Charlie replied. "But what about noise discipline?"

"I think they know we're here," Devans said.

Charlie hustled away. Down the line he pulled a grenade and shouted, "Fire in the hole!"

Red heard the grenade clatter across the ice. An explosion followed and water splashed down. The explosions crept closer as Charlie punched more holes in the creek. He then jogged to the other end.

From up the line to the right, Gunny Sawyer snapped a command: "Fix bayonets!"

The Marines passed the order, the younger voices pitched with nerves. The sound of so many bayonets sliding and locking sent a chill down Red's spine. He slinked his bayonet from its steel sheath and clicked the cold sharp metal down onto the barrel of his rifle.

Minutes passed without a hint of the enemy. The snow kept filtering down to the creek bed like sand in an hourglass. Mesmerized, Red, Charlie, and Devans watched the diamond dust swirling in the field ahead. The encampment had long vanished in the dark.

Gunny Sawyer moved down the line, keeping low. He stopped at Devans. "Bob, I need you to send a few men out to reconnoiter." His beady eyes blinked with impatience. "Tell 'em to go far enough to catch a whiff of the enemy, then get on back there."

Devans nodded dutifully.

Once the gunny had stepped out of earshot, Red spoke up: "That's a terrible damned idea!"

Devans hesitated, almost as if he was going to nod in agreement, but instead he grabbed his carbine from the lip and brushed away the snow. He flicked the safety off.

Red raised an eyebrow. "Where do you think you're going?"

"I'm not about to order someone else out there," Devans said, shouldering his carbine. He turned to Charlie and asked, "Want to come with me—maybe find that rocket launcher of yours?"

A grin cracked Charlie's face. "Would I!"

Charlie slapped Red on the shoulder and followed Devans out into the field.

Fifteen minutes passed, maybe more. Far away in the darkness came the patter of feet, the soft sounds of two men running on the fresh snow. Devans's shout pierced the darkness: "Here they come!" Red grabbed his rifle and tugged his T-shirt down from his mouth. Up and down the line, Marines raised their rifles and double-cocked their machine guns.

In the field ahead, two forms took shape against the blowing snow. Red recognized the husky silhouette of Charlie sprinting toward the line, followed by the diminutive shape of Devans farther behind. "They're hot on our heels!" Charlie screamed.

Bugles blared in the distance. Cymbals clanged. Voices wailed, "*Sha! Sha! Sha!*" and the sounds arose of hundreds of feet pounding the frozen earth. The enemy stampede seemed to shake the icy stream behind Red.

Charlie reached the Marine line and dove forward. He rolled over the lip and down into the creek bed. His helmet rattled away, but he quickly grabbed it. Red helped him to his feet, then spun back to his position.

Red's jaw sank at the sight before him. About thirty yards from the line, Devans was running sloppily, obviously winded. He glanced over his shoulder. "They're a hundred yards out!" Devans shouted forward. "Call for illumination!" The snow spun around him.

"Okay, get back here!" Red shouted.

A Marine bellowed for illumination rounds. Charlie took his place at Red's side, panting. "Come on, Sarge!" Charlie said, his voice shaking. A chorus of Marines' voices urged Devans onward. Devans was slipping and stumbling between glances at the enemy behind him. "They're nearing the bivouac!" he shouted. "Hold your fire! Let them come in closer!"

"Get out of there, Bob!" Red screamed.

Devans stopped looking back and bolted for the line.

Whoosh! Whoosh! Star shells arced through the darkness and burst above the encampment, causing Red to squint. The bluish light spotlighted Devans in midstride, his carbine in one hand, the other holding down his helmet. Behind him charged a horde of White Jackets in an arrow formation, their feet stirring a cloud of snow.

Devans was fifteen yards out, then ten yards, then five. Behind him, gunfire burst from the enemy ranks. Bullets zipped through the air. Devans leaned back like a baseball player to slide into the creek bed and Red rose up to catch him.

Crack!

Devans's head snapped forward in a spray of blood. His helmet flew off, his arms fell limp, and the young sergeant tumbled over the lip and into Red's arms.

Red sank to the ground under his sergeant's weight. "No! No!" Red shouted as he cradled Devans's body. The Marine line around them came alive with fire. "Bob?" Red shook his friend. "Come on, Bob!" But Devans's eyes remained fixed. Blood poured down Red's sleeves and over his parka. "No, God, no!" Red cradled his friend tighter.

Charlie glanced with terror between Devans and the onrushing enemy. Two Marines broke from the line and pried Devans from Red's grip. Red stood and tried to resist, but Charlie held him back. Blood covered Red's parka from chest to waist. Red's eyes bulged with horror as the Marines laid the young sergeant beside the creek. Charlie turned Red back toward the bank—the cloud of enemy troops was nearly upon them.

"There's nothing you can do!" Charlie stammered. "He's with the Lord."

Red's eyes narrowed with rage at the mention of God. He grabbed Charlie and hurled him to the ground. Charlie looked up in shock, his lip quivering. Red glared at him, then turned back to his rifle. Fifty yards away, White Jackets were emerging from the cloud and falling like dominos, dropped by Marine bullets. Charlie returned to his firing position without a word.

Red lowered his sights on a White Jacket and fired. The stock slammed his shoulder. A clump of padding burst from a White Jacket's coat, and the man crumpled. Red snapped off round after round, and brass shell casings pelted the Marine next to him. Red cursed, and spit dribbled from his lips. Charlie glanced over with fearful eyes. With a *ping*, Red's rifle kicked an empty clip into the air. He quickly stuffed a fresh clip into the chamber, let the bolt slam forward, and fired again.

Dead White Jackets began overlapping in the field. Fifty yards away, other enemy soldiers stopped charging forward and took cover behind their dead. Then, over the gunfire, a Marine shouted, "They're moving left! They're flanking us!" Another Marine screamed, "Watch right, watch right!" Red glanced from side to side. Like both horns of a bull, packs of White Jackets were wrapping around the Marine line.

A cry came from the right: "They're in the line!"

Red and Charlie lifted from their sights and turned. White Jackets were splashing down the creek, slowed only by the freezing water. The enemy began stumbling to shore, their padded pants and canvas shoes drenched. Behind the line, the young Marines stopped threading ammo belts, took up their rifles, and sprinted into the soaking enemy soldiers. Charlie peeled from the bank after them. "Get back here, Charlie!" Red shouted.

A Marine bayoneted a White Jacket against the creek bed. Another jabbed his rifle butt and sent a White Jacket tumbling into the icy water. Charlie and others waded into the fracas, firing from the hip. A large black Marine named "Big Daddy" Wiggins swung his rifle like a bat, knocking White Jackets into the creek and against the bank.

A crack rang out to Red's left—a Marine snapped from the bank and fell in a spray of blood. Red looked and saw that the man's face had been partially shot off. To the right, a machine gun stopped barking. Its crew had lowered the gun to the creek bed and were pouring canteens of water into the cooling jacket—the antifreeze had evaporated. A Marine darted to the creek to refill a canteen.

The Chinese spotted the break in the Marine line. A pack of White Jackets rose up from a pile of bodies and charged. Red fired until his rifle went empty, but the enemies were too many. The White Jackets dived onto the machine gun crew and knocked their gun aside. The Marines and the enemy grunted as they grappled on the stony ground.

Red tossed his rifle aside, drew his .45 pistol, and dashed toward a White Jacket who had wrapped his hands around a Marine's neck. Red blasted the enemy soldier off the Marine. More White Jackets leapt from the bank. Red fired as they landed and sent several sprawling. He ejected an empty clip and reached to his cartridge belt for a full one.

Atop the bank, a White Jacket officer appeared, an empty burp gun hanging from his neck. He jumped onto Red's back and wrapped his arms around Red's face, clawing at his eyes. Red's helmet went flying, and he dropped his pistol. The officer bit down on Red's right ear, straight through the cartilage. Red howled and flipped the officer from his back. The officer's burp gun was flung aside and clattered on the stones.

Clutching his bleeding ear, Red staggered to face the officer. The officer leapt to his feet and drew a short sword. His earflaps framed a dark face. Red slid his knife from its sheath. The officer snarled and thrust his sword. Red sidestepped as the blade darted past his chest, then swung his knife wildly and sliced the officer at the waist, cutting across the man's stomach through his jacket and belt. The officer's pants fell to his knees. He pedaled back, entangled.

Red lowered his knife and prepared to stab when a shot rang out from behind. A bullet zipped over Red's shoulder and knocked the officer backward into the creek. The officer floated, motionless. Red wheeled and glanced up. Against the bank, a helmetless Marine held a smoking carbine. Red nodded in thanks. The helmetless Marine turned back toward the field. Beside him, the machine gun crew lifted their weapon up the bank and swung it forward.

The gunner pulled the bolt and hammered away.

Red lowered his rifle to the snow. The hot barrel sizzled and steamed. His piercing eyes scanned the field for any enemy still moving. Beneath the star shells' flickering light, dead White Jackets lay scattered before him like stepping stones into the field. After thirty furious minutes of fighting, the surviving White Jackets had slipped away from the light and into the dark. Sporadic bullets snapped the trees overhead, but the attack was over, for now.

Red turned away from the bank, his chest heaving from exertion.

Horrific sights greeted him. A gut-shot Marine wailed and thrashed while a corpsman tore through layers of winter clothing trying to inject morphine. Another boy moaned against the bank, dying from a sucking chest wound. Beside the creek, a Marine shouted and struggled with his buddies. He wanted to execute the White Jacket prisoners who squatted by the water, but his buddies stood in his way.

Red couldn't see Charlie anywhere. The wounded and dead were being collected over by the road juncture, but Red couldn't leave his post to look.

Two Marines dragged a wounded man, his arms draped over their shoulders. Red stepped toward them and glanced under the wounded man's helmet and hood.

"Charlie?"

Teeth clenched in pain, a young face shook his head: "No." His buddies carried him away.

Another hour of darkness remained, time for the enemy to attack again. Up and down the line, battered Marines returned to their positions. Red's hands shook as he placed his last clips on the bank. From what he could see, about two-thirds of the detachment—forty men— remained standing. Behind the line, a Marine drifted between motionless White Jackets and bayoneted each body to ensure that each was truly dead. A slicing sound escaped as he thrust and withdrew his bayonet, again and again.

The gunny moved down the line. At each cluster of men he exhorted, "Go down fightin'—don't let 'em take you alive." During WWII, the gunny had been a "China Marine" at the American consulate in Tientsin, where the Japanese had taken him prisoner. For four years he endured the horrors of a POW camp. The gunny paused at Red. "No surrender, son," he added. "Save the last bullet for yourself." Red nodded, his throat tightening.

Alone in the shadows, Red traced his gloved fingers over his bloody right ear. He grimaced and began to remove a glove but then stopped and reeled back in horror. He held up his gloves. Devans's blood encrusted them. Red glanced down and realized that his arms and chest were crimson, too. Furiously, he pawed at his chest to scrape away the bloody crust. He turned to the bank, scooped up handfuls of soil, and rubbed the earth along his arms like sandpaper. He scrubbed harder and harder, but the crimson remained. Mere hours before it had been his birthday, his friends by his side. Now Charlie was missing, and Devans lay with his head on the creek stones, his eyes unblinking, his future with Audrey Johns vanished with his final breath.

Tears welled in Red's eyes. His lip quivered. He covered his ears, but the wailing of the wounded and the gunfire's snapping still reached him. He felt cold; his shoulders began shaking. Tears began leaking. Red sank to his knees. He gripped the sides of his face and began to choke up. He had never prayed before, but now he tried. "God, don't let me die, not here." He glanced upward, his cheeks streaked with tears. "I just want to see the sun come up one more time, just give me another day!" Red slumped against the bank and buried his face in his arms.

The wailing, the slicing, the snapping—all sounds seemed to fade. In a blur, Marines drifted by through the shadows.

A blue glow slowly stretched across the frozen creek. The glow crept over Red, from his feet to his arms to his face. Sounds vibrated across the ice, too, mechanical coughing, gears grinding, engines surging. In the distance, at Yudam-ni, Marines were starting trucks, jeeps, and tractors to warm the engines. Hushed voices muttered. It was 6 A.M., and the sky over the reservoir was turning pink beneath dark clouds.

A hand shook Red and he opened his eyes. The dim face of a young bazooka ammo bearer came into view. "Red, we're moving out on the double," he said. Red lifted his head and blinked the sleep from his eyes. Around him, Marines were stirring. *How's this possible?* Red thought. The White Jackets should have attacked by now.

Red stood shakily. In the dim light he gazed toward the encampment. Two hundred, maybe three hundred dead White Jackets stretched like a human roadway through the fields. The cold had contorted their arms and legs.

Marines broke from the bank and fell into a column behind Gunny Sawyer. The detachment had been ordered to reinforce a unit on the west side of the valley.

One by one, the surviving bazooka men gathered around Devans's body. One spread a sleeping bag on the ground. Together, several hands lifted their sergeant onto the bag and tucked him in. Red stumbled closer to see his friend's face for the last time. *Why him?* Red thought. *Bob was a better guy than me.* A Marine slowly zippered up the bag until Devans's cleft chin, upturned nose, and shy eyes vanished.*

Red grabbed his rifle and sleeping bag and took a place flanking Devans's body. He asked the others if they'd seen Charlie. "Yup," one replied. "He was helping the wounded." The man gestured back toward the road. Red sighed with relief.

The column began moving down the creek bed, away from the road. At the end, the creek bed opened into a field.

Four of Devans's men seized the corners of the sleeping bag and stood in unison. The bag sank in the middle from Devans's weight. They had been told their dead would be retrieved later, but the bazooka men weren't about to take a chance.

In step, with weapons jostling, the Marines carried their sergeant toward the light.

The detachment double-timed their march through the open field opposite Hill 1403. As dawn stretched across the valley, the gunfire popped more slowly.

With his now-bloody T-shirt raised over his face, Red moved rearward along the procession, looking for Charlie.

* Marine John Margee was Bob Devans's close friend from his hometown. At Wonsan, Margee was detached from Weapons Company to remain behind and guard supplies. He is certain: "If Sgt. Devans had survived Chosin, he would have become one of the subsequent heroes in the Corps."

Tired eyes looked blankly back, but none belonged to Charlie Kline.

At the tail of the column, two Marines backpedaled between nervous glances at the creek. Behind the column, an eerie fog had slipped through the creek bed and over the encampment. The fog was Marine vehicle exhaust, trapped at ground level by the frigid air.

Red kept pace with the rearguard Marines and asked if they had seen Charlie.

"Yup, he stayed back." One nodded toward the creek. "Said he needed to get his rocket launcher, then he'd catch up."

Red shook his head in exasperation. "He lost it at our bivouac, not the creek. That's where he's headed!"

Red unslung his rifle and set off toward the creek. Time was of the essence—in the fog, the White Jackets would surely swoop into the abandoned positions.

Red hadn't gone far when one of the rearguard Marines grabbed him by the shoulder. "No way, Red, you're not going back there."

Red shook the man's hand away. "Charlie's going to get himself killed!"

"Should we send someone looking for you next?" the Marine said. "Then someone else after that?"

Red glanced at the thin column of Marines that was slowly leaving them behind. His face twisted. If the White Jackets attacked now, his buddies wouldn't stand a chance.

Red shouldered his rifle and followed the rearguard Marine back to the column.

Exhausted and numb, the bazooka men struggled to carry Devans. Red grabbed a fistful of the bag and relieved one of the men. With every step forward, Red felt his sergeant's 120-pound body sliding. The turn of events seemed unreal to Red. The watermelons on Crete, meeting Liz Taylor on the beach—any good memory seemed to belong to another lifetime.

Ahead of Red, a Marine glanced at Hill 1403. "Oh, Lord," he muttered, his eyes locked. More Marine helmets turned toward the hill, and the column slowed in step. Red turned, too. His eyes went wide, his jaw dropped. Of all the hills in the Marine defensive ring, only 1403 had fallen, and now the morning glow revealed its conquerors.

White Jackets filled the hilltop. They stood on the crest, visible against the dark clouds. Others squatted on the slope and gazed like wolves down on the Marine column. The column slowed to nearly a halt, and the Marines stared back, entranced. The Chinese numbered in the hundreds, maybe the thousands. Red tightened his grip on the sleeping bag and felt a surge of defiance.

Why don't you come down and finish this? he wanted to shout at the Chinese.

What are you waiting for?

CHAPTER 34

A SMOKE IN THE COLD

Meanwhile, on Hill 1403

FACE DOWN, ED CODERRE LAY MOTIONLESS at the entrance of the gun pit. From down the line came rummaging sounds. He carefully opened one crusty eye.

Where he had last seen Tex, bodies lay scattered, and White Jackets squatted around the bodies, scavenging through the pockets. Enemy soldiers shook the contents from backpacks and pried boots from dead Marines, sliding socks off of stiff blue feet. *Dirty vultures!* Coderre thought, his teeth grinding.

To his right, Coderre heard mumbling. His nose sniffed the odor of garlic. Slowly, he turned his head and saw four White Jackets squatting beside him in the gun pit.

The nearest soldier ate a ball of rice with his bare hands in the sub-zero cold. His face was round, brown, and weather-beaten, although he probably was in his early thirties. Ragged black sideburns poked out from the side flaps of his padded cap. The soldier stopped in mid-bite. His eyes shifted in Coderre's direction.

Coderre lifted his head. There was no point in playing dead now. With a grunt, he rose to his elbows. The other White Jackets lowered their rice balls and looked at him. *There goes the Red Sox,* he thought.

Coderre began to rise to his knees but stopped with a grimace. Countless needles of pain coursed through his legs. He slumped onto his right side and ran a gloved hand down the backs of his thighs. His pants were ripped and crusty with blood, his flesh studded with shrapnel. Coderre could see a bloody black hole in his left calf. Then his eyes settled on his boots. Still unlaced, they had flapped open and taken in snow. He tried to wiggle his toes but couldn't—each foot felt like a block of ice.

Coderre's eyes filled with alarm. He needed medical care, urgently. He glanced out across the valley. At Yudam-ni, the peaks of Marine tents were visible above the fog, and black smoke rose from them. In the dim light, Coderre couldn't tell if the tents' stovepipes were billowing or if the tents were on fire. *Did the Chinese take the whole valley?* he wondered.*

Coderre turned back to face the gun pit. Having finished their breakfast, the White Jackets shivered with their hands tucked inside their sleeves. Ice encrusted their shoulders and canvas shoes.

They looked to be suffering as well and there wasn't a Chinese medic in sight. Coderre was certain: Once the Chinese realized that he couldn't walk, they'd put a bullet in his head. His eyes drifted to their weapons. He noticed several Tommy guns leaning against the pit, the same type that had fired at him on Hill 891 and shot him on 1403. How the enemy had come by American guns, he had no clue.

Coderre patted his parka and blinked with surprise. Both pistols were still in their holsters. One was loaded, but he didn't reach for it.

---

* How Company veterans agree that they never lost the battle for 1403. Sgt. Jack Coleman was in a reserve platoon that rushed up the left side of the hill and fought for hours after the defenses had collapsed on the crest. He insists, "We were not pushed off by the Chinese; our unit command used poor judgment in ordering us off prematurely."

He patted lower and found what he was looking for. Coderre reached into his pocket and removed his cigarettes and lighter.

The Chinese soldiers' eyes lifted. The others looked older than the first. Deep lines ran across their faces. One motioned for the Marine to toss him the pack. Coderre scowled and pulled his cigarettes closer. The soldier looked to his comrades in disbelief.

"Don't like it? Shoot me," Coderre said. "What do I care?"

The round-faced soldier chattered to his friends, as if translating, then crept toward Coderre. He thrust his head outside the pit and glanced side to side, then looked down at Coderre and whispered, "We no shoot you."

Coderre's eyes opened wide.

"You 4th Marines?" the soldier asked.

Coderre couldn't believe his ears. "No, but I know of them," Coderre replied. The 4th Marine Regiment were the legendary "China Marines" who had guarded America's installations in China before Pearl Harbor.

"We and 4th Marines—together," the round-faced soldier said. He intertwined his fingers: "Shanghai, 1937."

Coderre forced a grin and joked, "Sorry pal, I wasn't even born then."

The round-faced soldier smiled and translated for his buddies. The others nodded.

These guys are Nationalists, Coderre concluded. Suddenly, it made sense that they had Tommy guns. The Nationalists were America's allies, the troops of the Chinese government during World War II. America had armed and fought beside them. In fall 1937, they had defended Shanghai from the Japanese while the 4th Marines—a thousand men strong—guarded the international settlement inside the city.

Another Chinese soldier entered the pit. His neck slumped forward as if his head were too heavy. He squatted between the others. "You 4th Marines?" he asked Coderre.

Coderre shook his head. "Like I told your buddy—that was before my time."

The heavy-headed soldier nodded blankly. "USMC very good," he added. His smile was big and toothy.

The round-faced soldier nodded too. The men had all probably come from the same farming village.

During his days as a grocery clerk, Coderre had followed the Chinese Civil War in the papers. The war had ended in 1949 and the Nationalists had narrowly lost to the Communists, despite receiving $2 billion in American aid. What the papers didn't report was that the Communists gave the captured Nationalists a choice: Join their army or die.*

With his teeth, Coderre pulled his glove off his right hand. The round-faced soldier watched with curiosity. Coderre shook his pack of Lucky Strikes until one cigarette jutted from the others. He held the pack out to the round-faced soldier. The soldier smiled and drew the cigarette, half-nodding, half-bowing. Coderre flicked his lighter and lit the soldier's cigarette for him. Coderre then tossed the pack and the lighter to the others.

The other soldiers hesitated. They glanced over their shoulders, in obvious fear of their officers. After all, it was the Communists who had sent them to the Chosin without cold-weather gear, air support, artillery support, or medical support. Beneath their shoes, many Chinese soldiers went barefoot; each had been issued one pair of socks, and when a man wore through them there were no replacements.

One by one, the soldiers each drew and lit a cigarette. The last soldier nodded his appreciation and tossed the pack and the lighter back to Coderre. With numb fingers, Coderre struggled to flick the lighter.

---

* The Communists put former Nationalists through months of brainwashing called "thought reform" and field trips to study punishment against "reactionaries" or enemies of the Communist revolution. According to Marine historian Patrick Roe, "A former Nationalist officer described one of these in which the class attended a 'people's court' trial of an old peasant woman—a rich peasant, and therefore a reactionary—and her subsequent stoning to death." However, the brainwashing didn't always set with the older soldiers.

Finally the flame stood. He lit a cigarette for himself and took a warm drag.

Silently, in the cold, the soldiers and the lone Marine smoked and gazed upon the valley. Coderre knew the cigarette break was only a reprieve. His new friends weren't going to kill him, but they couldn't help him either.

A soft drone arose from the southeast, above the reservoir. Coderre's eyes rose with hope — he recognized the sound from his two months in combat.

Then his face sank as he remembered on which side of the lines he was.

The drone grew louder and clearer into a mechanical buzz. The Chinese heard it too. They stood and faced the sunrise, scanning the snowy hills.

His eyes full of alarm, Coderre glanced over his shoulder at the round-faced soldier and muttered one word: "Corsairs!"

The soldier's eyes widened. He turned to his buddies and shouted. The soldiers reached for their Tommy guns, then stumbled from the pit and peeled toward no man's land. The round-faced soldier glanced back at Coderre, just once, then disappeared behind the pit. Up and down the crest, Chinese soldiers fled.

Coderre rolled over to face the valley.

A black W shape had appeared against the clouds, its wings leveled toward him. Coderre knew the silhouette by heart. He had seen a Corsair up close while playing catch in the *Leyte*'s hangar deck.

The formation spread to reveal four Corsairs flying one after the other. Their propellers whirled and rockets dangled from beneath their wings. The cigarette shook in Coderre's hand. The Corsairs were racing toward him, almost level with the hilltop.

Coderre watched the lead Corsair's wings stretch wider and wider before him. He took a deep drag and braced for the burst of gunfire.

In a flash of navy blue, the Corsair roared overhead so close Coderre

could almost touch it. He saw oil stains on its belly and could have
sworn that he could feel the engine's heat. Another snarling Corsair
ripped overhead. Then came another and another. The snow swirled
and Coderre's clothes flapped. A deep purr trailed the planes.

Over no man's land, rockets ignited from the Corsairs' wings and
swooshed to earth. Behind the gun pit, explosions cracked and plumes
of fire billowed. Coderre glanced around with surprise—he was alone.
His eyes lowered on the left end of the line, where he had last seen
How Company. His mind screamed one word: *Go!*

Coderre clawed at the earth with his gloves and crawled on his elbows, dragging his feet behind him. Rocks edged through his parka
and dug into his knees. He winced but kept clawing at the snow. At any
second, he expected to feel the punch of a bullet in the back from a
Chinese soldier who hadn't fled.

The Corsairs were looping around—Coderre heard them coming
and flattened against the cold ground. As the planes roared overhead
he glanced over his shoulder and saw the pilots' helmets and white
stars on the planes' flanks. He heard their guns popping—the Corsairs
were now strafing no man's land.

Coderre kept crawling, past the stripped Marines' bodies. Beneath
his gloves, brass bullet casings appeared and cloth bandoliers and
bloody bandages. Coderre could see the edge of the hill ahead, where
1403 fell into a ravine. *There's home plate!* Fueled by hope, he clawed
harder. Coderre reached the edge, pulled himself over, and dropped
out of sight.

Coderre tumbled down the ravine. His helmet bounced away. His
arms and legs flailed at the snow. His body flattened scrub brush. With
a thud, he smacked against level ground, his heavy clothes softening
the impact. Around him, a series of folds led to some open space between 1403 and the neighboring hill.

Coderre lay crumpled in the shadows. He could hear the Corsairs
behind the hill, bleeding their guns dry. He didn't know if they were
navy or Marines, the Ks from the *Leyte*, or someone else. It didn't matter. Whoever they were, they were beautiful.

Snow clouds were gathering overhead, but all Coderre could do was watch. His legs felt frozen, and his head felt heavy and sleepy. He wrapped his arms around his shivering chest.

Behind a fold in the earth, muffled voices arose.

Coderre cupped an ear. The voices came from the north—Chinese territory. They grew louder. Men were moving between the hills. Coderre unzipped his parka, slid his left hand inside, and gripped the loaded pistol.

The voices became clearer. The language was vulgar, salted with four-letter words. Coderre grinned and relaxed—*They're Americans!* Four soldiers came into view. They carried carbines and wore green hip-length parkas.

"Help," Coderre called weakly, his throat cold and dry. The soldiers stopped and raised their weapons. "I'm a Marine." Coderre's voice cracked. "I'm a Marine!"

The soldiers kept their distance. "What unit?" one asked.

"How Company," Coderre replied. "7th Marines."

The soldiers lowered their rifles. Cautiously, one approached while the others stood guard. He was young and wore a battered helmet without a cover and his parka was short, unlike a Marine's. *They're army!* Coderre concluded.

The soldier glanced down at Coderre with pity. "You look like hell, pal." He waved the other soldiers over.

"Yeah, can't walk, either," Coderre replied.

The other soldiers crouched around Coderre. They were tired young men of the 7th Infantry Division. One had lost his helmet and wore a small-brimmed knit cap with the flaps pulled down over his ears.

Coderre told the men to keep quiet because the Chinese were holding the hill above. "Did you fellas come to our relief?" he whispered. He had heard that a three-thousand-man army task force had been moving up the east side of the reservoir.

The soldier shook his head; his buddies' faces went grim. The soldier said their unit had been cut off and overrun. With their backs to the reservoir, the four of them had escaped across the ice to try to reach Marine lines. They'd been behind the Chinese lines all night.

"So where are we?" a soldier asked.

Coderre told them that they were still north of the Marine lines. He explained that the Marine headquarters lay two miles away at Yudam-ni, unless the Chinese had taken the village. "They may hold the entire valley for all I know," Coderre added.

"One way to find out," the soldier replied. He and a buddy lifted Coderre to his feet. Coderre winced in pain, then looped his arms over their shoulders. The men started forward and Coderre did his best to hobble.

With a soldier on point and another watching the rear, the small band crept across the valley, toward the rising smoke.

Several hours later, that afternoon

Thick belts crisscrossed Coderre's chest and lashed his arms and torso to a stretcher as hands carried him from a tent. The cold stung his neck but he couldn't reach out to adjust the blanket. Coderre squirmed and raised his head, trying to glance backward. "Get these things off me!" he shouted.

"Wish we could," a Marine stretcher bearer replied. "Doc's orders. We can't have you thrashing around."*

One Marine carried the front of the stretcher and another carried the back. Behind them, another duo of stretcher bearers carried another wounded man. Marine tents slipped past on the right and stovepipes belched black smoke from each tent. The Marines still held Yudam-ni—only Hill 1403 had been lost—but now everyone in the encampment was counting the hours till darkness and wondering: *Can we hold out another night?*

---

* To this day, Ed Coderre regrets that he never recorded the names of the army soldiers who rescued him. If any of them should read this book, Ed requests that they please get in touch with him or with the author.

Coderre glanced down at the green blanket that draped his legs and feet. The army soldiers had delivered him to safety, and when the Marine docs had cut his boots away, he had seen his toes, black and swollen. The wind fluttered a white tag pinned to Coderre's chest. A doc had scribbled something on the tag. Coderre had heard him mutter "amputation."

A helicopter descended into the valley, its blades thumping and echoing. The craft was an HO3S, dark blue with a bulbous Plexiglas nose and tricycle landing gear. The spindly craft aimed for a clearing between Yudam-ni and the reservoir, where the stretcher bearers were taking Coderre.

"You're lucky, not many fellas are getting a lift outta here," one of the stretcher bearers said.

Coderre grunted. He'd never flown before and wasn't eager to start.

Screams drew Coderre's eyes leftward. On the edge of Yudam-ni, a whitewashed pagoda had become a field hospital and a man bellowed from within. Another emergency surgery was under way, maybe a young American with a bayonet wound through his gut. In the pagoda's front yard, rows of dead Marines lay on straw, and the wounded jammed the porch, their hoods raised. Behind the building, medical orderlies dumped rifles into a pile. Coderre looked away, his eyes heavy with remorse. He was done complaining.[*]

The stretcher bearers stopped on the fringe of the clearing and waited. The helicopter lowered its tail and hovered downward. Coderre had no clue where the chopper would be taking him, but he knew he'd be flying over hostile territory. He hadn't forgotten the Christmas light show he had seen the night before.

"So we're still surrounded?" Coderre asked the stretcher bearer.

---

[*] Another Marine evacuated that day was Sgt. Jack Allen, a wireman attached to How Company. He remembers seeing wounded Marines littering the hallways of the hospital in Japan. They held their fingers outstretched and Jack was told to steer clear of them—they had severe frostbite and if someone were to brush up against them, their fingers could snap off.

The man's face twisted. "Somethin' like that."

The helicopter settled down and snow pelted Coderre's face. In a crouch, the stretcher bearers carried him to the craft. Beneath whirling rotor blades, they slid him feet-first through the helicopter's narrow fuselage until his blanket-wrapped ankles jutted out the window on the opposite side.

With his lower legs beneath the rotors and a metal bulkhead above his face, Coderre didn't thrash or gripe. He was lucky, and he knew it. In a valley where more than nine thousand Marines were facing annihilation, about a hundred would be evacuated, and he was one of them.

From upside down, Coderre caught a glimpse of the stretcher bearers sprinting away, hats in hand. Other stretcher bearers approached carrying the second wounded Marine; the underpowered helicopter could only accommodate two casualties.

Coderre felt like a rider from the Alamo, only he wasn't leaving to summon help. The Marines in Yudam-ni had radios—the world knew that the Battle of the Chosin Reservoir was raging—yet there would be no relief force, not when every friendly unit in North Korea was fighting for its life.

In this frozen land, surrounded by one hundred thousand troops of the Chinese 20th and 27th armies, the Marines were on their own. To escape the Chosin Reservoir, it would take courage and more.

They would need a miracle.

CHAPTER 35

THE LOST LEGION

Five days later, December 3, 1950
Aboard the USS *Leyte*

THE SKIPPER SPREAD A MAP on a table and the squadron crowded closer.

Tom, Jesse, and others clutched notepads and wore leather jackets and green pants. It was 7 A.M. On the other side of the canvas partition, breakfast was being served, and the smells of coffee and pancakes spilled into the ready room. The pilots of Fighting 32, however, had bigger concerns than their empty stomachs.

Tom's eyes drifted to the map, to a body of water shaped like an inkblot and the words "Chosin Reservoir." The Marines there had been surrounded for six nights and the papers back home were now comparing the fighting to the Battle of the Bulge in WWII.

"Well, gents," the skipper said, his voice buoyant, "I've got good news—the Marines made it through the night." Tom, Jesse, and the others smiled with relief.

"They're still hanging by their fingernails," the skipper added. "That's all we know."

The pilots nodded.

"Word or no word," the skipper continued, "we're not going to sit around and wait."

Tom's eyes leapt with hope. Everyone wanted to defend the Marines at Chosin, and today was '32's turn, and he was on the roster. The *Leyte* would be putting up twenty-four planes for the biggest mission since the Yalu raids—if the weather didn't spoil it. According to the morning teletype, a massive snowstorm was blanketing eastern Korea. Conditions were so bad that the four Corsairs of '32's dawn flight had already diverted to strike the west side of North Korea, far from the Chosin.

"Cevoli." The skipper turned to his second-in-command. "Your six-ship will launch for the Chosin as planned, at 0840."

Cevoli nodded with relief.

"If Cevoli gets through to the Chosin," the skipper continued, "then Fowler's four-ship will follow in the afternoon sortie."

Dad Fowler nodded begrudgingly.

"Dang it!" Wilkie muttered, and Fowler's other pilots grumbled. Their flight was scheduled to launch at 2 P.M. and everyone knew the weather could worsen by then.

The skipper rattled off map coordinates, call signs, radio channels. He reviewed the changes to the roster. "Hudner, you're with Brown today," the skipper said. Jesse glanced at Tom and gave a nod. Tom smiled. Jesse's usual wingman, Koenig, had flown a recon mission the day before and had the day off.

The skipper glanced at his notes, his brow furrowed. He had no target photos to review, no strike pattern to choreograph. The *Leyte* was sending planes to the Chosin on blind faith; the fighting had gotten that desperate. Three days earlier, a reporter had asked President Truman if he would consider using the atomic bomb to seal off the border between China and Korea. "There has always been active consideration of its use," Truman answered.

The skipper turned to Dad: "Anything to add?"

Dad glanced around the table. "You can't attack ground troops without having a lot of crap flung at you, so I'd suggest we all review the escape and evasion brief."

The pilots nodded. Escape and evasion procedures were to be followed if a pilot was shot down, and everyone knew that the odds of that were mounting. Several days earlier, the *Leyte* had lost her second pilot of the war, a photo recon pilot named William Wagner.

"Okay, you have your mission," the skipper said. He tapped the map of the Chosin.

"Get there!"

Dressed to fly, Tom set aside his helmet and sat to review the list of escape and evasion procedures. Behind him, others checked their pistols and gear.

The skipper and Dad had refreshed the procedures in November after the *Leyte* lost a Skyraider pilot named Roland Batson. Batson had been shot down during a bridge strike and had belly-landed in a cornfield behind enemy lines. Dad's flight had seen the downed pilot waving up at them but couldn't communicate with him. They couldn't tell Batson that a rescue helicopter wasn't coming, that it was already too late in the day. They couldn't coordinate where he should hide for the night.

No one had given up on Batson, however. For days, the *Leyte* sent search planes. The skipper even took off with two spare fuel tanks and circled Batson's crash site for six hours. When he saw flashes from a signal mirror he called for a helicopter, but by the time the chopper reached the area, the mirror had stopped flashing. Batson was never seen again.

Tom slid his finger down the list that explained how to signal a downed pilot:

- Pilot has been seen: Fly low over pilot, rocking wings.
- Proceed in direction indicated: Drop wheels and fly in direction in which pilot should move.
- Use the right hand orbit to indicate that a rescue will be attempted . . . a left hand orbit to indicate that no rescue attempt is possible.

Tom's eyes devoured the list, although he knew it by heart. He hadn't forgotten the skipper's reaction to Batson's loss, either. After the failed searches, a young pilot had asked the skipper, "Why didn't someone just land and pick Batson up the first time? It was just a cornfield!"*

A hush fell over the ready room. "If tomorrow or the next day you see Batson," the skipper had replied, "even if he's waving up from a field of clover—you leave him there! It's bad enough to lose one pilot. We can't lose two. And if any of you try to land and pick someone up, I'll court-martial your ass." Tom had heard the skipper's warning and so had Jesse: A downed pilot was to be left where he was.

Tom set the clipboard aside and reached for his helmet. A man could prepare only so much for the unthinkable.

Meanwhile, at the Chosin Reservoir

Flurries drifted onto the snowy hillside at the southern entrance to Yudam-ni Valley. The snowflakes settled onto the piles of rocks across the slope. They settled onto the low bunkers scattered between the rock piles. They settled onto the corpses of the dead.

A plume of breath rose from a rock pile near the center of the line. Mittens clawed up from the snowy crust, then arms pried outward, then a helmeted head popped through. With a delirious swipe, Red

---

*The young pilot had a point. A Skyraider had a baggage compartment that could accommodate passengers, and Batson could have climbed inside—or a Corsair pilot could have flown Batson out on his lap. During WWII, similar rescues had succeeded. In 1944, German flak shot down P-38 pilot Dick Willsie, who crashed in a Romanian field. Pilot Dick Andrews then landed and took aboard his friend, and the duo flew to safety in Russia.

Parkinson brushed the snow from his helmet cover and hood. In the dim light, his face was pale and dirty. His eyes were heavy with sleep. Patchy red stubble marked his face, and his nostrils and mustache were encrusted with mucus.

Red slid from his snow-covered sleeping bag, careful not to wake the young Marine who dozed beside him. The Marine was seventeen-year-old Jack Danaher, a bazooka gunner and one of about forty survivors remaining in the detachment. His back was turned to Red, his helmet draped in six inches of fresh snow. On this sixth day of the enemy's siege, every minute of sleep was precious.

Red looked up and squinted against the flurries. Stormy gray clouds stretched in every direction, so low that they swallowed some hilltops. The air smelled lifeless and acidic. Red's face sank. *Forget any air support*, he thought. He peeked above the rocks and gazed up the slope, past a clump of White Jacket corpses. The Marine battle lines lay halfway up the hill. Two hundred and fifty yards higher stood the hill's crest, a dark curvy line against the ominous clouds.

Red's eyes scanned for movement above. A Chinese regiment—more than two thousand men—had been up there the night before. But no Chinese stirred. Red's eyes lifted with hope: *Maybe they're gone?* Two days earlier, he and a tired force of three hundred Marines had attacked this hill—named 1542—but had failed to win the crest. Instead, they had been forced to hunker in here, to maintain a toehold.

Red rolled over and glanced downhill. At the base, an endless column of Marines and vehicles filled a road. The column originated to the left in Yudam-ni Valley and inched through a string of small valleys before disappearing around a bend. The column was bound for the ramshackle American base at Hagaru, fourteen miles away. Red watched the column with longing eyes. He wished he were down there; riding or walking, it didn't matter.

The column was attempting a breakout. After six days under Chinese siege, the Marines had surrendered only Hill 1403 to the enemy, but the brass had ordered them out of the valley. More Chinese armies were approaching, and the situation could only worsen.

Now towers of black smoke rose from Yudam-ni. Around the valley, Marines were descending from the hills and burning their excess food, ponchos, even their souvenir Stalin posters, before joining the column. Red eyed the smoke and scowled. *Might as well ring a dinner bell for the Chinese,* he thought.

In an attempt to deny the Chinese any leftover supplies, some officer had put everyone on 1542 in danger. The Chinese would see the smoke. They'd know the Marines were bugging out and they'd attack. On 1542, Red and the tired three hundred weren't going anywhere anytime soon. They were the gatekeepers, with orders to hold the hill and shield the column until the nine thousand surviving Marines had passed.

Red grabbed his rifle and slid out from behind his fighting position. He crawled to the right and remained behind the line. Burst cans littered the snow and frozen food oozed from open lids. Beef stew. Ham and lima beans. Fruit cocktail. The air force had kept the Marines supplied, but the cold had ruptured any canned goods. Red and his buddies were now reduced to eating crackers, frozen grape jelly, and Tootsie Rolls.

Red stopped at a pile of rocks behind the others. "Gunny?" he whispered. "Don't shoot—it's Red."

"Yeah?" came a muffled voice.

Red leaned over the rocks. Gunny Sawyer lay on his back in his bag, his helmet tipped over his face as he savored every second of sleep.

"Is it okay if I go look for Charlie?" Red asked. Charlie Kline hadn't been seen since the creek bed.

"You're wastin' your time, son," the gunny muttered. "He's dead in a ditch or being marched to a camp in Manchuria."

Red bit his lip. During every lull in the action, Red had searched for Charlie at any aid station. "God as my witness, I'll come back," Red promised.*

---

* Red credited Charlie with leading him to his newfound faith in God. After Red had escaped the creek bed, he'd cracked open his pocket Bible and written in the inside cover: "Found my Lord, Nov. 28, 1950." He still has that Bible today.

The gunny raised the lip of his helmet and studied Red's face. Others had snuck from 1542 and vanished into the column. The temptation to desert was higher than ever—rumor had it that the American base was airlifting men to Japan. The gunny lowered his helmet. "Okay, Red, I believe ya."

Red slung his rifle and crawled away.

Red ambled toward the snow-packed road at the base of 1542. On the Marines' maps, the road was labeled as the "MSR"—Main Supply Route—although supplies weren't flowing these days due to Chinese roadblocks. With every step Red's pants crinkled, and he winced. Ice lined the inside of his pant legs and chafed his skin. Like many Marines, during the depths of night, Red had taken to urinating inside his pants. It had been too frigid for anything else.

Truck engines rattled and jeeps puttered as the column crept along the MSR. On both sides of the vehicles, tired Marines slogged through grimy snow. They were the walking wounded, with arms in slings and bandages over frostbitten ears, yet each still carried a weapon. The able-bodied men were ahead of the column, fighting to clear the way.

Through the flurries, Red searched the haggard faces for Charlie's. Beneath their helmets and hoods, the Marines looked old, even if they were young in years. Dark bags hung under their eyes. Their chins were tucked against the cold and their achy bodies were bent. They rubbed grimy mittens and chewed unlit cigarettes. Their icy parkas swished.

"Wake up, you lugs!" a sergeant shouted. "You can sleep when you're dead!"

Red leaned from side to side for a better view, but the faces were caked in dirt and camouflaged by stubble. A few eyed Red's blood-stained parka blankly. Red shook his head in frustration. He wouldn't recognize Charlie if he were standing in front of him.

Trucks and jeeps rolled by, their exhaust smelling faintly in the cold. Snow lined the jeeps' canvas roofs and Marines lay on their hoods, strapped to stretchers. Red watched their worried faces slide past. A perilous journey awaited them through frozen hills teeming with Chinese. Back home, Americans had heard of these Marines who were facing annihilation in northern Korea, and now the papers had given them a title: "The Lost Legion."

Red caught a flash of crimson beneath a truck's tailgate: an icicle of blood. He glanced into the truck's bed and his eyes went wide. Wounded men lay in three levels, separated by wooden boards. Marine engineers had created the additional floors to haul nearly seventeen hundred casualties. *Charlie could be in any of these trucks*, Red thought.

Horns honked. Brakes squealed. The column stopped, then started. "Keep moving!" An officer waved the vehicles onward. "Keep moving!"

Trucks passed with stiff bundles lashed to their bumpers. Red's eyes narrowed. The bundles were blankets wrapped around something. Boots with snowy soles stuck from a bundle. Then came another truck and more bundled boots. Then another.

Red's jaw quivered. *They're dead Marines.* He felt the urge to remove his helmet and thought of Devans. Red and the bazooka platoons had delivered their sergeant's body to headquarters but had received no assurances where he'd be buried—or *if*.

The Marines had suffered more than four hundred men killed in Yudam-ni and were bringing out all they could.

Red backpedaled from the road—he had seen enough. Such horrors had become commonplace across North Korea. In the west, the army and forces of democracy were also withdrawing, but no one was calling it a "retreat"—they were simply fighting back the way they had come.

Red paused at the roadside as the parade of men and vehicles rolled along.

Gunny's right, Red finally concluded. *Charlie's long gone.*

✳   ✳   ✳

Jack Danaher on the march to the Chosin

Red crawled back into his fighting position and found Jack awake and shivering. The youngster's hair was dark, and his nose was short and pointy. Red's chest heaved from the climb.

"Did you hear?" Jack's voice was high, his eyes filled with alarm.

Red shook his head.

"The entire Chinese army's comin' for us!" Jack blurted.

Red's face twisted. "Where'd you hear that crap?"

Jack said the fellows in the next hole had heard it from the men beside them. Red shook his head with a look of distaste. He expected such nonsense. Whittled by casualties, the detachment had taken on thirty shaky replacements—clerks, cooks, men from the 7th Marines band, even a handful of battered army soldiers who had escaped across the ice.

Red glanced down the line to trace the source of the rumor that had his young friend so riled. Several fighting positions over, on a rise, a Marine peered from a bunker with binoculars against his eyes. At his side another man worked a radio. They were glancing uphill. Red looked up, too.

Countless white hats now peppered the crest. Beneath each hat, a dark face glared down at the Marines. The White Jackets were awake.

The rumor bothered Red more than the sight of the enemy. He slapped Jack on the shoulder and slipped from their position.

Keeping low, Red darted to the bunker on the rise and ducked inside. The bunker, like the others on the hill, was made of dead White Jackets, stacked several high. Red was surprised to find the gunny there, crouched behind a Marine officer with binoculars. At the officer's side, a radio man clutched a map.

"What now?" The gunny looked perturbed to see Red.

"The boys are talking." Red shivered. "Is it true? The entire Chinese army's coming?"

The gunny glanced at the officer, and the officer lowered his binoculars and turned toward Red. "We don't know their numbers," the officer said, "but there's sizeable Chinese activity up and down the MSR—a whole mess of 'em."

He was implying that the Chinese were moving to attack the column. Red gulped. *Chinese attacking in daylight?* he thought. *This never happens.*

The officer swept his binoculars across the crest and past the glaring faces. He scanned a massive ridge to the left that angled down toward the road. Snow squalls drifted across its folds. If the Chinese were there, the weather was hiding them. The officer rattled off coordinates, and his radio man notated his map.

Red recognized the lingo as flyboy-speak. The officer was not just any officer, he was a forward air controller. A FAC, as men like him were called, was a Marine pilot embedded with ground units to call in air strikes. At the Chosin, the rules of engagement stipulated that any air strike within three miles of friendly troops had to be coordinated by a FAC to prevent friendly fire.

Red glanced at the stormy sky above the crest. The clouds seemed to be thickening and growing more ominous. Red's eyes welled up with concern. "Sir," he said, "do you think our flyboys will get through this weather?"

The FAC kept his eyes glued to his binoculars. "Doubtful. Even the birds are walking today."

Red glanced down, stunned. Ever since the creek bed, he'd clung to Devans's words: *If we stick together, we can't be beaten.* Red had bought into the rumors that the Marines would reach the base at Hagaru, spend the winter there, and then whip the Chinese in the spring. He glanced again at the column. The glorified wagon train was still crawling, likely destined for an ambush. Red shook his head with dismay.

Around him, the others remained quiet as snow flurries settled on their shoulders. They were the Lost Legion and they knew it.

Soon after, around 9 A.M. aboard the USS *Leyte*

With a throaty roar, Jesse's Corsair began its takeoff roll down the wooden flight deck. Behind him, a violent backdraft buffeted Tom's plane.

Tom toed the rudder pedals forward to hold the brakes. The wings shook as white smoke swirled into the open cockpit and filled Tom's nostrils with the smell of oil. On the tower to Tom's right, sailors and aviators held on to their hats.

Tom glanced past the whirling yellow-tipped propeller just in time to see Jesse's Corsair leap from the deck. All three wheels of Jesse's plane were in line with the horizon, by the book. Jesse banked rightward and climbed into a frosty blue sky where twelve Corsairs were assembling.

Tom's heartbeat raced. The forward deck was clear—he was next.

Waves slipped quickly past the carrier. The *Leyte* was steaming forward with all eight boilers burning and 150,000 horsepower churning.

Tom gave the instrument panel a last scan. *Oil pressure, normal! RPMs, steady!* The engine's pulse raced through the rudder pedals, stick, and seat. The outside air was only forty degrees, but warmth slipped through the instrument panel and warmed the cockpit.

Behind Tom's tail, a pack of Corsairs and Skyraiders sat with wings folded and propellers spinning. The noise of so many engines blended into one blasting drone. Helmeted pilots leaned from their cockpits and glanced forward. Some of their helmets were gold or white; others were navy blue with white symbols.

The deck boss hustled up to Tom's right wing. He wore goggles and a yellow shirt over a winter coat. His pants were khakis, the mark of an officer. He was known as "Fly One."

Tom's eyes lifted—*Here we go!* The collar of Tom's jacket—once black—was turning reddish at the edges with passing time and exposure to saltwater spray. Tom was becoming a veteran, even if he didn't notice it.

Fly One motioned Tom forward. Tom eased off the brakes and the Corsair's tires rolled slowly. Fly One backpedaled and stopped Tom parallel with the tower. The Corsair squealed to a halt. A drop tank and a napalm bomb shuddered beneath its belly, and eight rockets shook beneath the wings.

Tom pulled a lever and flaps lowered from the wings. He leaned from the cockpit and glanced forward. A little more than a football field away, the nose of the *Leyte*'s deck rose and fell in the waves. Sea spray leapt from the edge. Tom's eyes fixed on the right corner of the deck. He knew to aim for that spot to launch on an angle so that if his engine failed and he crashed, the thirty-eight-thousand-ton carrier wouldn't run over him.

Fly One raised a fist—*Hold brakes!* He twirled his other hand with a finger outstretched—*Rev it up!* Tom pushed the throttle forward. The Corsair's engine growled and the propeller spun faster. A steady

stream of white smoke blasted from the exhaust pipes on both sides of
the engine.

Static filled Tom's earphones. It was too hard to hear anything, so
Fly One would launch him by hand signal. From nose to tail, the
Corsair vibrated. The heavy prop blast wanted to lift the Corsair's tail,
so Tom tugged back on the stick to keep the tail glued down. His eyes
focused on Fly One's whirling hand.

Fly One glanced at the nose of the deck, gauging the sea. At the tip
of the deck, the number 32 had been painted in white. The 32 rose
and fell in the swells. Fly One needed to time his signal so that the
plane would leap from the deck as the ship was rising—otherwise the
pilot would fly straight into the waves.

The carrier nosed deeply down into a trough. Fly One snapped his
hand forward and ducked to the deck—Go! Tom released the brakes
and pushed the throttle. Furious noise filled the cockpit as 2,250 horse
power surged.

The Corsair barreled ahead, the right wing whipping over Fly One.
The fighter blasted past the tower and the onlookers. Tom pushed the
stick forward and the Corsair nosed up and onto her two front wheels.
Tom spotted the right corner of the deck and steered for it. Properly
aligned, he eased back on the stick and the plane dropped back to its
tail wheel. If a pilot tried to launch from two wheels he'd drop into the
sea from lack of lift.

The Corsair's nose blocked Tom's forward view as the deck slid past,
faster and faster. The tires rumbled across the wooden planks and the
windscreen shook. The Corsair crossed 60 miles per hour, 70, 75. The
acceleration sucked Tom back into his seat. The Corsair bounced on
her struts. The end of the deck was thirty yards away, twenty, ten. *Come
on, old girl!* Tom thought.

Blurry faces in colored skullcaps whipped past the wingtip. At 80
miles per hour, the Corsair sprinted across the number 32. *Whoosh!*
The deck slipped from beneath the tires and Tom felt his stomach lift.
Blue stretched around him and white-capped waves slid beneath his

wings. *Clunk, clunk.* The front landing gear flexed and Tom's vision turned smooth.

To build speed, Tom let the Corsair cruise with her nose high and her tail low. Thirteen feet of propeller clawed the air and wind rustled the cockpit. With his right hand firmly on the stick, Tom reached with his left and raised the landing gear lever, then the flaps. The gear sucked up—*clunk, clunk, clunk.* Tom passed the stick to his left hand and cranked the canopy shut. The cockpit turned still and the engine's hum steady.

When the speedometer needle ticked above 150 miles per hour, Tom banked to the right and pulled into a climbing turn to find Jesse.

The twenty-four *Leyte* planes climbed in formation through five thousand feet, on their way higher.

In the middle of the three squadrons, Tom peered leftward through his canopy. His eyes fixed on Jesse's wingtip. Side by side, the two planes soared upward. Just beyond Jesse's plane flew Cevoli and his wingman.

Tom held gentle backpressure on the stick. Reflections of the morning light floated across his canopy glass. Ahead, he saw ten Corsairs climbing across the sky, all '33 birds led by the *Leyte*'s air group commander. Normally, the commander oversaw all four squadrons from aboard ship, but he wasn't about to miss this mission.

As the armada punched through ten thousand feet, Tom snapped his rubber oxygen mask to his helmet. The Corsair began feeding him air and the sound of each breath filled his ears. An oxygen hose draped across his chest to the left and a radio cord dangled to the right.

At fifteen thousand feet, the planes of the lead squadron stopped climbing and lowered their noses toward the cloud-filled horizon. Cevoli's flight leveled off, too. Jesse glanced over to Tom, glad to see his wingman in place. The sun shone brightly on Jesse's plane; every rivet glimmered and every dent caught the light.

Tom's eyes snuck to his rearview mirror. Behind him, the silhouettes of two Corsairs bobbed against the morning sun. They were '32 birds, with white-tipped spinners. Beneath them motored eight Skyraiders, planes from '35, the boys who had busted the Yalu bridge.

The numb crackle of static remained in Tom's earphones. The flight was cruising under radio silence. An hour away lay the Chosin, buried somewhere beneath the clouds. Tom took in the sight of the twenty-three other planes around him. He had never seen so many white *K*s against blue tails. Beneath his mask, he grinned with pride.

Uncle Sam's fist was ready to strike.

CHAPTER 36

BURNING THE WOODS

An hour later, around 10 A.M.
On Hill 1542 at the Chosin Reservoir

FROM THE SAFETY OF HIS FIGHTING POSITION, Red gazed with concern at the MSR (Main Supply Route) down below. He braced himself for the next mortar shell to fall.

At the base of the hill, the column had stopped in its tracks. Trucks and jeeps idled; their drivers leaned out to peer around their windshields. Farther along the road, smoke rose from a burning vehicle.

Sergeants paced beside the column shouting orders and Marines took cover by the roadside.

"I saw that last one come down, I swear it," Red said. Jack nodded nervously. For fifteen minutes, Chinese mortar shells had rained down on the column. The enemy must have been short on mortars, because the shells were falling sporadically and inaccurately.

Still, a few had found their mark. A jeep was flipped over in a field, where it had run off the MSR. A truck had nosed into a ditch. Pink

trails of blood lined the snowy road where Marines had dragged their
wounded buddies to cover.

A whooshing sound fell from above. Red ducked but kept his eyes
on the column. A dark streak zipped down and slammed beside the
road. *Crack!* An orange explosion burst and a shock wave of black
smoke stretched at ground level.

Red raised his head to see if anyone had been hit. The smoke dis-
sipated and a small crater remained beside the MSR. Red shook his
head—even the near misses were trouble. As long as the shells kept
falling, the column wasn't going anywhere.

Jack elbowed Red and pointed to the left.

"It's true," the youngster muttered.

Red's eyes settled on the neighboring ridgeline and his face tightened.

In plain view, a stream of White Jackets snaked over the ridge. The
Chinese balanced rifles on their shoulders as they stumbled through
the snow. Others dragged Soviet machine guns on wheels. One Marine described the movement as resembling "picnic ants going across
a big frosted cake."

Jack clutched his rifle close. "They're flanking us," he whispered.

"No, they're headin' for the column," Red muttered. He twisted a
knob on the rear sight of his rifle to compensate for the new range—
seven hundred yards. At least the snow had stopped falling.

"You fellas seeing this?" Red shouted to the neighboring Marines.

"Yeah, we're tracking 'em," came a reply.

"I'm drawing a bead," reported another.

Red glanced around. The others had weapons aimed; all they
needed was the order to fire. But Gunny Sawyer was away, reporting to
the command post at the base of the hill.

To Red's left, two Marine replacements had hidden from sight. One
was a sergeant.

"Hey!" Red called.

The sergeant raised his eyes above cover.

"Can we fire?" Red asked.

"Are you crazy?" the sergeant said. "If you shoot, you'll stir 'em up!"

Red glanced uphill at the crest. It was true: If the Marines fired now, they'd bear the wrath of the two thousand Chinese above. Yet on the neighboring ridge, the enemy kept streaming toward the column.

Red raised his rifle and took aim. He still believed Devans's promise: *If we stick together, we can't be beaten.* Red's gloved finger tightened on the trigger.

Crack! Someone beat him to the first shot. Another rifle barked nearby, then another. Jack slapped his rifle onto the rocks and began snapping off rounds. Red blasted away too, and the smell of gunpowder filled the air. Everyone was firing—machine gunners, army soldiers, even the scared replacements. The cracking fire spread outward to the other companies.

On the neighboring ridge, White Jackets tumbled forward, their bodies stirring the snow. Near misses kicked up puffs of white. The enemy stumbled back uphill and fumbled to drag their machine guns with them.

Red glanced behind himself, hoping to see the Marine column escaping on the MSR.

"Of all the times!" he muttered.

The road had been cleared, yet the column still idled in place.

Seven miles ahead, near the front of the column, wounded Marines slid painfully from truck tailgates as bullets zinged overhead. Drivers leapt from doors; men rolled from jeeps. Bullets pinged against metal, and tires popped and hissed. Halfway through the journey, the Chinese had struck.

Marines steered their hobbling buddies away from the enemy fire. Bandaged and bleeding, the wounded men crumpled into a ditch to the left of the road, beneath a barren hill.

The column was stopped on the high ground between two valleys. The lead vehicle, a lone tank, idled, so low on ammo that its crew was

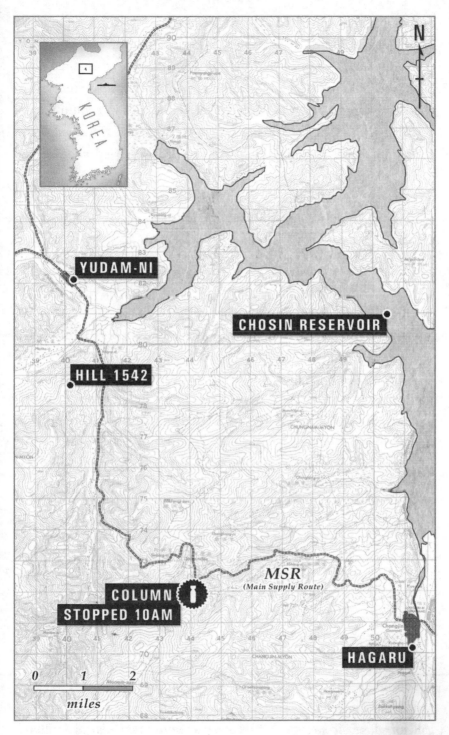

scrounging the column for more. Ahead of the tank, the empty road wound down toward a snowy valley. Behind the tank, the long train of men and vehicles dipped into another valley.

Furious enemy fire came from the right, where muzzles flashed across a snowy ridgeline. Five hundred White Jackets were up there, shielded by rocks and rises. From a patch of woods to the left, more Chinese troops poured onto the ridge. In packs, they scurried behind their firing comrades and expanded their lines.

Marines leaned defiantly from behind trucks and returned fire. Others rose from behind jeeps to launch rifle grenades. Everyone was fighting to buy time so that the able-bodied men ahead of the column could double back.

The badly wounded Marines never left their trucks. Beneath wooden ceilings they flinched and prayed as bullets raked the side rails. Shielded by a jeep, a colonel pulled his FAC officer close and told him to call for air support.

The FAC glanced at the low, stormy clouds and knew that air support was unlikely, but he snatched the radio handset anyhow. His radioman dialed in the American base at Hagaru. If any aircraft were nearby, the base's dispatcher would know.

"This is Dark Horse 14," the FAC announced himself. "We need close air support—it's damned urgent!"

He looked to the heavens and waited for a reply.

High above the clouds, frustration lined Tom's brow as he orbited behind Jesse. With his left wing tilted down, Tom scanned beyond his wingtip. Ten thousand feet below, storm clouds blanketed the earth, stretching in every direction.

Several planes ahead, Cevoli led the squadron orbit. The other two squadrons circled in separate patches of sky, everyone searching for a window to the ground. The American base had relayed the column's call for close air support but the pilots were powerless to lend aid. They hadn't glimpsed land since leaving the ship.

The storm over the Chosin seemed impenetrable. Even land-based Corsairs were turning back to their bases.

Again and again, Tom orbited, his eyes straining. He had set the radio so that he could listen to two channels at once—the Guard Channel for emergencies and the Squadron Channel to communicate with Cevoli. Both were silent.

Tom shook his head. Not a single mountain peeked through the blanket. The land below could be upstate New York in winter or San Francisco in the fog, it looked all the same. One thing was certain: A blind dive through the clouds would be suicidal over mountainous North Korea.

The radio squawked.

"Lead, I'm coming up."

Tom's eyebrows raised. The voice sounded familiar and it had transmitted over '32's Squadron Channel.

The voice spoke again. "That's Fusen Reservoir, sir. I can make out the shape."

Tom's eyes opened wide. *That sounds like Marty!* But just as quickly, Tom's brow furrowed. *It can't be.* Marty had launched at dawn with the flight sent to the other side of Korea.

"Roger that. Join up," a second voice said. That voice sounded a lot like Lieutenant Frank Cronin, the leader of the dawn flight.

Tom's face twisted. He wondered if he was somehow picking up chatter from nearly two hundred miles away. Tom checked the seal of his oxygen mask and took a deep breath. *Am I going nuts?* he wondered.

"P.A.N.! P.A.N.! P.A.N.!"

The second voice had returned, this time across the Guard Channel for all to hear. Tom tuned his ears. "P.A.N." meant: *Pay Attention Now!*

The voice announced his call sign and said, "Calling all planes, there's a break in the weather over the Chosin Reservoir—we'll hold position over the spot, just home in on us."

Beneath his mask, Tom grinned as he recognized Frank Cronin's call sign. He wasn't going nuts after all—he *had* been hearing Marty's voice earlier.

"Okay, we've got visual on you!" the air group commander radioed. He broke from orbit and steered '33's Corsairs north. Cevoli rocked his wings to tell his flight, *Form up!* Tom assembled beside Jesse. Jesse caught up to Cevoli and the trailing Corsairs tucked close. Cevoli gave chase and the Skyraiders fell in behind them.

Tom scanned the sky ahead. Far in the distance, the dawn flight orbited above the clouds. Their original target had been socked in by weather, so instead of returning to the carrier, they'd come looking for the Chosin. One by one, they dived and disappeared into the clouds.

As the armada neared the opening, Tom glanced to the left of his plane's nose. Sure enough, a small dark patch appeared like an island in the sea of clouds. The air group commander reached the patch first and led '33 in a dive through, two by two.

"Okay, boys," Cevoli radioed with excitement. "Let's go downstairs!" Cevoli winged leftward and his wingman dived beside him.

Tom was next. From almost overhead, he saw that the dark patch was actually a tube-like hole through the storm. Far below flickered the silvery ice of the Chosin Reservoir. Tom reached over to a bank of switches and flicked on the navigation lights.

Jesse glanced over, his eyes calm. He nodded to Tom, then snapped his head forward, and his Corsair peeled leftward. Tom followed him down.

Side by side, Tom and Jesse dived through the tube in the storm. Tom kept his eyes fixed on the green light that glowed in Jesse's wingtip. The cockpit turned dark around him. Nearby, Jesse's prop spun like a buzz saw.

Flurries slapped Tom's windscreen and gusts of snow slipped between the planes. Jesse's Corsair vanished, then reappeared. The green light rocked in the turbulence. Tom held his breath—the dark cloud seemed endless.

The first time Tom had flown with Jesse, he had worried that Jesse would lead him into a flock of seagulls, a ship's mast, or a low-flying Piper Cub.

But now Tom knew better. He could see Jesse's eyes fixed forward, steady and certain. Once, Tom had thought Jesse was a danger to his spotless career; now, after nearly a year together, Tom would follow him to the end of the world.

In a blur, the snowy clouds slipped behind, and Jesse and Tom pulled out into a silvery world of ice and snowy hills. Tom unsnapped his mask and let it flap to the side. A smile cracked his lips. They had found the Chosin.

The armada raced in loose formation above the ice. In the distance, wisps of white smoke rose near the foot of the reservoir. Stoves were burning at the Hagaru base and bulldozers were repairing the American defenses. Marty Goode and the dawn flight had already vanished beyond the hills.

Ahead of Tom and Jesse, Cevoli's plane began bobbing like a porpoise to signal—*Trail formation!* Cevoli's wingman dropped back and swerved behind his tail. Tom cut back on the power and slid in behind Jesse.

The radio squawked—a Marine dispatcher was calling from the base: "That was some piloting, Iroquois flight! Way to get through that ceiling."

The air group commander reported that the *Leyte* birds were ready to work.

"Good, we've got targets stacked up," the dispatcher replied. He rattled off a target and set of coordinates for each flight. Calls for help were coming in from around the reservoir.

The air group commander's four-ship left the formation first. Through his gunsight, Tom saw them peel left to pursue their target. The next four Corsairs banked right. Two more planes went left.

The dispatcher assigned the final target and Tom nodded with satisfaction. Cevoli steered the remaining planes rightward toward a gap in the hills where the icy reservoir met Yudam-ni.

* * *

Meanwhile on Hill 1542, Red hugged the slope as bullets snapped and splintered the rocks around him. At his side, Jack clutched his helmet with both hands. "Lord help us!" Red muttered. He wanted to rise and take a shot at the enemy but felt paralyzed. Spurts of green tracers zipped overhead so close that he swore he could reach up and snatch one.

Red's eyes clenched with frustration. At last glance, he had seen the crest and neighboring ridge awash in gunfire, all of it aimed toward the Marine line. Red and the others had succeeded in drawing the enemy's fury away from the column, but no one wanted to die like this.

One by one, the green tracers lifted. The spurts rose fifty feet above the Marines, then a hundred feet, then higher, as if the Chinese gunners had all drifted to sleep. Jack uncurled his hands from his helmet in surprise. Bullets stopped splintering the rocks, but gunfire still sounded.

Red raised his head and peeked uphill. The White Jackets were firing into the sky.

Whoosh!

A dark blur roared over Red and thunderous gunfire shattered the air. Red hit the dirt. Hot shell casings tumbled from above and thudded into the snow, sizzling. Casings clinked against Jack's helmet and slapped Red's back; Red shouted and squirmed in pain.

Another blur blasted over Red. He shielded his eyes and caught a glimpse of a W-shaped plane. Red hid his face as more casings rained down. He peeked in time to see a swath of orange tracers chew into the crest, tossing snow and dirt.

Another plane roared past and then another. Red buried his face in the snow and kept it planted. His arms began shaking, then his shoulders, then his entire body. Laughter slipped from his folded arms. "They're Corsairs, Jack!" Red shouted.

As the planes' purring softened, Red raised his face above the rocks. On the crest, the enemy was fleeing, their white hats dropping from sight. Against a backdrop of stormy clouds, four Corsairs were looping back around. White numbers stood out clearly on the planes' dark noses. Corsair 210 was up there, flown by Marty Goode. But it was the tails that caught Red's eye. Each sported a tall, white letter *K*.

Red and the others rose to watch the Corsairs.

"Well, that was close enough to part your hair," Jack muttered. Red laughed and shook his young friend's shoulder.

"It's the Ks!" a Marine shouted.

"They're *Leyte* birds!" added another.

At Crete, the Marines had watched these same planes fly too high and slow for their liking. But this was different. This was the best air show they had ever seen.

A rumble shook the valley behind the Marines. Red, Jack, and others whirled and glanced left as a new formation of navy planes raced over the column from Yudam-ni. The noise of fourteen engines filled the air. Corsair after Corsair thundered past at eye level, then Skyraider after Skyraider, each slung with ordnance, each wearing a white *K* on its tail, each in a hurry to free the embattled column.

Red took his rifle in his fist and raised it for the passing pilots to see. He shouted the first word that came to mind: "Hallelujah!"

Meanwhile, near the front of the column, Marines snapped off shots, then reeled back to cover behind their vehicles. They breathed heavily, beyond exhausted. The air smelled of gun smoke and diesel exhaust. Fifteen minutes had passed and no air support had come, only more White Jackets on the ridgeline.

The Marines glanced at the FAC officer behind a nearby jeep. As bullets pinged and dirt flung about, the FAC was just talking to the sky. With his handset over his mouth, the officer mumbled and looked to the dark clouds behind the column.

The Marines followed his eyes. The sky was blank.

Then a Marine lifted his helmet to hear over the gunfire. Others pried back their hoods and wounded men raised their faces from the

ditch. The sky was buzzing. Everyone glanced down the line of vehicles to the snowy valley. The buzz grew louder, then louder still.

A flight of blue planes suddenly burst into view. They peeled up
from the valley with a furious roar. There were Corsairs and Skyraiders, each with a white K on its tail. Lower than the hills, the planes
raced alongside the column. A cheer rose from the men and several
looked to the FAC. He had done it.

"No need for a dummy run, Iroquois flight!" the FAC shouted. "Enemy's in the open!"

With a rightward flick of their wings, the Skyraiders banked toward
the ridgeline. They were the flying tanks and the first target always
went to them. The Corsairs kept following the road, bound for a target
of their own. Marines had spotted Chinese troops ahead of the column, in a patch of woods, and the FAC had called it in. The enemy
were hidden beside the MSR, just waiting to spring another ambush.

Tom peered through his propeller as he raced across the snowy
landscape. Three planes ahead, Cevoli led the flight lower, almost
even with the treetops. Tom fought back a smile. He had seen the
Marines waving and knew that the Skyraiders behind him were chewing up the enemy ridgeline by now.

"We'll lead in with napalm to stir 'em out," Cevoli radioed, his voice
unusually serious.

Tom's face twisted. Napalm was the simplest fire bomb, just a spare
fuel tank filled with jellied gasoline and sealed with a white phospho-
rous detonator. Tom had dropped it on enemy buildings and vehicles
before, but never on troops.

The woods appeared ahead of Cevoli's plane, a field's length to the
right of the MSR. The tree line looked cold, brown, and deserted.

"Don't forget, the air's thin up here," Cevoli added as he barreled
in. "So keep your speed up, and climb out in a hurry!"

Tom gripped the throttle more tightly. He leaned forward and
squinted through his gunsight. His eyes widened with alarm.

White shapes began pouring from the woods. Two hundred White
Jackets raced like ants into the snowy field and formed a firing line.

Hundreds of flashes exploded—the enemy had come out for a clearer shot.

"Whoa," Tom muttered as he reeled back in his seat. "Watch it, Dick!"

Cevoli's rudder wagged furiously and his plane snaked through the air while bearing down on the Chinese. Tom held his breath—there were so many flashes. Just before Cevoli reached the enemy line, he released his napalm and climbed hard.

The egg-like napalm bomb tumbled end over end. In a bright flash, it cracked in front of the White Jackets and ignited. A three-thousand-degree wave of flame bubbled and rolled like an orange carpet over the middle of the Chinese line.

The enemy's padded uniforms burst into flames. Men fell writhing, fully engulfed, while others stumbled from the fire. Explosions crackled within the flames as the enemy's grenade pouches burst. A black cloud billowed from the boiling napalm.

At the ends of the enemy line, stunned survivors milled in circles, waiting for orders, but the bullets made the decision for them. Cevoli's wingman opened fire first. Orange bolts slanted through the frozen air and flattened men. Tufts of dirt and snow leapt as .50-caliber bullets chopped across the field. Cevoli's wingman burst over the enemy and through the black cloud, followed closely by Jesse.

Tom swooped across the field. A herd of White Jackets were sprinting for the tree line to the right, so Tom steered his glowing crosshairs onto them. Some soldiers tripped and fell, some stopped to fire up at him. Tom's eyes tightened as the woods stretched in his windscreen and rose up beside him.

He clenched the trigger. With a roar, yellow shock waves burst from his gun muzzles. His crosshairs shook as orange tracers spurted three hundred yards forward and chewed a path through the scattering troops. Bullets stirred the snow and Tom lost sight of his targets. He blasted blindly into the black wall of smoke and was momentarily swallowed. A burnt, oily smell flooded the cockpit. Tom felt a surge of heat beneath his feet and his wings rocked.

The Corsair punched out the other side. Tom hauled back on the stick and climbed through the thin air. The woods and fire sank far behind.

He released a long breath.

Over the snowy hills, Tom caught up as the flight looped back around. He wiped his nose with his sleeve. That harsh, burnt smell clung to his nostrils; he knew what he was smelling, and his face scrunched with disgust.

"Passing the lead," Cevoli radioed and broke from formation. Like a race car with a flat tire, he pulled off to the right. Tom and the others passed him on the inside.

Cevoli's wingman assumed the lead, Jesse pulled into second place, and Tom took third. Two planes later, Cevoli slid into last place. On the next attack run, his wingman would drop the napalm.

As the flight passed parallel to the woods, Tom glanced beyond his left wing. The fire from the napalm had boiled down and revealed a long scorch mark through the field where the snow had melted. The enemy were dragging their wounded beneath the trees.

"Lead, what do I do if no one's in the field?" Cevoli's wingman asked.

"Well, then dump it on the trees," came Cevoli's reply.

The flight crossed over the MSR during the final turn to target. Tom glanced beneath his wings. Below, Marines were taking cover behind vehicles and in ditches. Some lay sprawled, probably wounded, screaming, bleeding out as their buddies held them.

Tom might have known them. They might be the same boys who had thanked Jesse for the bottle of wine in Cannes, or the ones Tom had given a tour of a Corsair in the hangar deck. They might be the same ones who had tossed their love letters from the *Leyte* into the waves, to hide their mail from their mothers, to save them any shame if their sons died in battle.

And now they were dying. Tom was seeing it happen.

The Chinese had attacked a column of tired, frostbitten, wounded men intent on destroying them. Before the battle began, their general had ordered: "Kill these Marines as you would snakes in your homes!"

Tom's lip curled. The smell in his nostrils no longer bothered him.

Ahead, Jesse snapped his wings level to begin his attack. Tom could tell by the sharp, deliberate way that his friend was flying—Jesse was feeling the same way.

On the MSR below, a young black Marine and his buddies peeked from behind a jeep. The Marine was lanky and square-faced with a strong jaw. He and the others watched the Corsairs sweep over the snowy fields toward the woods, fifteen-thousand-pound machines sprinting so fast that the word NAVY was just a blur on their flanks.

The Marines shook their fists and cheered. "Come on, boys," the black Marine shouted. "Make it count!"

Popping noises resounded from the woods and flashes burst from the shadows. The enemy forces were firing through the canopy of branches at the onrushing planes.

The lead Corsair skimmed across the treetops and pulled up as a napalm egg tumbled down. The egg burst and a wave of fire spread across the canopy and showered down. The Marines on the MSR flinched and shielded their eyes. The heat wave licked their faces.

In the woods in front of them, burning napalm dripped from the treetops. Screams pierced from the shadows. Cloaked in flames, a lone enemy soldier ran from the woods and fell in the field. The Marines cringed but didn't look away.

Corsair after Corsair swooped down, six guns blazing, empty brass showering. More orange bolts zipped through the canopy. Bullets snapped branches and thudded into the trunks of trees and men. Tracers ignited flashes of leftover napalm.

A Corsair's belly almost scraped the treetops before it pulled up.

"That guy's a bachelor!" a Marine shouted. His buddies nodded. They claimed that they could tell if a pilot was married or not. The pilots who strafed longer and flew lower were bachelors; the married men supposedly played it safe.

Another Corsair strafed long and low. "There's another bachelor!" a Marine asserted.

Another Corsair pulled into a whistling climb at the very last second. "Definitely a bachelor!" a Marine said, laughing.

Finally, the sixth Corsair climbed away to re-form for another attack run.

"Thank God," a Marine said. "There's no married men flying today!"

On the high ground between snowy valleys, the exhausted Marines stood on the MSR and glanced around. The gunfire had ceased and the Skyraiders were purring off into the distance, to answer another call for air support.

Craters and scorch marks pocked the ridgeline beside the column. More than five hundred dead Chinese troops lay there, an enemy force "completely eliminated." The Marines would later give the battle a title: "The Great Slaughter."

Grunting and groaning, Marines pushed destroyed vehicles from the road. Trucks and jeeps crunched into roadside ditches. The men boosted the wounded back into trucks and the walking wounded fell into ranks. Everyone stood a little straighter. Snow-caked tires and treads began churning and the column rolled onward.

As the column passed the smoldering woods, the heat drew all eyes to the right. The woods crackled and trees shattered, showering glowing embers. Overhead, the Corsairs orbited to ensure that no enemy troops would emerge.

None did. No one ever entered the woods to count the dead, either, and Cevoli would later report the attack's results as "unobserved."

Cevoli broke from orbit and the others followed. A call had come to investigate troop activity on the eastern shore of the reservoir. Cevoli looped around, leveling his wings over the MSR. With five Corsairs following, he raced over the road, straight down the middle.

The Marines glanced over their shoulders. As the vehicles kept rolling, men stepped aside to watch. The Corsairs wagged their wings as they zipped overhead, and the Marines cheered and waved their helmets and gloved hands in reply.

The black Marine and his buddies waved as the first Corsair blasted overhead, followed by the second. A third Corsair approached, its wings wagging.

The black Marine looked up as the plane roared over him. Time seemed to slow. The plane's wing dipped toward the road and the black Marine saw the pilot, as clear as can be. A white helmet, a black face. The pilot was smiling and waving down at him.

Time seemed to accelerate. The Corsair blurred past. The black Marine wheeled in place and watched the plane race down the road.

The black Marine turned to one of his white buddies, who was still grinning and shaking his head in wonder.

"You saw him too?" the black Marine asked.

"See who?"

"That Negro pilot!"

"Really?" the white Marine replied. "I didn't know we had Negro pilots."

"I guess we do now." The black Marine smiled.

In a jeep ahead, the FAC rode in the passenger's seat and his radioman sat behind him. The FAC raised the radio handset as the Corsairs raced toward the reservoir.

"Well done, Iroquois flight," he radioed. "If we ever meet, I owe you fellas a beer!"

Farther down the road, the pilot of the last Corsair wagged his wings.

CHAPTER 37

INTO HELL TOGETHER

That night, December 3, 1950
Aboard the USS *Leyte*

CHRISTMAS MUSIC WAS PIPING throughout the cabin, a steward was dropping ice into glasses, and the flight surgeon was bringing the brandy—but Tom and the others were too tired to celebrate.

In clusters, he and a dozen squadron mates waited around a long table where the steward prepared the glasses. Tom puffed a pipe, and Jesse and Cevoli conversed somberly at his side. Their arms were folded, their voices hushed.

Tom's eyes admired his surroundings. This was the Flag Office, the admiral's dining room when he visited. The walls were pale green, the chairs white and fancy. A framed Pacific map hung on the wall. At the rear of the cabin, blackout shades covered portholes. Outside, the wind howled in the darkness, thick with flurries.

The *Leyte*'s captain had opened the cabin as a reward, a place for the pilots to enjoy a drink, and each squadron was given a turn to relax—or at least to try to.

"I just can't get it out of my mind," Jesse said. "That one guy running, all covered in fire. After everything, he bothers me the most."

Tom took a puff on his pipe. "The problem is you can't see the guys you saved today, like you can see that guy on fire."

Jesse nodded reluctantly.

"That's not the only problem with napalm," Cevoli said, lowering his glass. "From here on out, you'd better not get shot down."

Jesse's face sank, and Tom fiddled with his pipe. They knew what Cevoli was saying—a pilot couldn't drop napalm on the enemy and expect anything less than torture if he was captured. Rumor had it that helicopter pilots at the Chosin were now dressing like ground Marines so that if they were shot down they could deny that they were pilots.

Farther down the table, Dad Fowler and Wilkie burned through cigarette after cigarette, still rattled by the day's events. They had hit the Chosin, too, and returned to find a harrowing 57 mph wind racing over the flight deck. Wilkie surprised everyone by landing on his first try, when all the others, Dad included, missed and had to go around again.

And that wasn't all.

Dad rested a tired hand on Wilkie's shoulder. "Next time we drop napalm," he announced, "Wilkie's dropping first. He's our new napalm man."

The others nodded with approval. The flight had hit Chinese troops threatening the Hagaru base and Wilkie had laid his napalm the smoothest of everyone.

"Gee, thanks," Wilkie said and took a drag. "I hope I got lots of foxholes."

Dad grinned like a proud parent. Wilkie was becoming a professional before his eyes.

The familiar clinking of glass bottles sounded as the flight surgeon pushed his steel cart into the cabin. He walked from man to man and handed each a tiny bottle of brandy. Tom was too tired to pretend he wanted a scotch. Wilkie didn't ask for a gin and tonic. No one pestered

Wally Madden

the man for a rum and Coke. They just uncapped their brandies and dumped the contents into the glasses.

Jesse passed his bottle to Cevoli as usual. Tom and the others yawned as the stress of the day hit them. In another cluster, Marty slowly sipped the brown elixir. He had spotted the Fusen Reservoir that morning, he had dived through the clouds to confirm its identity, and he had led everyone to Chosin. But he brushed it all off as another day's work.

Cevoli's eyes lifted and he snapped ramrod tall. "Attention, CAG on deck," he blurted. Tom and the others set aside their drinks and turned toward the doorway.

A short thirty-five-year-old man with a round face and bushy black eyebrows entered. He was Commander Wally Madden, the air group C.O., who had led the aerial armada that morning.

"Relax, relax," Madden said calmly. "This will just take a sec." Madden was a WWII veteran and one of the few pilots on the *Leyte* who could fly as well as Dad. On the way to Korea, he had checked himself out on a Corsair by simply reading the manual.

"I just dropped by the CIC," Madden announced. "And thought you should hear this."

Tom and Jesse glanced at one another. The CIC was the Combat Information Center in the tower, where messages came in.

"The lead elements of the Marine column just rolled into Hagaru," Madden continued.

A collective sigh rose throughout the cabin. Tom and Cevoli grinned and even Jesse relaxed a little. That night, Dad Fowler would write to his mother: "Mark my words, history will show this to be the Marines' finest hour."

Madden raised a hand to silence the men. "Don't get too excited," he said. "Most of our guys are still out in the wild, so no letting off the gas now."

Tom nodded in agreement.

With a wave of his hand, Madden exited.

An outburst of conversation and backslapping followed. Normally, Cevoli would have been the first to call in the flight surgeon and cajole the man into another round of brandies. But not tonight. He stepped front and center. "Okay, fellas, let's wrap things up," Cevoli pronounced. "Tomorrow's gonna be a big one."

The pilots nodded. Nearly everyone was scheduled to fly. Tom slugged down his brandy and the others ground out their cigarettes in ashtrays. The pilots filed from the room as if they were ready to fly right now, in the dark.

In the hallway, Tom looked, but Jesse was already gone.

A little after midnight, under the light of a lone desk lamp, Jesse's pen swirled across the page. As he wrote a letter, his eyes fixed passionately on each word.

In the dark, Koenig lay in the lower bunk, under the sheets. The ship's hum coursed through the metal walls. Now and then Koenig checked his watch. Both he and Jesse were slated to fly the next day and needed eight hours of sleep, or else they'd be removed from the roster. There were plenty of hours of darkness remaining, but Koenig wasn't one to gamble.

Jesse slid aside a page after filling it with neat, upright cursive. He started writing a second. The incomplete drawing of his dream house was propped against the rear of the desk, yet he stayed focused on his letter. Koenig heard Jesse sniffling. He caught a glimpse of his roommate wiping his nose with his sleeve. Koenig closed his eyes and pretended not to notice.

Jesse gripped the pen tightly and wrote a third page, then a fourth. Finally, he set the pen to his desk and slid whatever he had written into an envelope.

The desk lamp snapped off and Koenig heard Jesse's footsteps in the darkness. Jesse climbed quietly to his bunk, careful not to rouse his roommate. But Koenig was still awake. Above him, a flashlight clicked on. Koenig saw a glowing light on the ceiling and knew that Jesse was reading his nightly Bible passages. He had stopped sniffling, too.

Some time passed, maybe thirty minutes, maybe more. Koenig stared at the ceiling and waited.

Finally, the flashlight clicked off and the room became dark.

Jesse was ready.

The following day, December 4, around 1:45 P.M.

An envelope sat in a wire basket on a table in the ready room. The basket was labeled OUTGOING MAIL, and the envelope was addressed to "Mrs. Daisy Brown."

Outside on the flight deck, Corsair 211 rolled slowly forward from the pack of planes. Its propeller whirled, its nose angled skyward. Inside the cockpit, Jesse gently pushed the throttle with his left hand, where his Rolex lined his wrist. The plane's nose blocked Jesse's forward view and, like blinders on a racehorse, its folded wings blocked any side view.

Jesse leaned outside the cockpit and the prop blast buffeted his goggles and helmet. To the right of the propeller, a yellow-shirted deckhand backpedaled and pumped his arms: *Forward!* Jesse let the Corsair creep until the yellow-shirt held both hands high: *Halt!* Jesse stepped on the brakes and the Corsair squealed to a stop almost beside the tower.

Behind Jesse, Tom waited in Corsair 205. The two had been paired again after one of the ship's "paddles," a senior pilot named Hudson, had complained that he was always on the platform and never flying. So Cevoli took Hudson as his wingman, assigned Tom to Jesse's wing, and bumped Koenig back to lead an ensign named McQueen.

Beside Jesse's propeller, the yellow-shirt wrapped his arms over his shoulders, then fanned his arms wide: *Spread wings!*

Jesse lowered a lever and the wings unfolded like drawbridges. As the right wing lowered, the blue sky appeared, then the top of the ship's tower, a clothesline of antennas, a billowing smokestack, then a flapping American flag.

As the wing settled fully, an incredible sight greeted Jesse. Up and down the tower, sailors and aviators crowded every deck, their arms draped over railings. Boyish awe filled their faces.

Marty, Wilkie, and other pilots watched from Vulture's Row, and Jesse's fan club crowded every other deck. The stewards had come out, as had cooks, mechanics, even snipes from the engine room. At the foot of the tower, the deckhands and the crash crew gazed up at the pilot in his cockpit. Everyone knew where the flyboys were headed and more men than ever had come out to show their support.

Now they could see that the next pilot was about to launch.

From behind Jesse, Tom saw it. On the tower, a man outstretched his arm and flashed a V-for-victory sign. Another man raised his fingers in a V. Then another, and another, until men on every deck were flashing Vs to Jesse Brown.

Tom thought the sign had died out after WWII and he'd never imagined that it would return during the Battle of the Chosin Reservoir. But it did.

Jesse looked up and extended a thumbs-up to the men on the tower. He turned back to his instruments.

It was time to go.

*   *   *

The ten Corsairs flew two by two over the wintery valley. Slants of sun cracked the dark clouds overhead and warmed the snowy hills in patches. From the perch of his Corsair, Tom leaned in his seat to scan the terrain five thousand feet below. Everyone knew that the Chinese occupied the hills leading up to the Chosin, yet from the air, the valley appeared cold and lifeless.

The hour-long flight had passed in silence. Ahead of Tom, the Corsairs of Cevoli and his wingman bobbed in the rough air. Beside him, Jesse flew tight-lipped. As the flight motored farther, the radio began buzzing with chatter. Tom could hear the excited voices of pilots from other squadrons—they sounded as if they were nearby. Jesse caught Tom's attention with a wave and pointed forward.

At the end of the valley, Tom saw it materialize—a sea of green tent peaks bristling the snow and countless wisps of rising smoke. A tiny village lay to the right and earthen defensive lines ringed it all.

The sight reminded Tom of a painting from a history textbook, of a Roman legion camp on the snowy fringes of Gaul. But this wasn't Gaul. To the left of the tents lay a dirt runway and behind the scene stretched an icy reservoir.

They'd reached the American base at Hagaru.

"This is Iroquois Flight 13," Cevoli radioed the base. "We're ten F4Us, checking in."

"Welcome back, Iroquois flight," the base dispatcher's voice crackled.

Cevoli relayed his flight's armament and fuel status. The dispatcher said he'd check and see if any targets were available. Tom's face scrunched: *A target shortage?* It made no sense, not when a hundred thousand Chinese were reportedly ringing the base. But as the flight came closer, Tom could see why targets were in short supply.

Beyond the base, countless blue aircraft orbited over the reservoir and the hills to the east. Like gnats, they circled in various levels. They were navy Corsairs, Marine Corsairs, and Skyraiders, too.

"So, we've got a decent aerial umbrella stacked up," the dispatcher clarified when he returned to the radio. "But we can use some road recon."

He described a stretch of road for the flight to patrol where ten thousand Chinese troops had been spotted that morning, moving toward Hagaru. Tom glanced at his kneeboard map. The course would take them up the MSR to Yudam-ni and then deeper into the wild. They'd be in enemy territory all the way. Tom reached and flicked his gunsight to life. Someone had to do it.

Cevoli banked left and steered the flight around Hagaru to avoid any planes taking off.

Beyond his right wing, Tom saw the airstrip on the fringe of the base. Silver C-47s idled on the dirt runway while lines of men poured from the transports. Replacements were coming in from bases in Japan, another platoon or so of the five hundred Marines who had volunteered to be airlifted in. Beside the planes, clusters of wounded men waited to be airlifted out. By the battle's end, more than four thousand men would leave Hagaru that way.

Cevoli leveled his wings toward the hills west of the base to begin the patrol. "There they are, boys!" he announced. "One o'clock!"

Tom edged forward in his seat for a glimpse. A dark line of vehicles and men snaked down from the snowy hills and inched into the base. Tom's eyes lifted.

The last of the Lost Legion were returning.

Once these Marines trickled in, the base's garrison would stand a fighting chance. Already, the two-thousand-man garrison had been joined by a relief force of four hundred Marines, soldiers, and British Commandos who had fought their way up from the south. Then a thousand survivors of the army's task force had limped in from across the ice. And now came the last of nine thousand Marines from Yudam-ni. Within the hour, the Marine air wing commander at Hagaru would radio the *Leyte* and *Philippine Sea* to say: "[I] saw the 5th and 7th Marines return. They thank God for air. I don't think they could have made it as units without air support. . . . Tell your pilots they are doing a magnificent job."

From his cockpit, Jesse glanced over at Tom. A smile stretched across Jesse's face. Tom nodded. They could both see the column of Marines snaking down from the hills, and they both knew it.

There was hope.

Ten minutes later

Against a backdrop of gray clouds, the two blue Corsairs dived toward the snowy mountains. Tom glanced at Jesse as their planes plummeted side by side. Jesse's helmeted head scanned back and forth, his eyes searching for a place to crash. He was going down, seventeen miles northwest of Hagaru, deep inside enemy territory.

None of the pilots had heard the gunshots over their engines. None had seen the weapons rise or fall from the snowy field. But now a vapor trail slipped from the belly of Jesse's Corsair: a bullet had punctured the oil line. With every passing second, the oil was bleeding, the friction was rising, and the plane's eighteen pistons were melting inside the engine.

High above, Cevoli leveled off the flight so he and the others could lend eyeballs to the search. Tom scanned the terrain beyond each wing. Rugged mountains stretched as far as the eye could see. The mountains bristled with woods and dipped into dark gorges. Patches of sun camouflaged the terrain, distorting its contours.

"Jesse, check your ten, might be a spot!" Cevoli announced.

Jesse glanced to his left. Tom saw it, almost level with his wing, a few miles north. A high, flat pasture lay atop one of the mountains. He could see down its full length. A mountain peak blocked the far end of the pasture and other peaks rose up to the left and right. But the near side lay open—an entrance.

"I'm taking departure," Jesse radioed Tom. His Corsair broke leftward and he steered for the high pasture. Tom peeled after him. Following a short chase, he resumed his place beside Jesse's wing.

"Let's run through the checklist," Tom said, trying to sound confident.

Jesse looked over, surprised to see Tom.

"Okay, Tom—go," Jesse replied.

"Jettison napalm. Belly tank. Salvo rockets."

The white napalm egg tumbled from Jesse's plane, followed by a spare fuel tank. A few seconds later, rockets launched from Jesse's wings and arced to earth.

"Flaps down!" Tom said.

Flaps dropped from Jesse's wings.

"Fuel pressure dump!"

Inside his cockpit, Jesse stepped on a pedal by his right foot and cleared the explosive gasoline vapors from the main fuel tank. "Check," Jesse said.

Tom glanced ahead. The pasture appeared to be about three hundred yards deep and as level a runway as they were going to get. But as they neared, Tom's eyes widened with alarm. The pasture was anything but smooth—small trees and boulders jutted from the snow. Jesse saw them too and steered toward the left side of the pasture where the land sloped uphill. The snow there looked white and flat.

"Canopy back and locked!" Tom continued.

Jesse's canopy slid backward and he lowered his goggles over his eyes.

How is he staying so calm? Tom wondered. He remembered Jesse as the same pilot who had incessantly read the Corsair manual back at Quonset Point. And it was Jesse who told one of the cockpit instructors, "I think that Corsair will kill me. I just have that feeling."

From above, Cevoli and the others watched the two black-blue fighters descend, side by side, into the pasture.

"150! . . . 140! . . . 130!" Tom called out their speed so that Jesse could keep his eyes on the pasture. As the Corsairs went lower, the pasture stretched around them and the trees and rocks became taller.

The propeller blades on Jesse's plane began to slow and show themselves until the four flat blades windmilled. His wings rocked—the plane was sinking. Jesse aimed for the slope and struggled to glide with a melted engine.

"120!" Tom called. "110! . . . 100!"

The white pasture and slope widened before them.

"Two hundred feet!" Tom shouted. "One hundred feet! Hold it steady—fifty feet—here you go!"

Tom gunned his throttle, hauled back on the stick, and climbed. He looked over his left shoulder and twisted to maintain a view.

Jesse's plane was bucking, struggling to keep its nose up, but without an engine pushing, the Corsair's wide wings lost lift, as if someone had cut the string that was holding the plane up. The twelve-thousand-pound fighter suddenly quit flying and dropped the final twenty-five feet to earth.

The nose slammed the slope in a burst of snow. Shattered propeller blades were flung in every direction, the engine ripped from its bolts and cartwheeled away, the tail smacked hard. Groaning, the Corsair skidded to a stop.

A cloud of snow embraced the fighter.

Tom orbited over the crash site, just above the mountain peaks. His eyes fixated on the cloud that obscured Jesse's plane.

Come on, Jesse, Tom thought. *Cue the radio.*

The snow slowly settled and Jesse's plane appeared. Tom inhaled sharply. Ahead of the cockpit, the Corsair's long nose was bent toward the right wing. It had bent so far that it nearly snapped off. Behind the tail stretched a path where the plane had skidded. The snow had

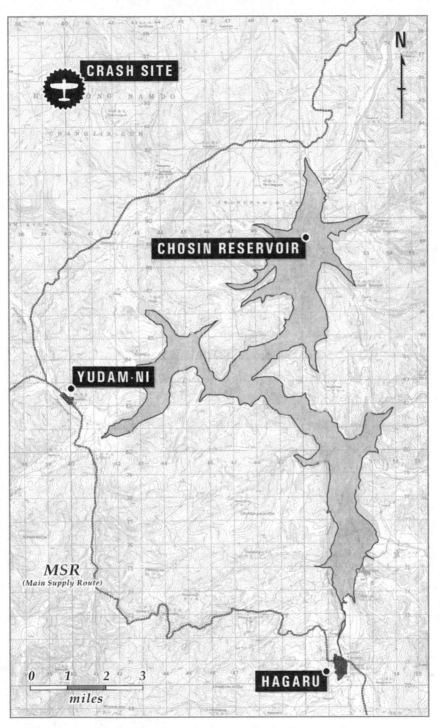

parted and revealed sheer rock beneath. Jesse's canopy had slammed shut and remained so.

Then Tom saw it. Inch by inch, the canopy cranked back.

Relieved voices flooded the airwaves. Tom had almost forgotten about the four pilots orbiting above him. Jesse waved but didn't leave the cockpit.

"What's he waiting for?" someone asked.

"He's gotta be hurt?" Koenig suggested.

Cevoli tried to call Jesse over the radio, but got no reply.

"I'm going upstairs to call for a helicopter," Cevoli announced. By calling from a higher altitude, he could beam a clearer transmission down to Hagaru. "Fellas, maintain orbit," Cevoli continued. "Tom, once Jesse gets clear, destroy the plane."

Tom agreed. He knew the rule: Never leave an intact plane and its technology in enemy territory.

Cevoli climbed from the circling planes into the dark clouds.

At separate altitudes, Tom and the others orbited. Minutes passed and Jesse kept waving.

Cevoli's voice crackled over the radio. He was still above the clouds. "Okay, a chopper's coming," he said. "But it's going to be twenty minutes or more. I'll keep you posted."

Tom's face twisted. If Jesse was hurt, he might freeze to death in that time.

Wisps of smoke began floating from the twisted nose of Jesse's Corsair. The plane's 230-gallon fuel tank lay just beyond Jesse's feet. Koenig called Cevoli to alert him to the fire, but Cevoli didn't reply. He had switched radio channels and was transmitting on the Search and Rescue channel.

"Come on, Jesse, get out!" Koenig radioed.

The smoke began pouring thicker and the wind carried it back into the cockpit. Jesse looked to be struggling. Tom's eyes tightened. He watched the nose of Jesse's plane and dreaded the thought of flames. *Lord, don't let him burn!* Tom prayed. The smoke rose from the pasture like a thin arrow pointing to Jesse's location. Tom's face sank. If he could see it, then the Chinese could, too. They were probably already on their way.

Tom took a deep breath. There was one last option.

The Tom Hudner who'd reported to Fighting 32 in December 1949 would have kept orbiting. From above, he'd have watched Jesse burn and told himself that there was nothing he could do. A downed pilot was to be left alone—the skipper had said so. It was his rule and he'd court-martial any man who broke it. It was probably the navy's rule too, written in some manual.

But this was not 1949.

Tom lowered his black-rimmed goggles.

"I'm going in," Tom radioed.

Above, Koenig and the others remained silent. Cevoli was still away and they either didn't understand what Tom meant or didn't want to encourage what he was thinking. So they watched.

Tom dipped his left wing and swooped down toward the pasture.

It was time to break the rules.

Jesse must have known that a Corsair had come to earth.

He must have felt the blast of wind at his back and heard the metallic crunch and the engine's whine as its propeller blades bent backward. In his rearview mirror, he must have seen the plane rushing toward him like an angry blue wave in a sea of white—sliding, metal screeching against rock—and he must have seen it stop in a violent lurch and toss a whiteout of powdered snow.

When the whiteout had settled, Jesse must have seen the plane sitting in the snow behind his right wing, a dark bird so out of place that it might have made him cry. Jesse didn't need to see the number on the nose or the face of the pilot behind the shattered windscreen.

He must have known who had come to try to save him.

High above, Koenig muttered in admiration: "Of all the guys, it would be Tom."

*   *   *

Tom lifted his head from the seatback and released a deep breath. His brow lifted with relief. "My God, it worked," he muttered. The windscreen had shattered, the props had folded backward, but Corsair 205 had held together. He had survived a carrier-style landing on a mountaintop.

Fifty yards ahead and to the left lay Jesse's plane, still smoking. Tom came to his senses and clawed at the latch on his chest. His shoulder straps released. He tugged his helmet's radio cord from a panel.

Tom cranked open the canopy and frigid air flooded the cockpit. *Damn, it's cold!* he thought. The pasture sat so high he could see the Chosin in the distance through the opening in the valley.

Tom lifted his arms to the canopy rails and pushed himself from his seat. A wave of pain shot up his back and he grimaced. Tom sank back down with a groan. He figured he had possibly fractured a vertebra. Eyes tight with pain, he stood again. This time he swung his leg over the rail, inserted a boot in a toe hold, and lowered himself down to the right wing.

Tom slowly slid from the wing and his boots sank into the snow. It was nearly a foot deep, but the powder was deceptive—the snow was thick beneath. The sun was gone, and dark clouds now rose around the peaks as if hungry to swallow the two men and their wrecked planes.

Tom took a step and winced, then managed a second step. Gritting his teeth, he stumbled around the steaming engine and kept going. Frigid wind whipped his tan flight suit and snow stuck to his goggles. Doubled over, Tom hobbled uphill toward Jesse in a race against time.

CHAPTER 38

ALL THE FAITH IN THE WORLD

On the mountaintop

FROM A DISTANCE the sight must have looked odd—the pilot plodding through the snow, his helmet still strapped, his goggles down, his life preserver flapping in the wind.

With every step, Tom panted. The air felt thin and the snow gripped his boots. He glanced at Jesse's plane and could see his friend sitting high in the cockpit, smoke rising around him. *Hang on, Jesse!* Tom thought.

Halfway between the planes, Tom stopped. His eyes locked on a pair of footprints that dotted the snow in front of him. *Chinese!* They might belong to one man, they might belong to a hundred men. The Chinese were known to march strategically in the same footsteps. Tom drew his .38 revolver.

His eyes followed the tracks to the end of the pasture. At the base of a peak sat a wooden shack with a boarded-up window. A farmer probably worked the pasture during the warmer months. The wind howled and Tom's helmet muffled his hearing. He could have sworn that he heard voices. Tom whirled, pistol in hand, searching. Dead trees creaked and snow swirled.

Tom raised the pistol skyward and fired. A crack echoed between the peaks. No one emerged from the shack or stepped from the trees. He fired again. Nothing. Tom holstered his revolver. He wasn't worried about the Chinese hearing his gunshots and discovering his location. All they needed to do was follow the smoke.

Tom plowed ahead and approached Jesse's right wing from the rear. Jesse waved weakly.

"Tom, I'm pinned," he called down.

"Don't worry, Jesse," Tom shouted up. "A helicopter's on the way." *All he needs is one good tug to get him out,* Tom thought. He stepped onto the wing. His snow-caked boots slipped on the metal and he slammed down. Tom picked himself up and shimmied up to the fuselage. The cockpit sat well above and behind the wing—he'd need to climb.

Tom inserted a gloved hand into a high handhold and leaned his left foot out from the wing. He kicked a spot in the fuselage and a metal foothold folded down. Tom rested his boot on the foothold. With his weight distributed between the foothold and the wing, he grabbed the canopy ledge and stood face to face with Jesse.

Tom's eyes sank at the sight. Jesse's lips were blue and his ears looked frozen and brittle. He was shivering wildly, his arms folded, his breath puffing. The cold had curled Jesse's fingers into claws. Jesse looked up with glassy eyes and said simply, "We've got to figure a way of getting out of here."

Tom nodded rapidly. "Let's see what's got you pinned." He raised his goggles and leaned into the cockpit. Wisps of smoke seeped through the shattered instrument panel. The smoke was the reason that Jesse couldn't close the canopy to escape the cold—it would asphyxiate him.

"It's this one," Jesse said, tapping his right thigh. Tom waved the smoke away and saw it: When the fuselage buckled, it had crushed

Jesse's knee against the part of the instrument panel that ran between his legs.

Tom's eyes narrowed. Jesse's helmet was lying next to his left foot. *So that's why he wasn't responding,* Tom thought. The helmet contained Jesse's microphone and earphones. His gloves lay on the floor as well, also out of reach. In Jesse's hurry to flee a potential fire, he had discarded his cumbersome gear and only then realized that he was trapped.

With one hand on the canopy rail, Tom grabbed the chest of Jesse's leather jacket with the other. Jesse's hands gripped the canopy ledge.

"On three," Tom said. "One. Two. *Three!*"

Tom tugged while Jesse pushed upward. Jesse's eyes clenched with pain, his bottom raised from his seat, but the metal gripped him fast.

Jesse lowered back into his seat. He leaned his head against the headrest and gasped. Tom surmised that his friend had internal injuries, a shattered back at least. He hated to try again, but one glance at the plane's nose reminded him that a fire could spark at any second.

"Okay, Jesse, let's try again," Tom said.

Jesse nodded.

Tom placed his full weight on the foothold and let his right leg dangle over the wing. He gripped Jesse and pulled, using his whole body for leverage. Tom strained, his arm shook, his right leg swung against the fuselage. Jesse groaned and pushed but his knee wouldn't budge.

Convinced that Jesse was immovable, Tom knew he had to buy time. "I'll be right back," he told Jesse. Tom lowered himself to the wing and slid down to the plane's broken nose. He scampered around to the empty engine cavity and fell to his knees. With gloved hands he shoveled snow into the cavity, toward the source of the smoke. After several heaps, the smoke settled into a trickle. Tom raised his goggles and squinted inside. He couldn't tell what was burning—it was probably the engine's residual oil. He didn't know if he had squelched the fire or just barricaded it off.

Tom scampered back to the wing and up to Jesse's side. Wisps of smoke still filtered through the instrument panel but less than before. "Fire's contained," Tom reported. "If it hasn't erupted by now I don't think it's going to." Jesse nodded, his teeth chattering. Tom unzipped his jacket and retrieved the black knit cap he always carried. "Hold still," he said. Jesse's eyebrows lifted. Tom flopped the cap over Jesse's head and pulled it down over his friend's frozen ears.

"Thank you," Jesse said.

Tom glanced down and tugged the silk scarf from around his neck. "Jesse, give me your hands," Tom said. Jesse raised his hands but averted his eyes — the sight was too painful. Tom wrapped Jesse's hands tightly in the scarf and Jesse settled his hands back to his lap.

"We're going to need an ax to cut you out," Tom said. "So I'm gonna go get a message to the chopper to make sure they bring one."

"Okay," Jesse nodded.

Tom slapped Jesse on the shoulder and climbed down. He couldn't believe it: Jesse's composure was settling *him* down.

As Tom plodded downhill, he noticed that the snow, the Corsair, the peaks, all were turning a deeper shade of blue. Time was slipping away.

Several miles to the southeast, they ran through a snowy field between two mountains, like a pack of upright wolves. White Jackets, a hundred or more. Their black sneakers crunched the snow and weapons bounced on their shoulders. They ran for the distant mountain, the one where the smoke had risen, where planes now circled.

Three thousand feet above the mountain, Koenig boiled with worry as he followed the planes ahead of him. Snowy peaks and valleys slid across his windscreen as the flight orbited rightward. Something was terribly wrong; fifteen minutes had passed and Jesse was still in the cockpit.

Cevoli swooped down from the clouds and slid back into the lead.

"Helicopter's halfway here," he reported, his voice high with hope. After an orbit or two he asked, "Where's Tom?"

"Lead, you might want to look down," Koenig replied.

Cevoli's right wing dipped for a better view. "Holy cow," he muttered.

Far below his circling friends, Tom lowered himself into the seat of his crashed Corsair and plugged his helmet's cord into a panel on the right. He squeezed the red button on the throttle and keyed the mic. "Iroquois flight, do you copy?" His chest heaved as he glanced upward.

"Go ahead, Tom," Cevoli replied.

"Jesse's alive but pinned inside," Tom said. "I think his back's broken. Tell the helicopter we need a fire extinguisher and an ax to extract him, and tell them to hurry, please."

Tom cupped his earphones tightly to hear the reply. "Helicopter's already in the air," Cevoli said. "I'll relay your message. If there's no ax aboard, there may be a delay while he goes back for one."

"Okay," Tom said, his face twisting. "Thanks for sticking around, fellas. Jesse's in rough shape—but he has all the faith in the world." Tom tugged the cord from the radio to return to Jesse's side. He had been gone long enough.

In his Corsair above, Koenig reached to his right and slid the radio dial to number 7, the Guard Channel. He couldn't wait for permission—Cevoli was on the horn with the helicopter. "Calling all transports," Koenig said. "If anyone's listening, fly over grid Charlie Victor 40-96 and drop a fire extinguisher—we've got two pilots down and they need one desperately."

Static crackled.

"Any transport, come in?" Koenig shook his head. The transport planes were probably on their way back to Japan.

Cevoli's voice returned to the airwaves. He sounded somber. "The chopper's turning around to get an ax," he told the flight. "The rescue's going to be a while." Koenig's jaw clenched at the news. In silence, the flight kept circling.

The radio hissed to life. Koenig's eyes lifted—someone was listening.

"This is Split Seam flight," a pilot announced. "Heard you've got pilots down?"

Koenig glanced toward the Chosin—in the distance, four Corsairs were approaching. Koenig checked his knee chart. "Split Seam" was the call sign of a Marine squadron called the "Devil Cats." Cevoli welcomed the newcomers and asked them to take up a wider orbit, three miles outside '32's circle. The Devil Cats peeled into a line and began prowling.

In no time, chatter burst across the radio.

"Enemy in the open!" a Devil Cat reported.

"Oh, I see 'em!" shouted another.

Koenig's eyes traced the commotion. In the direction of the reservoir, the Devil Cats were circling a field between two mountains.

"Iroquois flight, you have a serious Chinese problem!" the Devil Cat leader reported. "We're engaging."

One at a time, the planes dived toward the field with smoke puffing from their wings. Each plane disappeared behind a snowy rise, then rose again from the trees.

"Iroquois flight, this is Fire Guard," a new voice spoke. "Need more guns?" The pilot reported his heading, and Koenig spotted them—four Corsairs, coming from Yudam-ni.

They were more Marine planes—"Fire Guard" was the call sign of the "Black Sheep Squadron." Cevoli asked the Black Sheep to fall in with the Devil Cats.*

Again, the radio crackled. "This is Attack 35, coming on station." Two *Leyte* Skyraiders banked over from the Chosin to fall in with the

---

* Devil Cat pilot Al Graselli and Black Sheep flight leader Lyle Bradley remember hearing Tom on the radio and being impressed with his composure. Lyle and his fellow Black Sheep would later compose and sign a letter testifying to Tom's courage, and they'd send it up the chain of command.

Marine Corsairs. Cevoli welcomed the Skyraiders and urged everyone listening, "Keep 'em off our boys!"

On the mountaintop, Tom dangled from Jesse's canopy ledge and shivered. Without an ax to free Jesse's leg, there was nothing more he could do.

From the right, thumps of cannon fire sounded. Tom and Jesse glanced across the pasture, but a peak blocked their view. They caught sporadic glimpses of the fighting, when a Corsair climbed high or a Skyraider turned wide. Overhead, Tom could see his shipmates clearly. Their bent wings tilted toward him as they circled, a final line of defense. Tall in their seats, the pilots were silhouetted against the gray clouds. A steady roar of engines filtered down.

As the daylight faded, the temperature was plummeting. The sweat on Tom's skin froze like a layer of frost and he shivered.

Tom's eyes wandered to his watch. It was already 3:40 P.M., and darkness would arrive around five. Cevoli and the others still had an hour's flight ahead of them. If they were to reach the ship before dark, they'd need to leave. Tom gulped. *We're going to be alone soon.*

But he couldn't let Jesse quit.

Tom looked up. By the direction of their orbit, the others were signaling that a chopper was coming.

"Jesse, look," Tom said, pointing upward. "They're going clockwise."

Jesse glanced up. "Yes, they are," he said. His voice came labored, and his breathing was shallow.

Meanwhile, aboard the *Leyte*

Marty lowered his magazine and leaned forward from his seat in the ready room. He was on standby duty, suited up to launch in the event of a threat to the ship. His eyes settled on the teletype machine nearby. White letters trickled across the flickering green screen.

"Fellas, get over here!" Marty shouted to the others in the room. "*Leyte's* got a pilot down." The others crowded around as more words formed on the teletype.

ENS Brown, VF-32. Shot down.

Marty's eyes blinked wide, and the others looked to one another in disbelief. More words appeared.

LtJG Hudner, VF-32. Intentional crash landing.

"What?" someone muttered.

"This can't be right!" Marty said. The words kept trickling.

Both pilots awaiting evacuation.

Cevoli providing air cover.

Helicopter en route.

"Thank goodness!" someone said. Marty let out a sigh of relief. Cevoli's Corsairs could keep a Chinese army at bay.

"They had me worried for a second there!" another pilot added.

Marty lit a cigarette and settled his eyes on the screen. The others remained in place, but their chattering slowed. Everyone watched and waited.

On the mountaintop, Tom's arm shook along the Corsair's canopy ledge. His muscles ached and his knees quivered. In the cockpit, Jesse clutched himself, shivering silently. His head drooped forward. His puffs of breath were getting thinner. Forty minutes had passed since his crash and twilight was settling across the pasture.

Beyond the peaks, Cevoli broke from orbit and led the others down toward Tom and Jesse. Tom glanced forward and Jesse slowly lifted his head. Cevoli's wings stretched wider and wider as he descended.

Jesse had seen such a sight before. As a young sharecropper, he'd stood tall as a plane buzzed him in a cotton field, its pilot eager to see him run. But this plane was different. From a distance, the pilot began wagging his wings. He kept wagging them as he skimmed over a peak, over the pasture, and over Tom and Jesse.

Jesse raised his bundled hands in a feeble wave. Tom's face sank. Wagging wings sometimes meant "Good luck" and sometimes "Goodbye."

Hudson's Corsair roared overhead next, its wings wagging. Jesse raised his hand. Then came Koenig and finally his wingman, McQueen.

Tom glanced over his shoulder and watched the planes shrink away toward the Chosin. The last pilot wagged his wings as long as he could.

"They're still waving, Jesse," Tom said.

When he turned back, Jesse's chin had slumped to his chest. His eyes were closed. Tom could see his chest barely rising and falling.

With the planes gone, the wind wailed without competition. The clouds turned darker. Tom reached across his hip and felt his revolver. He debated the best course of action when the Chinese came: Should he shoot Jesse and then himself to avoid torture? Or take a chance as a POW?

He knew a POW camp would be brutal, but no one at that stage of the war knew that the communists routinely starved American POWs to death as a political statement. *

Tom glanced at his watch. It was nearly four o'clock. *Maybe the helicopter isn't coming after all,* he thought. In his hurry to aid Jesse, he had forgotten that helicopters lacked the performance to reach some of Korea's mountains.

Jesse slumped heavily forward. Tom reached out and shook Jesse's shoulder. Jesse raised his head and Tom released a long breath. Jesse's eyes slowly opened. They were glassy and blank. Then they closed again. *This can't be happening,* Tom thought. He wanted to slap his friend's cheeks to bring the light back into his eyes.

---

* For Americans held prisoner by the Chinese and the North Koreans, that winter would be known as "the starvation months," when more POWs died than at any other time. Overall, 38 percent of American prisoners died during the Korean War. In comparison, 34 percent died in Japanese camps during WWII, 14 percent died in North Vietnamese camps during Vietnam, and 4 percent died in German/Italian camps during WWII.

A weak voice uttered Tom's name.

"Yeah, Jesse?" Tom said.

With just his eyes, Jesse looked up at Tom. He drew a shallow breath. "Just tell Daisy how much I love her."

Tom nodded. Jesse closed his eyes and slumped heavily again. His breathing became so shallow that his shoulders barely rose.

Tom lowered his head. The finality was setting in.

Whomp, whomp, whomp. A bass sound traveled on the wind and Tom's eyes lifted to it. *Whomp, whomp, whomp.* The sound echoed across the pasture and grew sharper. Rotors were beating the air; an engine was whirring. Tom traced the sound ahead, behind a peak. He shook Jesse again, in the hope that he'd rally.

"Hey, buddy, hang in there!" Tom said. "The helicopter's here— I'm going to go flag him down."

Jesse's eyelids lifted heavily. He barely nodded.

Tom stumbled through the snow and stood fifty yards ahead of Jesse's plane. From the sound of it, the pilot was taking a roundabout approach to the mountaintop, not the obvious flight path behind Tom and Jesse, the one the enemy would expect.

In a furious burst of noise, the helicopter banked between the peaks in front of Tom, its blades whirling. The chopper was a bug-like HO3S. Tom pulled a short flare from his life vest, uncapped the top, and pulled a string. Red smoke puffed then spouted into a plume. Tom waved the smoking flare over his head. The smoke streamed toward the helicopter and revealed the wind's direction.

The helicopter pilot turned the glass bubble nose toward Tom and hovered closer. A circle of snow blasted outward and Tom shielded his face. Fifty yards away the craft lowered until all three tires had sunk into the white. The helicopter pilot looked up from his controls and paused at the sight of a pilot holding a flare with two crashed Corsairs behind him.

The helicopter's rotors slowed and the blades took shape. The pilot kept his engine running for fear that it wouldn't start up again at the mountainous altitude.

Tom tossed the flare aside. A door swung open from the right side of the helicopter and a short, stocky pilot jumped into the snow. The man wore a hip-length parka, paratrooper boots, and a black knit cap. Tom ran to greet him. Next to the cockpit, Tom stopped short with surprise.

The pilot's cheeks were balled thick against the cold. He was Lieutenant Charlie Ward, the jovial Alabamian who had once joked to Tom and Jesse that he didn't know the meaning of "fear" because he didn't understand big words. Over the engine, Ward shouted a one-word greeting: "Hi!"

Tom pointed to Jesse's plane and shouted, "We've got a pilot pinned inside and a fire in the nose. You have the ax?"

Ward nodded and slid open a door behind the cockpit. He handed an ax to Tom and grabbed a fire extinguisher for himself. The duo sprinted for the Corsair.

Tom hopped onto the wing. He glanced back and saw Ward stopped in his tracks, his eyes fixed on the pilot in the cockpit.

"Is that Jesse Brown?" Ward shouted.

"Yeah."

"Aww, shit."

Tom climbed to the cockpit and glanced inside. Jesse appeared unconscious; his breath had stopped puffing. Tom clutched the canopy ledge with his left hand, and with his right he choked down on the ax almost to the bottom. Tom's eyes focused on the outer fuselage, where the metal bulged in and pinned Jesse's knee. With a sidearm swipe, he hauled the ax back, then swung it forward.

Clang!

The steel blade skipped from the metal. Tom leaned and looked. The blade had barely made a dent. In a frenzy, Tom swung the ax again and again and again. Clang after clang sounded. The ax wasn't cutting, and worse, Jesse hadn't flinched.

More leverage! Tom thought. He lowered himself to the wing and raised the ax high over his head. Pain rippled up his back. Tom clenched his teeth and slammed the ax down against the fuselage. *Clang!* Tom's feet slid from under him and he slammed down onto the frozen wing. From his side, he glanced up to where the blow had landed. The ax had barely dented the frozen metal. Tom pounded the wing with his fists.

Ward reached to help Tom up. Instead of a hand, Tom handed him the ax. Having flown Corsairs during WWII, Ward climbed quickly to the cockpit. He leaned in to look Jesse in the face. "Hey, Mississippi— you hang in there, okay?" he said. "Hey, buddy?"

Jesse didn't stir.

In an outpouring of angst, Ward swung the ax blade against the Corsair again and again, but his frenzied blows had the same effect— barely a dent.

Ahead of the wing, Tom paced circles on the snow. Ward came down and grabbed Tom's shoulder to stop him.

"We need a cutting torch," Tom said. "They must have one at Hagaru!"

Ward shook his head and pointed a thumb back toward Jesse. "Jesse ain't moving. I don't want to admit it, but I think he's gone."

Tom looked away. He shook his head in denial.

Ward scanned their surroundings. The peaks had turned inky blue; soon they'd be black with night. "We gotta go," Ward said. "I don't have instruments for night flying." He looked Tom in the eyes. "You coming or staying?"

Tom glanced up at Jesse, slumped in the cockpit. If Jesse had been mumbling or even breathing, Tom's decision would have been easy. He'd have stayed.

"Decide quickly," Ward said. "But remember—you stay here, you freeze to death."

He hustled toward his helicopter.

From the ground, Tom looked up to the cockpit. "Jesse, we don't have the right tools to free you!" he shouted to his motionless friend.

"We're going to go and get some equipment. Don't worry—we'll be back for you!" But Jesse didn't stir.

Tom turned and followed Ward's footsteps to the helicopter. He opened the door to the fuselage, rolled inside, then shut the door and slumped against a bulkhead.

Up front, Ward glanced at Jesse through the glass and mumbled a quick prayer. He turned in his seat. "Ready?" he shouted to Tom over the whining engine. Tom didn't reply. He had crawled to the right and pressed his face against the window.

The helicopter lifted off—one wheel, then two, then three. Tom gazed down and saw Jesse still slumped in the twisted cockpit. His eyes remained locked on his friend as the helicopter nosed forward and flew over the wrecked Corsairs.

Ward guided the machine out of the pasture the same way Jesse and Tom had entered, through the opening in the peaks. He then pushed the control stick forward and flew down the mountainside to pick up speed. He glanced through the glass at his feet and his eyes went wide.

A column of White Jackets were climbing the slope. They ducked and held on to their hats as the helicopter's three tires buzzed over them. Ward tucked his neck and braced for the ping of bullets on metal. But no such sounds came. Ward slowly raised his head and his face loosened with relief. He'd realize later why the Chinese had held their fire—they had probably been afraid to draw more Corsairs.

Ward turned in his seat to see if Tom had seen the enemy troops, too. But Tom was leaning against the bulkhead, his arms wrapped around his chest, his eyes staring at his boots.

Ward thought about telling Tom what he'd just missed but thought better of it.

The fighter pilot behind him had already seen enough.

CHAPTER 39

FINALITY

Forty minutes later
Twelve miles south of Hagaru

IN NEAR DARKNESS, the helicopter touched down and a blast of snow shook the neighboring tents. The rotors slowed, then stopped. Crewmen emerged in heavy coats and tied down the blades. Inside the craft, Ward removed his earphones and shouted to Tom, "All clear!"

Tom slid the door open and winced at the bitter wind. A winter storm was swallowing any glimpse of the darkened sky.

A sea of pyramid tents surrounded the helicopter landing pad on three sides. There was no control tower, only a Marine radioman stomping around a jeep to keep his feet warm. Small arms fire sounded from hills to the right and left. Now and then a star shell flashed against the dark clouds.

This was Koto-ri, an American supply base below Hagaru, at the end of the valley. Far fewer Chinese were surrounding Koto-ri, and the base's four-thousand-man garrison had repelled the enemy's only attack so far.

Ward led Tom into the sea of tents. The tents fluttered in the wind like partially collapsed parachutes. Bundled Marines ducked inside and out. As he limped through the snow, Tom stared at the ground. *We left Jesse out there in this*, he thought.

Tom followed Ward into a long tent lit by Coleman lanterns. A wisp of warmth brushed Tom's face but he could still see his breath. The tent was crowded. More than a hundred fighting men were standing, eating from tins. Most were Marines, many were army, and a few wore the green berets of the British Royal Marine Commandos.

Ward approached a table where supply clerks dumped boxes of rations from a crate. He took a box for himself and offered one to Tom, who shook his head. Ward pointed to steaming cups of coffee but Tom declined those, too. Ward shrugged.

In the center of the tent, Ward found some space. He ate from a tin while Tom fiddled with his gloves, his eyes intense. "If we find a torch, can we go back first thing in the morning?" he asked.

Ward's face scrunched with frustration. "There's not a piece of equipment anywhere on this peninsula that could get Jesse out," he said. "You'd have to dismantle the damned plane."

Tom nodded, but his eyes stayed intense.

Ward leaned closer and his voice fell to a whisper. "Besides, these fellas are goin' the other direction," he said, gesturing to the nearby men. "Word is, once our troops in Hagaru regain their strength, they're fightin' here, then everyone's bugging out together."

Tom nodded reluctantly.

Between bites, the nearby Marines and soldiers eyed Tom with curiosity. His tan flight suit was dark up to the knees, wet from the snow. He still wore his helmet and he wasn't eating, as if he were itching to leave. Finally, a young Marine asked, "Sir, how'd you wind up in this mess?" The other Marines turned to Tom with anticipation.

"Crashed my plane up in the mountains," Tom said somberly. He motioned to Ward. "He came and rescued me." Ward shrugged and kept eating. For him, it was just another mission in a dangerous line of duty. The day before, his buddy and fellow chopper pilot Major Robert Longstaff had been killed attempting a similar rescue. As Longstaff hovered down toward the Marine column, a Chinese sniper had shot him between the eyes.

"Well, you're pretty safe here," the Marine assured Tom. The others nodded.

"A word of advice, though," the Marine added. "Avoid using the latrines after dark. It's like the Chinese got 'em zeroed in—the crapper's always the first thing to get hit!"

Ward laughed with the Marines.

Tom forced a smile.

By flashlight, a Marine led Tom and Ward to a small tent with a radio jeep parked outside. Tom and Ward ducked inside the tent. In sleeping bags, eight Marines slept on a dirt floor, helmets and rifles at their sides. Ward laid out his sleeping bag, the one he carried in his helicopter. Tom flapped up his fur collar and stretched out on the ground. He rested his helmeted head on the dirt.

"You sure we can't hunt you down a blanket somewhere?" Ward whispered.

Tom shook his head.

As he lay there, he kneaded his fingers to encourage circulation. The wind flapped the canvas above. Near the entrance of the tent, a flashlight clicked on and a young Marine slid from his sleeping bag. The bobbing light approached Tom. The Marine crouched with a sleeping bag draped in his arms.

"Sir, you'll need this." He set the bag beside Tom.

"I can't take your bag," Tom said.

"Sir, you'll need it a lot more than I will," the Marine said with a grin. "Besides, I'm on jeep duty tonight." He explained that every twenty minutes, he'd need to start the jeep's engine to pump electricity through the radio to keep it functioning.

"I'd take it," Ward muttered.

Tom reluctantly accepted the bag and thanked the Marine.

"Just give it back in the morning," the Marine said. "I don't sleep good at night, anyways."

Tom spread the bag and climbed inside. He pulled the edges around his face.

"Charlie," Tom whispered.

"Yeah?"

"Thanks for coming to get me."

Charlie paused. "You did good yourself, Tom."

"No," Tom said with resignation. "I'm gonna get court-martialed when I get back."

Ward rolled over. "Nahh," he muttered.

Tom stared at the ceiling. Outside, the wind was howling.

Three days later, December 7, 1950

A deckhand steered the Skyraider to a halt at the front of the flight deck of the USS *Leyte*. Other crewmen swarmed the plane, sliding chocks around the tires, and one darted to the right side of the fuselage and opened a small door. A pair of boots descended to the deck. They didn't belong to the pilot—he remained high in the cockpit, waiting for the engine to fully stop.

The deckhand steered Tom Hudner past the plane's tail. Tom paused and gazed across the empty rear deck. The early morning sun swept the wood and the deck crew scurried to reset the cables.

The carrier was back to business as usual.

Tom lowered his face and hobbled toward the tower. A deckhand opened a watertight door and Tom stepped inside, where an officer was waiting. "Lieutenant Hudner, the captain wants to see you on the bridge," the officer said.

Tom removed his helmet and tucked it under his arm. After three days on the ground, his hair was matted, his uniform soiled. And now he was going to be punished. *Let's get on with it*, Tom thought.

Captain T. U. Sisson

*　　*　　*

The sailors on the bridge worked like silent machines. One manned the wheel beside a large compass, while another scanned the horizon with binoculars. Men plotted the ship's course on charts with depth numbers.

A Marine guard opened a door that led from the catwalk and Captain Sisson stepped inside wearing a green parka. His face was round and ruddy, his nose pointy. He removed his tan ball cap, revealing a head full of gray hair.

Tom snapped a salute. Sisson handed his parka to a sailor and turned to Tom. "At ease, son," he said, his accent southern and thick. Tom lowered his shoulders a little.

Sisson's blue eyes were piercing. Golden wings adorned his left breast. As a young aviator, he'd flown search missions for Amelia Earhart over the Pacific, then during WWII he'd planned the carrier strikes for the invasion of North Africa and served as second-in-command of the carrier *Saratoga*.

Sisson slapped Tom's shoulder. "We're glad to have you back, son."

Tom's eyes opened wide with surprise.

"Personally," Sisson said, "I've never heard of a more wonderful act than what you pulled out there."

Tom's face softened. He thanked the captain.

Sisson meant it. Two days earlier, in a *Leyte* press release, he'd praised Tom's rescue attempt by saying: "There has been no finer act of unselfish heroism in military history. From the time of the first reports, we all prayed that our shipmate's life would have been saved thereby."

Sisson's smile faded. He told Tom that he'd sent two recon planes over the crash site that morning. "They saw Ensign Brown's body still in the wreckage," he added softly. "He'd been stripped of his jacket and gear."

Tom looked down at his feet. The finality was hard to accept. Jesse had become the navy's first black officer to die in battle.

"I've got a game call to make and I need your advice," Sisson continued. "We can steer close to the coast and launch a copter, and the flight surgeon can try to cut Jesse's body out. The question is: Do you think it can work?"

Tom shook his head slowly. "Sir, those mountains are teeming with Chinese and that helicopter makes an easy target. There's a good chance more men are going to get killed." After a pause, Tom added, "I know Jesse wouldn't want that."

Sisson stroked his chin. "I've got another plan. And I wish there was another way—but we can send a flight up there with napalm and give Jesse a warrior's funeral." Sisson studied Tom's face.

Tom's eyes met his. "I think Jesse would understand," Tom said.

Sisson nodded.

"And, sir," Tom added slowly. "Our squadron should be the ones to do it."*

---

* Pilot Herb Sergeant flew the recon mission that confirmed Jesse's death. He says it was "the saddest flight" he ever made. Another '32 pilot, Bryan Rudy, flew the funeral flight; he remembers that as they dropped napalm on Jesse's remains, one of the pilots recited the Lord's Prayer.

Sailors crowd the intercom as Captain Sisson announces
Jesse's death. Plane captain Carl Jeckel had his
camera nearby and took this picture.

Sisson nodded and turned to a sailor. "Get Dug Neill on the horn. Tell him to put together a four-plane strike." Sisson quickly corrected himself: "A funeral flight."

The enlisted sailors stood aside with the usual courtesy as Tom limped through the corridor. Their eyes lowered from his matted hair to his soiled flight suit. They may or may not have recognized him. That morning, Sisson had formally announced Jesse's death to the entire ship and concluded by saying: "The country needed Jesse Brown."

Tom passed through the mess hall, his helmet under his arm. Officers dotted the tables and stewards cleaned up from breakfast. Everyone looked, but no one said a word.

Tom approached the green curtain to the ready room, spread the flap, and entered. In a rush of green slacks and dark leather, the squadron stood from their magazines and board games.

Tom lowered his head. It was hard to face them, having returned without Jesse at his side. The pilots doused cigarettes and set their coffee mugs aside. In a bunch, they swarmed Tom. Koenig, Marty, and Wilkie slapped his back, and Dad Fowler shook his hand. So many voices overlapped. Cevoli gripped Tom by the shoulder, his eyes misty.

The crowd parted as the skipper barreled through. Tom's shoulders sank. *Here it comes,* he thought. He braced for the words *Your court-martial will convene on . . .*

With everyone watching, the skipper extended his hand. Tom shook it.

"Thanks for risking your life for Jesse," the skipper said. "We're all mighty proud of you."

Tom glanced around. The others were nodding, their eyes filled with gratitude.

"Cevoli says that what you did was the finest act he's ever seen," the skipper added, "and that's sayin' something." Just the skipper, Dad, and a few others knew how Cevoli had earned the Navy Cross during WWII: Flying his Hellcat off the coast of the Philippines, he had single-handedly strafed the Japanese super-battleship *Yamato.*

The skipper placed an arm over Tom's shoulder and steered him from the circle. "Be sure to get to sick bay to tend to that limp. And stay off your feet as long as you need."

Only later would Tom realize what had changed. The skipper's edict—"It's bad enough to lose one pilot. We can't lose two"—was based on the concept of a nameless, faceless downed pilot. But when that pilot was Jesse, everything changed. The skipper never mentioned a court-martial for Tom. He'd later write the squadron's combat history and record Tom's actions as "outstanding heroics."

The skipper departed to plot the funeral flight and Tom turned back to his friends. His brow was still furrowed, his thoughts far away, focused on someone Jesse had spoken about endlessly. Tom's mind now held a single question.

Does she know yet?

CHAPTER 40

WITH DEEP REGRET

A day later, December 8
Hattiesburg, Mississippi

ARMS LADEN WITH SHOPPING BAGS, Daisy followed her best friend, Snook Hardy, into the apartment building of Snook's parents. It was a Friday afternoon, around 4 P.M.

The girls shed their winter jackets. Underneath, they wore sweaters and skirts. Snook was tall and thin, and glasses encircled her cheerful eyes. Back when they were children, the two had lived next door to each other and worn a path through the hedge between their yards. Everyone called them "Pete" and "Repeat" because whenever one was seen, the other was nearby. The girls sank into couches and giggled as they slid paperboard boxes from the bags.

Daisy held up a colorful new dress. She had purchased it in preparation for her upcoming trip to the Bahamas with Jesse. Daisy's other bags contained Christmas presents for Pam. In a letter, Jesse had suggested specific presents Daisy should buy for their baby.

The phone rang and Snook bounded into the kitchen. "Yes, ma'am, she's here," Snook said, then shouted over her shoulder, "Tootie, your mama's calling!"

Daisy entered the kitchen and held the phone to her ear.

"Come home, child, you have company," her mother said simply. Her voice sounded strange. Daisy asked who had come to see her but got no answer. Daisy's eyebrows furrowed. She hung up the phone and turned to Snook.

"All she'd say is there's someone there to see me," Daisy said.

Daisy juggled her shopping bags as she shut the door of the green Wayfarer. The December shadows stretched from the clotheslines behind her mother's apartment. Daisy scurried along the path, her eyes sparkling. *It must be someone from* Life *magazine!* she thought. The magazine's photo essay on Jesse was due to be published that month. Daisy wondered if they had come for some photos of Jesse's hometown. She pattered up the back steps and into the kitchen.

Her mother, Addie, came to her side. Addie was robust, with a strong, oval face. Her eyes normally beamed, but not today. "Give me your bags, Daisy Pearl," she said, her voice shaky. "I'll take them upstairs."

Daisy's face twisted. She handed over the bags and her mother disappeared. Daisy heard murmuring, and she stepped into the living room. Her younger sisters and brother were there, and Jesse's close friend M. L. Beard, and a Caucasian woman who wore a Red Cross pin. Everyone turned to face her. In confusion, Daisy glanced from one somber face to the next.

M.L. approached Daisy. He was twenty-five and tall, but his thin mustache made him look older and wiser. His eyes were bloodshot.

"Shouldn't you be at home in bed?" Daisy asked. M.L. usually slept during the day because he worked nights, stocking a local department store while saving up for medical school.

The young man glanced at his feet and told Daisy that her mother had called him. He didn't look up. "When was the last time you heard from Jesse?" M.L. asked, his voice quivering.

"I got a letter from him today," Daisy said. "Why?"

M.L. walked over to the family's radio against a side wall. The radio was square and tall, like a small jukebox. Daisy's mother always placed her mail on top.

There sat what looked like a white postcard.

"We just received this," M.L. said. He took the postcard, passed it to Daisy, then turned away. Daisy saw M.L.'s shoulders bobbing. He was crying.

Daisy noticed that the "postcard" was actually a Western Union telegram. Her knees became weak. She lowered her purse to the floor. Her legs automatically carried her to the couch and she sat down. She glanced around the room again. Her siblings were crying and M.L. was looking away. The Red Cross woman had lowered her head. In the kitchen, Daisy's mother paced in circles with Pam in her arms.

Daisy gasped, and the telegram shook in her hands. She read a few words: *It is with deep regret* . . . She looked away and held the telegram at arm's length. Her tears began flowing as waves of horror came crashing down. Daisy peeked back at the telegram. Through blurry tears she read it.

It is with deep regret that I officially report the death of your husband Ensign Jesse Leroy Brown. . . .

The telegram fell from her fingers. Daisy buried her face in her hands and cried. Her muffled sobs filled the room.

She felt someone sit beside her and pull her close, but she didn't lift her head. She sobbed and sobbed into her hands. Her chest kept heaving.

After some time, Daisy lifted her face, sniffled, and sucked in air. She saw M.L. at her side. Someone handed her a handkerchief. She wiped her eyes and nose. Her rib cage ached. A vision of Jesse's parents entered her mind. John and Julia lived alone in the countryside, without a phone. Their children had all grown up and moved away.

Daisy staggered to her feet. M.L. moved to steady her, but Daisy waved him away. She retrieved her purse from the floor and rummaged through it. Daisy produced her car keys and moved for the back door. Her mother blocked her way with Pam in her arms. Addie shook her head. Her eyes were sad but stern. She had been widowed at the age of thirty and never imagined that this would befall her daughter too. The Red Cross woman pleaded with Daisy to sit.

"I've got to get to the Browns'," Daisy said, her voice shaking. "I want to be there before they get the news."

"Child, you're in no state to drive," her mother asserted.

Daisy turned to M.L. "Will you drive me?"

M.L. nodded. Daisy passed him the keys and led the way out the door.

Twenty minutes later, Daisy climbed the rickety steps to the Brown family's porch. Before she entered, the wails stopped her where she stood. Daisy nearly broke down herself but took a deep breath and entered the cabin. M.L. followed.

On one side of the room, John Brown sat rocking in his chair. His wife, Julia, sat across his lap. Her arms were locked around him and she sobbed with her face pressed against his shoulder. Julia glanced up and saw Daisy. She ran and embraced her and the two cried together. M.L. knelt at the side of Jesse's father. John Brown kept rocking, his eyes fixed blankly across the room.

Julia was gasping for breath and clutching her chest, so Daisy guided her to a chair at the kitchen table where Jesse and his mother had once played "the word game." Now, instead of a dictionary, a telegram sat on the table. Daisy moved the telegram out of sight and held Julia's hand.[*]

[*] The telegram to Daisy read: "It is with deep regret that I officially report the death of your husband Ensign Jesse Leroy Brown US Naval Reserve which occurred 4 December as a result of action in the Korean area. When further details are received concerning his remains you will be informed immediately. Your husband died while in the performance of his duty and while serving his country. I extend my sincere sympathy in your great loss. — Vice Admiral John W. Roper, Chief of Naval Personnel"

Daisy glanced over and saw John Brown still rocking, locked in a stupor. M.L. shook his head. Daisy stood. "M.L., bring Daddy Brown to the car," she said. "We're going to the doctor."

Daisy led Julia down the rickety steps toward the Wayfarer and M.L. followed with both of his arms wrapped around John Brown to keep him from collapsing.

This time, Daisy drove.

That night, Daisy clutched the railing as she climbed the back steps of her mother's apartment in the dark. Her mind felt hazy. *One last task*, she thought. M.L. followed close behind her. The doctor had given Jesse's parents sedatives and they had insisted they'd be okay.

Daisy staggered into the kitchen and heard more voices in the living room. Snook peeked into the kitchen and approached with open arms. After a long tearful hug, Daisy picked up the telephone from its cradle and cranked the handle. She huddled over the handset and asked for the long distance operator.

For some time, Daisy talked in a low voice, pausing only to wipe her eyes. Finally, she hung up and turned to Snook. "Now Jesse's brothers know," Daisy said. In search of better opportunity, Fletcher, Lura, Marvin, and William had moved to Chicago, where they lived in an apartment building owned by their uncle.

With Snook at her side, Daisy entered the living room. Her pastor, Reverend Woullard, was waiting with her family. The reverend shepherded Jesse's church in the country and the city church that Daisy attended. Daisy hugged the older man, then excused herself to freshen up.

As she started up the stairs, her feet felt heavy. The light bulb at the top began swirling. Tunnel-like darkness began squeezing her vision from the sides, turning everything blacker and blacker.

Daisy fell unconscious to the stairs.

CHAPTER 41

TO THE FINISH

Three days later, December 11
Northeastern North Korea

WITH DROOPING EYES, Red watched his shadow walk beside him. The shadow was hunched, dropping one foot in front of the other. Its breath puffed in the frigid air.

Red glanced up. The road ahead snaked downhill through a corridor of rock.

He glanced down again and kept hobbling. Red resembled a survivor of a polar expedition. His red beard had filled in and bristled with ice crystals. Dark bags hung beneath his eyes. Ice wrapped the bayonet of his rifle and his parka had turned black in spots.

Behind him, Jack plodded amid a line of twenty Marines. The youngster's black mustache was thick and unkempt. The men mumbled now and then. No one talked anymore—they lacked the energy to finish a sentence. Alongside them, drivers steered jeeps and hauled the wounded.

Yudam-ni lay seventy-eight miles behind the Marines. They had fought their way here, to Korea's eastern coast, in a grueling trek that the men were calling "the Big Bug-Out." Once sixty Marines strong, the detachment had been whittled almost in half, to thirty-five men. Among their losses was the detachment's only MIA—Charlie Kline. No one had seen him since the creek bed.

Red's eyelids sank as he slogged along. The cold masked his scent—he hadn't showered in fifty-three days. He sporadically slapped his cheeks to stay awake. Red caught glimpses of other units ahead, snaking downhill, and he heard orders shouted from units behind him, around the bend.

With every yard, the rock wall on the left diminished a bit. Red glanced to the side and his eyes widened. Far below lay a harbor partly ringed by snow-capped hills. Sunlight glistened on the sea and rows of American transport ships lay against the dark sand, their doors open.

Red almost bumped into the man in front of him. The column slowed and men wandered to the roadside. Their eyes feasted on the sights.

The road ahead wound down to a tent city on the beach where cranes transferred nets of cargo onto the ships. Marine units were marching through the tent city and onto the ships. Deeper in the harbor, more ships lay at anchor and planes buzzed in from aircraft carriers beyond.

This was the ramshackle port of Hungnam, and one of those ships would be Red's ride out of North Korea. Red and the men at his sides remained silent. At that moment, he knew it: *Devans was right.*

At the base of the hill, Red hiked faster, surging with a desperate rush of adrenaline. He panted and struggled to keep his footing. The gate to the tent city—the finish line—lay a field's length away.

Behind the gate, Shore Patrol sailors directed traffic, waving in each unit of Marines, urging them to move faster. The forces of democracy were evacuating North Korea and fourteen thousand fighting men were arriving from the Chosin, not to mention the units from other

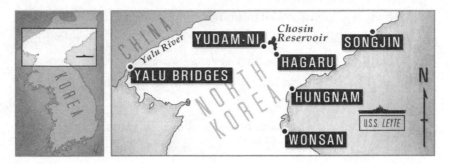

areas. Horns honked and jeep engines sputtered. Military interpreters shouted to crowds of North Korean refugees to remind them that they had to wait for the troops to board first. Time was of the essence—the army's 7th Infantry was holding a perimeter in the hills. About forty-five miles down the coast, Wonsan had cleared out the day before.

The gate bobbed in Red's vision. He swore he would collapse in joy when he crossed that line in the dirt. Then the gunny's Kentucky twang rang out: "Hold it up!" The men passed the word forward and Red's face sank. Everyone stopped and jeeps squealed to a halt. The men stood, wobbly.

Gunny Sawyer paced back and forth along the line. "Double column!" he shouted. "And look like Marines! Cinch them straps. Tuck in them loose ends. Stand like you've got a spine."

Red plodded into a line and fastened his icy chinstrap. Others straightened the bedrolls sagging on their buddies' packs. Wounded men hobbled from jeeps on frostbitten feet, using their rifle butts for balance. The wounded fell in and the two columns came to number roughly fifteen men in each. As the gunny passed to inspect them, Red and the others stood taller.

"Forward march!" the gunny called.

Sixty boots began thumping the snowy gravel. Red's eyes fixed on the ragged helmet cover of the man ahead. His eyes perked up and he raised his chin higher. In step beside the columns, the gunny started singing: "From the halls of Montezuma . . ." A chorus of voices picked up the tune: ". . . to the shores of Tripoli. We will fight our country's battles, in the air, on land, and sea. . . ."

The men sang as they marched through the gate. Young voices blended with older ones, northern voices with southern. From the corner of his eye, Red saw others watching—the SPs, the interpreters, refugee mothers with babies, squatting old men, bundled little boys and girls.

Inside the tent city, the song ended and the gunny called a halt. Red and the others lowered their last boot heavily. The wounded swayed, desperate to keep balance, and everyone fought to keep their backs straight. They once had been Boy Scouts and soda jerks and baseball players in sandlots. But now beneath the stubble and grime, they were veterans.*

Even the enemy was impressed.

Off to the side of the compound, hundreds of Chinese prisoners watched from the fence of a wire pen. Blankets were wrapped around their shoulders. They were loosely guarded and their casual posture suggested they had accepted their fate. They were due to be evacuated, too.

They had to be.

During the "Big Bug-Out," some Chinese prisoners had escaped from the Marine column and were "liberated" by their fellow Chinese. Marine patrols later found the escaped POWs machine-gunned in the snow. The communists had executed their own troops, believing them to have been "ideologically contaminated" during their captivity under the Americans.

Runners approached the gunny to deliver the unit's assembly orders. Red's eyes focused ahead and narrowed. Between the men and the ships lay a street, on both sides of which sat trailers. Their wooden side boards had been flapped up and turned into awnings. Marines were lining up beneath the awnings and someone was serving something—food or drink, Red couldn't tell.

---

* Red's Weapons Company marched to the Chosin with 188 men and reached Hungnam with 109. Ed Coderre's How Company began with 185 men and ended with 50. Among How Company's survivors were Wick and Tex, both frostbitten but alive.

The gunny returned. He pointed to a ship that was currently taking aboard tanks and told the men that they'd be boarding soon. The ship would carry them to Pusan, on the southeastern tip of South Korea. The gunny showed them where to assemble on the beach, two hundred yards away. "Y'all got ten minutes to grab a snack," the gunny said, raising a thumb to the trailers behind him. "Ten minutes, no more! Lotta Marines are coming in behind you."

Red and the others grinned.

Stretcher bearers approached and the gunny told the wounded to fall out to the side. "Everyone else stay on your feet!" the gunny added. "No plopping down—I ain't gonna drag your asses the last mile—it's un-damn-dignified!"

The men roared with laughter.

Red, Jack, and a few of their buddies hobbled toward a white trailer with a red awning. The line was short and a sign read: HOT COFFEE, FRESH BREWED. Inside, women wore green parkas and served coffee from stainless dispensers with spigots. A sailor walked up and placed his canteen around the spigot. The woman turned a handle and the coffee flowed. Steam rose from the canteen.

Am I dreaming? Red wondered. He was accustomed to melting snow in his mouth when he needed a drink. He and the others pried their canteens free and edged forward. Red unscrewed his canteen cap. A gritty, grinding noise sounded. Frozen saliva, dirt, and particles of food were caked around the canteen's rim. The others' canteens were just as filthy.

Red raised his canteen toward the spigot.

"Stop!" A woman reached from behind the counter and shielded the spigot with her hand, her face cringing with revulsion. Her co-workers leaned in to look at Red's canteen and reeled in disgust. "That's not sanitary," the woman snapped. "You're going to need to find a clean canteen."

Red turned to see if Jack and the others were putting him on. The others were muttering under their breaths—it was not a joke. Red glanced up at the woman and she glared down with disdain.

One of Red's buddies pointed to another trailer that was serving coffee a few spots down the row. "We're taking our business elsewhere," the Marine told the woman. She shrugged with indifference.

Red and his buddies walked to the Salvation Army trailer, where a perky young girl worked behind the counter, bundled against the cold. Jack held out his canteen. "Miss, will you still serve us with these?" He gestured to his canteen.

"You betcha," the girl said. "And we've got Oreos too!" She fanned her hand to a platter of cookies.

Red waited his turn and held his canteen up. His eyes followed the steam as the girl filled his canteen.

"Creamer?" the girl asked.

"Yes, ma'am," Red said.

The girl poured powder from a box. "Sugar?"

He nodded happily and she poured him sugar too.

Red capped his canteen and returned it to its case. He pulled off a mitten, reached for a few Oreos, and put them in his pocket. His fingernails were long and dirt filled the wrinkles on his hand, but the girl seemed not to notice.

Red and his buddies thanked her and hurried to their assembly point.

On a stretch of beach beside their ship, Red and his buddies dropped their packs and relaxed. They'd arrived early, even before the gunny.

Up and down the line of ships, Marines from other units climbed gangplanks to board. Trucks and tanks drove up the ramps and into the vessels' cargo holds. Cranes hoisted jeeps aboard. One hundred and eighty ships were already waiting or en route to Hungnam. Over nearly two weeks, the ships would take aboard 100,000 fighting men,

17,000 vehicles, and 91,000 civilians—most but not all of the refugees who had flocked to the harbor.

Red opened his canteen and took a sip of coffee. It was perfectly hot and bittersweet. He fished an Oreo from his pocket and crunched down on the cookie. His jaw had nearly forgotten how to chew soft food. The black crumbs clung to his stubble.

Jack and the others ate cookies and drank their coffee in silence.

They made no victory toast, nor would they. But there had been a victory of sorts at the Chosin Reservoir. The Marines, the army, the forces of democracy—roughly nineteen thousand men—had bested more than a hundred thousand enemy troops, nearly destroying the Chinese 20th and 27th armies.

"We shouldn't be leaving," a Marine commented. His eyes scanned across vast piles of supplies. "We should just regroup here."

Red shrugged. "Here or down the coast," he said. "What's the difference?" The others nodded. In a month, they'd get their wish. In January 1951, the 1st Marine Division would be returning to battle.

"Heya, look at that," Jack said. He pointed to a nearby ship and Red's eyes focused on the anchor chain. Halfway up the chain, two North Korean peasant boys were climbing to sneak aboard.

Their small faces were clenched. Their hands clutched the iron chains and their diminutive bodies dangled over the frigid blue water.

They might have been brothers. They were probably orphans. Whoever they were, they were desperate to escape the communists. Red glanced at the boys and knew exactly why the Korean War mattered. There, on the anchor chain, he saw why he had come to this miserable, frozen land and why Devans had given his twenty-one-year-old life.

"That about says it all," Red muttered.

At his side, Jack nodded.

CHAPTER 42

THE GIFT

Five days later, December 16
Hattiesburg, Mississippi

THE MORNING SUNSHINE STREAMED through the windows and into the apartment's living room. From outside on the porch, Daisy's voice trickled through the glass, as did the soft, somber voices of strangers.

Local folks, blacks and whites, men and women, dotted the sidewalk in front of Daisy's mother's apartment. Some were coming to see Daisy, while others were leaving. Ever since the local paper had announced Jesse's death on the front page, a constant stream of visitors had come to the projects to express their condolences. For many white visitors, it was their first visit to Hattiesburg's all-black neighborhood.

During a lull between visitors, Daisy entered the apartment with a covered bowl in hand. She set it on the kitchen counter with the others. Almost every visitor had brought banana bread or a casserole or their mother's recipe for this or that.

Daisy sank down onto the couch. She had never expected to become a twenty-three-year-old war widow. She wasn't angry at Jesse for leaving her, nor at God for taking him. When a writer for *Ebony* magazine asked how she was coping, Daisy said, "I guess it was the will of the Lord to take him. I'm glad, proud that he died fighting as a navy flyer. He would have wanted it that way more than anything in the world."

Still, Daisy's heart felt hollow.

The house was silent. Her mother was out and Pam was napping. Daisy was glad that Pam was asleep. She had never cried more over her daughter than she had that week. Anytime Pam had heard an airplane fly over, she ran for the windows shouting, "Daddy! Daddy!"

Daisy's mother entered through the back door and set a small sack on the kitchen table. She emptied the contents and a pile of mail poured forth. Citizens across the nation were writing to Daisy to express their sympathies. Even Tom Hudner had written from the *Leyte* to tell Daisy of her husband's bravery, but the letter went missing in the deluge of mail.

Daisy's mother leafed through the pile surreptitiously. Whenever she found a newspaper, she tore it in two and threw it in the trash. She couldn't bear to let Daisy see what the papers were saying—it was too terrible.

The story of Jesse and Tom had become front-page news across America. The papers were all quoting a navy press release that had been wired from the *Leyte* immediately after the crash, before Tom had returned to the ship. The press release got the story wrong, and so did the papers.

In Tom's hometown, the Fall River *Herald News* wrote, "The 26-year-old Hudner landed in the same field and ran to Brown's help knowing, the Navy said, that his own chances of escape were slim. But Brown was dead when Hudner reached him. Hudner radioed for a helicopter to take Brown's body back to friendly territory."

In Hattiesburg, many black folks read the *Afro-American* newspaper's account: "Navy rescue planes rushed to the scene of the crash, but Brown's plane became enveloped in flames before he could be removed from the cockpit. . . . the Marine helicopter arrived and Ensign Brown was removed from the plane. He was dead."

Daisy's mother thumbed through the envelopes to see who had written. She didn't realize that her efforts to protect her daughter were in vain. Daisy had already gathered clues from her visitors, who openly lamented the senseless, gruesome way that Jesse had died. She had heard how her husband had died alone, before anyone could reach him. And she surmised what no one would tell her—that Jesse had burned to death.

"It's for you," Daisy's mother said as she set an envelope on the coffee table in front of her daughter and then hurried away. Daisy sat up, curious. "I'm going for a walk," her mother announced from the kitchen. The back door opened and closed.

Daisy picked up the envelope. Her eyes went wide. She recognized the handwriting and the return address: "Fleet Post Office San Francisco, USS *Leyte*, VF-32—Ensign Jesse L. Brown."

The tears began streaming. Daisy slowly opened the envelope and unfolded four handwritten pages.*

At Sea, Sunday Nite
3 December 1950

Daisy held her mouth and shook her head. Jesse had written this on the night before his death:

My own dear sweet Angel, I'm so lonesome I could just boo-hoo.
But I try to restrain myself and think of the fun we're going to have
when we do get together, so only a few tears escape now and then.
I love you so very much, my darling.

---

* Daisy made Jesse's last letter available to readers following the Afterword of this book.

Daisy could hear Jesse's voice in her mind. She held the letter closer.

The last few days we've been doing quite a bit of flying, trying to slow down the Chinese communists and to give support to some Marines who were surrounded. . . . Knowing that he's helping those poor guys on the ground, I think every pilot on here would fly until he dropped in his tracks.

Daisy's eyes raced left to right.

Don't be discouraged, Angel, believe in God and believe in Him with all your might and I know that things will work out all right. We need Him now like never before. Have faith with me, darling, and He'll see us thru and we'll be together again before long too.

Daisy flipped through the pages. Jesse spoke of the past they shared and of the future he longed for with her. It was as if he had a premonition that they might part.

I want you to keep that pretty little chin up, Angel, come on now, way up. I want you also to be confident in this and that is: Your husband loves his wife with all his heart and soul—no man ever loved a woman more.

Daisy turned to the final page. The end was coming.

Darling, I'm going to close now and climb in the rack. I honestly dread going to bed, but I usually dream of you, so I'll manage to make it until we'll share our bed together again—darling, pray it'll be soon.

Daisy's eyes savored each word.

I have to fly tomorrow. But so far as that goes my heart hasn't been down to earth since the first time you kissed me, and when you love me you "send" it clear out-of-this-world.

Daisy gripped the letter tightly.

I'll write again as soon as I can. I'll love you forever.
Your devoted husband
lovingly and completely yours
forever
Jesse

Daisy clutched the letter to her chest. She leaned back against the couch and closed her eyes. New tears slipped down her cheeks as a look of calm settled across her face. She knew that this letter was a blessing, a means to hear Jesse's voice again and again for the rest of her life.

Through her tears, Daisy thanked God.

Soon after

Each morning before their shifts, they came up to the corridor in the *Leyte's* tower.

They were white sailors, black sailors, men in T-shirts from the boiler room. This was officer country, a place where the average sailor never ventured. Stewards in white high-collared coats, deckhands in colored shirts, each came with an envelope in hand.

At a steel door, each man knocked. The door opened and each handed over his envelope.

Officers came up too, holding envelopes. Tom knocked on the steel door. So did Koenig, Marty, and Wilkie. Some didn't have as far to walk. Captain Sisson came from the bridge and handed over his envelope.

*   *   *

Every morning, Commander Wally Madden approached the steel door and stepped inside without knocking. This was his office, and every morning he shook his head in awe.

His staff had placed the morning's collection on his desk, and each day the pile of envelopes cascaded like a landslide across the desktop.

The envelopes contained cash. Everyone in Squadron 32 had heard Jesse say, at one time or another, that his dream was to provide his daughter with an education, so the *Leyte*'s crew had taken up a collection to create a scholarship for baby Pam. As the air group CAG, Madden had been chosen as custodian of the funds.

The ship's crew didn't normally take up collections. They couldn't possibly do it for every casualty. But, as Madden explained in a *Leyte* press release, "We felt this way about the loss of Jesse. He was a hell of a swell guy. We figured that his little girl was going to have a rough row to hoe without any daddy, so we wanted to do something for her in his memory."

Some sailors gave one dollar, some a couple of quarters. Someone leaked that Captain Sisson had contributed forty dollars—equivalent to nearly four hundred dollars in present-day money.

In the end, nearly every man on the *Leyte* knocked on that steel door with an envelope in his hand.

Six weeks later, February 3, 1951

A crowd of civilians cheered as the line of pilots descended the gangway of the *Leyte* and stepped onto the pier of North Island Naval Air Station in San Diego. The sun shone brightly, the temperature was in the low sixties. After three months at war, the *Leyte* had returned.*

Dignitaries waved from a grandstand. A navy band belted out

---

*While en route to San Diego, Captain Sisson received a message from Elizabeth Taylor's manager. The starlet had been following the *Leyte* in the papers and asked if she could greet the crew in San Diego. But Sisson didn't want the crew to be whistling and cat-calling the actress when they should be remembering the men they had lost in battle. He politely declined Elizabeth's offer.

marching music as drum majorettes high-stepped to the beat. Behind the crowd, sailors opened a telephone trailer for the pilots to call home.

The crowd parted as the skipper, Cevoli, and Dad led the squadron through. The pilots wore green tent caps and leather jackets, and they carried sea bags over their shoulders. Beyond the distant hangars, a navy transport was waiting to fly them to Quonset Point.

As the squadron filtered past, the crowd searched the pilots' faces for friends or loved ones. Female sailors batted their eyelashes and dignitaries stepped down from the grandstand, eager to pose for pictures.

But the men of Fighting 32 remained in line. Marty grinned at some of the female sailors but didn't make a pass. Wilkie eyed the telephone trailer but didn't dart away to call his wife. Tight-lipped, Tom passed the clamoring dignitaries.

He carried two sea bags—one his, the other Koenig's. Koenig followed behind, arms wrapped around a box. The *Leyte* had sailed to war with nearly three thousand men and three had been killed in action. The box belonged to one of the fallen.

It was heavy with books—Plato's *Five Great Dialogues*, and *Love Poems, Old and New*, and Jackie Robinson's life story. There was a well-worn Bible and the drawing of a red, single-story dream house that would never be built.

Eyes set forward, the squadron left the crowd and the carrier behind. The collar of Tom's jacket had turned reddish all the way through. So had the others'. They were a squadron of veterans now, far from the days of Cannes. This time, the skipper didn't need to ask.

Everyone stuck together.

CHAPTER 43

THE CALL FROM THE CAPITAL

Almost two months later, March 31, 1951
Fall River, Massachusetts

UNDER THE CEILING LIGHT in his bedroom, Tom scribbled a note at his desk. He sporadically sipped from a glass of scotch. The window behind him was dark except for the light of the streetlamps on High land Avenue. Tom had returned to his parents' house from Quonset Point. It was a Saturday night and his parents were away at dinner.

Envelopes lay piled on his desktop, some open, some sealed. A sack of unopened mail sat on the floor nearby. The balsa planes were long gone from Tom's ceiling and the Boy Scout poster was stripped from the walls. But Tom's Horatio Hornblower book remained on his dresser.

For months, countless black citizens had written to thank Tom for trying to save Jesse. Some letters contained photos or good luck charms. One woman sent a strip of silk taffeta, her prized possession, for Tom to use as a scarf. For weeks, Tom had come home every week-end to answer the mail. He responded to each letter with a quick note and a clarification: "I'm no hero, I just did what was right to do."

The phone rang. Tom lowered his pen. *At this hour?* It rang again. Tom walked into his parents' bedroom and picked up the phone.

"Mr. Hudner, I'm trying to reach your son, Tom."

Uh-oh, Tom thought. "This is he."

The man introduced himself as the White House naval liaison officer. He was a lieutenant commander and he sounded all business. "Lieutenant," he said. "You've been approved to receive the Medal of Honor for your actions in northern Korea."

Tom's heart skipped a beat. The Medal of Honor was the military's highest award. It was so rare that Tom had yet to see anyone wearing one. Tom lowered himself to his parents' bed and kept listening. He had heard rumors that Sisson had nominated him for a medal but never believed them—until now.

"In two weeks, the president will be presenting the medal to you here in Washington, on April 13," the commander added. "It'll be a brief ceremony. Your travel and lodging arrangements will be forthcoming. Any questions?"

"No, sir." Tom's voice was low.

"Good. This will be the first Navy Medal of Honor since World War II."

The commander hung up and Tom sat, stunned. He knew the medal came with responsibility—he'd be placed on a pedestal as a figurehead of the military.

Tom's face sank as his thoughts raced to Mississippi. He lowered his head. *What will Daisy think of this? Jesse's gone and I'm getting an award?*

Two days later, Hattiesburg

Seated behind a gray plastic dashboard, Daisy clutched the Wayfarer's metal steering wheel as she drove. Snook sat beside her on the striped fabric seat. It was a Monday afternoon, and the two were running errands.

"So are you going to Washington?" Snook asked over the engine's purr. The White House had invited Daisy to attend the Medal of Honor presentation, all expenses paid.

"I don't know," Daisy said. "It's just going to bring it all back."

Snook nodded slowly.

It had been a long and sad winter. First came Jesse's memorial service at the high school. Then came Christmas, when Jesse's cousin Ike and his wife, Gwen, came home, distraught. Then Jesse's mother died. Thirty-one days after her son's death, Julia collapsed while making her bed. The coroner said that she had died from a stroke, but the family considered her a casualty of the Korean War, killed by the stress of Jesse's death. John Brown's depression only deepened.

"Someone should represent Jesse at the ceremony," Daisy said, thinking aloud. She glanced over at Snook. "The problem is, I've got no one to go with me. Will you come with me?"

Snook shook her head vigorously. "No way am I flying in some airplane to some strange city to somethin' with all those upper-class folks. . . . Are you sure *you* want to go to all that?"

Daisy sighed. It did sound intimidating.

Ten days later, Daisy looked timidly at her toes as she paced through the aircraft's aisle. She wore a long tan coat and a small hat. Behind her, the sounds of revving aircraft engines snuck through the plane's open door. It was just another busy day at Hattiesburg Airport. From seats on both sides of the aisle, white passengers glanced up at Daisy. Businessmen dipped their newspapers and women lowered their makeup cases. In those days, it was uncommon to see a black person flying.

Daisy wanted to turn and flee back to the terminal. She had never traveled alone before. *You're representing Jesse!* she reminded herself.

Daisy dropped into a seat beside a round window with the curtains spread. Behind her, baggage thumped as it was loaded aboard.

Daisy took a deep breath and fastened her seatbelt.

The following afternoon, Friday, April 13, 1951

From the back seat of a Cadillac, Daisy glanced side to side with wonder. To the left stretched the National Mall, its green lawn warm in the mid-afternoon sun. On her right stood the stately buildings of Washington, D.C., every other one with wide steps and tall stone columns.

Daisy held a bouquet of roses on the lap of her coat. The bouquet was a gift from the secretary of the navy, who would be present at the ceremony.

At Daisy's side sat her escort, Seaman First Class Clara Carroll. Clara was a young black woman, too. Her navy uniform flowed into a skirt and she wore a white hat with a short brim. Her face was round, her chin was thick, and her hair curled behind her ears. The White House had arranged for Daisy to stay with Clara because most of Washington's hotels didn't permit black guests.

Daisy beamed as she gripped the roses. Already, she was overwhelmed by the navy's generosity. Earlier that morning at Quonset Point, the air group had announced their scholarship for Pam. The *Leyte*'s crew had raised $2,700, equivalent to more than $24,000 in present-day money. It was more than enough to pay for Pam's college education. The skipper had traveled to New York City and invested the money in a fund so that when Pam turned twenty-one, the money would go to her.*

Daisy hadn't forgotten Jesse's instructions for herself, either. His life insurance money had arrived, and she knew that he wanted her to

---

* The air group's scholarship announcement read: "In the collective units comprising our democratic society, there are those who through individual ability, perseverance and exemplary character earn the whole hearted respect, admiration and friendship of those who know them. Ensign Jesse L. Brown was such a person."

spend it on her education and become a teacher like his mama. But Daisy was hesitant to spend the money on herself. She had Pam to raise in addition to something Jesse had never anticipated—his father now needed her care, too.

"Have you met Lieutenant Hudner before?" Clara asked Daisy.

Daisy's face scrunched. "I'm sure I have, I just don't remember him because Jesse and I lived off base. All I really know about him is what the papers said—he tried to save Jesse, but Jesse had already passed."

Clara nodded.

"He was very brave to try," Daisy added.

Beneath the covered entrance to the White House, the driver opened Daisy's door. She stepped from the car. A navy-colored dress peeked from beneath her tan coat and she wore white gloves. Her hair was curled beneath a hat with a scalloped brim, and a borrowed mink stole draped her shoulders. From behind a wrought-iron fence, tourists snapped photos. The spring air was crisp.

A White House staffer led Daisy forward. Two Marines opened the double doors for Daisy and stood ramrod straight in their dress blues. Whenever the Marines were around, it meant that the president was near. Daisy could see a chandelier inside and a small army of staffers waiting to greet her.

She took a deep breath and stepped inside.

Tom and his family funneled into the White House Cabinet Room behind the presidential secretary, a man in his forties. Tom wore his navy blue uniform with the usual black tie and white shirt, and his hair was swept back.

Tom's family admired the long table where the president held meetings. Thick leather chairs surrounded the table and light poured in from tall windows beside it. Tom's mother was all smiles in her thickest fur wrap. His father stood quietly content in a gray three-piece suit. Tom's sister and brothers were there along with his three uncles and their wives.

Tom's face scrunched and he turned to the secretary. "Where can I find Daisy Brown?" he said. "I really need to talk with her."

The secretary told Tom that Daisy was waiting outside but that Tom couldn't go out yet—he needed to meet the president first.

"Okay," Tom muttered.

He had tried to find Daisy at the hotel but she hadn't been there, either. Tom's uncle stood quietly by. He knew why Daisy wasn't at their hotel, but he held his tongue to not spoil Tom's day.

The uncle was from Tom's mother's side and his last name was Brown, like Jesse's. He'd decided to come to Washington at the last minute and called the stately hotel on 16th Street, where the White House was housing the Hudner family. The uncle told the reservations clerk the reason for his visit and asked, "You've heard about Jesse Brown, the colored pilot who died in Korea?"

After a pause, the clerk replied, "I'm sorry, Mr. Brown, but we're all filled up."

Tom's uncle found this odd. So he called a friend in Washington and asked him to try to make a reservation for the same night. His friend called him back. "You're all set to stay there," the friend said. "The problem was that when you said your last name was 'Brown,' they thought you were a Negro, someone from the Hattiesburg Brown family."

"Everyone, please gather around," the secretary said. Tom and his family congregated. The secretary told Tom's family that they could watch the ceremony from the stairs behind the president. He then turned to Tom and said, "Just a warning, but expect to see a lot of cameras—far more than usual." The secretary sounded annoyed at the thought. Tom knew why the media were turning out.

Two days prior, President Truman had made a controversial decision.

With the battle lines in Korea seesawing along the 38th parallel, Truman's administration was suggesting peace talks with the communists. General MacArthur, however, wanted to bomb targets across the Yalu and airlift Nationalist Chinese troops from Taiwan into China. He'd even written to Congress to request authority to expand the war, with complete disregard for the Soviet Union's defense pact with China.

Truman had little choice. Rather than watch the legendary general spark World War III, he fired MacArthur.*

The door to the Cabinet Room opened and Tom turned. From the hallway, the president's snappy midwestern twang sounded.

"I want to meet this young man!" Truman said loudly. "Where is he?"

When Tom and President Truman stepped onto the porch, thunderous applause erupted. Countless flashbulbs popped and Tom blinked. Dignitaries lined the sides of the staircase and more than three hundred people crowded the Rose Garden lawn below.

Truman flashed a cheery grin and waved to the crowd. His face was round, his nose sharp, and he wore wire-rim glasses. A red tie provided a splash of color to his gray suit. Few presidents had ever made as many big decisions as he had. Truman had authorized use of the atomic bombs to end WWII, he'd ordered the desegregation of the military, and he'd committed American forces to the war in Korea.

Tom scanned the faces along the staircase. Halfway down, on the right, he spotted Daisy. She was facing him and smiling, tight-lipped

---

* Truman's peace talks would founder over the POW issue. The forces of democracy had captured vast numbers of Chinese and North Korean soldiers, and the communists wanted them returned as terms of a cease-fire. But the forces of democracy held that the POWs should be able to choose to return to a communist land or not. Over this issue, the negotiations would melt down and the war would rage for two more years.

but friendly. She held a bouquet of roses in the crux of her arm and was clapping. Tom released a breath of relief. Daisy stood between Clara and a middle-aged black officer. A thin mustache lined the officer's oval face; he was Lieutenant Dennis Nelson, and during WWII he'd become one of the navy's first twelve black officers.

Truman turned to Tom and asked, "Shall we?"

Tom smiled and nodded.

Truman descended the stairs, followed by Tom and his family.

Truman stepped to the podium, where microphones were waiting. Tom took his place at the president's side.

Cameramen hunkered down behind movie cameras and photographers raised hand-held still cameras. Reporters flipped open notepads. More cameramen climbed ladders in the background. Behind the press pool, a large portrait of Jesse in his uniform stood on an easel. The White House staff had enlarged the photo so that the journalists could capture Jesse's likeness for their stories.

Truman glanced nervously at the press pool. He was in no hurry to face their questions. The American Legion's commander had just come out against his decision to fire MacArthur, and MacArthur himself had gone silent in Tokyo.

Truman looked across the audience and began in a steady voice: "The President of the United States takes pleasure in presenting the Medal of Honor to Lieutenant Thomas Jerome Hudner Jr., United States Navy."

Applause sounded.

When the crowd quieted, Truman recited a summary of Tom's actions while Tom stood at attention, his eyes locked forward. Admirals and generals dotted the crowd of men in fedoras and women in shin-length dresses. Captain Sisson was among the brass too. In the background, the Washington Monument stood tall against a blue sky.

Truman's voice lowered as he read the final line: "Lieutenant

Hudner's exceptionally valiant action and selfless devotion to a ship-mate sustain and enhance the highest traditions of the U.S. Naval Service."

The president removed a felt-covered box from the podium. He opened the box, revealing the bronze, star-shaped Medal of Honor. "You earned this," Truman said to Tom. "This is the greatest honor anyone can get." He draped the medal around Tom's neck and snapped the blue ribbon closed.

"Thank you, sir," Tom said.

Truman shook Tom's hand but didn't let go. His eyes lowered to the medal. With his free hand he lifted the medal from Tom's neck and said, "I would rather have this than be president."

Tom grinned.

A cameraman shouted from the press pool: "Mr. President! Can you stay there so we can get some close-ups?"

"Sure," Truman said. "Let's do even better." He turned to Daisy and called, "Mrs. Brown—would you be willing to join Lieutenant Hud-ner and me?"

Daisy, President Truman, and Tom during the White House ceremony

Daisy nodded. She descended the stairs like a princess. Truman wrapped his arm around her and steered her close. Daisy glanced at Tom and smiled; not a single tear had slipped from her eyes.

She's just like her husband was, Tom thought. *An extraordinary person.*

Truman turned to face the press with Daisy on his right and Tom on his left. "Okay!" he said loudly. "Get your shots, movie men."

The journalists laughed. Cameras flashed and movie cameras panned on their tripods. Daisy had never been under a brighter spotlight. *So this was Jesse's world,* she thought. Her husband was special, she had always known it. But not until she was the only black person on the White House lawn did she understand his accomplishments.

Daisy smiled across the sea of cameras and didn't blink.

The president's secretary indicated that Truman needed to be going. The president nodded and shook Tom's hand heartily. Truman then turned to Daisy and said, "Mrs. Brown, the nation is grateful for your husband's sacrifice."

"Thank you for remembering him, Mr. President," Daisy said. She explained that she had brought a photo of Jesse and left it with his secretary.

Truman's eyes turned moist. He shook Daisy's hand and said simply, "Thank you."

The president began to climb the steps. A chorus of voices shouted from the press pool: "Mr. President!"

Truman stopped and gave them a wave. "Sorry, gents, this is not the time or the place." Truman wheeled to resume climbing and caught his foot on a step. He lost his balance and was about to fall when Lieutenant Nelson—the black officer—snagged him by the arm. Truman regained his footing and paused, flustered.

"Don't worry, Mr. President," Nelson said. "There's still someone supporting you today."

Truman chuckled, as did everyone in earshot. The president bounded up the remaining steps.

Tom stood alone with Daisy as the brass and dignitaries dispersed. Nearby, the journalists were boxing up their cameras. Tom's family watched from the steps with Clara and the White House staff. A few admirals lingered for a chance to speak with Tom, but everyone gave Tom and Daisy space.

"There are some things I've been wanting to tell you," Tom said softly. "There's just no easy way to do it."

"Tom, it's okay," Daisy said. "Say whatever you need, I'll be all right."

Tom glanced at his toes. "Jesse was so calm through it all, I've never seen anything like it," he said. "When we were on the ground, he was calming me down, when I should have been the one calming him down."

Daisy cocked her head. "How could he have calmed you? The papers said he passed before you reached him."

Tom looked up with surprise. "Oh, they got that all wrong." New life flowed into his eyes. "Jesse was alive. We were together for forty minutes—I was up along the canopy and we were talking."

Tears welled along Daisy's eyelids. She shook her head in disbelief.

"When I left the plane to wave in the helicopter," Tom added, "that's when he let go."

Daisy squeezed the bouquet of roses tightly.

Tom looked Daisy in the eyes. "He was thinking of you. He even gave me a message to tell you."

Daisy gulped.

Tom's voice choked. "He said, 'Just tell Daisy how much I love her.'"

Daisy lowered her head and her tears flowed. Tom glanced away, his eyes blurry. Everyone watching became emotional, and some wiped their eyes.

Sniffling, Daisy pulled herself together. She blotted her eyes with a handkerchief. But Tom's head remained lowered. Daisy could tell how much Jesse's death still weighed on him.

"So, Jesse wasn't alone," Daisy said, her voice warming. "That means so much, Tom."

Tom didn't look up. "I'm just sorry the result wasn't happier," he muttered.

Daisy ducked to see Tom's face. "Tom?"

He finally looked up.

"I'm just so grateful that you tried to save him," Daisy said. "Jesse was lucky to have a friend like you."

Tom's face slowly loosened and his shoulders lowered.

After a pause he said, "Well, I guess we'd better be going."

Daisy agreed. Cars were waiting to whisk them to a dinner. That weekend they'd do a radio show together, in Baltimore; then the next month they'd travel to Chicago to be honored by the *Chicago Defender* newspaper. During the years, Tom and Daisy would make numerous appearances together to perpetuate Jesse's legacy. This was just the first.

Tom and Daisy turned and walked up the steps. Behind them, the press pool had thinned and the portrait of Jesse had come into sight.

On the steps, Clara took her place at Daisy's side and asked, "How are you holding up, Mrs. Brown?"

"I'm doing as well as I can," Daisy said. "This is the price of marrying an exceptional man."

CHAPTER 44

THE MESSAGE

Six days later, April 19, 1951
Fall River, Massachusetts

TOM WAVED SHEEPISHLY from the black Cadillac convertible as it cruised Main Street. Around him, a crowd of all ages waved and cheered. More than forty thousand citizens of Fall River filled the sidewalks and spilled into the street. The townspeople were backed up against the storefronts; some had to stand on their toes for a glimpse of the officer in the navy blazer and white hat.

From the back seat of the convertible, Tom glimpsed children, businessmen, housewives, immigrants—even his childhood bully-turned-friend, Manny Cabral, might have been there. It was a brisk, gray Thursday afternoon and the city's largest celebration since WWII had begun, an event that the town fathers had named the "Hudner Day Parade."

Tom's eyes darted about with confusion, even discomfort. He couldn't fathom why so many people had turned out to see him. Police officers jogged in front of his car while navy officers flanked its sides. Tom's parents and sister, all smiles, sat in a separate Cadillac behind Tom's and a marching band followed several lengths behind. Farther back stretched a motorcade of dignitaries, and behind them came the marching soldiers of an all-black National Guard unit.

Tom continued waving, his smile tight and awkward. This was only the beginning, and he knew it. *Life* magazine wanted to interview him. Officials from a war bond campaign wanted to put his face on posters and the Baltimore Urban League had asked him to speak at their youth rally. Invitations to a quiz show and a movie premiere were forthcoming.

Tom hadn't yet committed to a thing. Secretly, he wanted to put his newfound notoriety behind him. On his blazer he wore a small blue award ribbon to represent the medal, but nothing more. Around his neck, Tom wore his navy-issue black tie—he had left his Medal of Honor at home.

A roar bellowed from behind. Tom glanced over his shoulder as four Corsairs raced low over the parade route, then over his head. White *K*s stood out on their tails. Their noise rattled the glass store-fronts and caused children to cover their ears. Another four Corsairs buzzed Main Street, then came another four. The crowd cheered.

As the Corsairs sped away, Tom shook his head in wonder. His friends were at the controls, including Cevoli, Marty, and Wilkie—all flying to salute him.

I really don't deserve this, Tom thought.

At the end of the parade route, the vehicles stopped in the city's South Park. Tom stepped out of the Cadillac and headed over to a stage set against a hill of barren trees. A cold bay of ocean lay downhill. Behind Tom, the crowd funneled into the park.

A cluster of dignitaries lined up on the stage to greet Tom. He shook hands with the mayor, representatives from the state, and even the commander of Quonset Point, a rear admiral who'd later say in his speech: "I am very proud to wear the uniform that Tom Hudner wears."*

At the end of the receiving line waited a cluster of women. Beneath their hats they wore their hair in buns. One of the town fathers introduced them to Tom as the town's Gold Star Mothers. They'd each lost a son in war, most in WWII, a few very recently in Korea. Tom stepped into the half-circle of women and warmly shook each mother's hand. With teary eyes, one mother told Tom how brave he was for trying to save Jesse. Another pulled him close and hugged him tightly.

Tom could sense their grief, the same emotional wound that had killed Jesse's mother. Yet the women all looked at Tom with admiration. Each wanted to shake *his* hand. As Tom conversed with the Gold Star Mothers, he began to realize the powerful responsibility that came with the medal.

Someone has to speak for those who paid the ultimate price.

Eager faces of all ages watched Tom step to the wooden dais. Against the backdrop of barren trees he addressed the crowd.

"This has been one day I shall never forget," Tom said. "Concerning the incident that happened in Korea last December—just as sure as I am standing here now, if I had been down, it would have been Jesse Brown who would have helped me out."

Tom kept his remarks short, then concluded by saying, "To the fellows there now and to those who will never come back from this horrible conflict, I want to thank you all. And to this committee and the people of Fall River—God bless you all."

*   *   *

---

* Massachusetts congressman John F. Kennedy would attend a subsequent function in Tom's honor. Incidentally, as a teen at Andover prep school, Tom had played intramural football with George H. W. Bush, who later became the forty-first president. And at the Naval Academy, Tom knew his friend's roommate, a young man from Georgia who would become the thirty-ninth president, Jimmy Carter.

For the day's final presentation, a judge from the city's superior court stepped forward, carrying a silver bowl. "Lieutenant Hudner," he said into the microphone, "I'd like to present these gifts to you on behalf of the grateful citizens of your native city, Fall River."

Tom grinned as the judge handed him the silver Paul Revere–style bowl. Tom looked closer and his eyes went wide. Inside the bowl was a check in his name for $1,000 — equivalent to about $9,000 in present-day money. Tom shook his head in disbelief.

When he returned to his seat, Tom examined the silver bowl as the ceremony wrapped up. One of the town fathers tapped him on the shoulder, leaned in, and asked in an excited whisper, "So, how are you going to spend all that money?"

The next day, the sounds of aircraft maintenance echoed through the hangar at Quonset Point as Tom climbed the steps to Fighting 32's briefing room. Clad in his leather jacket and green slacks, Tom moved with a bounce in his step. He carried an envelope containing his check from the city of Fall River.

Tom entered the squadron briefing room and set the envelope in the outgoing mail bin. The envelope was addressed to Mrs. Daisy Brown, T-116 Robertson Place, Hattiesburg, Mississippi. Inside, Tom had signed the check over to Daisy. His decision had been easy.

If the Leyte's putting Jesse's daughter through college, then Daisy should go, too.

Tom dropped into a seat beside his buddies and readied a pen to take notes. The skipper was coming, the briefing about to begin. Tom was back.

Five months later, Labor Day weekend, 1951

In a dark blur, the Corsair raced low over the hidden inlets of the Massachusetts coastline. The mid-morning sunlight stretched over cottages and train stops nestled behind the beaches. From his seat in the Corsair's cockpit, Tom flew with a mischievous gleam in his eyes.

Marinas stocked with sailboats zipped beneath his right wing, so close his wingtip nearly clipped their masts. Tom had never flown this low before—never stateside, anyway.

It was September 1, the Saturday of Labor Day weekend. Everyone had gone home from Quonset Point for the holiday, so Tom had seized the opportunity to pursue a personal mission, one he'd been considering since his first flight with Jesse.

Tom thought of Jesse often, and Daisy, too. Daisy had written Tom a gracious letter and had used his gift to enroll at Alcorn College, about three hours from Hattiesburg. She was in classes now, on her way to becoming a home economics teacher.

One day she'd remarry, after waiting seven years. She'd find someone whom Jesse would have approved of, an army medic named Gilbert Thorne. From the start, Gilbert would admit to Daisy, "I know I can't take Jesse's place, but I'll do the best I can for you." Gilbert would love Pam as if she were his own and together the family would move to Germany on a deployment. There, in a quaint village, Daisy would secure her dream job, teaching kindergarten to the children of military parents. And there, she'd buy a red Sunbeam convertible and race the autobahn.

But that was all to come. On the horizon, Tom's target appeared. His eyes tightened. Ahead and to the right lay swaths of green grass along the coastal cliffs. Neat clumps of trees dotted the green. This was it.

Tom nudged the throttle forward and steered the Corsair lower.

A golfer flexed his knees and the spectators turned silent. He swung his club and hit the ball. As the ball rolled to a stop, the spectators clapped politely. The golfer waved, then walked to make his next shot and the small crowd followed, talking buoyantly. The Acoaxet Country Club's annual golf tournament was in full swing.

Tom's father was on the green, wearing khakis and his polo shirt with the club logo on the front pocket. He and several friends had founded the club in 1919, and he never missed a tournament.

Tom Senior didn't see the black W-shaped silhouette diving from the sky behind him. None of the club members did. But the silhouette stretched larger and larger, aiming straight for them.

Tom leaned to see around his gunsight and steered the Corsair's nose at the crowd on the golf course. As a boy, he'd spent his summers at the club, sailing from its beach. Back then, he loved everything about the place. But lately, he had become frustrated with certain members— namely, his father's friends. In Korea, the battle lines were locked in a bloody stalemate around the 38th parallel, yet his father's friends had stopped following the news. They were back to worrying about the stock market and their golf scores, as if young men weren't still dying in Korea, as if there wasn't even a war going on.

Rather than sit idly by, Tom had written a letter to the Fall River newspaper in which he encouraged his neighbors to extend the same support they had shown him to the troops overseas.

"With all the cold, the mud, the blood and horror they are living in," he wrote, "there is never anything so demoralizing or dangerous as the feeling we at home don't have too much interest in what they're doing and going through."

Tom didn't know if the letter had an effect or if anyone had even read it. So he devised another way to get his message across.

He held a shallow dive, just like a strafing run in Korea.

Gotta be low enough! Tom thought, his eyes tightening as the crowd slipped closer. *They need to see that this is a navy plane.*

The crowd must have been applauding a well-placed shot, because no one heard the sound of the twelve-thousand-pound plane bearing down on them from behind.

With a furious roar, the Corsair ripped over the crowd at 250 miles per hour, flattening the sea grass and blowing hats from heads. Golfers dropped their clubs and spectators sank to their knees, soiling their clean khakis. The plane's thick shadow whistled across the green and kept going.

The spectators glanced up and saw a flash of curved wings, a white star, and the word NAVY on the plane's flank. A puttering sound trailed the Corsair's tail.

The plane kept running out over the sea, now low above the waves.

From their hands and knees, the golfers and spectators scowled.

"Who the hell is that?" someone shouted.

"He should be grounded!" yelled another.

Someone chuckled nervously. One by one, the faces turned to Tom's father. He was cowering on the green like the rest of them, a grin lining his face. The others glared at him and shook their heads. Tom's father just shrugged.

The perturbed golfers and spectators stood. They pranced around, trying to clean their knees off. In his cockpit, Tom could see them through his rearview mirror. He broke out in laughter. They looked just like storks.

Tom remained low and fast over the leaping waves. He almost shook his head with wonder.

Jesse was right.

He should have done this long ago.

AFTERWORD

AFTER THE BATTLE OF THE CHOSIN RESERVOIR, the Korean War raged for an additional two years and seven months along the 38th parallel, the prewar border. Neither side gave or gained much ground.

Four months before the war ended, **Joseph Stalin** died, having seen his dreams of communist expansion crushed by the free world. After his death, with the Soviet Union gripped in a leadership struggle, the Chinese and North Korean communists abandoned their demands for mandatory prisoner repatriation and returned to the peace table.

In July 1953, the Korean War concluded after claiming five million lives — nearly thirty-seven thousand of them American. Of the communist prisoners captured by U.N. forces, 30 percent of the North Koreans elected to remain in the south, and 70 percent of Chinese prisoners chose not to return to communist China.

Today, the Korean War is often called "the Forgotten War." But the men who fought there know it by a different name: The Forgotten Victory. Today, thanks to the United States and United Nations forces, some fifty million South Koreans live in freedom.

*   *   *

In January 1955, **Dick Cevoli** was on duty in Florida when his wife, Grace, gave birth at Quonset Point. Their fourth child—Richard Jr.—was born mentally disabled.

After hearing the news, Cevoli took off in rough weather in a Cougar jet to hurry home. When a priest entered Grace Cevoli's hospital room, she thought that something had happened to her baby. Instead, the priest delivered the news that Dick had crashed and died.

Today, a post office in East Greenwich, Rhode Island, is named in honor of Dick Cevoli.

After his tour in fighters, **Marty Goode** became a navy helicopter pilot. Whenever he came in to land, sailors and aviators would line Vulture's Row to see a helicopter land like a fighter.

Marty later became a navy test pilot at Sikorsky and retired as a commander, far from his humble beginnings as an enlisted seaman. Along the way, he met a beautiful Hungarian artist named Paula at a theater performance. Then and there, Marty's days as a ladies' man ended; he was certain that Paula was the girl he'd been looking for. He married her and adopted her two young daughters from a previous marriage.

These days, Marty and Paula go out weekly to dance the Argentinian tango.

Bill Koenig remained in the navy and became a master naval parachutist and commander who oversaw the development of ejection seats and escape systems.

In civilian life, Koenig remained close with the Brown family. In 2005, he took Jesse's granddaughter, Jessica, on a special trip to Oceana

Naval Air Station so she could see why her grandfather had loved carrier aviation. Together, they visited Navy Fighter Squadron 32. The squadron's pilots suited up Jessica in flight gear and showed her how to preflight an F-14 jet.

Today, Jessica calls Koenig "Uncle Bill."

Richard "Dad" Fowler commanded the carrier *Ticonderoga* during the Vietnam War and retired as a rear admiral, the equivalent of a two-star general.

Anyone who knew him wasn't a bit surprised.

Bill "Wilkie" Wilkinson foresaw a career full of separations from his wife, Mary, so he transitioned to the Naval Reserves in 1952. While continuing to fly fighters on weekends, he took a weekday job with American Airlines and became a commercial airline captain when he was only twenty-four years old. Thirty-five years later, he made his final flight for American as a 747 pilot.

Today, Wilkie and Mary enjoy sailing a twenty-foot sailboat from their home in Maine. During quiet times at sea, Wilkie reflects on his life, and his thoughts sometimes roam back to the Yalu bridge strike and the North Korean children he flew over.

He hopes their lives turned out okay.

During a layover at Norfolk Naval Base in 1954, Wilkie reported for dinner in the officers' club and was seated two tables away from **the skipper—Dug Neill**. To Wilkie's surprise, the skipper invited him to his table, and afterward the two went out for beers, like old friends. The following year, Marty Goode bumped into the skipper at Naval Air Station Key West and enjoyed the same hospitality.

Both Wilkie and Marty would later come to the same conclusion:

The pressures of leading a squadron had altered the skipper's personality, making him stern for a reason—out of concern for his young pilots.

The skipper would later become a university professor.

John "Red" Parkinson had trouble readjusting to civilian life. He drifted by day and at night he couldn't sleep under blankets for fear he'd be caught unprepared.

Then in 1952, everything changed. While driving to his uncle Anton's farm, Red was crossing a four-way intersection when another driver's brakes failed. The other driver broadsided Red's car and rolled it. Red emerged with scrapes but was otherwise okay. He noticed that the other driver was a pretty twenty-one-year-old girl with hazel eyes and curly blond hair. Her name was Virginia.

In the hospital, the two struck up a friendship. Red borrowed a friend's car to drive Virginia home. Two years later they married and settled down on a dairy farm.

Every November 27, on the anniversary of the Chosin Reservoir battle, Red climbs a hill near his farm at night. In the cold, he sits and remembers.

Red hadn't seen **Charlie Kline** since Yudam-ni but never forgot how Charlie had steered him to his faith. In tribute, Red began volunteering with the Gideons International, the organization that had given him his pocket Bible during his Marine days.

In 1985, Red attended a Gideons convention in Philadelphia as a delegate. As Red was introduced to the audience, a man stood abruptly at the rear of the hall, nearly flipping his chair. "We finally got ya!" the man shouted. Red looked closely and saw the thick chin and wide grin of fifty-six-year-old Charlie Kline.

Charlie hadn't died at Yudam-ni after all. He had been searching for his bazooka when the Chinese came, so he took shelter in a culvert. After three days in hiding, he escaped but with both lungs damaged by the cold. The Marines transported Charlie in the column to Hagaru, then airlifted him to Japan and hospitals from there.

In the middle of the Philadelphia convention hall, Red and Charlie embraced to thunderous applause. Until Charlie's death in 1999, the two were inseparable.

On a brisk October day in 1955, **Sergeant Bob Devans**'s remains were returned from North Korea to his hometown of Wilkes-Barre, Pennsylvania, during one of the few postwar exchanges of remains. As his coffin was lowered into the earth, his brother, sister, father, and mother were present.

And so was his high school crush, Audrey Johns.

During his fourteen months in naval hospitals, all ten of **Ed Coderre**'s frostbitten toes were amputated. Due to his war wounds, Coderre was never able to play for the Red Sox; he became an accountant instead. In 1977, he and his wife, Wanda, took a cruise to Cozumel, Mexico. On the beach, Coderre was hesitant to remove his shoes and reveal his toeless feet, so he went for a walk.

At a nearby baseball field, he took a seat in the stands as players were arriving for a pickup game. He and the players discussed their mutual love of baseball. When one of the teams found itself short a player, they asked Coderre to join them. He did, and on his first at bat, he hit a line drive. Coderre rounded the bases safely to third, running on just his heels. The Mexican players were too busy cheering to notice.

Today, Coderre still loves the Red Sox.

In 1952, the Marine Corps awarded **Lieutenant Robert Reem** a posthumous Medal of Honor. His widow, Donna, accepted her late husband's award from the secretary of the navy. Later, in an interview with *Coronet Magazine*, she explained that she had begun teaching Sunday school as a way of moving forward after her husband's death. "If you didn't have something to cling to you'd be lost," she said. "I believe I'll see Bob again."

Charlie Ward received the Silver Star for rescuing Tom from the mountaintop. After a long Marine career that had begun before Pearl Harbor, Ward retired in 1964 as a major. He settled in Pensacola and lived there for ten years. After a career fraught with danger, Ward was killed in a jeep accident at age fifty-six.

Fletcher Brown became a mechanic in the air force during the Korean War, and **Lura Brown** served in the 82nd Airborne, a unit held stateside in anticipation of a Soviet attack on Europe. Both men later followed their mother's wishes and sought higher education. Fletcher earned an MBA from Pepperdine and Lura studied horticulture at UCLA.

In 2000, the brothers and Daisy represented Jesse at a Korean War commemoration in Sacramento. A tall, black Marine in his seventies approached them. Five decades earlier, he had been the square-faced Marine who had watched Jesse fly at the Chosin.

"I can still see him overhead," the Marine said, as his eyes filled with tears. "If it hadn't been for him and the others, none of us would have gotten out alive."

In 1966, **Tom Hudner** attended a Christmas party in Miramar, California. He was a captain then in rank, and navigator of the carrier *Kitty Hawk*.

Across a crowded room he saw a striking brunette, a tall, Jackie Kennedy look-alike. Tom's friend told him that the brunette's name was

Georgea Smith. She was a widow whose husband, a pilot, had been killed three years earlier.

Tom's friend tried to steer him toward any other woman. Georgea had three children—and she was taller than Tom, too. But Tom had already made up his mind. As Georgea was slipping on her jacket to leave, he stopped her at the door.

Two years later, they married and had a son together, Thomas Jerome Hudner III.

After thirty years of service, in February 1973, Tom delivered a speech just days before his retirement from the navy. At the Boston Navy Yard, with Daisy Brown in the audience, he dedicated a new frigate—the USS *Jesse L. Brown*.

In civilian life, Tom served as a state commissioner for veterans' affairs, as president of the regional USO, and as treasurer of the Medal of Honor Society. During his many speeches to military officers, veterans, and schoolchildren, he always remembered his last words to Jesse: "We'll be back for you!"

For more than sixty years, Tom's promise went unfulfilled. Ever since the war, relations hadn't thawed between America and the North Korean regime, and the U.S. military had been unable to search for the remains of its nearly eight thousand MIAs, Jesse Brown included.

Then, in summer 2013, at the age of eighty-eight, Tom decided to take matters into his own hands.

His family tried to dissuade him. His fellow veterans urged him to reconsider. The U.S. State Department advised Tom that they'd be powerless to protect him. But Tom had learned a lesson in wartime: Sometimes you have to break the rules.

In July 2013, in a drizzling rain, Tom stepped off a plane in North Korea. Officers of the North Korean army were waiting for him and his traveling party.* Two days later, in the capital of Pyongyang, Tom clipped his Medal of Honor around his neck. Soldiers led him into a

---

* Author's note: My staff and I accompanied Tom Hudner on his ten-day journey to North Korea and have posted our photos and video on my website: www.AdamMakos.com.

conference room, to a seat across from a North Korean colonel and his staff. For sixty-three years, Tom had waited for this moment.

With cameras of the world media rolling, Tom asked the North Koreans to begin a search for Jesse Brown's remains.

At first, the North Korean colonel remained silent. He glanced at his notes where his reply had been prewritten. News of Tom's arrival had already coursed through the ranks of the North Korean military, the government, and into the ear of the nation's new, thirty-year-old Supreme Leader—Kim Jong Un.

The colonel began to read a message from the Supreme Leader to Tom.

Kim Jong Un was impressed that Tom had come so far, after so long, to keep a promise to a friend. In tribute to Tom, the North Korean leader granted approval to his army to resume the search for the remains of MIA American servicemen—beginning with Jesse Brown.

Back in Hattiesburg, eighty-six-year-old **Daisy Brown** was following Tom's journey to North Korea and the tremendous outpouring of national support. A news network sent a camera crew to Daisy's home to gauge her reaction. "I never dreamed that this would happen," Daisy said in an interview, "and yet if it's successful, I'm sure that it'll bring some closure to us and they can bring him back and give him a final resting place."

With renewed hope, Daisy waited. Sixty-three years had passed since Jesse's death and she knew it could take longer, even decades, for anyone to locate two burnt Corsairs in a range of desolate mountains. Most of all, Daisy was thankful to Tom for trying.

In July 2014, after a long illness, Daisy died in her home. But before she passed, she told her daughter, **Pamela Brown**, that she had decided where Jesse should be buried if his remains ever returned to his native soil. At first Daisy had thought Jesse should rest in Mississippi, in a quiet cemetery under a shady tree. But then the schoolteacher in her had a better idea.

Daisy decided that Jesse should one day rest in Arlington National Cemetery so people of all ages and races could visit his grave and be inspired by his story. Because, to Daisy, her husband isn't done serving his fellow man.

In her last days, when she looked around her, Daisy came to one final conclusion:

The world needs Jesse Brown and Tom Hudner, now more than ever.

At Sea
Sunday Nite
3 December 1950

My own dear sweet Angel,

I'm so lonesome I could just boo-hoo. But I try to restrain myself and think of the fun we're going to have when we do get together, so only a few tears escape now and then. I love you so very much my darling.

I've been trying to get a chance to write you for the last three days but without much success. I'd like to write you every night. I love to tell you that I love and adore you, and, although I never quite succeed in getting it across, I like to try and tell you how much I care and how much you really mean to me. So you see, my darling, not only do I like to hear you tell me that you love me but I like telling you also that you're the sweetest woman in the world. I love you angel and I want you to know that my heart belongs to you

It was a little past midnite when I started this, but who cares. We're in love and thats what matters, not the time Right darling?

The last few days we've been doing quite a bit of flying trying to help slow down the Chinese communists and to give support to some marines who were surrounded when the Chinese launched their big drive. Knowing that he's helping those poor guys on the ground, I think every pilot on here would fly until he dropped in his tracks. This morning we were flying in weather so bad we could hardly see each other at times — snowing yet the air was full of planes. Navy planes for close support of the troops, Air force transport dropping supplies by

Jesse's last letter home to Daisy

parachute, etc. We know a few of the marine officers down on the ground because they were with us in the Med. But my biggest hope still is that somehow, thru the mercy of God, this war can come to a close without us getting into an all out war with China.

Know what darling? I love you with all my heart and soul. I'm so deeply and completely in love with you until nothing else in life matters to me at all except you angel. Occasionally Lee Nelson will show me a certain portion of one of his letters from Lee. The reason I mention that is because her letters to him always remind me of yours to me and mine to you. I guess people who are really and truly in love do think quite a bit alike — different couples I mean. As for us, our thoughts and mind seem to run exactly alike and I know that it isn't just a coincidence. When we were married darling, our bodies, minds, hearts, and souls were also wed. I guess that is why making love to you is such an exquisite joy, because we belong to each other and we give ourselves to each other without reservations at all. In Lee's letter to Lee she was telling him how she needed him and how she was praying and trusting in God to bring him home soon.

Darling, heaven alone can know how much I need you and how badly I want to see you. I need you and want you angel far more than I have the ability to express. If only my heart could talk — if only my hungry, lonely, arms could enfold you darling, I love you with a passion that is beyond description. I love you with a true love, an everlasting love, a love that says that I am yours alone, only yours darling, and that I always shall belong to you. Sweetness, my very soul is dedicated to you.

I'm so lonesome for you and I need you so much darling. I guess you've always thought I was a big cry baby, but honest darling you're my weakness and I can't help it. I love you so much darling, and even though usually it seems that instead of tears flowing from my eyes they flow down into my heart and stay there and hurt, sometimes this loneliness just wrings the tears of my aching heart. Often when I climb into my rack at nite all the loneliness of the day seems to descend upon me and I'm haunted by seemingly a thousand sweet memories of you. Then all the tears that I've been holding back all day long refuse to be held any longer, and I just lay there in loneliness and misery and cry my heart out. I pray so earnestly to God to see my tears and grant that thru His pity and mercy we may be together again soon. Then I feel His comfort and yours and I go to sleep

Oh darling, please, please try and realize what you mean to me and try and understand how much I care. I need you so much darling. Please help me Dassy, please my darling.

Don't be discouraged angel, believe in God and believe in Him with all your might and I know that things will work out all right. We need Him now like never before. Have faith with me darling and He'll see us thru and we'll be together again before long too. I want you to keep that pretty little chin up angel, come on now, way up. I want you also to be confident in this and that is. Your husband loves his wife with all his heart and soul — no man ever loved a woman more.

You know how I feel now? I feel like I feel when we've just laid in each others arms a long time just talking. We usually kiss and whisper sweet words of love to each other and say softly over and over "I love you angel." Then after vowing all over again to always love each other we're ready for the loving

of our lives. That is one of the times when our loving
is sweet and gentle. Thats the way I'd like to love you right
now angel, sweet and gentle. I'd like to whisper sweet things
in your dainty ears, kiss your sweet lips, play in your
hair and caress your smooth skin, frame your beautiful
face in my hands — hold you close and enjoy the thrill of you
taking my breath away — raise up at times just so I can
look at you and admire you

    Darling, I'm going to close now and climb in the
rack. I honestly dread going to bed, but I usually dream
of you so I'll manage to make it until we'll share our
bed together again — darling pray that it'll be soon. I have
to fly tomorrow. But so far as that goes my heart hasn't
been down to earth since the first time you kissed me, and
when you love me you "send" it clear out-of-this-world.

    I'll write again as soon as I can. I'll love you
forever.

Your devoted husband
lovingly and completely yours
forever
Jesse

ACKNOWLEDGMENTS

I'D LIKE TO EXTEND MY DEEPEST THANKS to the following people for their help with *Devotion*:

To Tom Hudner, the gentleman I met in the hotel lobby eight years ago. Thank you for entrusting me with your story and allowing me to accompany you on your mission to North Korea. You're a real-life "Captain America" who has given us all a timeless gift an example worth emulating.

To Daisy Brown Thorne. A half-century after you lost Jesse, I asked you to relive the memories of your times together, for this book. On July 6, 2014, soon after we completed our work, you left this earth. I'll never forget your words after one particularly long interview: *I just love talking about Jesse.*

To the supporting stars of *Devotion*, in order of appearance: Lura Brown, Fletcher Brown, Marty Goode, Bill Koenig, Halley Bishop, John "Red" Parkinson, Ed Coderre, and Bill "Wilkie" Wilkinson — your stories are each worthy of a book of its own. Thank you for giving *Devotion* humor, poignancy, and depth.

To Tom Hudner's wife, Georgea Hudner, thank you for your faith in this book from the start. When your husband decided to travel to North Korea, you could have dissuaded him—as many wives would have—but you encouraged him to fulfill his promise to Jesse. You're proof that beside every great man stands a great woman.

To Pamela Brown Knight—Jesse's daughter—whose blessing made this book possible. As Daisy's protector, you could have said "enough" and our history-gathering would have ended. Instead, you welcomed me to Hattiesburg and opened the doors to your family's history. You're everything one would expect from the daughter of Jesse and Daisy Brown.

To Marine Sergeant Dick Bonelli, one of the legendary warriors of Fox Company at the Chosin Reservoir. In 2013, when Tom Hudner returned to North Korea, he included Dick in his traveling party to represent the Marines. Although *Devotion* lacked the pages to cover their adventure, I assure you—*Bonelli was there*.

To the veterans' families and friends, thank you for the stories, photos, and documents you shared that enriched this book. Special thanks to: Sue Burton, Steve Cevoli, Ed Coderre, Jr., Wanda Perkowska Coderre, Dr. Frank Cronin, the Danaher family, Don Devans, Kelli Fernandez, Richard C. Fowler, Ellen Franks, James Hudner, Mary Hudner, Phillip Hudner, Rick Hudner, Thomas Hudner III, Audrey Johns, Jamal Knight, Jessica Knight, Jim and Diane McMichael, Jenny Parkinson, Edward Sisson, Charlotte Ward, and Karen Ward.

To my dedicated agent, David Vigliano, who guided *Devotion* into the hands of the team at Ballantine Books. To my editors, Ryan Doherty, who recognized the power of this story and coached me through its early days, and Mark Tavani, whose deft hand polished the manuscript to its final form. To the president and publisher of Random House, Gina Centrello, and the publishing team at Ballantine Bantam Dell: Libby McGuire, Jennifer Tung, Richard Callison, Susan Corcoran, Greg Kubie, Quinne Rogers, Betsy Wilson, Evan Camfield, and everyone on the sales and marketing team, thank you all for bringing *Devotion* to the world.

To this book's aviation advisor, Rob Collings, a modern-day Corsair pilot with the Collings Foundation, and to Valada Flewellyn, who works tirelessly to preserve Jesse Brown's history through her traveling exhibit A *Pilot Lights the Way*. Thank you Valada, for guiding my first visit to Hattiesburg and introducing me to your friends Daisy and Pamela Brown.

To the historians and researchers of the Marine Corps Archives, the USMC History Division, the Naval History and Heritage Command, and the National Archives: Francis Alexander, Rita Cann, Jenny Crabb, Lisa Crunk, David Fort, Joe Gordon, John Hodges, Kenneth Johnson, Kara Newcomer, Nathaniel Patch, Kevin Pratt, Jonathan Roscoe, and Nancy Whitfield.

To the early readers who lent a discerning eye to this manuscript: Dianne Castelli, Franz Englram, Joe Gohrs, Patty Gohrs, Jaime Hanna, Tricia Leupp Hoover, Carolin Huber, Tony Hughes, Elizabeth Makos, Betsy Rider, Peter Semanoff, Agata Twarowska, Kyle Warren, and Bob Windholz.

To the experts, friends, and supporters who contributed in a myriad of ways: the Honorable Ray Mabus, Bill Bartsch, Jennifer Baxter, Lt. Andrea Cassidy, Mark "Goober" Connolly, Richard Downes (Coalition of Families of Korean & Cold War POW/MIAs), Herbert Fahr Jr. (USS *Missouri* Association), Mary Faria (*The Herald News*), David Friant, Craig Fuller, Joe Galloway, Chip Gibson, Matt Hall, Paula Hancocks, Gareth Hector, Steve Herman, Jeff "Growler" Hogan, Chester Makos (7th Infantry), Jean Lee, Kevin "Joker" Mastin, Ken McLaurin (USS *Leyte* Association), Joseph Pickard, John Powers, Dan Sheahan (Fall River Main Library), Lindy Smith, Dave Stecker (Quonset Air Museum), Anthony "K-Bob" Sweeney, Justin Taylan (Pacific Wrecks), Pauline Testerman, Joanna Williams, Vickie Wilson (Johnson Publishing Co.), Richard D. Winters, Bill Woodier, and Le Grande Van Wagenen (USS *Leyte* Association).

To Marcus Brotherton, the veteran author and coauthor of twenty-five books who mentored my writing. From the first chapter to the last, you were always trimming, sharpening, and sharing the tricks of your trade to help me become a better writer. I'm lucky to count you as a friend.

To my grandfather Mike Makos, who passed away during the process of this book. You always told me about those postwar years when Soviet fighters intercepted your B-17 off the coast of Japan. Only now do I realize the dangers you faced.

To my sisters, Erica Makos and Elizabeth Makos, and my mother, Karen Makos, thanks for being my proofreaders and toughest critics. Your feedback helped shape this book. To my dear friend Helga Stigler, thanks for looking out for me from afar.

To my grandparents Francis and Jeanne Panfili, who brought countless lunches and dinners to my brother and me during those endless days and nights at our desks. Your love and encouragement always lifted our spirits.

To my dad, Robert Makos, and my brother, Bryan Makos, who led our research team and even traveled to North Korea for this book. Your task was lofty: to conduct interviews and gather historical facts across three continents, seven countries, and both sides of the Korean War. Few could have done the job that you did.

Lastly, thanks to you, the reader, for purchasing *Devotion*. I hope this story will inspire you and remain in your mind. If you find yourself hungry to learn more, you'll find film of Tom's trip to North Korea, an eerie ghost story from Daisy, and other bonus content on my website: www.AdamMakos.com.

On behalf of Tom, Daisy, and the heroes of *Devotion*, I now pass the torch to you. Keep the flame alive. The legacy of great men and women lies in your hands.

BIBLIOGRAPHY

THANK YOU TO THE MEN AND WOMEN of the Greatest Generation who granted us interviews for this book and shared their letters, diaries, personal memoirs, and written accounts.

Due to the space limitations, I could not list every name or describe every face in the manuscript, yet still you contributed, both in the spotlight and behind the scenes. Your memories enriched *Devotion* and honored your comrades, friends, and family.

My deepest thanks go out to:

Jack Allen (H&S/3/7, 1st Marine Division)
Halley Bishop (Flight Deck Corpsman, VF-33)
Robert Blackington (Pilot, VA-35)
Richard Bonelli (F/2/7, 1st Marine Division)
Ira Bossert (USS *Leyte*)
Lyle Bradley (Pilot, VMF-214)
Fletcher Brown (Jesse Brown's brother)
Lura Brown (Jesse Brown's brother)
Harry Burke (F/2/7, 1st Marine Division)

Hector Cafferata Jr. (F/2/7, 1st Marine Division)

Richard Cantrell (Pilot, VA-35)

Roland Christensen (Jesse Brown's flight instructor)

Edward Coderre (H/3/7, 1st Marine Division)

Jack Cogdell (Pilot, VF-31)

Jack Coleman (H/3/7, 1st Marine Division)

Robert Duncan (H/3/7, 1st Marine Division)

Robert Ezell (F/2/7, 1st Marine Division)

Sam Folsom (Pilot & Operations Officer, MAG-12, USMC)

William Gelonek (Pilot, VF-32)

Martin Goode (Pilot, VF-32)

Albert Grasselli (Pilot, VMF-212)

Daniel Holland (CO, 7th Marine Regiment Forward Air Controllers)

John Homan (H/3/7, 1st Marine Division)

James Hudner (Tom Hudner's brother)

Mary Hudner (Tom Hudner's sister)

Phillip Hudner (Tom Hudner's brother)

Rick Hudner (Tom Hudner's brother)

Thomas Hudner Jr. (Pilot, VF-32)

W. Carl Jeckel (Plane Captain, VF-33)

H. Newt Key Jr. (Pilot, VF-32)

William Koenig (Pilot, VF-32)

John Margie (H&S/3/7, 1st Marine Division)

Ken McLaurin (USS *Leyte*)

John Mills (I/3/7, 1st Marine Division)

Jack Mitchell (USS *Leyte*)

John Mitchell (H&S/3/7, 1st Marine Division)

Robert Molson (USS *Leyte*)

William Morin (Wpns/3/7, 1st Marine Division)

Gene Morrison (Pilot, VMO-6)

Clifford Myer (H&S/3/7, 1st Marine Division)

William Parish (Pilot, VF-31)

John Parkinson (Wpns/3/7, 1st Marine Division)

Peter Pitz (Pilot, VF-33)

Walter Rathmann (USS *Leyte*)

Stan Roberts (USS *Leyte*)

Pat Roe (H&S/3/7, 1st Marine Division)

Bryan Rudy (Pilot, VF-32)

William Sallada (Pilot, VF-33)

Herbert Sargent (Pilot, VF-32)

Roy Shaul (H&S/3/7, 1st Marine Division)

Darrell Smith (Pilot, VMF-312)

Richard Stack (Pilot, VF-32)

Dell Thomas (Pilot, HU2 Helicopter Utility Squadron, USS *Leyte*)

Daisy Brown Thorne (Jesse Brown's wife)

William Wilkinson (Pilot, VF-32)

Official Documents and Reports

1st Lt. Charles C. Ward, HO3S-1 SN 122522, Accident Report. 1948.

1st Marine Air Wing Historical Diary. November–December 1950.

1st Marine Division Historical Diary. November–December 1950.

2nd Lt. Charles C. Ward, SBD-5 SN 28740, Accident Report. 1944.

7th Marine Regiment, 3rd Battalion, Special Action Report. October–
      December 1950.

Army Field Manual FM 23 32 "Rocket Launchers." 1949.

Attack Squadron Thirty Five Historical Report. July–December 1950.

Cmdr. Richard L. Cevoli, F9F-6 SN 128278, Accident Report. 1955.

Corsair Serial Number 82050 Aircraft History Card. 1950.

Corsair Serial Number 97231 Aircraft History Card. 1950.

Ens. Carol R. Mohring, F4U-4 SN 81357, Accident Report. 1949.

Ens. Carol R. Mohring, F4U-4 SN 80950, Accident Report. 1950.

Ens. Jesse L. Brown, F4U-4 SN 97231, Accident Report. 1950.

Fighter Squadron Thirty One Historical Report. July–December 1950.

Fighter Squadron Thirty Three Historical Report. July–December
      1950.

Fighter Squadron Thirty Three Operational Report. October
      1950–January 1951.

Fighter Squadron Thirty Two Historical Report. July–December 1950.

Fighter Squadron Thirty Two Operational Report. October
　　1950–January 1951.

*Inadequacies Noted in the System of Control of Close Air Support
　　Aircraft.* 1951.

Lt. (JG) Robert O. Davis, HO3S-1 SN 122709, Accident Report. 1950.

Pfc. Edward Coderre NAVMED Report, USNH, Newport, R.I. 1950.

Presentations of USS Leyte Officers, Air Group Three. 1951.

Production Inspection Trials of the Model F4U-4 Airplane. 1948.

Report of Sixth Fleet Exercises. July 15–20, 1950.

*Substance of Statements Made at Wake Island Conference on 15
　　October 1950.* Compiled by General of the Army Omar N.
　　Bradley.

USS Boxer Action Reports. October 1950.

USS Leyte "32's News" Ship's Newspapers. 1950–1951.

USS Leyte Action Reports. October 1950–January 1951.

USS Leyte "Daily Press News" Releases. October–December 1950.

USS Leyte Deck Logs. May–December 1950.

USS Leyte Korean Cruise Book. 1950–1951.

USS Leyte Six Fleet Mediterranean Cruise Book. 1950.

USS Leyte War Diary. 1950.

USS Missouri War Diary. 1950.

USS Philippine Sea Action Reports. October–December 1950.

USS Valley Forge Action Reports. November–December 1950.

USS Worcester Six Fleet Mediterranean Cruise Book. 1950.

USS Wright Deck Log. April 4, 1950.

VF-14 Aircraft Action Report. June 19, 1944.

VMO-6 Action Report. October–December 1950.

Books

Applebaum, Anne. *Iron Curtain.* New York: Anchor, 2012.

Appleman, Lt. Col. Roy E. *East of Chosin.* College Station: Texas
　　A&M University Press, 1987.

Atkins, Edward. *On Which We Serve*. Bloomington: WestBow, 2011.

Bartsch, William H. *December 8, 1941: MacArthur's Pearl Harbor.* College Station: Texas A&M University Press, 2003.

Beach, J. M. *Gateway to Opportunity: A History of the Community College in the United States*. Sterling: Stylus, 2011.

Brown, Lt. Col. Ronald J. *Whirlybirds: U.S. Marine Helicopters in Korea*. Washington, D.C.: U.S. Marine Corps, 2003.

Cagle, Malcolm W., and Frank A. Manson. *The Sea War in Korea.* Annapolis: Naval Institute, 1957.

Cohen, Yohanan. *Small Nations in Times of Crisis and Confrontation*. Albany: State University of New York Press, 1989.

Courtois, Stéphane, Jean-Louis Panné, Andrzej Paczkowski, Karel Bartosek, Jean-Louis Margolin, and Nicolas Werth. *The Black Book of Communism: Crimes, Terror, Repression*. Ed. Mark Kramer. Trans. Jonathan Murphy. Cambridge: Harvard University Press, 1999.

D'Amato, Donald A. *Images of America: Warwick*. Charleston: Arcadia, 1996.

Doss, Erika L. *Looking at* Life *Magazine*. Washington, D.C.: Smithsonian Institution, 2001.

Drury, Bob, and Tom Clavin. *The Last Stand of Fox Company*. New York: Grove, 2009.

Edwards, Paul M. *Korean War Almanac (Almanacs of American Wars)*. New York: Facts on File, 2006.

Field, James A., Jr., and Ernest M. Eller. *History of United States Naval Operations: Korea*. Honolulu: University of the Pacific Press, 2001.

Fletcher, Gregory G. *Intrepid Aviators: The American Flyers Who Sank Japan's Greatest Battleship*. New York: NAL Caliber, 2013.

Forero, Lt. Col. L., Maj. C. Bailey, Maj. W. Cunningham Jr., Maj. C. Ebbingar, Maj. J. Stone, Maj. R. Bondel, Maj. W. Drake, Maj. T. Garrett, Maj. Y. Lim, and Maj. R. Watford Jr. *Battle Analysis, Wonsan, Rear Area Operations (3rd Infantry Division,*

Korea, November 1950). Rep. no. AD-A152745. Fort Leaven-
worth: Combat Studies Institute, 1984.

Foss, Christopher F. *Artillery of the World.* New York: Charles Scrib-
ner's Sons, 1981.

Gaddis, John L. *The Cold War.* New York: Penguin, 2005.

Goncharov, Sergei, Litai Xue, and John Lewis. *Uncertain Partners:
Stalin, Mao, and the Korean War.* Stanford: Stanford University
Press, 1995.

Gugeler, Russell A. *Combat Actions in Korea.* Washington, D.C.:
U.S. Army Center of Military History, 1970.

Hallion, Richard P. *The Naval Air War in Korea.* New York: Zebra,
1986.

Hammel, Eric M. *Chosin: Heroic Ordeal of the Korean War.* New
York: Vanguard, 1981.

Hannings, Bud. *The Korean War: An Exhaustive Chronology.* Vol. 1.
Jefferson: McFarland, 2007.

Hoyt, Edwin P. *The Bloody Road to Panmunjom.* New York: Stein
and Day, 1986.

Jacobs, Bruce. *Korea's Heroes.* New York: Berkley Medallion, 1961.

Kirkland, Richard C. *MASH Angels.* Short Hills: Burford, 2009.

Krylov, Leonid, and Yuriy Tepsurkaev. *Soviet MiG-15 Aces of the
Korean War.* Oxford: Osprey, 2008.

Lech, Raymond B. *Broken Soldiers.* Urbana-Champaign: University
of Illinois Press, 2000.

Leue, Capt. David. *Korean Combat: The Four Freedoms Betrayed.*
Lexington: n.p., 2013.

Lewis, Jack. *Chosen Tales of Chosin.* North Hollywood: Challenge,
1964.

MacGregor, Morris J., Jr. *Integration of the Armed Forces, 1940–1965.*
Washington, D.C.: Government Printing Office, 1981.

Meyers, Bruce F. *Swift, Silent, and Deadly: Marine Amphibious
Reconnaissance in the Pacific, 1942–1945.* Annapolis: U.S.
Naval Institute, 2004.

Miller, William L. *Two Americans: Truman, Eisenhower, and a Dangerous World*. New York: Alfred A. Knopf, 2012.

Milligan, Sean P. *Quonset Point, Naval Air Station*. Charleston: Arcadia, 1996.

———. *Quonset Point, Naval Air Station*. Vol. 2. Charleston: Arcadia, 1998.

Montross, Lynn, and Capt. Nicholas A. Canzona. *U.S. Marine Operations in Korea: The Chosin Reservoir Campaign*. Vol. 3. Washington, D.C.: U.S. Marine Corps, 1957.

Nalty, Bernard. *Winged Shield, Winged Sword, 1950–1997: A History of the United States Air Force*. Honolulu: University of the Pacific Press, 2003.

O'Donnell, Patrick K. *Give Me Tomorrow*. Cambridge: Da Capo, 2010.

Owen, Joseph R. *Colder Than Hell*. Annapolis: Naval Institute, 1996.

Parker, Lt. Col. Gary W., and Maj. Frank M. Batha Jr. *A History of Marine Observation Squadron Six*. Washington, D.C.: U.S. Marine Corps, 1982.

Rackham, Oliver. *The Making of the Cretan Landscape*. Manchester: Manchester University Press, 1997.

Roberts, John. *The Aircraft Carrier Intrepid*. Annapolis: Naval Institute, 1982.

Roe, Patrick C. *The Dragon Strikes*. Novato: Presidio, 2000.

Russ, Martin. *Breakout: The Chosin Reservoir Campaign, Korea 1950*. New York: Fromm International, 1999.

Sandler, Stanley, ed. *The Korean War: An Encyclopedia*. New York: Routledge, 2013.

Sauter, Jack. *Sailors in the Sky*. Lincoln: University of Nebraska Press, 2011.

Schnabel, James F. *Policy and Direction: The First Year*. Washington, D.C.: Center of Military History, 1992.

Schneller, Robert J. *Breaking the Color Barrier: The U.S. Naval Academy's First Black Midshipmen and the Struggle for*

Racial Equality. New York: New York University Press, 2005.

Sears, David. *Such Men as These*. Cambridge: Da Capo, 2010.

Simmons, Gen. Edwin H. *Frozen Chosin: U.S. Marines at the Changjin Reservoir*. Washington, D.C.: U.S. Marine Corps, 2002.

Spurr, Russell. *Enter the Dragon*. New York: Newmarket, 1988.

Stewart, Richard W., ed. *American Military History*. Vol. 2. Washington, D.C.: Dept. of the Army, 2010.

Summers, Col. Harry, Jr. *Korean War Almanac*. New York: Facts on File, 1990.

Taylor, Theodore. *The Flight of Jesse Leroy Brown*. New York: Avon, 1998.

Thompson, Warren. *F4U Corsair Units of the Korean War*. Oxford: Osprey, 2009.

———. *Naval Aviation in the Korean War*. South Yorkshire: Pen & Sword, 2012.

Tooker, D. K. *The Second Luckiest Pilot*. Annapolis: Naval Institute, 2000.

Wagner, Robert F., Arthur Capper, Joseph Cavagan, and Hamilton Fish, comps. *Lynching Goes Underground*. N.p.: n.p., 1940.

Walker, Jack D. *A Brief Account of the Korean War*. N.p.: n.p., n.d.

Warren, James A. *American Spartans*. New York: Free Press, 2005.

Weapons: An International Encyclopedia from 5000 B.C. to 2000 A.D. New York: St. Martin's, 1990.

Magazines

"ALNAVS, NAVACTS in Brief." *All Hands*, Nov. 1946: 62–63.

Black, Charles L. "Briefing off Wonsan." *Flying*, Feb. 1951: 24+.

———. "A Carrier Goes to War." *Flying*, Dec. 1950: 24+.

———. "Korean Strike: From the Back Seat." *Flying*, Jan. 1951: 16+.

Cavendish, Richard. "The Greek Civil War Ends." *History Today*, 1999. *HistoryToday.com*.

Elliott, Lawrence. "Widows of Honor." *Coronet*, Sept. 1953: 59–61.

Farrell, Sean. "Not Just Farms Anymore: The Effects of World War II on Mississippi's Economy." *Mississippi History Now*, Mississippi Historical Society, Sept. 2001.

Grasselli, Maj. Albert, II. "Chosin to CQ." *Foundation*, Fall 1997: 30–33.

Hemingway, Al. "Airman Down in Korean Hills." *Military History*, June 1995: 54–60.

Herring, George C., Jr. "Lend-Lease to Russia and the Origins of the Cold War, 1944–1945." *The Journal of American History* 56.1 (1969): 93–114.

"How Could Soviet Attack Come?" *Life*, Feb. 27, 1950: 20–29.

Kaiser, Helen. "Pioneering Spirit." *Wilkes*, Fall 2010: 12.

Kerr, Frank. "At the Reservoir: Through the Eyes of a Combat Photographer." *Leatherneck*, Dec. 1990.

Lashmar, Paul. "Stalin's 'Hot' War." *New Statesman Society* 9, no. 388 (1996): 24.

"The Last Days of a Navy Pilot." *Ebony*, Apr. 1951: 15–17.

Lester, Connie. "Economic Development in the 1930s: Balance Agriculture with Industry." *Mississippi History Now*, Mississippi Historical Society, May 2004.

"Lieutenant (jg) Thomas Hudner, Jr. Medal of Honor." *Life*, May 26, 1952: 131.

"Public Relations Is an All Hands Job." *All Hands*, Aug. 1950: 2–5.

Rasula, Col. George. "Chapter 74." Ed. Byron Sims. *Changjin Journal*, 2009.

"Refugees: Innocents' Day." *Time*, Jan. 9, 1950.

Rose, P. K. "Two Strategic Intelligence Mistakes in Korea, 1950." *Studies in Intelligence* (2001). *CIA Library*. Center for the Study of Intelligence, Apr. 14, 2007.

Schneller, Robert J., Jr. "Oscar Holmes: A Place in Naval Aviation." *Naval Aviation News*, Jan.–Feb. 1998: 26–27.

Schoeni, Lt. Comdr. Arthur L. "Fire Bombs Blaze a Trail of War." *Popular Mechanics*, July 1951: 108+.

Skates, John R. "German Prisoners of War in Mississippi, 1943–1946." *Mississippi History Now*. Mississippi Historical Society, Sept. 2001.

Tooker, Lt. Col. D. K. "The Jesse Brown Story." *Foundation*, Spring 1993: 8–18.

"We Finally Got Ya!" *Pentecostal Evangel*, Jan. 10, 1999: 30–31.

Weathersby, Kathryn. "To Attack, or Not to Attack? Stalin, Kim Il Sung, and the Prelude to War." *Cold War International History Project Bulletin* (Spring 1995): 1–9.

Weems, John E. "Black Wings of Gold." *Proceedings*, July 1983: 35–39.

Newspapers

"Ask Medal for Pilot Who Tried to Save Brown." *Chicago Defender*, Dec. 23, 1950: 1.

Baldwin, Hanson W. "'Cold War' Involves Mediterranean." *New York Times*, Jan. 18, 1948: E5.

———. "The Landing at Inchon." *New York Times*, Sept. 18, 1950: 4.

———. "Prolonged Fight Seen." *New York Times*, Jan. 4, 1950: 2.

———. "Red Threat to Asia Gains." *New York Times*, Dec. 18, 1949: 27.

"Both Races Honor Hero in Mississippi Ceremony." *The Afro-American* [Washington], Oct. 9, 1951: 14.

Brindley, Thomas K. "Congressional Honor Medal Is Presented to Lt. Hudner." *Herald News* [Fall River], Apr. 13, 1951.

———. "Honor Medal Man Hudner Awaits Further Navy Orders." *Herald News* [Fall River], Apr. 14, 1951.

"Clue Said to Back U.S. Baltic Charge." *New York Times*, Apr. 27, 1950: 17.

"Cmdr. Cevoli's Funeral Is Held." *Providence Journal*, Jan. 1955.

Culshaw, Peter. "How Jazz Survived the Soviets." *The Telegraph*. Telegraph Media Group, Nov. 14, 2006.

Daniell, Raymond. "Communism, Held in the West, Strikes in the East." *New York Times,* Dec. 26, 1948: E3.

Debro, Joseph. "Welcome to Segregated California." *San Francisco Bay View,* Oct. 5, 2012.

"Ens. Brown's Widow, Pal to Be Cited." *Chicago Defender,* May 5, 1951: 1.

"Ensign Brown's Widow Sees Truman Award Highest Honor to Navy Pilot." *Chicago Defender,* Apr. 21, 1951: 1.

"Ensign Hudner Receives Wings." *Herald News* [Fall River], Aug. 17, 1949.

"Fall River Navy Flier Risks Life to Rescue Fellow Pilot in Korea." *Herald News* [Fall River], Dec. 6, 1950: 1–2.

"1st Tan Navy Flier Dies in Korea Crash." *The Afro-American* [Baltimore], Dec. 16, 1950: 1+.

"Flying Cross Is Awarded to 10 Men on Baltic Plane." *New York Times,* Apr. 25, 1950: 14.

"40,000 Cheer Tom Hudner in Parade." *Herald News* [Fall River], Apr. 20, 1951: 1.

"Helped Make History Over Clark Field." *Providence Journal,* 1945.

"Hero Gives $1,000 Gift to Killed Pilot's Kin." *The Afro-American* [Baltimore], Apr. 28, 1951: 1.

"Heroic Flyer of Korean War Now Carrier Boss for Viet Missions." *Herald News* [Fall River], May 3, 1966.

"Hudner Qualifies as Carrier Flier." *Herald News* [Fall River], Apr. 5, 1949.

"Hudner Tried to Save First Negro Naval Officer Ever to Lose Life in Action in Any U.S. Campaign." *Herald News* [Fall River], Dec. 11, 1950.

James, Edwin L. "Vital Facts at Issue in Dispute Over Plane." *New York Times,* Apr. 23, 1950: B3.

Johnson, Richard J. "New Forces Moved Directly From U.S." *New York Times,* Aug. 1, 1950: 1.

Leviero, Anthony. "U.S. 'Not at War,' President Asserts." *New York Times*, June 30, 1950: 1+.

"Leyte Pilots Raise $2,700 for Late Buddy's Daughter." *The Afro-American* [Baltimore], Apr. 28, 1951: 19.

Lieberman, Henry B. "Chou Brands U.S. China's Worst Foe." *New York Times*, Oct. 1, 1950: 48.

"Lt. Hudner Grateful for Fete, Proud to Be Fall River Man." *Herald News* [Fall River], May 3, 1951.

"Lt. Richard Cevoli Wins Navy Cross." *Providence Journal*, 1945.

"Morale of American Soldiers Is High Declares Lt. Hudner." *Herald News* [Fall River], Feb. 5, 1951.

"Naval Hero Honored at City Youth Rally." *The Afro-American* [Baltimore], Dec. 11, 1951.

"Navy Is Commissioning Destroyer Escort in Memory of Man Hudner Tried to Save." *Herald News* [Fall River], Feb. 16, 1973.

"Negro Navy Pilot Killed in Korea." *Hattiesburg American*, Dec. 9, 1950: 1.

"New Communist Frontiers." *New York Times*, Dec. 12, 1949: 32.

"New Year, New Chance." *New York Times*, Jan. 1, 1950: 6.

"No Troops of Peiping in Korea, Limb Says." *New York Times*, Sept. 19, 1950: 11.

"North Korea Warns of Fight for Unity." *New York Times*, Oct. 18, 1949: 20.

"Now It Can Be Told: Fire Bombs Ignited Pyre of Airman Jesse Brown." *The Afro-American* [Washington], Mar. 6, 1951: 3.

Perry, Tony. "Remains of Camp Pendleton Marine Killed in Korean War Identified." *Los Angeles Times*, Aug. 10, 2013.

"Pilot's Widow to Be Honored by President." *The Afro-American* [Baltimore], Apr. 14, 1951: 15.

"Richard L. Cevoli Takes Bride in Dixie Kiefer Chapel." *Providence Journal*, 1946.

"Russian Killed by American in Patrol Clash in Germany." *New York Times*, July 10, 1949: 1.

"Russians Fire B-29 by 'Error' in Korea." *New York Times*, Sept. 17, 1945: 1+.

"Russians Irk Navy; Fired at Two Planes." *New York Times*, Mar. 2, 1946: 2.

"Scenes From Fifth Annual Robert S. Abbott Award Presentation." *Chicago Defender*, May 12, 1951: 4.

"Sec. Chapman Backs Truman Policy Here." *Chicago Daily News*, May 5, 1951.

"6-to-9 Month War Foreseen in Korea." *New York Times*, July 17, 1950: 10.

"Soviet Fliers Gun U.S. Vienna Plane." *New York Times*, Apr. 23, 1946: 5.

"To Annapolis." *Herald News* [Fall River], June 7, 1943

"Truman Presents Top Medal to Navy Flier Who Landed in Enemy Area in Rescue Try." *New York Times*, Apr. 14, 1951: 4.

"U.S. Planes Were Shot Down." *New York Times*, Apr. 11, 1948: 32.

Wersinger, Tammie. "Richard Fowler Jr. Gave His Best to Every Task." *Orlando Sentinel*, Apr. 25, 2011.

Winslow, Walter G. "A Beacon for All to See." *Milwaukee Sentinel*, Sept. 21, 1952: 2.

"World News Summarized." *New York Times*, Aug. 1, 1950: 1.

Websites and Other Sources

"Apr 16, 1947: Bernard Baruch Coins the Term 'Cold War'" *This Day in History*. The History Channel, www.history.com/this-day-in-history/bernard-baruch-coins-the-term-cold-war.

Barnes, Michael. "An Overview of the Korean War." *The Authentic History Center*, www.authentichistory.com/1946-1960/2-korea/1-overview.

"Berlin Airlift." *History.com*. A&E Television Networks, www.history.com/topics/cold-war/berlin-airlift.

"Desegregation of the Armed Forces: Chronology." *Harry S. Truman*

Library and Museum, www.trumanlibrary.org/whistlestop/study_
collections/desegregation.

Howard, Sally. "Postcards From the Age." *Social Planet*, 2012, http://
bmisocialplanet.tumblr.com/post/16118086170/postcards-from
-the-age.

"Jul 5, 1946: Bikini Introduced." *This Day in History*. The History
Channel, www.history.com/this-day-in-history/bikini
-introduced.

Koenig, William H. "On Jesse's Wing." 2007. MS.

"Letter from Feng Xi (Stalin) to Kim Il Sung (via Shtytkov)," Oct. 8,
1950, History and Public Policy Program Digital Archive, Archive of the President, Russian Federation, http://digitalarchive
.wilsoncenter.org/document/112862.

"M20 3.5in Rocket Launcher and Manuals." *Korean War Online*,
www.koreanwaronline.com/arms/bazsup.htm.

"Newsletter of the USS Leyte Association." *Leyte News* (1990–2012).

North Atlantic Treaty Organization. *The North Atlantic Treaty*.
Washington, D.C.: NATO, 1949. Official Texts. Dec. 9, 2008,
www.nato.int/cps/en/natolive/official_texts_17120.htm.

Skelton III, William P. "American Ex-Prisoners of War." *Department
of Veterans Affairs*. Independent Study Course, released Apr.
2002.

Smitha, Frank. "Communists Win China's Civil War." *Macrohistory
and World Timeline*, www.fsmitha.com/h2/ch24cld8.htm.

"World War II Naval Glossary and Terminology." *Valor at Sea*, 2002,
www.valoratsea.com/glossary.htm.

NOTES

CHAPTER 6

42 **Tom nodded politely, despite his doubts:** After middle school, Tom attended the prestigious Andover Academy prep school. He served as president of his senior class and captain of the track team. At the end of the senior year, Tom's classmates voted him "Most Respected," and in the top three for the categories "Best Athlete," "Most Popular," "Most Modest," and "Most Agreeable."

CHAPTER 8

51 **Tom Hudner steered:** Tom's car was spotless, for being a decade old. Aviators in those days had an image to maintain and never drove a second-rate or secondhand car.

57 **Marty introduced himself:** Marty Goode remembers: "I was one of three fellows in the city of New York that passed that exam and was taken into the flight program. I'll never forget during the round of tests they gave, this lieutenant said to me: 'Do you really want to fly in the navy?' I said, 'Yes, sir.' All these pictures of navy fighter planes were on the wall. 'Can you name the planes?' he asked. I read off what I thought the names of all these planes were. He said, 'That's fine, you've passed, you're in.' Years later, when I thought about it, I had all those names wrong. They must have really needed pilots!"

CHAPTER 9

60 **"atomic bomb monopoly":** "How Could Soviet Attack Come?" *Life*, Feb. 27, 1950.

CHAPTER 11

78 **"If I had done anything right":** Theodore Taylor, *The Flight of Jesse Leroy Brown* (New York: Avon, 1998).

80 **Jesse chuckled but decided to leave:** Jesse would tease Daisy about saying "Anathens" for months to come, and Daisy remembered that her husband even let his brothers in on the joke and that Lura and Fletcher teased her in good fun.

80 **The recent headlines had set her emotions:** Compounding Daisy's worries were the funeral announcements she saw every week in the papers. The remains of boys killed in World War II were still coming home from Europe and the Pacific, five years after the fact.

80 **saga of the lost "Baltic Plane":** Edwin L. James, "Vital Facts at Issue in Dispute Over Plane," *New York Times*, Apr. 23, 1950.

81 **"Perhaps we will have to get":** "New Year, New Chance," *New York Times*, Jan. 1, 1950.

CHAPTER 12

88 "an armed attack against one": North Atlantic Treaty Organization, *The North Atlantic Treaty* (Washington, D.C.: NATO, 1949). Official Texts, Dec. 9, 2008, www.nato.int/cps/en/natolive/official_texts_17120.htm.

CHAPTER 13

96 "Little Stalins": Anne Applebaum, *Iron Curtain* (New York: Anchor, 2012).
96 "An iron curtain has descended across": John L. Gaddis, *The Cold War* (New York: Penguin, 2005).

CHAPTER 14

99 "could be pulled through a wedding ring": "Jul 5, 1946: Bikini Introduced," *This Day in History*, The History Channel, www.history.com/this-day-in-history/bikini-introduced.
99 "Hey, hurry up so we can": William H. Koenig, "On Jesse's Wing," 2007, MS.

CHAPTER 19

143 "police action": William L. Miller, *Two Americans: Truman, Eisenhower, and a Dangerous World* (New York: Alfred A. Knopf, 2012).

CHAPTER 21

158 The *Leyte* had just steamed 4,700: One of Fighting 32's newest pilots, Bill Wilkinson, remembered how the squadron ferried their Corsairs from Norfolk airfield to the *Leyte*: "We parked for about an hour, then taxied 1.5 miles through the naval base streets to the *Leyte* pier. Police blocked traffic for us as we flapped our wings over stop signs, etc. We folded our wings at the dock and a crane lifted our Corsairs aboard."
162 Not a minute later, Dad: The veterans still remember the hotel with disdain. The author has chosen to withhold the hotel's name out of respect for the present-day employees who have no ties to this incident.

CHAPTER 23

173 "The United States Government": Henry B. Lieberman, "Chou Brands U.S. China's Worst Foe." *New York Times*, Oct. 1, 1950.

CHAPTER 24

178 "All I see is a white helmet": Koenig, "On Jesse's Wing."
188 "If I have to bail out": Ibid.

CHAPTER 25

193 **"Enemy flak isn't very accurate"**: Charles L. Black, "Briefing Off Wonsan." *Flying,* Feb. 1951.

CHAPTER 26

200 **"Bean soup with crackers, grilled beef"**: Charles L. Black, "A Carrier Goes to War." *Flying,* Dec. 1950.

201 **"I believe that formal resistance"**: *Substance of Statements Made at Wake Island Conference on 15 October 1950,* compiled by General of the Army Omar N. Bradley.

CHAPTER 27

206 **Sasebo had once been an Imperial:** During WWII, Sasebo was home to a Japanese POW camp that held 245 American prisoners, mostly civilians captured on Wake Island. The POWs were forced to build a dam in the mountains, during which 113 perished.

207 **"Never hoppon, Joe!"**: Jack Sauter, *Sailors in the Sky* (Lincoln: University of Nebraska Press, 2011).

CHAPTER 28

214 **"volunteers"**: Paul M. Edwards, *Korean War Almanac (Almanacs of American Wars)* (New York: Facts on File, 2006).

214 **"stragglers"**: P. K. Rose, "Two Strategic Intelligence Mistakes in Korea, 1950," *Studies in Intelligence* (2001), *CIA Library,* Center for the Study of Intelligence, Apr. 14, 2007.

215 **"I'll be careful"**: Lawrence Elliott, "Widows of Honor," *Coronet,* Sept. 1953.

216 **"Gentlemen, you may soon be fighting"**: Bud Hannings, *The Korean War: An Exhaustive Chronology,* vol. 1 (Jefferson: McFarland, 2007).

218 **"will reverberate around the world"**: Ibid.

CHAPTER 29

230 **"Our naval pilots have been given"**: Malcolm W. Cagle and Frank A. Manson, *The Sea War in Korea* (Annapolis: Naval Institute, 1957).

237 **His record was intact:** A day later, Wilkie would write to his parents about the mission while camouflaging the reason he didn't drop his bomb, for fear that the skipper might read his mail. "My bomb didn't release," Wilkie wrote, "don't think I pressed the pickle [button] hard enough. God that made me mad. . . . I didn't have the guts to drop it on the city as I went by. I just can't bomb or shoot at something that isn't

military. I'd probably have killed 50 innocent people that didn't want this
war in the first place. . . ."

CHAPTER 30

241 **a lieutenant named Tarshinov:** Leonid Krylov and Yuriy Tepsurkaev, *Soviet MiG-15 Aces of the Korean War* (Oxford: Osprey, 2008).

245 **"bridgehead":** "Letter from Feng Xi (Stalin) to Kim Il Sung (via Shtytkov)," Oct. 8, 1950, History and Public Policy Program Digital Archive, Archive of the President, Russian Federation.

246 **"hug the enemy":** Patrick C. Roe, *The Dragon Strikes* (Novato: Presidio, 2000).

246 **"First Phase Offensive":** Eric M. Hammel, *Chosin: Heroic Ordeal of the Korean War* (New York: Vanguard, 1981).

247 **"Second Phase":** Ibid.

247 **Now the U.S. 8th Army:** The forces of democracy called their attack the "Home by Christmas Offensive." It lasted just a day and covered roughly fifteen miles before enemy resistance brought it to a standstill.

247 **"There's nothing special about me":** "Last Days of a Navy Pilot," *Ebony.*

248 **"He's one of the best pilots":** Ibid.

248 DIEU ET PATRIA: Pilot Lee Nelson designed '32's patch and chose the words "Dieu et Patria." The words were half-French and half-Latin in tribute to the squadron's cruise with the Dancing Fleet.

248 **"The key to Jesse's popularity":** "Last Days of a Navy Pilot," *Ebony.*

CHAPTER 32

256 **"Maybe we'll see a saber tooth tiger":** Patrick K. O'Donnell, *Give Me Tomorrow* (Cambridge: Da Capo, 2010).

CHAPTER 33

284 **the cold had contorted:** The army's preeminent WWII historian, General S.L.A. Marshall, was recalled for duty in Korea. He'd later conclude: "The fighting at the Chosin Reservoir was the most violent small unit fighting in the history of American warfare." Tony Perry, "Remains of Camp Pendleton Marine Killed in Korean War Identified," *Los Angeles Times,* Aug. 10, 2013.

CHAPTER 35

298 **"There has always been active":** Gaddis, *Cold War.*

300 **Pilot has been seen:** *Fighter Squadron Thirty Two Operational Report,* October 1950–January 1951.

304 **"The Lost Legion"**: Frank Kerr, "At the Reservoir: Through the Eyes of a Combat Photographer," *Leatherneck*, Dec. 1990.

310 **Normally, the commander oversaw:** The air group commander, or "CAG," that day was Cmdr. Wally Madden, who had flown F4F fighters in WWII. Another veteran in the formation was Maj. William Powell Jr., who led a flight of '33 planes. Powell was an active-duty air force pilot on exchange duty with the navy. He, too, had flown in WWII, as a P-40 pilot in the Philippines, where he was ultimately captured when the islands fell.

CHAPTER 36

313 **"picnic ants going across"**: Martin Russ, *Breakout: The Chosin Reservoir Campaign, Korea 1950* (New York: Fromm International, 1999).

316 **The FAC glanced at the low:** The author's staff interviewed Captain Dan Holland, a FAC, who called in air strikes during the attack described on the column.

325 **"Kill these Marines"**: Ibid.

325 **a young black Marine:** Thanks go to Jesse's brother Fletcher for sharing this black Marine's eyewitness account with the author.

326 **"The Great Slaughter"**: Lynn Montross and Capt. Nicholas A. Canzona, *U.S. Marine Operations in Korea: The Chosin Reservoir Campaign*, vol. 3 (Washington, D.C.: U.S. Marine Corps, 1957).

CHAPTER 37

336 **"[I] saw the 5th and 7th"**: Richard P. Hallion, *The Naval Air War in Korea* (New York: Zebra, 1986).

CHAPTER 39

362 **"The country needed Jesse Brown"**: "Last Days of a Navy Pilot," *Ebony*.

363 **"outstanding heroics"**: *Fighter Squadron Thirty Two Historical Report*, July–December 1950.

CHAPTER 40

366 *It is with deep regret*: "Last Days of a Navy Pilot," *Ebony*.

CHAPTER 41

372 **"ideologically contaminated"**: Russ, *Breakout*.

CHAPTER 42

377 **"I guess it was the will"**: "Last Days of a Navy Pilot," *Ebony*.

377 **"The 26-year-old Hudner landed"**: "Hudner Tried to Save First Negro

Naval Officer Ever to Lose Life in Action in Any U.S. Campaign," *Herald News* [Fall River], Dec. 11, 1950.

377 **"Navy rescue planes rushed":** "1st Tan Navy Flier Dies in Korea Crash," *The Afro-American* [Baltimore], Dec. 16, 1950.

378 *At Sea, Sunday Nite:* "Last Days of a Navy Pilot," *Ebony.*

381 **"We felt this way":** "Leyte Pilots Raise $2,700 for Late Buddy's Daughter," *The Afro-American* [Baltimore], Apr. 28, 1951.

382 **The crowd parted as the skipper:** Earlier that morning, a handful of '32's pilots had ferried Corsairs from the carrier to the air station. They then rejoined the squadron on the pier to collect their belongings.

CHAPTER 44

397 **"I am very proud to wear":** "40,000 Cheer Tom Hudner in Parade," *Herald News* [Fall River], Apr. 20, 1951.

397 **"This has been one day":** Ibid.

397 **"To the fellows there now":** Ibid.

400 **"With all the cold, the mud":** "Lt. Hudner Grateful for Fete, Proud to Be Fall River Man," *Herald News* [Fall River], May 3, 1951.

PHOTO CREDITS

pp. ii–iii: Bill Wilkinson
pp. 4, 57: Martin Goode
pp. 12, 146: Thomas J. Hudner, Jr.
p. 19: Daisy Brown Thorne
pp. 26, 39, 41, 45, 62, 70, 72, 79, 87, 93, 174, 225, 236, 330, 360: U.S. Navy
p. 31: Lura Brown
p. 46: Courtesy of the Jesse Leroy Brown family
p. 95: Richard Fowler
pp. 105, 125, 165, 305: John E. Parkinson
pp. 108, 362: W. Carl Jeckel
p. 110: Halley Bishop
p. 138: Ed Coderre
pp. 139, 175, 274: U.S. Marine Corps
pp. 167, 391: National Archives
p. 181: Bill Wilkinson
p. 412: U.S. Navy, via *Ebony*
pp. 414–17: Daisy Brown Thorne, via *Ebony*

FIRST INSERT

Teenage Tom Hudner with his siblings: Thomas J. Hudner Jr.
Nineteen-year-old Tom during a visit home: Thomas J. Hudner Jr.
Daisy holds Pam: Courtesy of the Jesse Leroy Brown family
Jesse as an ensign: U.S. Navy
Jesse and Daisy with Pam: Courtesy of the Jesse Leroy Brown family
Marty Goode aboard the *Leyte*: Martin Goode
Jesse in the Quonset Point chapel: U.S. Navy
A *Leyte* LSO signals: U.S. Navy
Marty catches the last cable: Martin Goode
Fighting 32 during the Mediterranean cruise: U.S. Navy
Leyte deckhands prepare a Corsair: U.S. Navy
The beach at Cannes: W. Carl Jeckel
Elizabeth Taylor, Nicky Hilton, and friends: U.S. Navy
Elizabeth Taylor dines with the officers: U.S. Navy
6th Fleet Marines practice: U.S. Navy
Red Parkinson and his platoon: John E. Parkinson
A Marine aims an M20 Super Bazooka: U.S. Marine Corps
Ed Coderre during a visit home: Ed Coderre
Enjoying watermelons on Crete: John E. Parkinson

Marines assemble aboard the *Leyte:* U.S. Navy
Red Parkinson naps: John. E. Parkinson
Jesse during a stop in Tennessee: Courtesy of the Jesse Leroy Brown family
Jesse plays with Pam: Courtesy of the Jesse Leroy Brown family
Bill Wilkinson during flight training: Bill Wilkinson
Wilkie's photo of a practice flight: Bill Wilkinson
Jesse and Koenig in their cabin: U.S. Navy, via *Ebony*
On the *Leyte*'s first day at war: U.S. Navy
Squadron 32 at the front of the pack: Bill Wilkinson
Tom in the cockpit: Thomas J. Hudner Jr.
Sailors muscle a Corsair onto an elevator: U.S. Navy
"Dad" Fowler as a Hellcat pilot: U.S. Navy, via Richard E. Fowler Jr. family
Dad Fowler launches down the center line: Bill Wilkinson

SECOND INSERT

Marty and others review maps: U.S. Navy
Sisson and the skipper with captured flags: U.S. Navy
Jesse's buddies carry him: U.S. Navy, via *Ebony*
At anchor in Sasebo harbor: U.S. Navy
Black Market Alley: U.S. Navy
Artillery pounds Hill 891: U.S. Marine Corps
Chinese soldiers captured near 891: U.S. Marine Corps
A Skyraider returns from a mission: U.S. Navy
Jesse as seen through a windscreen: U.S. Navy
The *Leyte*'s special mission planes: U.S. Navy
The bridges of the Yalu: U.S. Navy
Cevoli and Jesse play backgammon: U.S. Navy, via *Ebony*
Jesse checks the rockets: U.S. Navy, via *Ebony*
Jesse up high on the *Leyte*'s tower: U.S. Navy, via *Ebony*
Jesse in the cockpit of a Corsair: U.S. Navy, via *Ebony*
Leyte deckhands clear the deck: U.S. Navy
The Chosin Reservoir: National Archives
Stalin propaganda poster: U.S. Marine Corps
Marines press onward: © David Douglas Duncan, Harry Ransom Center,
     University of Texas
Daytime firefight at the Chosin: U.S. Marine Corps
Marines watch an airstrike: U.S. Marine Corps
Nicolas Trudgian's *Off to the Chosin:* ValorStudios.com
Gareth Hector's *Wingmen to the End:* ValorStudios.com
An HO3S at Hagaru: U.S. Marine Corps
Matt Hall's painting *Devotion:* Mall Hall and ValorStudios.com
During the withdrawal: © David Douglas Duncan, Harry Ransom Center,
     University of Texas
Marines manage to smile: U.S. Marine Corps
Marines follow the precipitous trails: U.S. Marine Corps
Ed Coderre's parents visit him: Ed Coderre
The *Leyte* returns to San Diego: U.S. Navy
Red Parkinson strums a guitar: John E. Parkinson

ABOUT THE AUTHOR

ADAM MAKOS is a journalist and the author of the *Sunday Times* bestseller *A Higher Call*. Inspired by his grandfathers' World War II stories, he has interviewed countless veterans from World War II, Korea, Vietnam, and present-day battles. In pursuit of a story, Makos has flown a World War II bomber, accompanied a Special Forces raid in Iraq, and organized an expedition into North Korea in search of an MIA American serviceman. He lives in Denver.

adammakos.com
@AdamMakos